Northern Ireland at the Crossroads

Also by Marc Mulholland

TO CARE ALWAYS: A History of Holywell Mental Hospital, Antrim, 1898–1998

Northern Ireland at the Crossroads

Ulster Unionism in the O'Neill Years 1960–9

Marc Mulholland
Lecturer in Modern British History
Hertford College
Oxford

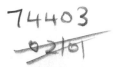

First published in Great Britain 2000 by
MACMILLAN PRESS LTD
Houndmills, Basingstoke, Hampshire RG21 6XS and London
Companies and representatives throughout the world

A catalogue record for this book is available from the British Library.

ISBN 0–333–76075–1

 First published in the United States of America 2000 by
ST. MARTIN'S PRESS, INC.,
Scholarly and Reference Division,
175 Fifth Avenue, New York, N.Y. 10010

ISBN 0–312–22835–X

Library of Congress Cataloging-in-Publication Data
Mulholland, Marc, 1971–
Northern Ireland at the crossroads : Ulster Unionism in the O'Neill years 1960–9 /
Marc Mulholland.
p.   cm.
Includes bibliographical references and index.
ISBN 0–312–22835–X (cloth)
1. Northern Ireland—Politics and government—1969–1994.   2. O'Neill, Terence,
1914– 3. Unionism (Irish politics)   I. Title

DA990.U46 M78   1999
941.60824—dc21
99–046717

This book is printed on paper suitable for recycling and made from fully managed and sustained
forest sources.

10   9   8   7   6   5   4   3   2   1
09   08   07   06   05   04   03   02   01   00

Printed and bound in Great Britain by
Antony Rowe Ltd, Chippenham, Wiltshire

Contents

Acknowledgements

This book is based upon my PhD thesis completed at the Queen's University of Belfast in 1997. I explicitly repeat only some acknowledgements here, but naturally I am grateful still to everyone who helped in that venture. I was principally supervised by Dr Alvin Jackson, and he has taken a valuable and welcome interest in my work since. A source of seemingly endless fresh ideas and inspiration, Dr Jackson was good enough to take my own few notions seriously and always offered much to improve them. Any scholarly values and original thought in this work owe an immense amount to his careful and good-humoured attention. I was also lucky enough to enjoy the temporary supervision of Ms Sabine Wichert. I hope that I have taken on board some of the academic rigour, fairness and carefully grounded speculation Ms Wichert did so much to inculcate in me.

This book has benefited greatly from those who took the time and effort to talk with me about their participation in the events described. To those listed in the bibliography, and others who wish to remain anonymous, I am very grateful. The Ulster Unionist Party provided me with access to their archive and put me in touch with many valuable contacts. Their open and courteous help was gratefully received. A special mention must go to Lady O'Neill of Lymington, Hampshire, who not only allowed me access to the papers of Lord O'Neill of the Maine but also treated me with extraordinarily generous hospitality and warmth. My visit to Lady O'Neill's beautiful home and garden in the New Forest shall remain for me an enduring and happy memory.

In the course of my research I have made many demands on the staffs of libraries and research institutions: Queen's University Main Library, especially the Special Collections; Belfast Central Library, especially the Newspaper Library; the Linen Hall Library, both its Irish section and the invaluable Political Collection; the London School of Economics; the Bodleian Library at Oxford, the British Library, both at the British Museum and Colindale; the Public Records Office at Kew; and the Public Records Office of Northern Ireland. I am grateful to George Friel for providing me with video footage of Terence O'Neill.

My fellow historians have done much to ease the hard slog of research and writing. I thank Brigette Anton, Noel Armour, Jonathan Hamill, Kathy Hirst, Patricia Horton, Gill McIntosh, Ben Novick, Senia

Pašeta, John Regan, Rosemary Richey, Alan Scott, Diane Urquhart, and Patricia Horton. I am particularly grateful to Eoin Magennis, Ciaran Crossey and Kenneth Darwin who read and commented on a draft of this book. Their observations improved it greatly. Thanks too to my commissioning editor at Macmillan, Aruna Vasudevan, and copy-editor Janey Fisher.

For freely given and helpful advice I must also thank Peter Blair, Roy Foster, David Hayton, Peter Jupp, Oliver Rafferty, Donal Lowry, Bob Purdie, Nini Rodgers and Brian Walker. My PhD examiners, Professor Paul Bew and Professor Ronan Fanning, provided much very helpful advice on how it might be turned into a book. All remaining mistakes in this volume are my own.

My brothers and sisters – Kathleen, Ciaran, Padraig, Deirdre, Niall, Ita, Áine and Breandán – have provided much support and borne my soliloquising on Terence O'Neill with admirable patience. My parents, Ita and Dominic, naturally have been a tremendous support to me over these three years and much longer. From them I have received not only a sympathetic ear, unjustified confidence in my abilities and much appreciated injections of cash, but also the virtues of hard work, critical distance, empathy, historical imagination and accessible prose. If I have learnt only inadequately, it is not from want of their love and attention. To my parents I dedicate this book.

List of Abbreviations

BBC	British Broadcasting Corporation
CDU	Campaign for Democracy in Ulster
CSJ	Campaign for Social Justice
ICTU	Irish Congress of Trade Unions
IRA	Irish Republican Army
LEA	Local Education Authority
NHS	National Health Service
NIC	Northern Ireland Committee [of the Irish Congress of Trade Unions]
NICRA	Northern Ireland Civil Rights Association
NICS	Northern Ireland Civil Service
NIEC	Northern Ireland Economic Council
NIHC	Northern Ireland House of Commons (*Hansard*)
NILP	Northern Ireland Labour Party
PD	Peoples Democracy
PEP	Programme to Enlist the People
PRO	Public Records Office
PRONI	Public Records Office of Northern Ireland
RDC	Rural District Council
RUC	Royal Ulster Constabulary
SPA	Special Powers Act
UA	Unionist Association
UP	Unionist Party
UCDC	Ulster Constitution Defence Committee
UDC	Urban District Council
UFU	Ulster Farmers' Union
USC	Ulster Special Constabulary
UTA	Ulster Transport Authority
UTUA	Unionist Trade Union Alliance
UTV	Ulster Television
UUC	Ulster Unionist Council
UVF	Ulster Volunteer Force
WHC	Westminster House of Commons (*Hansard*)

Introduction

> I doubt whether there is any other country which has shown such universal political stability as Ulster.
>
> Brian Faulkner, January 1963.[1]

> The signs and portents were in the skies of Northern Ireland ... but none of us, although we may have seen signs of the gathering storm, had the least conception that instead of a wind of change were going to be met with a hurricane.
>
> Edmund Warnock, Unionist MP, December 1968.[2]

This book assumes that Northern Ireland's conflict is basically one between competing ethnic identities: Irish nationalists and Ulster unionists. Both are somewhat ambivalent in their sense of nationality. A substantial number of catholics have historically accepted partition and the link with Britain as an accomplished fact. A substantial number of protestants acknowledge a definite, if subordinate, Irish identity. Such ambiguity may best be explained by the problems of self-conceptualization posed by sharing political territory with an opposition ethnic group. Neither community is able to achieve equilibrium and rest secure in its national identity. Ambivalence makes not for compromise but a tendency towards militant assertions of communal identity. Incompatible and competing identities, as both lay claim to the same 'narrow ground', make for chronic polarization, extremism and conflict.

After partition, on the basis of the military, political and moral defeat of the catholic nationalist community,[3] a certain equilibrium was attained. Devolution successfully insulated Britain from the remnants of the irksome Irish problem and simultaneously underpinned the pan-class alliance built up to resist Irish Home Rule. Severe economic straits, southern irredentism, restrictions on Stormont's legislative powers and over-mighty local government in Northern Ireland produced a veritable 'factory of grievances'.[4] Provincial politics was reduced to an obsession with the border, sectarian lobbying over those few resources in the government's gift, indolent ministers, conservative civil servants, an immiserated but hopelessly divided working class, and a sullen, uncommunicative hostile catholic minority.

Stormont's acceptance of the post-war welfare state, against its better Tory instincts but a necessary sop to protestant workers attracted to local variations of Labourism, changed the situation. Though still hardly a stunning economic success, Northern Ireland participated in the post-war economic boom. The 1950s saw the development of a more confident Unionism. Rising living standards in the North widened its differential with the South, thus reinforcing partition. Catholics came to recognize the durability of the Northern Ireland state and were increasingly content to accept its advantages. Nationalists looked to the workings of demography and later the Common Market to undermine the border gradually. The IRA border campaign only served to undermine traditional militant nationalism. In this atmosphere an assimilatory unionism, ambitious to include catholics in British political culture, could at last prosper. From the mid-1950s it always seemed likely that the next Prime Minister, raised from a political generation not active at the time of partition, would respond to the prevalent spirit of liberalism. This Prime Minister proved to be Captain Terence Marne O'Neill.

While most historians consider O'Neill to have been a 'well-meaning liberal'[5] others have been less sure and David Gordon has gone as far as to condemn him as 'the most reactionary of all the Unionist Prime Ministers.'[6] It has been pointed out that O'Neill's reforms amounted to very little, something O'Neill himself acknowledged.[7] Terence O'Neill's understanding, political skills, even personality, have attracted considerable comment, usually to his detriment.[8] Much of this opinion rests on O'Neill's autobiography, no great masterpiece of self-revelation. Its anecdotal structure, overweening interest in foreign visits and name-dropping, and the rather Colonel Blimpish opinion-ating strike the reader as, variously, snobbish, bizarre, myopic and inappropriate.[9] Further, O'Neill's intense retrospective antagonism to his own political party and, in reality, electorate, must be nearly unique in the memoirs of a political leader. Nevertheless, one sees in this work a humour, self-deprecation and ironic detachment which indicated, if not a great mind, an open and liberal instinct. O'Neill, furthermore, held on to power for six and a half years in a period of rapid change and incessant plotting. O'Neill as a politician is worth renewed attention.

This book is not a biography of Terence O'Neill but, given the paucity of detailed historical research on the period, neither is it an examination of Ulster Unionism at the roots. Rather it steers a middle course, following chronologically the high politics of unionism, at least from 1963, but attempting to place this in the context of popular unionist consciousness and the actual structures and personnel through which any political leadership must operate: the cabinet, civil service and party. Inevitably Terence O'Neill takes centre stage, but the second tier, Brian Faulkner and William Craig, are also considered. Below this, at the level of the parliamentary party and unionist *apparatchiks*, individuals of necessity blur somewhat, but I have attempted to delineate and provide examples of all the principal trends. Other formations in society, the nationalists, the Northern Ireland Labour Party, Paisleyism, the middle class and so on, are treated in so far as they are relevant to Ulster unionism.

In researching this thesis I have employed such government and private papers as are available. More importantly I have had access to Terence O'Neill's private papers and have interviewed a number of contemporary participants/observers. This was underpinned by an exhaustive scouring of the local press, particularly the *Belfast Telegraph* and the mysteriously under-used *Unionist*. This unusual level of dependence on the press has obvious drawbacks. My day-by-day trawl through the papers had the advantage, however, of re-enacting the political drama as most of the contemporary population followed it. If this does not negate hindsight, it at least forces one not to consider events teleologically. When surfacing from immersion in the 1960s, it always came as something of a shock to recall the disaster that overtook Northern Ireland in the years following. This may indicate a lack of skill in reading the runes on my part, but it reinforces the point made by the epigraph. The actions of politicians in the 1960s must be judged on the basis that none knew then what the outcome would be.

1
Peoples and Parties in a Decade of Flux

Terence O'Neill, in one famous moment of indiscretion, was undiplomatically frank as to his hopes and aims as a Prime Minister.

> The basic fear of Protestants in Northern Ireland is that they will be outbred by Roman Catholics. It is as simple as that. It is frightfully hard to explain to a Protestant that if you give Roman Catholics a good job and a good house they will live like Protestants, because they will see their neighbours with cars and TV sets. They will refuse to have eighteen children, but if the Roman Catholic is jobless and lives in a most ghastly hovel he will rear eighteen children on national assistance. It is impossible to explain this to a militant Protestant, because he is so keen to deny civil rights to his Roman Catholic neighbours. He cannot understand, in fact, that if you treat Roman Catholics with due kindness and consideration they will live like Protestants in spite of the authoritarian nature of their church.[1]

So gratuitously paternalistic was this statement that, ironically, its centrality to the entire O'Neillite project has been somewhat obscured. Sam Napier, Secretary of the Northern Ireland Labour Party, explained O'Neillism to a southern Irish politician in 1966. The 'Captain wished to make certain concessions to Catholic professional and middle-class people in the North with a view to weakening the Anti-Partitionist cause. He felt that once the better-off Catholics were given some share in the spoils they would turn in favour of the regime.'[2] This more considered judgement brings home the peculiarity of pre-Troubles Unionism. Leaders hoped and believed that they could broaden the basis of unionism to include catholics, and to escape the sectarian dichotomy. The end product – catholic insurrection, the IRA's war against Britain, and intense sectarian conflict restrained from open civil war only by a massive and semi-colonial military commitment – was evidently far from what O'Neill anticipated. This chapter examines the processes at work in both communities in Northern Ireland, in particular as expressed by their main political parties, to explain why O'Neillism seemed a viable project, and to suggest its inherent weaknesses.

Sectarian discord seemed to be dissipating in the early 1960s. In Northern Ireland, as in the Republic, there was a broad 'reaction against the political in favour of the socio-economic'.[3] The increasingly liberal broadcast media from the 1950s strove to blur religious differences, while remaining obsequious to the state.[4] A little later the editorial columns and letter pages of Northern Ireland's profuse press took up this conciliationist refrain.[5] The most obvious change was in the catholic community. Virtually all catholics hoped for improved community relations (97 per cent) and in 1967 70 per cent believed that relations had improved over the previous five years (only 47 per cent of protestants agreed).[6] It is clear that catholics were optimistic and happy with the direction in which politics was moving in the 1960s. Given the massive catholic mobilization of the civil rights movement and the development thereafter of virtual uprisings in certain areas, this bears closer examination.

Catholics

In the May 1955 Westminster general election two abstentionist Republican candidates were dramatically elected for the Westminster constituencies of Fermanagh-South Tyrone and Mid-Ulster. Emboldened, the IRA launched Operation Harvest, a largely cross-border campaign of guerrilla raids.[7] Ironically this republican offensive set the scene for O'Neill's premiership. Failing to galvanize the catholic minority, IRA actions served merely to discredit nationalist obduracy, even when expressed peacefully. A catholic social study conference in Garron Tower in 1958 expressed the dissatisfaction of middle-class catholics with negative politics and a lack of engagement with the northern state.[8] Increasingly abstentionism was abandoned, as when Eddie Richardson provided a South Armagh MP at Stormont in 1958 for the first time in eight years.[9] The Republican vote in the 1959 election collapsed. By the end of 1961 a 'silent revolution'[10] had transformed the Stormont House of Commons from a quiescent rubber stamp to a cockpit of politicking awash with all-night sittings, censure motions and lengthy debates.[11] A pattern of Nationalist accommodation to the Northern Ireland state was clearly emerging from 1958.

The failure of the IRA border campaign, called off in 1962, served only to emphasize the lack of militancy amongst northern catholics. In this space ecumenism developed to weaken the protestant/catholic dichotomy. The Second Vatican Council, which ran from 1962 to 1965, modernized the Roman Catholic Church and watered down its objections to liberal democracy. As Rafferty has pointed out, this 'facilitated ... a re-evaluation by the catholic community of its relationship with the state and protestant population.'[12] In his Lenten Pastoral of 1966 Cardinal Conway urged that 'the life of the community be enriched and strengthened by the participation, in one way or another, of all its members.'[13]

Certainly, it was the catholic community that appeared to move much the farthest from traditional attitudes in the 1960s. Tim Pat Coogan, editor of a southern Irish newspaper, found that 'the secret wish of most Northern Catholics is not for union with the South (entailing a fall off in social benefits) but for an end to discrimination and a fairer share of the Northern spoils. This truth may be unpalatable to us in the South, but it has to be faced.'[14] Poll evidence indicated a fairly broadminded attitude amongst catholics to nationalist verities. Of those who identified themselves as nationalist, only 30 per cent favoured a completely independent united Ireland, a substantial 20 per cent preferred the status quo and the greatest number, 50 per cent, favoured a united Ireland linked to Britain.[15] No doubt generous economic and welfare benefits were important factors in this, but so too was a real affinity with British liberal democracy.

Were catholics, thus, assimilating into British culture? Admittedly parallel state institutions continued to socialize catholics into a sense of alienation, yet catholic schools and even catholic health services were compatible with full acceptance of citizenship in other countries. Moreover, catholics were far from insistent on separate institutions, accepting them rather as a given fact. A full 69 per cent of catholics favoured integrated education, surpassing support amongst Anglicans and Presbyterians.[16] Nor were catholics religiously exclusive; an overwhelming 96 per cent thought the ecumenical movement a good thing.

Whilst conciliatory, however, catholics were largely non-assimilationist in that they clung to a basic Irish identity. In 1968 76 per cent of catholics identified themselves unambiguously as Irish with only 15 per cent preferring the potentially more flexible label of British. The contrast to protestant uncertainty was marked.[17] Irish nationalism, moreover, was often expressed in traditional forms. Thus in 1966 tens of thousands marched or lined the route in West Belfast to commemorate the 1916 Easter Rising.[18] The following year 15,000 filled the same road to celebrate the victory of catholic Glasgow Celtic over protestant Rangers in the Scottish Football Association final. Gerry Fitt, referring to his recent capture of the West Belfast Westminster seat from the Unionist Party, made the connection explicit. 'We have beaten our opponents in politics, sports and in every other field they dare to confront us,' he crowed 'and I have no doubt this will be a continuing trend in years to come.'[19] Gaelic Athletic Association sport also expanded in this period, with Down bringing the All-Ireland Football cup across the border for the first time in 1960, a feat repeated in 1961 and 1968. Gates at Gaelic matches reached new all time highs.[20] The Credit Union, which expanded rapidly from its foundation in 1960, was a non-sectarian movement but attracted mainly catholics. Its stress on co-operation was seen as better suited to the catholic ethos than protestant individualism.[21] The first leader of the movement, John Hume, rose to prominence as a civil rights leader.

The preservation of a catholic nationalist identity was not incompatible with increased assimilation, but it set certain limits. Two prominent catholics, J. J. Campbell and Brian McGuigan, criticized their own community for failing to integrate into civil society, but equally lambasted Terence O'Neill for failing to appoint members of the minority to statutory boards. A southern journalist, expecting to find them 'warmly approved by the Catholics of Belfast', instead 'heard them called "Castle Catholics for begging for crumbs from the Government's table", heard it asked, "just who do they think they represent?"'[22] Catholics may have been pragmatic about their nationalist ambitions, but they showed precious little willingness to integrate into the unionist establishment.

Rather, catholics in the 1960s looked to seize the moral high ground as progressive and modernizing. Old strategies of voluntary segregation were thus put under very considerable strain but, until the Civil Rights Movement, an alternative was not clear. Not surprisingly, traditional nationalism was wracked with crisis.

Many, including crucially Terence O'Neill, assumed that catholics had wearied not only of the Nationalist Party, but also of Irish nationalism itself. Upon closer inspection, however, the genuine moderation of the catholic community was but one face of a protean character.

Catholic consciousness was a curious amalgam of moderation and militancy. Whilst protestantism tended towards theological assertiveness, even aggression, catholics as a rule were non-dogmatic in religion. Albert McElroy, Liberal Party leader and Presbyterian Minister, went as far as to say that he had 'met Irish Catholics who were political bigots, but never any who were religious ones.'[23] Yet there was a certain superiority in this stance that annoyed even liberal protestants: catholics were not inclined to debate with erring brothers. In some respects a similar attitude existed in their politics. A substantial 67 per cent of catholics still believed that the border would disappear, most expecting this to take place between ten and twenty years. The mechanisms they expected to operate were pacific but automatic. Many looked to improved economic performance in the south and north-south co-operation to render partition superfluous, 65 per cent of catholics (70 per cent of Nationalist voters) believed that entry into the Common Market would hasten reunification, more again looked to differential birth-rates.[24] The practical merits or demerits of reunification were rarely considered.

In an often penetrating discussion recorded in April 1969, Michael Farrell and Eamon McCann, socialists and civil rights leaders, discussed the nature of catholic identity. Said Farrell:

> I have repeatedly found ... that if you urge Catholics to accept Protestants as their brothers, this is always welcomed with a cheer and a clap. They are very devoted to the idea of not being sectarian even when in practice they may not have much opportunity to do this.

McCann was blunter still: 'Everyone applauds loudly when one says in a speech that we are not sectarian, we are fighting for the rights of all Irish workers, but really that's because they see this as a new way of getting at the Protestants.'[25]

Nationalist opinion consistently scorned liberal attempts to make the creed of unionism acceptable to catholics. 'The Nationalists of Northern Ireland will not forswear their allegiance to their native land' insisted a Nationalist Senator.[26] The *Derry Journal* agreed that the 'ideal of a free united Ireland is not for sale at any price'.[27] Brushing off Unionist overtures to catholics the *Irish News* reminded them that the 'conviction of the minority in the ultimate unity of our country is a much prized one. That is why they don't join the Unionist Party'.[28] Though technically a campaign for 'British rights for British citizens',[29] the civil rights movement is better seen as a way morally to embarrass the unionists, particularly in British eyes. Even the middle-class Campaign for Social Justice directed all their attention at exposing Stormont's maladministration rather than attempting to promote practical catholic progress in business, the professions or the state.[30] Civil rights agitation was primarily an exercise in constructing a catholic self-identity, at once oppressed, risen, reasonable and militant.[31] It is often observed in the Irish context that political actors attempt to seize upon the past to validate their actions in the present. It is just as important, however, to present oneself as in tune with modernity and future trends. 'In this modern world of ours', noted the nationalist *Irish News*, 'the label reactionary is one with which no party, no politician, no spokesman wishes to be associated.'[32] Long labelled as backward looking, wedded to antiquated economic and political mores as encapsulated in the dismal Irish Republic of the 1950s, catholics were keen to be cast as the progressives and to depict unionists as the reactionaries.[33]

The Civil Rights Movement, thus, did not represent a true desire to accept a British identity on the part of catholics, nor did its eruption cut across a sustained development in that direction. The *Guardian* journalist, Harold Jackson, observed cynically, but with some truth that:

> The Civil Rights Movement ... had a firm foundation in its demand that United Kingdom standards should apply to all citizens ... But this perfectly legitimate struggle masked the fact that it did not really touch on the heart of the crisis, which had a far more mystic basis. What the Catholics were really looking for, though they did not admit this even to themselves ... was the best of both worlds – the freedom of spirit and action implicit in nationalism allied to the economic benefit of the £100 million a year with which the English taxpayer bolstered the province's ailing economy. Clearly this is not the sort of demand capable of rational expression because it has no rational basis. Any attempt to translate it into political terms could thus only falsify.[34]

It is more accurate to say that catholics genuinely held themselves to be Irish but with a special relationship to Britain by virtue, certainly, of the economic benefits, but also of a recognition of unionist rights and their own sense of affinity with British culture. This need be no more hypocritical than the much-commented-upon multi-layered nature of protestant identity. However, Irishness was prone to slide into articulation through uncomplicated all-Ireland nationalism, particularly as more subtle concepts such as joint sovereignty remained much under-developed. Militant nationalism became increasingly attractive as the boundaries of catholic identity were threatened first by O'Neill's ambitions to assimilate all citizens into a unionist consensus, then by the breakdown of established patterns of unionist 'oppression' in favour of Westminster-led amelioration.

Protestants

John Taylor, leading a path-breaking delegation to meet a Fine Gael group in Dublin in 1963, asserted that, protestants were 'Ulstermen who are Irishmen and Irishmen who are British.'[35] In theory this multi-layering and flexibility of identity made unionism uniquely suited for absorbing the Irish nationalist minority in Ulster. In practice, though unionists were aware of the changing nature of catholicism and the opening out of catholics attitudes, they were far from sure how to react. The prospect of a reformed Roman Catholicism and pragmatic minority politics shook certainties. Ultimately a divide appeared between those who wished to continue in the tracks of communal polarization and segregation and those who were prepared to appeal to catholics and assimilate them into unionist political culture. In 1971 Frank Wright observed:

> The most decisive political cleavage within Unionism has been between those who on the one hand want and believe it to be possible to achieve Catholic support for the Union, and those on the other hand who believe that Catholic unionism would be undesirable, impossible, or too conditional to depend upon.[36]

The 1960s were indeed a period of struggle between assimilatory and segregatory unionism.

While Vatican II and the ecumenical movement, for a small minority, inspired hope that Roman Catholicism might cease to be a threat to liberty, no unionist accepted this as an accomplished fact.[37] A strongly 'liberal' unionist summarized his community's *weltanschauung*:

> Basically the Partitionist fears the exclusiveness of Roman Catholicism, its claims to absolute truth and the consequences that seem to follow from that position. ... [The] claims of the Catholic and his church make it difficult for them to be tolerant of what might be called liberal society – the society which, for this discussion, may

be described as trying to make a distinction between the responsibilities of the Church, whether it be Roman Catholic or Protestant, and the State.[38]

As long as catholics presented a stony face of non-co-operation, unionists knew how to react. But with minority attitudes apparently softening, unionists faced tactical, strategic and even existential choices. The *Unionist* newspaper positively welcomed old-fashioned statements of nationalist intransigence as 'it lets us know where we stand – just in case any loyalists were being talked into a false sense of trust.'[39] Unionism was defined by negatives, principally its opposition to Roman Catholicism and Irish nationalism. A positive British nationalism, whilst not absent, remained under-developed.[40] The apparent weakening of its enemy threw its own self-identity into crisis, thus the anomaly of Paisleyite loyalist reaction developing before a sustained nationalist challenge to the Union.

For traditional unionists assimilatory ideas were based upon a dangerous illusion. Even a policy of 'leaning over backwards' warned James Molyneaux, Deputy Grand Master of the Orange Order, would not 'transform nationalists into loyal and responsible citizens of Northern Ireland.'[41] Any attempt threatened to weaken unionist unity by shearing off the 'extremists'. By shifting the emphasis of politics away from the constitution it raised the possibility of legitimizing class-based parties such as the NILP. Unreliable catholics, moreover, would colonize the party and state. 'Normalization' of politics implied an acceptance of the end of one-party rule, and the creation of a cross-party, cross-community stable pro-Union majority. Yet a non-unionist government, in segregatory eyes, was inherently untrustworthy. Catholics would never be loyal enough to be allowed to control, even indirectly, the levers of power. Protestant unity was the imperative for segregatory unionism.

Despite the admonitions of Edward Carson, devolution in Northern Ireland had never greatly deviated from a segregatory model that excluded catholic Irish nationalism from the public cultural sphere.[42] In the 1950s there was even an attempt to slow the catholic birth rate through social engineering. The Family Allowance Bill of 1956 was justified to the Parliamentary Unionist Party by

showing that the exclusion of the first child from family allowance during the past decade had had the effect of discriminating against smaller families and in favour of larger families. As Unionists had a greater percentage of smaller families and Nationalists a much greater percentage of large families this discrimination had led to an upsurge in the Nationalist birth-rate.[43]

The Bill, which proposed a lower rate of allowance for children after the first two, was dropped on the insistence of Westminster Unionist MPs fearful of British reaction.[44]

The IRA Border Campaign of 1956–62 dissuaded the government from radical initiatives and helped prolong the life of traditional, segregatory Unionism.[45] In October 1959 assimilatory unionists – those who hoped to eventually win catholics to unionism – were provoked into a premature demonstration and badly mauled. Sir Clarence Graham, Chairman of the Standing Committee of the Ulster Unionist Council, and Brian Maginnis, the Attorney General, had suggested that catholics be invited to join the Unionist Party.[46] Lord Brookeborough insisted, however, that catholics, loyal to an inveterately anti-unionist church intent on interfering in civil matters, were never likely to be good unionists.[47] Maginness was left isolated in the party and, while Unionist Associations could, and some did, admit catholics to membership, they had clearly been discouraged from doing so.[48] The assimilatory tendency in unionism had been exposed as being without organization, and potential supporters were demoralized or scared off.[49] The early 1960s saw an actual decline in the influence and membership of the one avowedly 'liberal' unionist organization, the Unionist Society.[50]

Conciliation was not the preserve of assimilatory unionists however (thus the difficulty of applying a simple liberal-reactionary gradient). In the aftermath of the IRA's defeat segregatory unionists seemed to consider granting concessions in a spirit of *noblesse oblige*. The 'Orange-Green talks' of 1962–3 were between traditionalists on both sides.[51] In August 1962, a leading Nationalist Senator, in a speech to an Ancient Order of Hibernian's rally in Omagh, proposed, as a means of removing discrimination, to meet Senator Sir George Clark, Grand Master of the Orange Order. To general surprise, Sir George Clark agreed to private but formal discussions 'relating to the good will of Ulster's people.'[52] Clark met Lennon, in secret, on 18 October 1962.[53] In early 1963 the Orange Central Committee appointed representatives for regular meetings with nationalist leaders.[54] By February, however, it was clear that fundamental problems of principle had arisen.[55] It became known that the five-point agenda submitted by the nationalist delegation included references to discrimination in employment and housing. The Grand Lodge believed that to discuss such allegations would be to admit their basis in fact. This was deemed unacceptable. Further discussions between Clark and Lennon in June failed to cut the Gordian knot.[56]

Shortly afterwards Green representatives received an ultimatum: no more discussions until they recognized of the legitimacy of the Northern Ireland state.[57] This was a practically impossible demand and in all likelihood was a deliberate ploy on the part of the Orange Order to extricate itself from a difficult situation. Discontent on both sides rapidly spread.[58] In December Clark refused to comment on prospects for renewed talks in 1964 and Lennon simply observed that he had heard nothing since writing to the Orange Order in June.[59]

This interesting attempt at rapprochement between the established sectarian camps failed because, from the unionist point of view, in the absence of an effective nationalist offensive or sustained interest from outside the state, they had really very little to gain from compromise. Unionist ultra, Norman Porter, articulated the basic zero-sum assumption: 'I cannot see any value in having the talks, because the only basis on which the Nationalists will have negotiations is of them gaining something and us losing something.'[60]

The rapid exhaustion of initiative from segregatory unionism left the field to those prepared to pursue an assimilatory path. Though powerful, even dominant, in civil society, this trend was seriously under-represented in the party. With admittedly copious exceptions, middle-class protestants in the late 1950s and early 1960s did largely accord to the assimilatory unionist model. They were self-confident, optimistic of improving communal relations, suspicious of protestant populism, in favour of British norms, hostile to Irish nationalism and catholicism but willing to accommodate the reform of both. Amused contempt for Orange coat-trailing was a particularly noticeable characteristic.[61] Whilst the protestant middle class might scorn loyalist pageantry, however, this did not translate into an active desire to compromise with the minority. Barritt and Carter's description of small-town middle-class consciousness rings particularly true:

> We find that in going to a provincial town we are referred time and time again to the same small group of Catholics, as being 'interested in co-operation'; and most of these will be professional and business men of liberal outlook. ... [The] younger Protestants, in the higher social classes, while not liking a display of political sentiment (and perhaps making fun of the Orange Order) take the

British connection very much for granted. If there is to be any bridgebuilding, they expect it to be from the Catholic side.[62]

Not only was the political consciousness of the protestant middle class circumscribed, but its impact on official Unionist structures was severely limited. There were only two or three hundred regularly active party members most of whom were aged stalwarts set in their ways.[63] It was apparent that the moderate middle class simply was not becoming involved. As Bob Cooper remembers:

> It was very difficult to get people to join the Unionist Party, particularly substantial business people, professional people. ... In most Unionist Associations ... the number of lawyers, the number of doctors, accountants would have been tiny. They were small business people, in the main, and in the rural areas, farmers and so on. It was very, very difficult to get [professionals] to join the Unionist Party or to have anything to do with politics at all. As far as they were concerned politics was a nasty sort of game...[64]

The 1960s were a period of blurring boundaries in Northern Irish society. As we have seen this was only partially reflected in established political structures. It did create, however, an opportunity to remake the political landscape. The Northern Ireland Labour Party, the Liberal Party, and elements of the Civil Rights Movement all attempted to establish new political alignments on the basis of the apparent exhaustion of the old sectarian dichotomy. The most important experiment, however, was that attempted by Terence O'Neill. As Prime Minister from 1963 to 1969 he evolved an assimilatory strategy designed to foster a new pluralist culture based upon acceptance of the Union. This very process, however, threatened the political certainties of both catholic and protestant communities, and indeed challenged their self-identities. In a familiar response, both sides reacted by reinforcing their boundaries.[65] That catholics were slower to respond in this way is obvious, and partially accounts for the dynamic of the period. But most striking in the longer view, certainly apparent by August 1969, was the fearful symmetry of both communities retreating into militant political segregation.

2
The Origins of O'Neillism

Born in London on 10 September 1914, Terence Marne O'Neill was socialized into a political family. His maternal grandfather had been a Liberal Home Ruler and Gladstone's Irish viceroy. His paternal grandfather was a leading Tory Unionist. The union of his parents sent ripples of political scandal.[1] Terence's father, Captain Arthur O'Neill, unwillingly inherited the Mid-Antrim seat. O'Neill was three months old when his father, serving in the Second Life Guards, became the first MP of the First World War to be killed in action.[2] Many contemporaries believe that O'Neill's aloof and lonely manner may have derived from his lack of a father figure in youth.[3]

Terence O'Neill had a pride in his Ulster genealogy, though more particularly the illustrious history of the O'Neill clan, 'the oldest traceable family left in Europe'. Descent could be traced back to a Tyrone Prince killed in battle in 1283, but by tradition the line included Niall of the Nine Hostages, High King of Ireland from c.379 to c.409 AD. Terence was not directly descended from the Ulster kings but rather from a branch of O'Neill's founded by a nominee of the English after the 'flight of the earls'. He was a descendant of Edward Chichester, brother of James I's Escheater-General of Ulster from 1689 and later Lord Deputy of Ireland. Chichester's grandson married Mary O'Neill, of Shane's Castle, and his great grandson became heir to the Antrim estates of the O'Neill's. Terence's branch only adopted its present name from the mother's side in 1855 when the original line died out.[4]

O'Neill spent the first seven years of his life in London in a comfortable house run by ten servants paid for by his grandfather, Lord Crewe. Most summer holidays were spent in Shane's Castle, the O'Neill family home in Ulster.[5] In 1922 his mother was remarried to the British consul in Addis Ababa and consequently the young Terence spent an exotic year in Abyssinia, 'the happiest ... of my life.'[6] O'Neill went to school at West Downs in Winchester, then Eton, where he was by his own admission an indifferent student.[7] Upon leaving school he spent a year abroad in France and Germany, a politicizing experience which led him to support Churchill's crusade against appeasement and set him against members of his family and social circle.[8] Still he had little concern for politics in Northern Ireland.[9]

After a stint working in the City, in 1939 his aunt secured O'Neill a job as ADC to the Governor of South Australia. However, within a few weeks war broke out and he returned to join the socially prestigious Irish Guards.[10] Whilst waiting for the invasion of Europe, he married Jean Whitaker, of a wealthy and long-established family owning Lisle Court estate near Lymington, Hampshire.[11] Once in Europe O'Neill served as the intelligence officer of the 2nd Battalion, where he was noted by his fellow soldiers as 'the most tolerant of men and quite a Francophile'.[12] O'Neill suffered tragedy in the war. He lost a close friend, David Peel, who had been his best man at his marriage, as well as both his brothers, Lord O'Neill with the North Irish Horse in Italy and the Hon. Brian O'Neill with the 1st Battalion of the Irish Guards in Norway.[13] Nevertheless, some of his exploits – notably a gourmet picnic near the frontline and adopting a POW as a personal servant – bring home the socially rarefied atmosphere in which he did his bit for king and country.[14]

By 10 September 1944 the Guards had reached the Dutch frontier. Here O'Neill was injured, hit on the sciatic nerve by shrapnel during shelling. As they were temporarily cut off, O'Neill was tended in a local house by the Ten Horn family, near Nijmegan in Holland. His some-what mannered old-world politeness and diffidence left an impression. When O'Neill and his wife revisited in 1964 Mrs Ten Horn reminded Jean O'Neill: 'We had waited so long for liberation that nothing was too much. Your husband was forever apologising for troubling us.'[15] Captain O'Neill was evacuated back to England and the war came to a close before he could return to active service.

His mother's family opposed O'Neill entering politics but he was deter-mined and hoped to secure a Westminster seat.[16] At the end of 1945 he and his young family finally came to live in the north of Ireland, in a converted Regency rectory near Ahoghill, Glebe House.[17] Here he lived until the 1970s as a country gentleman.[18] Only at the age of 31 did the future Prime Minister of Northern Ireland settle down in the province. In October 1946 the Stormont constituency of Bannside became vacant. Relying on the prestige of his family name, he secured the nomination and was returned unopposed in November 1946.[19] He had neither previous reputation nor experience with the Unionist Party.

There was little sign in O'Neill's personal life of any particular sympathy with the catholic minority. Notoriously in the 1950s he placed an advertisement in a Belfast newspaper seeking a protestant housemaid.[20] This, he explained unapologetically in 1972, was because on previous occasions there had been 'some trouble' over catholic staff, so they had 'advertised for a person of the Protestant religion to stop Catholics turning up'.[21] His daughter, Anne, born 1947, reminiscing in 1969 of her Ahoghill childhood, recalled that she was warned to steer clear of catholics as dangerous rowdies.[22] The image of an aloof ascendancy family is inescapable.

Perhaps because Stormont was evidently second best, O'Neill made little mark as a backbencher. He briefly courted controversy in 1947, when ideas of dominion status were current in unionist circles, by advocating, in a speech to his constituency party, home rule for Scotland. The following day a local paper's headline read, 'O'Neill in favour of Scottish Nationalists.'[23] Having lived most of his life in England, O'Neill was somewhat unfamiliar with the intricacies of Ulster politics, as he was himself later to admit.[24] The impression gained is that of a British constitutionalist to whom the passions of Irish nationalisms were quite alien.

O'Neill's lack of political nous, not to mention the shallowness of his support amongst the Unionist rank and file, probably accounted for PM Brookeborough's unwillingness to promote him too rapidly. In February 1948 he was appointed Parliamentary Secretary to William Grant, Minister of Health.[25] Grant hailed from a working-class Belfast background, but despite their obvious differences O'Neill was stimulated by his energy.[26] Grant died in August 1949 to be replaced by Dame Dehra Parker who, notwithstanding her liberal inclinations (and the fact that she was his aunt), irked O'Neill as she kept him in the shadows. In 1953 he was moved to the even lower-profile post of Chairman of Ways and Means (Leader of the House).

In 1954 George Hanna, Minister of Home Affairs, asked him to become a joint Parliamentary Secretary for Hanna and Dehra Parker at Health. He was unwilling to move back, but did so specifically to deal with the controversial Rent Derestriction Bill Parker hoped to introduce.[27] This was considered by some a dangerous provocation of traditionally Unionist-voting workers.[28] O'Neill showed his facility in negotiating the timetable of the bill with his opposite number at Westminster, Enoch Powell, but he failed utterly to salve inner party tensions.[29] The Attorney General,

Edmund Warnock, went public with his criticism of the bill, prompting a demand for his resignation from Brookeborough.[30] In the resultant reshuffle Terence O'Neill, aged 42, finally reached Cabinet level as Minister of Home Affairs. Six months later O'Neill took on the Finance portfolio, divesting himself of Home Affairs shortly afterwards.[31]

O'Neill thus found himself holding not merely nominally but, with the economic crisis of the early 1960s, in reality the most important ministerial portfolio after the Prime Minister. Decline of employment in traditional industries – heavy engineering, textiles and agriculture – meant that between 1945 and 1959 Northern Ireland suffered an average unemployment rate of 7.4 per cent compared to 3.0 per cent in Scotland and 1.7 per cent in the United Kingdom as a whole.[32] Average wages were about 80 per cent of the UK level.[33]

Towards the end of 1954 a working group of Stormont and Whitehall civil servants convened to discuss the Northern Ireland economy. Though British Ministers found the resulting report 'inconclusive and depressing', it posed the crucial question 'whether the circumstances of Northern Ireland are so exceptional as to be unique' and thus deserving of higher levels of Treasury aid than that offered to even depressed regions of Great Britain.[34] The Northern Ireland delegation, hampered by conservative officials from the Ministry of Finance, presented a poor case. However, the potential for an ethnic explosion in Northern Ireland spoke to the British government more eloquently than any Unionist minister.

Increasingly apparent was a worrying shift in Northern Ireland's domestic politics; not an incipient fragmentation of the unionist bloc on class lines, but signs of revolt amongst the nationalist minority. Sectarian tensions were kept at boiling point throughout the 1950s by provocative Orange marches through catholic areas, indulged by the Stormont government.[35] Since 1951 the IRA and splinter groups had been increasingly active. A number of paramilitary operations were carried out, most spectacularly an arms raid on Armagh barracks. In 1955 Sinn Fein, standing IRA felons as candidates, polled 152,310 votes in Northern Ireland and elected two to parliament, Tom Mitchell for Mid-Ulster and Phil Clarke for Fermanagh and South Tyrone. Both refused to take their seats.[36]

The British government was concerned at what this rise of militant nationalism might mean. In 1955 a Minister advised:

there are strong arguments for affording Northern Ireland special assistance. The Province remained in the United Kingdom because the majority of the inhabitants fiercely desired this. The Union creates particularly tiresome problems for the Government of the United Kingdom and they are not merely domestic but on occasion affect our relations with Commonwealth countries, notably Australia, and foreign allies, notably the US, in which persons of Irish descent cherish a deep rancour against Northern Ireland and against partition. Nevertheless it must be recognized that the possession of Northern Ireland is of capital importance in the defence of Great Britain. The gravity of the loss of the naval base at Queenstown in the Irish Republic was acutely apparent during the last war. If this had been accompanied by the loss of Northern Irish harbours, aerodromes and shipbuilding capacity, the results might well have been disastrous. It is important to remember this since inevitably Northern Ireland is apt to be a nuisance to United Kingdom departments whose members may sometimes be in danger of allowing their attitude to Northern Ireland problems to be unconsciously influenced by this. If we desire to retain Northern Ireland – and so far no responsible person has contested the view that the advantages in favour of this course are overwhelming – it is most important politically to be able to demonstrate that Northern Ireland benefits from the Union. Indeed, the only remedy for the unrest, rancour and violence which rend that unhappy country is to make life north of the Border more desirable than life south of it.[37]

Rab Butler supported this in a memorandum. Extra help for Northern Ireland, he believed:

can be justified on the grounds of her exceptional geographical position, and of the long history of severe unemployment there. Moreover, Northern Ireland's internal dissensions can best be resolved by making it a desirable mode for the anti-partitionist minority. Prosperity will not of itself solve the Irish question, but it should do something to dilute rancour, and if a generation can grow up in reasonably prosperous circumstances which are clearly dependent on Union, it is just possible that one day the ending of partition may cease to be the foremost thought in the minds of the minority, and that there may emerge a coherent opposition prepared to accept Union, without which political life in Northern Ireland is unlikely ever to flourish. At any rate if nothing is done there seems a distinct risk that matters will get worse.[38]

The Secretary of State agreed with the terse observation that '[S]uch a high level of unemployment [as exists in NI] where there is a large and potentially violent dissident minority may easily lead to violent civil disorders.'[39]

The British analysis gave priority to political and defence considerations. They were chiefly concerned to pacify a dimly understood but feared catholic minority. It was with these considerations in mind that the British government made two crucial concessions. Firstly a Development Council in 1955, headed by Lord Chandos, was established to 'to promote new industries and to reduce unemployment in Northern Ireland'.[40] Much more importantly, the Joint Exchequer Board, a civil service committee that mediated between the Treasury and the Northern Ireland government, promulgated the principle of leeway in 1955.[41] This created what Arthur Green, Assistant Secretary in the Department of Finance, called an 'expenditure based system' in which the British 'subvention' would be determined not by an abstract formula but by the perceived merits the case made by Stormont.[42] The expenditure-based system allowed the Stormont government effectively to spend beyond its own means to make up leeway.

At first this new system did nothing to change the rigid framework of economic policy evolved under Brookeborough. This was centred upon a wide range of grants and inducements to encourage foreign investment. The Industries Development Acts were 'the principal instrument of Government policy in the period since the end of the last war'.[43] Between 1945 and 1951 a total of £75.17 million was spent by the Northern Ireland government on industrial subsidization. Between 1952 and 1957 this went up to £139.29 million and it shot up to £292.25 million between 1958 and 1963.[44] Though there was to be an enormous expansion in the money spent on regional policy inducements after 1963, Brookeborough's government had largely set the pattern in the 1950s.

None of this, however, took advantage of the implicit British promise of funding for special projects. The Chancellor of the Exchequer emphasized to the Stormont team, with some impatience, that 'United Kingdom Ministers would be willing to help in whatever way might be necessary when they saw the Northern Ireland Government taking the initiative.'[45] Large-scale social spending, however, was alien to Stormont's *modus operandi*. Policy remained firmly in a rut of subsidies to established employers with only minor unemployment relief or house building schemes. Unionist ministers simply could not imagine substantial environmental investment. In a remarkable memorandum, illustrative of his tendency to sometimes wildly speculative thinking, Terence O'Neill warned in 1958 that an employment crisis loomed and that desperate measures were required:

> All ideas should be considered. ... For good measure I will put one up to be shot down – perhaps with some scorn and derision. Can Lough Neagh be drained? It would be equivalent to a new county. Have engineers – possibly Dutch engineers – ever been consulted? The Government could possibly lease it out in 100-acre farms. County Neagh would have no mountains or bogs and might be quite fertile, it could be planted with trees and people and a new town could be built at its centre. (Strangford is smaller and has salt water and tide but could perhaps also be considered.)[46]

This strikingly reveals O'Neill's characteristic combination of grandiose vision and naivete, as well as a tendency to pronounce before thinking which often tested his civil servants' nerves. As such, it prefigures, if rather comically, his contribution to Irish history. But it indicated too an immediate problem – the simple difficulty of responding imaginatively to an intractable employment problem even with an awareness that Britain would ultimately pay well above the odds to secure quiet in the province.

O'Neill's gloomy predictions proved correct. Crisis in Belfast shipbuilding and marine engineering employment, which contracted by 11,500 or 40 per cent between 1961 and 1964, inflicted much pain on politically important protestant working-class communities.[47] The labour and trade union launched an effective campaign of agitation that, as it was primarily directed against treasury restraints in Britain, attracted some unionist sympathy.[48] There was a severe slippage in the Unionist vote in the general election held on 31 May 1962. Though they won no new seats, the Northern Ireland Labour Party (NILP) vote reached 26 per cent, up from 16 per cent in 1958. They nearly equalled the Unionist vote of 67,450 in Belfast, winning 60,170.[49] Only just over 60 per cent of the total votes were cast for the government.[50] Unionists had seen this coming. In February Harry West noted that 'many people in Belfast had got their minds filled with the economic position of the country and seemed to forget the great and important issue of the election – their constitutional position.'[51] Brookeborough named Labour as 'the enemy at the gate'. The persistent rate of unemployment – at 8 per cent – was proving the Unionists' greatest weakness.[52]

Under pressure from a developing trade union campaign and Labour vote, Brookeborough flailed defensively:

> I hope that trade unionists and those men who suffer from unemployment and redundancy will accept the fact that my heart bleeds for them. I understand their situation and will do everything I can to solve it. I cannot go beyond that and I cannot make any promises I cannot accomplish.[53]

Aristocratic bleeding hearts were not best calculated to stem the advance of Labour amongst the protestant working class.

Terence O'Neill, as Minister of Finance, had been clearly identified with the government's minimalist approach, and as such had come under heavy criticism.[54] His penny-pinching rhetoric, however, had frequently been wrapped in patriotic injunctions to his fellow citizens to inculcate the virtues of 'self-help' rather than rely on handouts.[55] O'Neill was probably inspired by 'Self-help', written by Scottish author Samuel Smiles (1812–1904) and republished on its centenary in 1958.[56] Enthusiastically he adopted Smiles' nostrums on civic responsibility and entrepreneurial initiative which, O'Neill argued, had underpinned nineteenth-century industrial revolution in Belfast.[57] This both flattered the protestant self-perception ('work-ethic') and appealed to the regional patriotism as espoused by some assimilatory unionists keen to transcend divisive British or Irish labels.[58]

His relative youth, high office, and increasingly veteran status began to raise O'Neill's political stock. Though he was often condemned for complacency, his urbane and languid manner at least implied a certain self-confidence and authority. A tussle with the British minister, Selwyn-Lloyd, over the National Insurance Surcharge indicated that he might be something more than the British Treasury's poodle.[59] Nor was he afraid to pinch some of the NILP's more popular ideas, such as Ulster Bonds.[60] Partially as a result of his failure to get on with Douglas Harkness, the permanent secretary at the Ministry of Finance,[61] O'Neill 'concluded that he should take a stronger personal hand in relations with the Treasury in London'.[62] By lunching with senior Treasury officials in the London Saint James Club, he built up a personal network of influence.[63]

O'Neill likewise developed semi-independent and quasi-unofficial connections and allies in the Northern Ireland Civil Service (NICS). His friendships with Bloomfield, his Private Secretary who he took with him from department to department, and Cecil Bateman, later Secretary to the Cabinet, appeared warmer than with his political colleagues.[64] The higher reaches of the NICS were at this time developing a more assertive and autonomous role in relation to their political masters.[65] O'Neill acted as champion of the NICS. He was beginning to emerge as a serious power broker, even a future Prime Minister.[66]

In May 1961 the British and Stormont governments had established a joint working party on Northern Ireland's economy chaired by Sir Robert Hall. Britain by 1960 was convinced that the problem of Northern Ireland's unemployment was more or less insoluble.[67] London, therefore, was not keen to participate in yet another working group, but realized that Brookeborough needed an initiative for political reasons.[68] The report of the working party was published in October 1962.[69]

The Hall report, despite the contemporary vogue for regional planning, was unadventurous and suggested little more than lower wages and higher emigration.[70] This was not simply a report in the mould of Isles and Cuthbert.[71] It was significant because its preparation was the arena for a struggle between the Northern Ireland government and the British exchequer. Ironically, Stormont's success in limiting the IRA campaign and the failure of catholics to lend it militant support had undermined British fears of adverse political consequences to economic lag in Northern Ireland. In contrast to the mid-1950s, when the Chandos Council and the principle of leeway had been conceded, they were no longer concerned that high unemployment in Northern Ireland would create sectarian disorder or a catholic uprising. The evolution of global military strategy, moreover, made Northern Ireland rather less crucial to the defence of Great Britain. Westminster, therefore, refused any substantial response to Brookeborough's plea for further economic succour.[72]

The Hall working party had divided between the respective governments, and little common agreement was arrived at.[73] The Northern Ireland proposals were profoundly defensive, principally wage subsidies to bolster pre-existing jobs.[74] It was designed to defend the interests of labour and local capital. The Treasury rejected them outright. Brookeborough's public disappointment was palpable and bitter.[75] He ended his speech on the Hall Report in Stormont by announcing a crucial shift in emphasis: 'A good deal of hope – perhaps exaggerated hope – has centred on what might come out of this Committee's deliberations. We must now turn our thoughts to making further inroads on the problem by our own continuing efforts.'[76]

Spurned by Britain, the ideology of 'self-help', frequently espoused by Minister of Finance O'Neill, suddenly came into its own.

The scope of Brookeborough's personal failure was obvious. His reputation as a Prime Minister had largely depended on his contacts with the British elite. It was clear in the aftermath of the Hall Report debacle that his ability in this regard was spent. A new professionalism and a greater dependence on Northern Ireland's own resources were widely deemed to be appropriate. Brookeborough's public image, as a country gentleman running a part-time Cabinet with a light touch, was a declining asset.[77] The passing of the pre-war political generation in Britain meant that Brookeborough's influence in high political circles in Britain could only wane.[78]

After Hall the mood was one of disillusionment in the reliability of the British government and a feeling that the local government had proved itself insufficiently professional and adventurous. Facing a strong threat from the NILP, the demoralized Unionist Party was looking for a new inspiration and leadership. Now, in this crucial period of unrest, O'Neill pitched in with a post-Brookeborough agenda. Delivered to a Belfast Unionist Association on 29 November 1962, this became known as the Pottinger speech.[79]

O'Neill had for many years espoused the benefits of 'self-help'. In the Pottinger speech he revisited this theme, at first as an 'ourselves alone' riposte to the British rebuff delivered by the Hall Report.[80] 'Self help' he defined as a new public spirit: innovation and energy from entrepreneurs, loyalty and flexibility from workers, an end to carping.[81] He argued that 'to make full use of our advantages' the attractions of Northern Ireland for industry, and especially for the managerial personnel who would come with it, must be promoted and improved.[82]

This led O'Neill on to the real substance of his talk. Northern Ireland was part of the United Kingdom, and it was the responsibility of the UK government to ensure that all areas enjoyed similar prosperity.[83] Regionalism was enjoying a country-wide renaissance after the 1950s.[84] Worried by overheating in the prosperous south-east, threatening the national balance of payments, the British government was attempting to redirect investment to peripheral regions of higher unemployment where there was more slack to be taken up. Until now this had been perceived as a threat by unionists, who saw their province losing its margin of advantage to Scotland, Wales and northeast England in the inducements it could offer. O'Neill, however, turned this on its head:

> The United Kingdom needs the Ulsterman, the Scot, the sturdy Durham miner, the tough Merseyside factory worker, if it is to

continue to be the great, rich, diverse nation it has always been. I spoke of the allies of our struggle of 1912. I believe we have allies today, in every part of the United Kingdom which protests against the 'concentrated economy'.[85]

This was an alternative programme to Brookeborough's failed economic policy.

Brookeborough had gone to Britain relying on charm, contacts and special pleading to win resources from the exchequer. He called in old debts built up during the war and requested stop-gap aid to overcome specific political and economic crises. British interest in a seemingly backward, archaic and irredeemable political and economic backwater had steadily waned, however, as expectations amongst the Ulster populace waxed. With the Hall Report the inexorable scissors finally closed, and Brookeborough's credibility was cut short. Nothing appeared able now to check the NILP's advance amongst traditionally unionist workers besides drumhead politics. This strategy, in turn, threatened to alienate still further a broad swathe, particularly among the better educated. Sheelagh Murnaghan, a catholic Liberal, in 1962 won a Queen's University seat in a straight fight with a Unionist. The graduate electorate had a large protestant majority. Unionists were terrified at the prospect of the middle class joining the electoral desertion.[86] Brookeborough's strategy had reached an impasse.

Terence O'Neill's 'self-help', in contrast, envisaged Northern Ireland pulling its weight as part of the United Kingdom. The province would demand United Kingdom aid not as a charitable stop-gap, but as a right of citizenship. O'Neill was explicit that he believed that the principle of leeway had come to supersede that of 'step by step'.[87] A new progressive thrust to local policy – the political rationale of the 'expenditure' based subvention system now favoured by the local civil service – would renew the validity of claims on the British exchequer. This was recognizable O'Neillism.

O'Neill's new rhetoric was made possible by a revolution in the outlook of the Northern Ireland Civil Service (NICS). It was becoming clear that the 1955 agreement on leeway meant that the civil service could now propose ambitious development.[88]

In 1960, in an attempt to resolve a long-running dispute between Stormont and the Belfast Corporation over the city's boundary, a survey of the Belfast region by an independent consultant was authorized. This tactical ploy was immediately seized upon by the NICS who considerably expanded the remit.[89] The services of an eminent planner, Sir Robert Matthew, were engaged. The Matthew Plan attracted virtually no comment in Stormont before its publication and discussion on the topic in Cabinet barely featured, the Ministers' attention being fully consumed by the Hall Report. When Ministers finally received a copy of the Plan, their response was one of surprise and some confusion.[90] Discussion for such a vast project was minimal. Yet when the Matthew Plan was published on 26 February 1963, in the dying days of Brookeborough's tenure, it was clearly of the greatest significance:

> [It] placed our feet firmly on a path from which we were never to turn back, the path of a positive, activist approach to the physical and economic problems of the province ... it is true to say that his Belfast Regional Plan represented the undisputed origin of a huge programme of government involvement and of the assumption of government of responsibility for the physical development of the country; and secondly that the popular impact of the plan coincided with (if it did not actually fire the starting pistol for) a whole series of other important departures in public policy.[91]

Matthew represented a huge plan of investment, especially in the creation of a 'new city' between Lurgan and Portadown and the designation of a series of growth points: Bangor, Newtownards, Downpatrick, Antrim, Ballymena, Larne and Carrickfergus. Northern Ireland transport was also to be revolutionized, with the planning of a motorway and road network much in advance of the British equivalent. Here too an energetic NICS took the lead with politicians trailing behind.[92] What was remarkable was the lack of political impetus for these measures. They were created autonomously by an ambitious NICS which saw the opportunity to win funds for pet projects. Indeed, Britain proved much more willing to pay for such expansionary schemes than for the modest, but essentially negative, proposals presented by Brookeborough and rejected by the Hall Report. O'Neill did not create his economic policy; he simply recognized the spontaneous appearance of one.[93] O'Neill's economic revolution was civil service created. His skill was in astutely recognizing its political potential in the post-Hall atmosphere and seized the opportunity to become its champion.

By February 1963 Brookeborough was under siege. He condemned rife rumour-mongering in the party and demanded of his restive MPs 'two requirements – support in Parliament and Unionist members to be

Unionist and not get on the Socialist bandwagon.'[94] Discontent over part-time and thus amateur ministers had long simmered. It finally boiled over when Lord Glentoran, Minister in the Senate, was revealed as a director of a bank benefiting from government contracts.[95] Ten rebels in the Parliamentary Unionist Party openly demanded that he divest himself of this compromising tenure.[96] The sub-text was obvious. A more professional Cabinet operating by British standards was required and the ageing, genteel Brookeborough was not the man to lead it.[97]

Two days later the *Belfast Telegraph* admitted that it 'share[d] the view which, as is reliably reported, is held by a growing number in Parliament that the Minister of Finance, Captain Terence O'Neill, is proving his fitness to take command.'[98] It reported that, though strong support existed in the Parliamentary Unionist Party for both Brian Faulkner, the hard-line Minister of Home Affairs and J. L. O. Andrews, the affable Minister of Commerce, support was strongest for O'Neill.[99] This may have been exaggerated, but it serves as a useful corrective to the idea that O'Neill enjoyed virtually no support outside the ranks of the big house magic circle.[100]

Probably Brookeborough's illness, a duodenal ulcer, saved him from overthrow by stirring sympathy and indicating that he was likely to retire on his own initiative soon enough.[101] The attacks continued, however, and on 1 March, following three emergency Cabinet meetings and an angry Ulster Unionist Council Standing Committee, Glentoran resigned the controversial directorship.[102] Only now could Brookeborough be admitted to Musgrave Hospital, from where he emerged 11 days later.[103] However, he apparently still felt worried about his health[104] and at 74 he no doubt felt his age.

On 23 March Lord Wakehurst, the Governor, was telephoned by Lady Brookeborough asking him to meet Lord Brookeborough at Stormont House. Upon his arrival Brookeborough announced his resignation due to ill health and because 'he could step down without loss of face seeing that he had mastered the revolt within the Unionist Party'.[105] A discussion was held on the possible successor. Wakehurst later opined that he 'and Lord Brookeborough were of one mind in considering the Minister of Finance and acting Prime Minister, Captain Terence O'Neill, as the obvious choice.' As Brookeborough pointedly refused to suggest a successor, however, the retiring premier's unwillingness to recommend O'Neill is evident.[106]

Captain O'Neill was forewarned, before both Faulkner and Andrews, and called to the Governor's house at 6 p.m. the following Monday. Even with this head start he 'felt it necessary to consult the Chief

Whip (Mr Craig) as to whether he could give an assurance (of a parliamentary majority) if sent for.'[107] Craig later denied helping O'Neill into power,[108] but he certainly carried out a straw poll amongst Unionist members of the Stormont Commons, the result being allegedly 16 votes for O'Neill and nine each for Faulkner and Andrews.[109] Though comfortable this was hardly an overwhelming victory for O'Neill. Support in the broader party, particularly amongst the younger layers, however, was probably greater.[110]

It was not simply O'Neill's self-promotion as a pragmatic modernist that ensured his accession. His lineage undoubtedly gave him the leverage he required with the Unionist hierarchy.[111] A 1961 profile commented that O'Neill 'is probably closest in charm, background and general nature to the present premier.'[112] On his succession in 1963, the *Irish Times* characterized him as the representative of the 'ruling class' in Northern Ireland, and declared him the head of the 'O'Neill – Chichester-Clarke caucus in the North's politics'.[113]

It was not quite as simple as this, however. O'Neill was himself not a landowner. Nor was he titled: when his elder brother died in the war his nephew became Lord O'Neill. The Antrim O'Neills were not consistently prominent in the unionist elite, certainly in contrast to the landed elite of south and west Ulster.[114] The gentry during the 1960s considered O'Neill to be somewhat inferior in social status, if a cut above bourgeois unionist leaders.[115] O'Neill, thus, straddled the old landed elite in unionist politics, accustomed to rule, secure in their authority, contemptuous of populism, and the restless, technocratic, modernizing middle class.[116] Crucial to O'Neill's appeal to the unionist 'magic circle' were his social standing and military credentials. Nevertheless, Jack Andrews, also from an illustrious background and distinguished career, and though he was Glengall Street's (the Party's HQ) favourite, lacked O'Neill's drive and ambition for power.[117] This it was that proved crucial.

That Terence O'Neill's entertained assimilatory ideas on the virtue of winning catholics to unionism was known to selected acquaintances in the public sphere,[118] but it was not prominent in his public persona at the time. Certainly he had exhibited signs of an assimilatory approach. In 1960 he told the Cullybackey Twelfth demonstration, for example, that: 'Education, health and prosperity are all above and beyond any divisions that may be in our community.'[119] Never was he more explicit than this, however, and his liberal credentials stemmed more from an evasion of sectarian rhetoric rather than an embracing of its contrary. O'Neill enthused liberals by his youth, his undoctrinaire approach to politics and economics, his evident compatibility and ease with British norms and expectations, and his lack of an Orange and populist reputation. He was seen not as an original thinker, but open to influence from the liberal intelligentsia outside the Unionist Party.[120]

He never made an explicit pitch for assimilationist support, and his renowned Pottinger speech, delivered in November 1962, appealed more to regional Ulster pride and a desire for economic vitality. In a lesser speech addressed to the Young Unionist Conference in February 1963 he was still more general and reflective on the nature of unionism. He called for a forward-looking Northern Ireland, emulating the confidence of the Republic of Ireland. To this end he advocated a regional, Ulster patriotism. Unionism should shed its defensive posture and develop its unique strength: in contrast to British parties it united the classes rather than set one against the other. 'It is that unity which is our greatest asset and which we must struggle to preserve. In this little country of ours we cannot afford the struggle of pitting man against man, class against class.' This was an important statement of O'Neillism.[121]

Modernization normally implied a political evolution towards the British model. But such a bi-polar, class-orientated structure could only be to the advantage of the NILP. O'Neill proposed modernization based upon a transcendence of the border issue, as in effect resolved in Unionism's favour, by a shared Ulster identity. The Unionist Party, already a pan-class alliance for the purposes of defending the Union, would maintain itself by uniting all classes around a pragmatic, regional patriotism. O'Neill's liberalism at this time was primarily a device to retain pan-class unity in the face of a socialist challenge: 'We do not want the class struggle introduced into our midst. There is too great a similarity between the aspirations of a Unionist and a [trade] union to allow that to happen.'[122] Ulster's mission, one that would recast the Unionist alliance in a progressive mould and thus win back the active participation of the professional classes, was economic and technocratic. Announcing his ambition, for the first time, to 'change the face of Ulster',[123] he intoned visionary advances in the Harland and Wolff Belfast shipyard, Shorts aircraft factory, linen manufacturing, synthetic fibre, agriculture and 'above all' new industries.

> All these things are possible if we work together as a community . . .
> With confidence, with unity, with vision we can advance into the
> future and show the world that small countries like Switzerland and
> Denmark are not unique in their achievements.[124]

O'Neill's regional patriotism was non-divisive, indeed virtually apolitical. It would attract the middle classes and even, he quietly hinted, the catholic minority.

The similarity to the project of Seán Lemass, Taoiseach of the Republic of Ireland from 1958, is striking. Lemass similarly hoped to dislodge Irish nationalism from its anglophobic groove. Instead patriotic mobilization was to be directed to winning for Ireland a place as an economically vibrant and socially modern small nation. Terence O'Neill, as British-unionist as he undoubtedly was, preferred this Irish model of development to British class politics. His role as Prime Minister was to mobilize Ulster's patriotic energy for economic development. His weaknesses in comparison to Lemass are equally obvious. Lemass had carefully prepared his ground. Fianna Fáil was psychologically ready, after returning to power in 1957, for a radical programme of modernization under the auspices of the Whitaker Plan.[125] O'Neill made no such impression on the Unionist Party.

Secondly, Lemass had a homogenous nation behind him. Northern Ireland, in contrast, was profoundly divided. O'Neill may have hoped to turn Unionism away from a defensive alliance but the very reason it existed was that the catholic minority was disloyal to the state itself. The defensive orientation of Unionism was thus not as archaic as O'Neill liked to believe and could not simply be wished away.

O'Neill's initial goal was not to create a united Ulster, but rather reunite an increasingly fragmented Unionism to see off the NILP's challenge. Nevertheless, assimilatory unionists had no choice but to support him. They backed O'Neill because they were too weak to raise their own champion, and as O'Neill himself was to muse years later, 'The moderates can only succeed when they are in power.'[126] Rallying behind O'Neill in power was assimilatory unionism's only chance to end the confessional basis of Unionism.

3
Changing the Face of Ulster

In a speech to the Annual General Meeting of Ormeau Unionist Association early in 1965 Terence O'Neill explained that he had approached his premiership with a 'businesslike and systematic plan of action'. First, to 'survey our problems and pinpoint our opportunities' in economic and social policy. Thus a series of reports: Matthew on physical planning, Benson on transport, Wilson on economic development, and Lockwood on education. Second, to overhaul the machinery of government: reorganise ministries, establish an Economic Council and reach a concordat with the trade unions.[1] This imposed a retrospective order on the first two years of O'Neill's government, but it has some validity. This chapter analyses O'Neill's attempt to modernize the structures of devolved administration in Northern Ireland.

The structure of government

Both to maintain continuity and because of the dearth of talent on the backbenches, O'Neill began moderately enough, making few changes in his Cabinet. His rivals for the leadership held the top jobs – J. L. O. Andrews had Finance and Faulkner added Commerce, a speciality close to his heart, to the portfolio of Home Affairs. Chichester-Clarke, O'Neill's cousin, was made Assistant Whip. Aware of his poor links with the party, O'Neill brought Bill Craig, Chief Whip and a personal ally, into the Cabinet.[2] A month later Craig took over Home Affairs and Chichester-Clark became Chief Whip.[3]

From the start O'Neill attempted to professionalize the political administration of the province. He first lanced the boil of discontent that had bedevilled Brookeborough's last days by announcing a

28

Cabinet code of conduct. This allowed Ministers to hold business directorships only if they clearly avoided conflicts of interest.[4] Cabinet colleagues were soon to find that, in contrast to Brookeborough, who appointed ministers and left them to their own devices, O'Neill kept a close eye on all the ministries.[5]

O'Neill's work ethic was often commented on. In 1964 he told an interviewer that, on average he worked 15 or 16 hours a day:

> I think that these days any Prime Minister – and indeed any Cabinet Minister – must expect to have to reduce his personal and private commitments to a minimum. If he is putting private inclinations before his public duties he is not doing his job properly. ... The days of the amateur, part-time man in public life are a thing of the past.[6]

O'Neill's passion was for politics. Even when retired he filled his available hours by 'read[ing] newspapers, all day almost, and biographies, particularly of politicians. I don't have much time for music. ... I used to ride a lot, but it went out of my life a long time ago, as did shooting game. And I never had the patience to fish. I've never been to Croke Park in my life.'[7] Lady O'Neill remembers that even while abroad her husband would every day, if possible, attend the local library to catch up on all the available British and Irish newspapers.[8] He was a meticulous, efficient and conscientious politician, but not a skilled party 'boss' adept at small talk, social interchange and patronage. The contrast to the shooting, fishing, genial and popular Brookeborough is striking.

O'Neill's firmest relations were with apparatchiks like himself. A 1961 profile noted that 'when presented with a file requiring a decision, he ... likes to pursue the problem back through the various civil servants who have contributed to it.'[9] In April 1962 he jocularly commented that 'I hope I don't appear frivolous in saying that what I most enjoy is arguing things out with my civil servants.'[10] Indeed, O'Neill in his autobiography speaks most warmly not of party colleagues, but of his senior aides, Ken Bloomfield, his Private Secretary, and Cecil Bateman, Secretary to the Cabinet.[11]

O'Neill rapidly established the team through which he really intended to govern. He hoped to inculcate the professional methods of Whitehall, rather than the more traditional 'court' system.[12] Within 24 hours of Brookeborough's resignation, Sir Arthur Kelly, his Cabinet Secretary and grey eminence, was replaced.[13] Cecil Bateman, an

economics graduate, succeeded Kelly.[14] O'Neill rearranged the layout
of Stormont and introduced new telephones so as to facilitate closer
communications with his staff.[15] This consisted of the Cabinet
Secretary (Cecil Bateman and, from 1965, Harold Black), Private
Secretary (Jim Malley) and assistant secretary to the Cabinet (Ken
Bloomfield, O'Neill's former companion in Finance). Also important
was Tommy Roberts, O'Neill's press secretary. Almost every day this
group would gather in O'Neill's room for a lengthy and ill-organized
'bull session'. Bateman and Black dealt with relations with Whitehall,
Malley was the political fixer and Bloomfield wrote most of O'Neill's
speeches. Between them, they established a quasi-presidential style of
government that circumvented the Cabinet, over which O'Neill found
himself incapable of exercizing firm control.[16]

In July 1964 Terence O'Neill felt confident enough radically to
reshape the Cabinet and structure of government he had inherited
from Brookeborough. John Andrews, aged 60, left the Ministry of
Finance and the government to be replaced by the long-serving Ivan
Neill, previously Minister of Labour and Minister of Education.
Herbert Kirk, a liberal, moved from Labour into Education. Bill Craig,
at 39 the youngest in the Cabinet and a crucial O'Neill ally, moved
from Home Affairs to the Ministry of Health and Local Government.
As he retained transport, it was clear that this was to become a new
Ministry of Development, the key to O'Neill's new 'planning'
regime.[17] Health and Local Government was reformed into Health and
Social Services when the Ministry of Development came into being in
January 1965.[18] The creation of two new ministries was, as O'Neill
proudly recorded, 'the first major alterations to the structure of the
government since its inception.'[19] As a consequence the civil service
apparatus was radically shaken up.[20]

Terence O'Neill was frustrated at the impediments imposed by the
rigid 1920 Government of Ireland Act on restructuring the Stormont
administration. The two new departments were delayed by some six
months. This, he complained, made it 'practically impossible for a
Prime Minister to keep pace with modern thought.'[21] O'Neill, as
Minister of Finance, had made clear his preference for the Canadian
model of devolution, in which state legislatures were clearly subordinate to central government, with shorter sittings and less
quasi-sovereign pomp than Stormont.[22]

Nevertheless, though Terence O'Neill recognized that the structure
of devolution in Northern Ireland was unwieldy, he never went further
in rationalizing it. To do so would require a bill at Westminster and

Unionists entertained a morbid dread of throwing the constitution into the melting pot. Once the 1920 Government of Ireland Act was back in the British political arena it was feared that the opportunity would be taken to do away with Stormont altogether and push Northern Ireland towards unity with the republic.[23]

Economic planning

Early 1963 saw the peak of the unemployment crisis. The loss of 800 jobs in one month from shipbuilding and marine engineering coinciding with atrocious, virtually arctic, weather pushed unemployment up to 54,583 in February (11.2 per cent and 13.7 per cent of males), the highest since 1952.[24]

O'Neill saw the border settlement as an established fact, reinforced particularly by the 1949 Ireland Act which guaranteed no change without the consent of Stormont, and thus put economic policy as his first priority.[25] He was a genuine enthusiast for external investment as the only permanent remedy and was prepared to sacrifice the interests of local employers to this end.[26] By 1963 foreign interest in investment opportunities in Northern Ireland was at its lowest ebb for years.[27] O'Neill candidly admitted to the Coleraine Chamber of Commerce that the limit of cash incentives to private investors had been nearly reached.[28]

In October 1963 O'Neill raised in Cabinet, as a non-agenda item, the idea of an economic plan for Northern Ireland.[29] This was more a Prime Ministerial than a Cabinet initiative as O'Neill had already secured the services of Professor Thomas Wilson, 'a distinguished economist and a patriotic Ulsterman'.[30] The Cabinet generally welcomed O'Neill's proposal, though not in a manner which indicated any enthusiasm for economic planning *per se*. They were more concerned with Wilson's suitability 'on constitutional and political grounds' (conservative in economics, strongly unionist and pro-devolution).[31] Brian Faulkner, Minister of Commerce, was most openly sceptical.[32]

O'Neill replied to the discussion by summarizing the expected advantages of a plan. Intrinsic economic merits did not bulk large. First, 'we must not only be active but be seen to be active'; 'Secondly, an improvement in confidence, both internally and externally, could be expected. This had clearly resulted from the Whitaker Plan in the Republic'; and 'Thirdly, it would be unfortunate if the Treasury, in considering the well-documented claims of other areas, could not take into account a similar survey for Northern Ireland.'[33] Prominent in his justification to the Cabinet, therefore, were the two enduring concerns of O'Neill at this time: Northern Ireland's public image, particularly in comparison to the Republic of Ireland, and the extraction of resources from the British exchequer.[34]

The Economic Plan was announced in parliament on 22 October 1963, not as part of the Queen's Speech, but as O'Neill's gloss upon it. Thus it was firmly attached to his personal prestige.[35] Wilson's Report, with a White Paper as a companion piece, was published in February 1965.[36] Two main growth targets were proposed and accepted: 65,000 new jobs (30,000 in manufacturing, 30,000 in service occupations and 5000 in construction) and 64,000 new houses, all by 1970. This was to be financed by £445 million public investment and a projected £455 million private investment. No clear indication was given of how this figure was arrived at and there were no output or productivity targets. Few dramatically new projects were envisaged. Instead, the concentration was on fulfilling the accepted ideas of limiting the physical growth of Belfast, developing alternative growth centres and expanding industrial training facilities.

O'Neill's planning has justly been judged 'blatantly cosmetic'.[37] Speaking of the Economic Plan in 1969, Wilson noted that while the failure of the first British National Plan had affected Scottish development his own report survived intact because 'it did not lay "excessive stress" upon detailed forecasts and targets'.[38] In other words it was so 'indicative' and vague that it was immune to the vagaries of the economic climate.[39] As Ronnie Munck has commented, the Wilson Plan 'lacked any serious economic calculation. ... The 1960s do appear to mark a shift in the mode of regulation of the Northern Ireland economy, but there does not appear to a watershed as clear-cut as 1959 in the South.'[40] This somewhat misses the point, however. O'Neill knew what he was doing and his intention was never to adopt planning, but rather to steal the modernizing, technocratic clothes of the NILP and, more important still, to construct new levers for winning a greater British subvention.

This latter was the key to O'Neill's economics. Brookeborough's cosy relationship with the Tory grandees of post-war Britain had been seen to fade, culminating in the cathartic humiliation of the Hall Report. O'Neill set out to develop a new persuasiveness around the theme of regionalism.

Throughout most of the 1950s regional development had been ignored in British economic policy. Lord Hailsham's appointment as Minister for the North East in January 1963 dramatically signalled a turn of attention to the backward periphery. In November 1963 a programme of new towns in Scotland and north-east England and an extra £230 million for the peripheral British regions was announced.[41] Most unionists feared the competition for resources.[42] O'Neill however saw opportunity in the renewed enthusiasm for regional growth.

In December he spoke at a banquet in the Guildhall, London. Here he appealed to the 'nation' to use Ulster's unrealized potential to achieve UK growth targets.

> If we are to achieve a fast rate of economic growth, we must bring more of the under-used resources of these areas into use. And when I say 'we' I mean the whole nation. In a very real sense Britain needs the success of Northern Ireland, of central Scotland, of the north east of England to achieve its own essential rate of progress. Without us you will be a car trying to win a Grand Prix with a missing cylinder.[43]

The economic logic may have been dubious, but O'Neill was skilfully exploiting current British obsessions with growth rates, bottlenecks and overheating in the south of England region.[44]

O'Neill believed that Northern Ireland was uniquely placed to benefit from regional planning: 'We have a head start in all this activity. Ours is a closely knit community with its own Parliament and its own distinctive and well established machinery of government.'[45] He predicted that, 'using means closely attuned to our own particular needs', Northern Ireland would achieve economic and social parity with Britain within 46 years.[46]

O'Neill was concerned to communicate his message directly to the British audience. In July 1963 he met with Westminster political Fleet Street correspondents in the Mayfair home of Lord Robert Grosvenor. Also present were Ken Bloomfield, Tom Roberts (Northern Ireland's chief information officer in London) most of the Ulster MPs and a number of Tory dignitaries.[47] O'Neill often met British Ministers, in low key meetings, no doubt hoping to raise the profile of Northern Ireland through a process of osmosis.[48] He courted assiduously the British political and economic elite. In July he hosted a reception in the Hyde Park Hotel, organized by Sir Francis Evans of the London Ulster Office, for 150 dignitaries from industry, politics, diplomacy, radio, television, journalism and the City.[49] Evidently this was a successful venture and it was decided to expand it the following year.[50] This time 400 attended a 'bash' in Claridges, including the British Prime Minister Sir Alec Douglas Home, government and shadow Ministers, and a clutch of business and media tycoons.[51] The Claridges gathering became an annual fixture of the O'Neill years and was held every year up to 1967. Most were grand affairs even by London standards. The emphasis was on conviviality and practical dealing.[52]

This was not the limit of O'Neill's British charm offensive. In Cabinet, as a non-agenda item, O'Neill supported the notion of Ulster Weeks, 'in which Northern Ireland manufacturers and agricultural producers would be invited to co-operate in a concentrated sales and publicity campaign' in Great Britain.[53] The first Ulster Week was held in Nottingham in October 1964. Thirty Ulster commercial firms and organizations were involved, 40 travel agents had Ulster displays, 200 shops stocked Ulster goods, poster sites were booked and O'Neill made a television broadcast. Northern Ireland flags and red hands – rendered in a suitably modern abstract style – adorned the city.[54]

Brookeborough's administration had been characterized by demands for Band-Aid subventions to support employment in traditional industries. This strategy had reached its nemesis with the Hall debacle. O'Neill grasped the new approach emerging from the mandarins of the Northern Ireland civil service, which was to seek finance for modernizing projects ostensibly with the aim of harnessing positively the province's potential so as to contribute to national growth. The results were impressive, as public expenditure per head in Northern Ireland rose from a mere 88 per cent of the English level in 1959–60 to 118 per cent in 1969–70.[55]

For O'Neill the *ad hoc* basis of fiscal relations with the British Treasury, based upon individual projects, was a positive boon. Stormont were able to adopt ambitious plans – the New City, new university and Economic Plan – quite beyond the resources of the local economy.[56] Well might the British exchequer feel uneasy, bombarded as they were by sophisticated pitches disingenuously dressed in modish British notions of 'self-sufficiency', 'regional development' and 'planning'. They were being hoisted by their own petard.

Recognizing NIC-ICTU

O'Neill's economic policy created political difficulties as well as opportunities. Prominent amongst these was the 18-month battle with the trade union movement over recognition.[57] Since its establishment in the 1940s, Stormont had refused to recognize the Northern Ireland Committee of the Irish Congress of Trade Unions (NIC-ICTU) as a body based in another jurisdiction. With Captain O'Neill's emergence as the new Prime Minister came hope of a new chance for a resolution to the impasse.[58]

In April 1963 the Northern Ireland government was approached by Belfast Chamber of Commerce who asked that an equivalent forum to the British National Economic Council be established in the province.[59] The government agreed that a Northern Ireland Economic Council (NIEC) be formed. Such quasi-corporatist economic policies were linked with the maintenance of good industrial relations. The NIC seems to have deliberately decided to pick a fight on what it considered strong ground: the NIEC nominations.

As early as April 1963 the ICTU had established an internal commission to consider the structure of the Congress.[60] This envisaged autonomy for the NIC in matters pertaining only to the North.[61] The Congress was evidently moving towards autonomy for the NIC as a palliative to the demands of its northern membership.[62] Congress realized that in any confrontation with the government business interests would counsel compromise for the sake of tri-partite economic arrangements. It therefore planned to bargain recognition in return for the NIC's autonomy that was probably inevitable anyway.

In May 1963 the government asked for six trade union representatives for the NIEC. Defiantly a conference called by the NIC in July included Billy Blease, NIC chairman, in the delegation. As he held no other position in the trade union movement, for the government to accept him would be tantamount to recognition. After a long delay, suggesting indecision, the government formally rejected Blease's nomination. In response, the trade unions declared a boycott on the NIEC.[63]

At a Cabinet meeting on 20 September the Minister of Labour, Herbert Kirk, intimated that backbench opinion remained hostile to compromise.[64] At O'Neill's insistence a lengthy statement was published setting out the government's considered position:

> The Government ... cannot accept or endorse a situation in which a body in another state has the power to discuss and decide upon affairs which are solely the concern of Northern Ireland or the United Kingdom as a whole. ... In these circumstances the Government cannot contemplate recognition of the Northern Ireland Committee unless radical changes take place which will assure the complete absence of any possibility of interference from outside the United Kingdom.[65]

As tempers soured, the deadlock seemed complete.[66]

With the evident decline of the Conservative administration at Westminster, the prospect of a Labour government began to loom large in Unionist calculations. On 11 March Herbert Kirk urged compromise on the Cabinet. Non-recognition, he insisted, 'provided the government's critics with a very effective propaganda weapon.' Crucially:

> It is now known that the leaders of the British Labour Party have been well briefed on the Northern Ireland Committee issue and have been specifically asked to put pressure on the Government here to recognise the Northern Ireland Committee. If the Labour Party is returned to power in Westminster the unions expect this pressure to be exerted to the full.'[67]

Faulkner, rather unwillingly, accepted compromise in principle but urged that nothing be done quickly. The Cabinet decided to enter into negotiations to secure the NIC's 'effective autonomy'.[68]

There followed a long period of grassroots soundings. It was not until 20 April 1964 that it became known a change in government thinking had occurred.[69] On 23 April the Parliamentary Unionist Party approved the opening of direct negotiations with the NIC, only Edmund Warnock (St Anne's, Belfast) remaining adamantly opposed to compromise.[70] On 9 August the ICTU published the proposed amendment to its constitution.[71] This fell well short of full autonomy for the NIC. It was still required to implement decisions of an all-Ireland executive and conferences. Even purely Northern Ireland decisions were subject to a veto if all-Ireland trade union interests were at risk. Contentious issues once loudly advertised by unionists, such as the make-up of the Executive Council, the method of the NIC's appointment or references in the ICTU constitution to the all-Ireland 'nation' were not even broached.

During the course of three working parties the government secured amendments which at least implied that NIC autonomy was automatic, rather than discretionary, provided that it adhered to ICTU discipline.[72] This was little comfort for the unionists, however, as was clear from the extremely long Cabinet discussion on recognition on 25 June. The Minister of Labour, Herbert Kirk, urged on pragmatic grounds that the extent of autonomy conceded be accepted as grounds for recognition.'[It] would be better to accord recognition freely, on the basis of a reasonable compromise,' he argued, 'rather than to accord it later under pressure from a possible Labour

Government in London.' Faulkner was not convinced. Ivan Neill, until 1962 long-serving Minister of Labour, conceded that non-recognition could not be maintained without 'a serious loss of prestige' but he 'felt bound to say ... that a settlement on the terms suggested could be represented as a victory for the ICTU.' After an exhaustive, and at times near despairing discussion, the Cabinet finally accepted the inevitable.[73]

On 30 June a 75 minute meeting of the Parliamentary Unionist Party approved recognition of the NIC on the basis of the amended constitution. O'Neill recorded that 'many Unionist MPs were too frightened' to attend.[74] A month later the Annual Conference of the Irish Congress of Trade Unions, significantly held in Belfast, unanimously and triumphantly approved the amended constitution.[75] Almost another month elapsed before O'Neill announced the full and formal recognition of the NIC as the trade union centre in Northern Ireland.[76] The impasse was finally at an end.

By delaying for so long the Unionist government considerably weakened its bargaining position. It was true, before as after the change in the ICTU's constitution, that the southern dominated National Executive Council could not impose unpopular policies at will on the NIC for fear of provoking a split.[77] As before, however, the National Executive Council could push the NIC in certain directions as it saw fit[78] and it continued to appoint the Northern Ireland Officer.[79] The NIC and the Northern Ireland conference were even more clearly subordinate to the all-Ireland conferences of Congress.

The recognition crisis lasted over a year. Terence O'Neill displayed many traits he would apply to later, less successful reforming efforts – an unwillingness to confront opposition in his Cabinet or parliamentary party, failure to prepare public opinion, dependence on British pressure – all of which made him seem inconsistent to Unionist insiders and a lone reformer to the world at large.[80] Faulkner led doubters in the Cabinet, though, as he was relatively favourable towards the trade union movement, this was probably due to bloody-minded opposition to O'Neill as much as to ideological scruples.[81] O'Neill's chief obstacle, however, was backbench and rank and file opinion. O'Neill hoped that by concentrating on economic modernization he could bypass the sclerotic and suspicious political structures of the Unionist Party. The recognition crisis, born out of an attempt to establish a Northern Ireland Economic Council, showed clearly that the economic could not blithely move ahead without impinging on the political sphere.

Benson, Matthew and Lockwood

Specific reforms were in the context of infrastructural modernization and were tailored to attract British funds. In November 1963 the Eccles Report proposed that the Electricity Board become the province's sole supplying authority.[82] There was immediate resistance from Belfast and Derry Corporations, who feared that loss of their autonomy would mean their subsidizing rural areas through higher electricity costs.[83] Eventually a compromise was agreed in which separate facilities would remain with a co-ordinating control centre to which the corporations would nominate representatives.[84]

The Ulster Transport Authority (UTA), a government body that ran trains, buses and road freight in Northern Ireland, endured chronic net losses. In 1963 these jumped from about £60,000 to £306,736, the losses on the railways being £457,777 but on the roads only £45,172.[85] The Northern Ireland government had long decided that severe cuts were required in the loss-making railways and had set up a review body to prepare public opinion.[86] The Benson Report, when published in July 1963, counselled that all rail lines but three – Belfast to Larne Harbour, Belfast through Portadown to the border and Belfast to Bangor – be closed, freight services be abandoned, and steam trains be phased out, all over three years. This required the closure of both rail links to Derry (one through Portadown, the other through Coleraine and Ballymena); from Goraghwood to Newry; from Newry to Warrenpoint; from Dungannon to Coalisland; Knockmore Junction to Antrim; and Coleraine to Portrush. A total of 1100 jobs were expected to be lost.[87]

The UTA was to be broken up and privatized over three years, beginning in 1965, and the railways were to be replaced by a motorway and trunk road programme costing £120 million. An ambitious target of 100 miles of motorway by the mid-1970s was announced.[88] The M1 would by mid-1968 connect Belfast to Dungannon via the New City while the M2, due to be completed by 1970, would snake north of Lough Neagh linking Belfast, Antrim, Ballymena, Coleraine and Derry. Dual carriageways would ultimately link Derry, Omagh and the New City. In 1965 Belfast City Council and the Ministry of Development jointly appointed a firm to produce a plan for the Belfast urban motorway and ring road, a project first agreed in principle in 1945.[89] The entire road programme gave Northern Ireland an infrastructure considerably in advance of that of Britain. Presented with a *fait accompli*, British Prime Minister Douglas Home, though irritated, felt unable to force Stormont to renege on its promises.[90] By the mid-1960s the roads programme was consuming 25 per cent of all capital expenditure in the public sector.[91] Given the chronic shortage of housing, to become so politically explosive, this was hardly a wise allocation of resources.

The government's attention had been turned to environmental policy by the demands of a Dutch industrialist, Roelof Luitje Schierbeek, managing director of British Enkalon. In negotiations leading to the establishment of an important textile plant at Antrim in 1963, he had demanded access to fresh water, clean air, skilled workers, recreational and social facilities, a site of 293 acres and better communications with Belfast. The imperious requirements of multinational capital shocked the Northern Ireland government into a sudden realization of the importance of physical planning.[92]

A blueprint for the Greater Belfast region, but with implications for the rest of Northern Ireland, had been produced by Sir Robert Matthew, presented to ministers in October 1962, and published in summary as a Command Paper in February 1963.[93] It recommended the limitation of growth of the Belfast urban area and the preservation of green spaces. Alternative centres of growth to Belfast were to be encouraged, particularly Antrim, Ballymena, Carrickfergus, Larne, Bangor, Downpatrick and Newtownards. Most spectacularly the Portadown - Lurgan area was to be developed into a New City. O'Neill, as we have seen, trumpeted it as the centrepiece of his 'changing the face of Ulster' speech to the Ulster Unionist Council on 5 April 1963.[94] Matthew put Northern Ireland, in some respects, ahead of Great Britain in physical planning, but its implementation was conservative. The idea of a Ministry of Planning, for example, was rejected.[95] Its bold rhetoric, however, cast lustre on a cyclically improving economic situation.[96]

An outline plan and report was published in December 1965. It was expected, by 1981, to cover 6000 acres and have a population of 100,000. Targets included 26,000 new jobs, half in manufacturing, 18,750 new houses, 16 primary and eight secondary schools, 25 new churches, and a 1000 bed regional hospital. It was to be a 'motor-car city' with a modern and efficient infrastructure, 'stronger and more varied than ... most of the twenty-one established and designated new towns of GB.'[97] With such grandiose ambition, it was worrying that there was a planning staff of only 36, compared to the average of 200 in Britain.[98]

A primary recommendation of the Matthew Report was the centralization of planning powers presently dispersed between 37 local councils.[99] Influential business bodies backed centralization.[100] Wary of local government's jealous defence of its prerogatives the Cabinet struggled to find a formula which would 'combine the maximum degree of centralisation and uniformity with the preservation of a reasonable amount of local influence and interest.'[101] On 24 March 1964, after much consultation, a 'revolutionary' White Paper on planning was published which advocated one central planning authority, ten local development committees (for the six counties, plus Belfast, Belfast Harbour, Derry and the New City) to preserve accountability, and machinery for public hearings.[102] Wrangling with local authorities held up progress and full centralization was not achieved until 1973.[103] Nevertheless, a series of regional plans were produced covering County Fermanagh (1963), the New City (1964), Antrim (1965), Ballymena (1966), Derry (1968), the Coleraine-Portrush-Portstewart triangle (1968) and Belfast urban area (1969).[104] These were facilitated by interim planning legislation, the New Towns Act (NI), the Land Development Values (Compensation) Act (NI) and the Amenity Lands Act (NI), all passed in 1965.[105]

The government was keen to reduce in size the enormously cumbersome machinery of local government. There were at least 74 local authorities including a confusion of indirectly elected boards and there were considerable difficulties in attracting capable staff and councillors. In October 1965 William Craig submitted to the Cabinet a memorandum advocating a complete review of local government over five years.

> One message running through much of the professional advice received by Government in recent years – from Matthew, Benson, Wilson, Lockwood amongst others – it can be summed up as the need for Northern Ireland to streamline and modernize its administration. Much has been done, and more is mooted, in spheres of central government and statutory bodies; the unchanging face of local government, by contrast, is appearing more and more an anachronism. ... Public opinion is also ready to see changes and the business world in particular is becoming highly critical.[106]

Though worried that the issue could become another 'political shuttlecock' the Cabinet acceded to Craig's request.[107]

The task of drawing up reform plans was entrusted to Dr John Oliver, a senior civil servant at the Ministry of Development. There was virtually no input from parliament or the councils themselves. Whilst this was no doubt to avoid stirring up opposition from vested interests, it was also designed to exclude consideration of gerrymandering and the restricted local government franchize. Indeed, Craig announced that the franchise was explicitly excluded from Oliver's remit.[108] Two White Papers were published, in December 1967 and July 1968,[109] but the entire project was overtaken by the civil rights movement and scrapped.[110] In 1970 Patrick Macrory reviewed, and gutted, the political authority of local government.[111]

In November 1963 the government established a committee, headed by Sir Joseph Lockwood, to report on higher education provision, specifically whether a second university was required. Faulkner wanted the university to be located in the New City to help it 'get off the ground'. Other ministers agreed that the New City was their preferred site but decided against attempting to dictate to the committee.[112]

The Lockwood Report proposed measures to accommodate 12–13,000 full-time students by 1980, 4000 part-time and 3000 trainee teachers. Student numbers at Queen's were to be capped at 7000 and a university precinct developed. Queen's would specialize in applied sciences and technology while a second university – to cater for 5–6000 students and open in October 1968 – would develop biological sciences, agriculture, social sciences, humanities and teacher training. A Regional Technical College should be established in Belfast. This would associate with the Art College and a proposed college of commerce to form a further education Ulster College. The report rejected Armagh, Derry or the New City as a location for the new university in favour of Coleraine. It cited as justification the advantages of a green field site, synergy between student and tourist accommodation in Portstewart and Portrush, and the proximity of Aldergrove international airport.[113]

Lockwood's committee strongly advocated the complete closure of Magee College in Derry.[114] Aware of the powerful lobby Magee could muster, however, the Cabinet was loath to take this fateful step. Terence O'Neill went as far as to suggest the total scrapping of the second university project in favour of developing Queen's University in Belfast.[115] He was talked out of this, but the problem of Magee remained.[116] In due course a compromise was worked out with Magee's trustees whereby its future was assured as a campus of the new university.[117]

Lockwood had proposed divesting Queen's of its agricultural faculty, which the university ran hand in hand with the Ministry of Agriculture. Harry West, the Minister of Agriculture, argued vigorously for the status quo, as did his civil servants and Queen's University.[118] Chichester-Clark argued that depriving Coleraine of the Agriculture faculty would detract from its whole *raison d'être*. Terence O'Neill, however, made it clear that Queen's retention of the faculty was the *quid pro quo* for its accepting the new university, and the government caved in.[119]

Less dramatic was an intensification of existing industrial policy, with attempts to attract new industry particularly strong from 1964. Government incentives were much increased to this end.[120] This had a particular impact on the textile sector, as factories working synthetic fibres displaced the chronically declining linen industry. Also in 1964 an Industrial Training Board was established which soon covered most of industry. By 1970 eight government centres were processing 3000 trainees per annum.[121] In late 1962 a considerable slum clearance plan for Belfast had been agreed upon. House building accelerated across the province though with bottlenecks, particularly in Belfast, due to local authority bureaucracy and sectarian demographic and electoral considerations.[122] The persistence of slum housing and the new high rises, notably Divis Flats in Belfast, had by the late 1960s become centres of agitation and an organizing focus for radicals and republicans.[123] Nevertheless, by 1969 the output of new houses had risen by 40 per cent in five years and, at 12,000 per annum, was ahead of the economic plan.[124]

The flurry of reports and reforms in the early to mid-1960s indicated an interventionist government far from Brookeborough's 'maximum assistance but minimum interference' with private property.[125] Yet the vision they encapsulated was distinctly apolitical. In 1965 the Ulster Unionist Council offered a £25 prize for a teenager's essay on 'The Ulster I would like to see in the seventies'. The winner was Tom Paulin, a 16-year-old pupil of Annadale Grammar School.[126] His vision, imaginatively cast as a *News Letter* editorial from 3 April 1977, was of new industries, new towns, physical planning, a developed road system, the Belfast urban sprawl curbed, air traffic, full employment, and better housing. In common with most of the 200 or so entries, politics barely featured except as an unexceptional blurring of old divisions.[127] This was the O'Neillite ideal – practical, planned economic development rather than a political revolution. Bland it certainly was, but it is likely to have chimed with most of the population.

Stealing Labour's thunder

The relative success of O'Neill's economic strategy since becoming Prime Minister was now to be tested in a make or break electoral competition with the Northern Ireland Labour Party. Brookeborough had left a Unionist Party reeling from a substantial loss of support to the NILP and a government on the defensive. One party activist complained that 'Nowadays everything is looked at from the point of view, "Is it politically expedient or are we going to get attacked by these socialists?"'[128]

Terence O'Neill set out to defy such defeatism, propounding, as we have seen, a newly refurbished concept of unionism as a pan-class movement based upon a progressive and regionalist consensus. O'Neill emphasized the traditional support given to unionism by the working class.[129] A Workers' Charter was presented in his first Queen's Speech.[130] In the same speech O'Neill informed the country that he had asked Professor Wilson to draw up an economic plan. His strategy was clear to observers. As the *News Letter* observed: 'The Government's wholehearted acceptance of the principle of economic planning was greeted with ironical Labour cheers ... the Government had stolen their thunder.'[131] The 'stolen thunder' phrase was quoted in O'Neill's autobiography with some relish.[132]

Terence O'Neill was particularly aware of the Labour challenge in Belfast. In a speech to Bloomfield Unionist Association he warned that 'the Labour opposition in Stormont must be taken seriously, and the challenge in Belfast must be met and overcome. He wanted to see the [Unionist] Party in Belfast going over to the attack. If they failed it would be unhealthy for the Party, who had always drawn its support both from the city and from the outside.'[133]

Organizational measures were taken to counter the NILP threat. With the personal blessing of O'Neill, the Unionist Trade Union Alliance (UTUA) was established.[134] Prompted by the controversy over the recognition of the Irish Congress of Trade Unions, hundreds had joined the UTUA by the time of its first General Meeting on 30 September 1963.[135] The UTUA's secretary was Nelson Elder, a former member of the NILP. He had pressed for a unionist trade union organization in frustration at the inactivity of the Ulster Unionist Labour Association. Nelson appeared to antagonize traditional members of the party, who attempted at one point to force his resignation from the party.[136]

In February 1964 the UTUA, now with 1200 members, decided to launch a new trade union. The Ulster Workers Union, as it was to be known, was hoped to start with 2000 members. Anxious to avoid aggravating rivals, it planned not to poach members, but to organize those currently outside the union movement. The target members were not craft workers but the unskilled, professional and semi-professional.

Though ostensibly non-political, it was likely to affiliate to the British TUC rather than the ICTU, oppose wildcat strikes and seek co-operation with employers.[137] The union was due to be launched in April 1965, but there is no evidence that it got off the ground. Nevertheless, that the attempt was made at all indicates the importance O'Neill's Unionist Party attached to winning back influence from the NILP and its trade union allies. To the same end the Ulster Labour Unionist Association was reinvigorated and 10,000 homes in the Belfast estates were circulated with a message from Terence O'Neill appealing specifically to trade unionists.[138]

The NILP were a new and difficult challenge for Unionism because of its successful carving of a niche in protestant working-class culture.[139] O'Neill's premiership did not prevent Labour's expansion outside its heartland. Eight new constituencies were represented at the 1964 Annual Conference, representative of strong growth over the previous six months.[140] By April 1964, when the NILP nominated no less than 150 candidates for the municipal elections, it was organized in 40 out of the 48 Stormont territorial constituencies.[141] Paddy Devlin told his branch that in a matter of weeks new branches had been established in Down, Tyrone, Fermanagh, Armagh and Antrim. Membership had doubled since the 1962 election.[142] This in part reflected support for Labour in blossoming middle-class suburbs and dormitory towns around Belfast.[143]

O'Neill's progressive reforms were vindicating NILP policy in the eyes of many, rather than undermining it. In line with political culture in Britain, there was a strong public interest in the left's programme of renewal. The NILP's 1964 policy document, *Signpost to the sixties*, sold its entire print-run of 2000 in advance and another 5000 had to be printed.[144] In conjuncture with Conservative Central Office, the Unionist Party was forced to produce a response to the Signposts document for its election candidates.[145]

The NILP, thus, was growing strongly under the first two years or so of O'Neill's premiership. This very success, however, involved a risky new strategy that brought its own internal strains in tow and badly disorientated the party. In the late 1950s and early 1960s the NILP catered almost exclusively to its protestant constituency. All four of its MPs were evangelical protestants and in the 1962 election not one of its 14 candidates was catholic.[146] Failure to increase the number of its Stormont seats in 1962 persuaded the party to pursue catholic votes more determinedly.[147] This was encouraged by a considerable influx of new party members, many of them catholic.

This new turn, however, lay uneasily on the old guard. At grassroots level long-standing members, some who were sympathetic to the loyalist populism of Paisley, were disturbed at the influx of catholic members.[148] The MPs, particularly Billy Boyd and David Bleakley, represented staunch protestant areas and themselves had cut their political teeth in the fierce reaction to nationalist labour following the 1949 split. These MPs were not above a bit of Union Jackery in their own constituencies.[149]

These tensions reflected the difficulty in creating a balance between contrasting pressures at least as much as personal predilections or prejudices. They were ripe for a destructive explosion, which duly came after the November 1965 general election. The unexpected source for this was a controversy over sabbatarianism. NILP councillors, including Billy Boyd MP, voted with the Unionist right wing, against party policy, to keep the city's play-centres closed on Sundays. This sparked an eight-month internecine war that pitted the party's ideologues and headquarters – striving to reach out to catholics – against a parliamentary party anxious to retain their protestant base.[150]

As early as June 1965 there was speculation that Terence O'Neill would call an early Stormont election to capitalize on turmoil in Labour ranks.[151] There was relatively little Unionist optimism, however, that the NILP was as yet seriously on the defensive.[152] Since the election of a Labour government in Britain, the NILP centred its criticism of the Unionists on any lapse from parity with Westminster measures.[153] O'Neill attempted to turn this back on Labour. In what was widely seen as the opening shot of the campaign, O'Neill, during a speech to Court Unionist Association, lambasted the NILP's toadyism. 'I believe it is right that we should do what we think is best', he argued, '...bearing in mind the particular circumstances in Ulster, and not least the views of those who return us to parliament.' Implicitly criticizing the liberalization of gambling and alcohol licence laws in Britain, he maintained the right of Stormont to legislate with an eye to Ulster's own social mores.[154]

In a late night adjournment debate in Stormont, O'Neill, angrily banging the dispatch box for effect, launched a carefully prepared broadside against Labour on the same theme. By the judgement of Barry White, the *Belfast Telegraph*'s political correspondent, it was a wildly over-the-top performance, producing 'alternate amazement and amusement' in the almost empty House. Bleakley later announced his party's willingness 'to fight an election on parity ... [We] stand four-square with Her Majesty's Government in social and economic legislation.'[155] O'Neill seemed prepared to risk pursuing the novel strategy of appealing to Ulster patriotism against British monolithism. This indicates the high stakes for which O'Neill was playing, but it proved too dangerous a path to follow to the end.

On 27 October 1965 the election was set for 25 November.[156] There was no pressing need for this. Parliament still had two years to run, the government's current programme of legislation was far from dealt with and no burning issues required an expression of public opinion. O'Neill's intention was primarily to attack Labour. He hoped to catch them still weakened by party splits and before its stock was raised by British Labour's expected success in the forthcoming Westminster election. An electoral success would strengthen him against his critics in the party and local government and serve to validate his bridge-building policy, particularly the summit with Lemass.

Terence O'Neill announced at the outset that Belfast would be the main battleground.[157] The Unionists contested only two Nationalist held seats, but in Belfast Unionist met Labour in 11 straight fights and one three-cornered contest. At the outset, however, Barry White reported that 'the candidates against sitting Labour MPs hardly hope to dent their rising majorities.'[158] O'Neill himself was unwilling to predict major reverse for Labour and admitted that its support was still growing.[159]

In his first major election speech, O'Neill signalled the abrupt abandonment of his putative strategy of highlighting the contrast between the Unionist Party and the NILP on parity with Britain. Instead he concentrated on economic achievement, promised that unemployment could be defeated and rebuffed Labour accusations that Unionists were only in favour of step-by-step with British Conservative administrations.[160] The Unionist manifesto, *Forward Ulster to Target 1970*, was primarily economic in tone.[161] In a later election platform O'Neill trumpeted Unionism as the vehicle of modernization: 'Socialism is rooted in the class struggle of the thirties; Nationalism is bogged down in the emotions of the twenties; only Unionism turns its face to the promise and hope of the seventies.'[162]

Disaster hit the NILP campaign, which was already being disrupted by dismal weather, when on the 21 November William Purdy, Bleakley's election agent, suddenly died. Labour election work in the Victoria constituency was called off for a week in sympathy. The Unionists meanwhile concentrated on six marginals: Victoria, Pottinger, Woodvale (all held by the NILP), Duncairn, Clifton and Willowfield. Terence O'Neill personally canvassed.[163] O'Neill, who was never comfortable with electoral glad-handing, toured only Unionist houses and talked in the main with active party members.[164] Nevertheless, such a Prime Ministerial intervention was unprecedented.

The election was not without incidents reminiscent of the 1964 Westminster general election. There was a spurious IRA threat to ministers and some low-key paramilitary activity.[165] A unionist mob attacked a Liberal Party meeting in Derrygonnelly, County Fermanagh, while in Derry the President of North Ward Unionist Association, and a USC officer, explained his pulling down of Liberal posters as being in the interests of road safety.[166] In general, however, the campaign was low-key and good-natured. Vivian Simpson, despite the serious reverse suffered by his party, the NILP, afterwards admitted it had been 'one of the cleanest elections fights I have ever taken part in.'[167]

This can be explained at least partially by the campaign conducted by O'Neill's Unionist Party. It was largely free of traditional appeals to rally around the constitution and scare stories about the opposition. In a full-page press advertisement for the Unionist Party no mention was made of the border.[168] Terence O'Neill explained his approach to the election in an interview with the *Belfast Telegraph*.

> I don't want to see merely a richer Ulster, I want to see a *better* Ulster – more tolerant, more cultivated, more concerned with great issues that transcend the local scene – in short, not merely richer materially but richer spiritually. No one can accuse us of having fought an emotional, gimmicky campaign. We have been trying to put serious issues in a serious way; without underestimating the intelligence of the voter. If people are not ready to vote for this up-to-date approach it will be very sad.[169]

Though sectarian or inflammatory rhetoric was avoided, so too was any direct reference to 'bridge-building' that might have produced a healthy controversy. O'Neill expressed the hope that catholics would vote Unionist on the strength of its economic programme, the main plank of the manifesto. This left both catholics and the Unionist Party largely unmoved. Denis Kennedy reported:

> For turning away from the blood and thunder of Old Ulster, Captain O'Neill has substituted not a challenging vision of the New, but a diet of economics which is a good deal less intoxicating.
>
> There must be some sympathy for him in this dilemma. Having stuck to his promise not to fight on the old slogans he found

himself, at Crossgar last week, following Mr Basil Kelly who had told the electors of East Down that he was, and they should be, Unionist because his father had fought off Sinn Fein attacks on his small farm in Monaghan half a century ago.

Worse, not better was to follow. Introducing the Prime Minister, the chairman remarked that there was some doubt as to who the National Democrats were.

'He had a story - one farmer asked another.

'"What is a National Democrat?"'

'"I'll tell you. It is another name for the papishes."'

O'Neill's subsequent lecture on the economy was received with 'torpor' from the audience.[170]

On polling day Terence O'Neill conducted a last minute tour of Victoria, Pottinger and Willowfield.[171] The turnout of voters, at 60 per cent, was the lowest on record. The NILP lost its Victoria seat, held by David Bleakley, and its Woodvale seat, held by Billy Boyd, to the Unionists.[172] The Unionist vote in Belfast, where turnout was a mere 45 per cent, actually fell from 67,350 to 62,646, but the Labour vote fell further from 60,170 to 43,363: a 6 per cent swing to the Unionists. In the country it was 10 per cent, mainly because South Antrim, a safe Unionist seat, was unusually contested. Councillor Kidd, for the NILP, blamed arctic weather conditions and transport problems for the debacle and, fundamentally, the party's milk and water brand of socialism.[173]

For the defeated MPs the loss after years of strenuous work in Stormont was a devastating blow. David Bleakley, his voice choked with emotion, gave vent to his bitter disillusionment with the voters.[174] Sam Napier, NILP secretary, was no doubt correct when he mournfully admitted that, the Unionist and Nationalist parties having pilfered the centre-left economic and social policies of the NILP, Labour was left with insufficiently distinctive policies and an apathetic electorate.[175] O'Neill, through design and good fortune, had succeeded in anaesthetizing, not galvanizing, the electorate.

O'Neill's response to the result – 'I am very well satisfied with the dramatic drop in Labour support in Belfast' – confirmed his strategic objective in the election.[176] The *Belfast Telegraph* greeted the result as a singular triumph for the Prime Minister: 'Any fears he may have had, and he seems to have had some, of not being able to overcome rank and file resistance to his re-education of Unionism should be dispelled.'[177] No doubt there was some truth in this. Ironically, however, it was the political middle ground, the NILP who actually took a decision to support O'Neill against his own right wing, which had been squeezed by the Unionist offensive. Though the guns of those who decried O'Neill's leadership qualities had been temporarily spiked, the ranks of the right of the party had been not diminished but increased by the election. Moderate Billy Boyd, for example, was replaced by John McQuade, an 'obsurantist' semi-Paisleyite nominated by the reactionary Court Unionist Association.[178]

Labourism was far from dead in Northern Ireland. In the 1966 Westminster election there was a large swing from the Unionists to the NILP. In seats where there was a straight contest, the swing averaged at 7 per cent to the NILP, well above the United Kingdom average.[179] The Unionist share of the vote dropped from 63 per cent to 61.6 per cent. In Belfast it fell 1 per cent to 55.6 per cent. The NILP overall won 72,613 votes, or 12.1 per cent. Though not calamitous for the Unionists, it did something to reverse their crushing of Labour in November 1965.[180] However, a demoralized Labour Party had failed to field candidates of stature and a real opportunity to win Belfast East was lost.[181]

In the 1967 council elections the NILP were trounced, their vote in Belfast dropping from 29.6 per cent to 20 per cent, a 5.5 per cent swing in the Unionists' favour. All 28 of the NILP's Belfast candidates were defeated and it suffered severe reverses in Derry and Newtownards. The Unionist Party picked up five seats in Belfast, four from the NILP, giving it its biggest ever majority. All three NILP seats fell to the Unionist Party in Castlereagh. Labour suffered from having being tainted, in protestant eyes, by its identification with the Campaign for Democracy in Ulster and Harold Wilson's impatient hostility to Stormont. O'Neill, evidently, had succeeded in aping Labour's economic and social policy sufficiently to convince protestants who supported Labour as the UK government to support the constitutionally safe Unionist Party in Northern Ireland contests.

Ironically the eclipse of the NILP was followed in fairly short order by an economic downturn that exposed the limits to O'Neill economic 'revolution'. Unemployment reached a post-war trough in March 1966 when the monthly figure dipped to 29,475, or 5.9 per cent.[182] The Wilson Plan was ahead of target until British economic difficulties forced a six-month pay freeze and tax hikes beginning in July 1966.[183] Shorts aircraft factory was hit by redundancies and only a joint loan of £6 million from Whitehall and Stormont in December 1968 kept it afloat.[184] Faulkner alerted an emergency Cabinet meeting in August 1966 to a 'serious and urgent financial crisis' for Harland

and Wolff shipyard due to unremunerative contracts and poor productivity. It was on the brink of bankruptcy and closure. The government was dragged reluctantly into investing money and undertaking a reorganization.[185] In September 1966, in the midst of the conspiracy to oust O'Neill as Prime Minister, it was announced to a stunned Stormont that Harland and Wolff, employing 12,000 workers, was being bailed out by the government to the tune of £3.5 million. Strings attached to the government loan made the rescue operation a partial nationalization.[186] This crisis was, O'Neill later claimed, 'the most traumatic experience' of his premiership.[187] Job losses from the yard continued.

The 1967 budget was noticeably tighter than in recent years.[188] In August that year unemployment soared to 7.7 per cent, compared to 2.4 per cent in Britain.[189] With Northern Ireland resources stretched to the limit there was a flurry of visits to Westminster begging for funds to cover public works.[190] In 1968 the Treasury forced cuts in Ulster's lavish road building programme.[191] Brian Faulkner, influenced by the distinctly leftist Northern Ireland Economic Council, proposed a radical plan for public-private partnerships to establish enterprises in peripheral areas, where he admitted industrial progress had been negligible even before the credit squeeze.[192] In the end only an attenuated plan for Omagh, Enniskillen and Newry was approved.[193]

Terence O'Neill's struggle to change the face of Ulster, thus, enjoyed only a transient success in setting the economy on an upward incline. Its most signal achievement was to shift Treasury expenditure onto a higher level within the framework of a revivified home rule. This was to persist in the form of administrative devolution long after the political apparatus, which O'Neill failed to reform for fear of upsetting the constitutional status quo, had been swept away by direct rule.

What were the consequences of O'Neill's plans to 'change the face of Ulster' for community relations? Economic development could not be neutral in an environment of sectarian political economy. Resource allocation within the province would always have political implications. Thus the ambitious plans of physical development detailed in the Matthew Report, and which O'Neill appropriated as his administration's leitmotiv, soon became embroiled in communal controversy. For a substantial number of catholics, 1965 was the year in which O'Neill's bridge-building rhetoric seemed exposed as hollow.

The centrepiece of O'Neill's new Ulster – the New City – was tainted from birth with sectarian bitterness. Catholics were already aggrieved at the new city's location in the protestant east of the province. The crowning insensitivity came with its naming. On 6 July 1965 Ministers Faulkner, Craig, Kirk and Fitzsimmons concertedly pushed for the new city to be named 'Craigavon', after the unionist hero and first Prime Minister of Northern Ireland. Terence O'Neill was unhappy, fearful that such a name would 'divide the community', but his tentative objections were overwhelmed.[194] In the House the same day Craig announced the decision with a triumphal flourish. The Opposition was incredulous.[195] One member of the planning team was 'too shocked to speak' when informed about the choice.[196] The bitter reaction of one catholic citizen in Portadown was perhaps typical of his community: 'What's it got to do with us? We're not the Government. They're the Government. They do what they like. It's a wonderful way to lead to better understanding, I must say.'[197] Even Orange Grand Master, George Clark, thought the choice unwise.[198]

When the government appointed Samuel McMahon, former chairman of the Ulster Unionist Council executive committee, as leader of the New City commission, Nationalist leader, Eddie McAteer, queried, 'Wind of change, how are ye?'[199] The *Belfast Telegraph*, too, was driven to wonder whether O'Neill's liberalism was more than skin deep.[200] Perhaps to appease soured catholic and assimilatory unionist opinion, Frank Guckian, a prominent catholic businessman in Derry, was also appointed to the New City commission, much to the discomfort of the nationalists.[201] The entire nine-person commission, however, negated this moral advantage. Few of the appointees had any relevant expertise and one government supporter judged it fit only 'for running a Unionist garden fete.'[202] At least three were active unionists and another an Orange Order Master, but Craig admitted that others might have unionist 'sympathies'.

More serious still were the implications of economic and physical planning for the north-west. Derry had long felt excluded from development, and indeed up to 1966 it received a disproportionately small share of advance factory space, an investment attraction wholly in the gift of the government.[203] The Benson Report on transport reorganization, published on 17 July 1963, had dealt a particularly severe blow to Derry. It proposed that both rail links to Belfast be closed. The response was a united chorus of outrage and despair from Derry's political and civic leaders.[204] One line was reprieved.

The cause of Derry was considerably boosted by the dramatic resignation statement of Geoffrey Copcutt, head of the design team working on the 'New City' between Portadown and Lurgan.[205] In a 7000-word statement he called for the brakes to be taken off Belfast's development and Derry also to be given priority. He argued that development of Derry, rather than raising a new city, 'would indeed be an earnest of the sincerity of the desire to prepare Ulster for the twenty-first century.' In a later statement he proposed allowing Belfast to double in size, streaming new developments to Derry and establishing Armagh as an administrative centre.[206] He ended with a general indictment of Northern Ireland's administration: 'I have become disenchanted with the Stormont scene ... Stormont, on the basis of my brief but deep acquaintance, has shown signs of a crisis-ridden regime – too busy looking over its shoulder to look outwards.'[207]

In a tortuously worded section, Copcutt alleged that 'religious and political considerations' were perverting demographic development plans for the New City.[208] Some years later Copcutt confirmed to *The Times* that 'during the planning of the city ... he was told by a source close to the Northern Ireland Cabinet that the Ulster Government would not countenance any scheme that would upset the voting balance between Protestants and Roman Catholics in the area.'[209] Indeed, sections of the Unionist Party were demanding that Ballymena be developed as the 'new city'.[210] The *Church of Ireland Gazette* articulated their rationale. It feared that South Down and Fermanagh, with catholic majorities and where unemployment was high, would provide many of the migrants. An influx of catholics would risk Unionist seats in Armagh. It would thus be better to build up Ballymena as the Antrim Unionist majorities were over-whelming.[211] Unionist MPs expressed private concern with the 'political implications' of the New City site.[212] County Armagh Unionist Association complained that Unionist-controlled councils would only be able to allocate less than half the required 20,000 new houses, the rest being in the remit of the Housing Trust.[213] Unionists feared an uncontrolled increase in the local nationalist electorate.

The government evidently took on board these concerns. Thus, while in the first report on the New City it had been made clear, following Matthew, that most of the projected new population would come from the predominantly catholic south and west of Northern Ireland, in the second report this was de-emphasized in favour of re-housing Belfast residents. It was now explicitly stated that 'the proportions of families in the different community groupings will be similar to that of the Province as a whole.'[214] Other planning decisions seemed to militate against catholic immigration. Out of 28 schools planned, only five were for the catholic voluntary sector.[215] Urban redevelopment was clearly being manipulated so as not to upset the communal balance of power.

Copcutt concentrated minds on the apparent exclusion of Derry, and his third and final statement was more about this than the New City. Londonderry Corporation, controlled by the Unionists, quickly supported him.[216] The debate was reflected at Cabinet level, with the rural ministers expressing grave doubts on the entire Matthew-originated strategy. Harry West (Enniskillen) and Chichester-Clark (South Londonderry), when Wilson's Economic Plan was being reviewed, 'expressed concern about the implication of the "growth centre" policies for the more remote areas of the province. ... It might be desirable to slow down the pace of events in the east, and to allow development to proceed more evenly over the province as a whole.'[217] They were over-ruled by the technocratic majority, however.

On 9 December 1964 a detailed plan and report on the New City was published. Comparing the plan with the Matthew Report, Geoffrey Copcutt drily commented that the 'attempt to channel one in three of all new manufacturing jobs in the next sixteen years to Lurgan-Portadown is incompatible with the promise given that all urban areas will receive a proportionate increase.'[218] When the Wilson Report was published on 2 February 1965 it made only a fleeting reference to Derry and Enniskillen and none at all to Omagh, Cookstown and Strabane.[219] Well might the north-west despair at O'Neill's new Ulster.

It was the question of a second university that gave focus for outrage at the apparent government disregard for Derry. There had existed widespread support for the expansion of the small University College in Derry, Magee.[220] In February 1965 rumours began to circulate that Coleraine would prove to be the site. An action committee to secure the second university for Derry was established by a group of business people and professionals.[221] This University for Derry committee organized a rally to show the unanimity of opinion in the city across political and religious lines.[222] One and a half thousand turned out and were addressed by 16 speakers, including four MPs and the Unionist mayor, Albert Anderson. Eddie McAteer expressed the hope and defiance of this unprecedentedly united movement: 'The Government might be able to slap down the men of Derry. They might even be able to slap down the men of Londonderry. But they cannot slap down the united men of Derry and Londonderry.'[223]

On 10 February the Lockwood Committee on higher education finally reported. It recommended that Northern Ireland's second university go not to Derry nor even Armagh, the favourites, but to the small protestant town of Coleraine.[224] The University for Derry action committee proposed a general strike in the city and a motorcade from

Derry to Stormont.[225] The motorcade, involving up to 1000 vehicles, went ahead on Thursday 18 February. The Lord Mayor, Albert Anderson, and Nationalist leader, Eddie McAteer, shared the leading car in a striking symbol of unity.[226]

Indeed, unionist support for Derry's claims was widespread. A poll of Unionist backbenchers, taken just before the publication of the Lockwood Report, found them six to one in favour of the second university going to Derry.[227] Dr Nixon MP told his North Down Unionist Association that the government had made its greatest mistake in 40 years. Moreover, he suggested that political bias was at work: 'You cannot run away ... from Derry City where the population is 60 per cent Nationalist and 34 per cent Unionist. You cannot maintain Ulster this way.'[228]

In March a marathon debate in Stormont on the Lockwood Report stretched over 18 hours and two days in which 33 MPs spoke. Only five were in favour of Lockwood's recommendation: O'Neill, the Minister of Education and the three MPs whose constituencies abutted Coleraine; 17 favoured Derry as a location, three Armagh and eight were, at best, neutral.[229] When the vote was finally held at 3 a.m. on 5 March the government won by 26 votes to 18. Desmond Boal voted with the opposition and three other Unionists, Dinah McNabb (North Armagh), Dr Robert Nixon (North Down) and Mr David Little (West Down) abstained on what amounted to a vote of confidence in the government.[230] The government won on the day but obviously only by coercing a reluctant backbench.[231]

Nevertheless, Derry Unionists were not prepared to indulge in lengthy confrontation with their own government. In a letter to the press on 22 February, Albert Anderson announced that 'the time for demonstrations is now past'.[232] Sufficient steam, Derry Unionists felt, had been released. Edward Jones, the Londonderry MP and Attorney General, who was under attack for voting with the government, insisted that the local party close ranks in the face of the nationalist enemy.[233] For unionists in Derry, the logic of sectarian zero-sum politics beneath the froth of pro-university agitation was never forgotten.

Almost immediately after the high-point of the motorcade had passed, the facade began to crack to reveal a murky and disreputable conspiracy. Raymond Wolsley, a leading businessman and president of the Junior Chamber of Commerce in Derry, disclosed that two years previously he had resigned from the executive committee of the North Ward Unionist Association because two leading Unionists in the city opposed the siting of a second university in Derry.[234] Ivan

Cooper, formerly of the Derry Young Unionists, revealed that a year previously he had helped compose a resolution for the Unionist Annual Conference calling on the government to raise Magee College to full university status. When its content leaked to the press, a successful campaign was raised in Derry Unionist circles to have it withdrawn.[235]

The controversy exploded in May when Dr Nixon, Unionist MP for North Down, delivered a highly controversial speech to Londonderry Middle Liberties Young Unionist Association. In it he attacked the 'nameless, faceless men from Londonderry' who advised the Unionist leadership in Stormont against establishing a second university in Derry or even attracting industrial development there:

> men from this city went to Stormont and said under no circumstances must industrial development come to the Derry area ... there are Unionist people who say that Derry is a Papist city and therefore it must get no industry or university and must be allowed to run down, and men who sit beside me in Stormont say this about Derry.[236]

Terence O'Neill and Major Gerald S. Glover, president of the City of Londonderry and Foyle Unionist Association, quickly denied the allegations, as did Lockwood himself, but the Unionist Derry Alderman, Campbell Austin, expressed his deep concern and asked for details.[237] To protect the confidentiality of his sources, Nixon refused to produce substantiating evidence and was expelled from the Parliamentary Unionist Party.[238] He remained unrepentant: 'everyone agreed that these gentlemen existed, but it would be impolite to say so.'[239]

On 27 May Nationalist MP Patrick Gormley named the seven 'faceless men' in Stormont. They were: Gerald S. Glover (president of the City of Derry and Foyle Unionist Association and ex-Lord Mayor), Rev. John Brown (prominent Orangeman and Magee lecturer), Rev. Professor R. L. Marshall (retired Magee professor), Mr J. F. Bond (described by Gormley as a 'solicitor to the Unionist Party'), Dr Abernathy (head of the Apprentice Boys of Derry), Robert Stewart (a businessman) and Sidney Buchanan (editor of the *Londonderry Sentinel*). Gormley claimed that two 'honourable gentlemen', a clergyman and a businessman, had refused to join the conspiracy and were prepared to give evidence to a tribunal if asked. All nine had attended a secret meeting over two years previously to discuss the implications of industrial growth and a second university in Derry:

In a bid to preserve Unionist monopoly it was decided that the viewpoint of the local party should be against economic planning for the Foyle region, and that would include university development. ... The Cabinet, the Civil Service and several members of this House were all parties to the conspiracy against Derry. ... A few months ago in Derry Guildhall the Prime Minister was blamed by two leading educationalists for not being fair to Derry, an old university town, his answer was: 'What could I do when the Derry Unionists do not agree on this point?'[240]

Gormley had produced a convincingly detailed charge sheet. Bill Craig, Minister of Development, virtually conceded the existence of a unionist conspiracy in Derry when he argued that informal approaches were quite acceptable, and denied only that the government had been unduly influenced.[241]

The Londonderry and Foyle Unionist Association flatly denied all allegations, but there was much disquiet amongst the membership.[242] Three senior ' unionist members of Derry Corporation initially supported demands for an inquiry.[243] All were forced by the Party to retract.[244] On 22 June a Derry delegation met O'Neill to demand an investigation.[245] O'Neill refused an inquiry, but significantly refused to confirm or deny whether a deputation had ever been received from Derry requesting that industry or the university be channelled away from the second city. Nothing had been said to Lockwood's committee 'that could be regarded as a direction.'[246] This was a virtual admission that the secret cabal had existed and behaved as alleged.

Earlier that month, Robert Nixon, defending his conduct before North Down Unionist Association, gave details of an occasion when he had been part of a delegation of seven Unionist MPs meeting O'Neill over the future of Magee College. 'It was at this meeting that the Prime Minister himself told us that leading Unionist citizens in Derry were against new industries and the new university coming to Derry, and indeed that the siting of Coolekeeragh power station there was against their advice and wishes.'[247] In May 1966 Terence Woodland, a lecturer at Magee College, spoke at a press conference for Ruth Morrow, a rebel Unionist Independent standing in a local government by-election in the Unionist-controlled North Ward of Derry. Woodland quoted a statement made to him by J. O. Bailie, secretary of the Unionist Party, and overheard by two witnesses: 'Don't blame Lockwood. Don't blame the Government or Mr Jones [Unionist MP for Londonderry]. Blame your own Unionists in Derry. They passed a resolution and pigeonholed it. They never sent it on to Belfast.'[248] A prominent protestant clergyman attacked the 'Faceless' conspiracy. He remembers a prominent Unionist declaring that, 'We don't want any more industry here because if we upset the applecart the RCs will come in and swamp us.'[249]

The evidence that important Derry Unionists lobbied against the second university coming to Derry (as well as much investment) is overwhelming. It is harder to judge what impact this had on the final decision on where the second university be located. Some hints, however, were coyly suggestive. 'It is ... essential', the Lockwood Report gravely opined, 'that the development of the new university should be able to proceed smoothly and successfully through the planning and later stages unaffected by political considerations, either at local or central level.'[250] The Committee listed, *post facto*, as one of its criteria that the local authorities of the area be 'able and willing to support the establishment of a university and that in doing so ... not be influenced by other considerations which could impede development and progress.'[251] In the light of the facts considered this appears to be justifying the exclusion of Derry on the grounds that the local Unionist elite were so partisan in not wanting the university in Derry that they would have prejudiced its success had it gone there. Thus were disinterested outsiders able to excuse acquiescence in the most narrow-minded bigotry. As for the impact of 'faceless men' lobbying on the government, again hard evidence is lacking, but the brief comment by the Minister of Health and Local Government to his Cabinet colleagues in June 1964 – that the location of the university in 'Londonderry would raise political difficulties' – must surely have referred to local unionist pressure.[252] Derry was perhaps the starkest example of how the unionist siege mentality in the periphery held up modernizing reform in the centre.

Scholars who have examined O'Neill's economic, infrastructure and physical planning programme, even those hostile to unionism, have failed to prove anything but, at worst, the sectarian ramifications of planning decisions when taken in Northern Ireland which would be neutral in a mono-ethnic environment.[253] It is safe to assert, however, that sectarianisn malice tainted the very decision process.

How successful was O'Neill's economic modernization? In the 1958–70 period Northern Ireland's economy grew at an average of 4.9 per cent per annum, compared to 3.6 per cent in the UK as a whole and 2.3 per cent in the 1948–58 period. O'Neill's regional growth policy played no small role in this. From 1958 to the end of the 1960s public expenditure per head of population had doubled, with particularly large increase in housing stock, roads, education and training.[254] By 1969 almost 29,000 new manufacturing jobs had been created compared to Professor Wilson's target of 30,000. However, taking into account the continuing decline in traditional industries, the net gain was only 5000.[255] Despite industrial successful diversification, with new light engineering, electronics and man-made fibre plants, unemployment remained well above that in Great Britain.[256] Regional policy, moreover, may have featherbedded local industry and actually inhibited economic 'catch-up' with the West European economies.[257] The British government massively propped up Harland and Wolff and particularly Shorts. Harold Wilson scornfully referred to the latter as a 'soup kitchen'. While relatively minor cases of discrimination attracted much attention, this disproportionate pampering of the protestant working class went largely unremarked.[258]

Most economic success resulted from a continuation of Brookeborough's industrial development policy, if intensified. There was some success in diverting new enterprises to the growth centres outside Belfast.[259] Many of these closed, however, in the turbulent economic conditions of the 1970s. Specific projects likewise had chequered results. The road building programme was undoubtedly impressive but, combined with the ravages of urban redevelopment, its impact in disrupting and uprooting traditional communities gave rise to increasing opposition. Some schemes were reversed.[260] The most spectacular failure was of the Craigavon New City. By 1980 its population, supposed to be 100,000, stood at only 57,000.[261] Much of the housing and infrastructure was shoddy and the local council embodied not communal accord but extreme sectarian polarization.[262] In 1978 special government funds were cut off and redirected to Belfast and Derry city centres.[263] Antrim new town fared little better.[264] People had simply failed to relocate in the numbers expected. Similarly, the second university at Coleraine failed to stand in its own feet and in 1985 was merged with the Jordanstown campus polytechnic and Derry's Magee College.

Politically the Unionist Party was always uneasy with the principle of such a high level of state intervention. As the sheen of Labour's 'white heat' revolution dimmed the traditional Toryism of most Unionists began to assert itself. In March 1968 the assimilatory Unionist MP, Roy Bradford, wondered whether the principle of 'parity, right or wrong, has become a sacred cow which is running out of milk.' He condemned the 'malign osmosis' of the O'Neill years in which socialist concepts of egalitarianism and welfare culture had permeated unionist thought: 'we are swimming in the effluent of socialist parties.' The speech was the culmination of backbench mutterings over a number of weeks criticizing the constraints of parity. These came from both 'right' – John Taylor and Joe Burns – and 'left' – Bradford and Phelim O'Neill. Selsdon man, as a counter to O'Neill's changing face of Ulster, was making his tentative appearance in Ulster unionism.[265] Those in favour of a greater exercise of Northern Ireland autonomous powers had powerful support in the Cabinet from Bill Craig. Craig indeed, was the first to warn of 'a danger that socialism will permeate our policies' and railed against 'wasteful approach to social and welfare schemes – an extravagant blanket use of public funds.'[266]

Craig's desire for greater Ulster autonomy from British economic policy drew sustenance from the Cabinet's secret and tentative negotiations with Whitehall which, had they been consummated, would have meant a huge leap towards effective dominion status for Northern Ireland. The ballooning subvention to Northern Ireland, a result of the *ad hoc* 'expenditure based system' conceded in the mid-1950s and ruthlessly exploited by O'Neill, greatly worried Whitehall bureaucrats. Clearly the only bar to Stormont's profligacy was the (often lacking) political will at Westminster to resist its demands. Developing Treasury thinking preferred an increased but fixed revenue for Northern Ireland, calculated on the basis of population plus top-up allowances linked to unemployment levels. All previous parity agreements would be superseded and Stormont would be free to allocate resources as it saw fit. The Stormont Cabinet expressed interest but O'Neill, acutely aware of the advantages of *ad hoc* arrangements, made clear his preference for the status quo.[267] Further negotiations were halted by the outbreak of the Troubles.

In March 1968 O'Neill unambiguously backed parity in parliament.[268] Doubts evidently remained in the party however. His Minister of Finance, Herbert Kirk, delivered a carefully researched rejoinder to the critics of parity in a speech to the Belfast committee of the Institute of Bankers in Ireland. He emphasized that parity was a reciprocal relationship with obligations on Northern Ireland's side. It could not spend as it liked and send the bill to Westminster.[269] Nevertheless, considerable Unionist criticism met the budget statement in May 1968, with Burns, Brooke, Ardill, Scott and McQuade, all of the right of the party, complaining that the country was 'taxed to the hilt.'[270] In June Terence O'Neill was forced to justify the province's financial relations with Great Britain to the backbench 66

Committee.[271] The extreme complexity of Northern Ireland's relationship with the Treasury,[272] the result of a thicket of conventions and, more importantly, an attempt to hide the British subvention, allowed self-delusion as to Northern Ireland's self-sufficiency to run riot on the Unionist backbench. It was to return to haunt O'Neill in 1968.[273]

O'Neill's regional policy, successful at extracting resources from Britain, was at a political cost. As Harold Wilson remembered,

> our members were very concerned with the very great increase in financial assistance from the Westminster exchequer to Ulster, and without constitutional reform and more liberal policies it was becoming more difficult to justify to MPs, and to some members of our Cabinet, the large sums we were being asked to vote.[274]

If Northern Ireland wanted Britain to pay for a British standard of living, it could not ignore British pressure for political normalization.

4
Bridge-Building

For an Ulster politician, Terence O'Neill was unusually attuned to liberal ideas within Northern Ireland and public opinion in Britain and beyond. He maintained close connections with a number of British journalists[1] and was an avid reader of the press, particularly *The Times, Financial Times* and the *Economist*.[2] As Minister of Finance he was acutely aware that the Republic of Ireland sold itself as dynamic and economically progressive much more effectively than did the North.[3] O'Neill realized that a poor image abroad threatened overseas investment and goodwill from Britain. The Hall Report debacle convinced him that Northern Ireland must project more positively if it was to attract Treasury largesse. This required a change in the traditional Ulster mind-set. With striking brevity he warned those 'completely absorbed by internal affairs' that 'in some ways the image of a country outside its boundaries is indivisible.'[4]

In an interview with Roy Lilley of the *Belfast Telegraph*, O'Neill set his own philosophy against 'negative Unionism':

[In] the past there have been times when perhaps our political thinking has been concerned too much with the 'No Surrender' and 'Not an inch' theme. Today we have to persuade the people of Northern Ireland that we have forward looking policies which will improve social conditions. This is positive Unionism – something which young people can support. There is a great deal to be achieved in the social sphere. I want all sections of the community to feel committed to the task. It is important to convince more and more people that the Government is working for the good of all in Northern Ireland – not just those who vote Unionist.[5]

Clearly his 'self-help' ideology was developing a new inclusiveness. O'Neill consciously connected Northern Ireland's move into the 'progressive age'[6] with youth:

> Unless we can appeal to the sort of people who admire the Beatles then as the party gets older we will be able to appeal to nobody. The future depends on the younger population and not on old men. This was an error into which the party had been falling in recent years.[7]

O'Neill recognized that relaxing public attitudes on communal relations threatened to leave the Unionist Party behind if it did not respond. The government had to prove its continuing vitality and relevance in the face of the NILP and a modernizing Nationalist Party.[8]

O'Neill lacked Brookeborough's rapport with the common people and perhaps to counter this embarked on a series of high profile 'meet the people' tours of provincial towns. The first visit was to Larne, a predominantly protestant town, in May 1963.[9] It became gradually clear that O'Neill hoped to use such tours not merely for 'distributing bones' to his supporters,[10] but to encourage a collective and regional pride in economic development. 'Our future', he said while visiting Newtownabbey, 'can only be bright if we develop and maintain a unity of purpose in Ulster.'[11] It was over a year later, however, before O'Neill's 'inclusive' meet-the-people tours covered a principally catholic community. Even this was less than completely official, as he accompanied his wife on a National Trust party to Rathlin Island.[12]

O'Neill made a more substantial gesture to catholics on the death of Pope John XIII. He joined with Londonderry Corporation and Portadown Urban District Council in publicly sympathizing, while Belfast City Hall flew its flag at half-mast. Assimilatory unionists, who had been losing hope in O'Neill's administration, were heartened, if only briefly.[13] Generally, however, O'Neill went out of his way to appeal not to catholics, but to the party's traditionalists. On 18 December he enlisted in the Apprentice Boys of Derry (though he absented himself from the traditional burning of Lundy).[14] For over a year O'Neill made no explicit acknowledgement of catholic grievances.[15]

In fact, O'Neill did not see the problem of communal relations as being directly amenable to governmental action or even rhetoric. He was rigorously *laissez faire* in the religio-political sphere, if not in the economic, and firmly believed that intervention from above could only aggravate sectarian tensions, never ameliorate them. Catholics, he believed, would come in time to accept the economic sense of the Union, and until then all that could be profitably done was to 'think and speak of each other with charity and understanding.'[16] 'If you wish to spend your lives talking about discrimination,' he once admonished hecklers, 'then you can be sure that relations in Northern Ireland will get worse and worse. If you wish them to improve, then for a time the discussion must be put to one side. In that way relations will slowly improve.'[17] Here was O'Neillism in a nutshell.

Frustrated by his abdication of responsibility moderate catholic opinion boiled over. On 3 April 1964 J. J. Campbell, a senior lecturer at St. Joseph's Training College, Belfast, and Brian Mck. McGuigan, a solicitor, both established assimilatianist catholics, published previously private correspondence with O'Neill. The first letter, dated 19 August 1963, expressed disillusion at O'Neill's failure to reciprocate the goodwill of conciliationist catholics. It specifically demanded that representatives from the minority community be appointed to the Northern Ireland Economic Council. 'If our fellow-Catholic critics are proved to be right, that our efforts are futile, then we shall be forced to reconsider whether there are other means within the constitution and the rule of law by which our rights as citizens are to be won.' In a second letter, on 5 March 1964, O'Neill's failure to directly address the minority was criticized. The third letter, dated 26 March, regretted O'Neill's failure to appoint catholics to the Lockwood committee on higher education.

The *Belfast Telegraph* reported that, ironically, O'Neill had been anxious that both the NIEC and the Lockwood Committee have catholic nominees. Three leading catholics had been approached, but were unable to serve. More importantly, however, 'whatever aspirations the Prime Minister may have in this direction, clearly he has not the advantage of an open and active support of a major body of opinion within the Unionist Party towards such ends.'[18] O'Neill, in his reply to the catholic critics, obviously had his eye firmly on recalcitrant unionists. 'We have bent over backwards to be fair', he told a Young Unionist rally in Fermanagh,

But I will not pretend that it is a healthy or progressive thing for any part of the community to constitute itself an exclusive and closed society. For forty years a separate educational system has continuously and deliberately fostered a sense of separate identity. Yet it is *we* who are told that any move must come from *us*. We are being asked to open doors which have never been closed.[19]

This critique of catholic separatism, and particular the invidious impact of the segregated education system, was a commonplace of assimilatory unionism. However, in response to a plea from the most co-operative section of catholic middle class, O'Neill's rebuke can only have dispirited unionists desirous of improving community relations.

O'Neill's failure to strike out steadfastly in an assimilatory direction soon built up disillusionment amongst liberal unionists.[20] Perhaps in recognition of his crisis of legitimacy with the unionist left, O'Neill began preparing for a gesture to catholics in early 1964. On 15 April it was revealed that O'Neill intended to visit a Roman Catholic school whilst on a 'meet the people' tour of Ballymoney.[21] No previous premier had dared visit such an establishment of the minority community. A front page article carried by the *News Letter*, the daily closest to the Unionist Party, on 17 April bore all the hallmarks of a leak from the Prime Minister's office to prepare public opinion,[22] and deserves extensive quotation:

> The Northern Ireland Government is likely in future to give more overt backing than hitherto to a policy of encouraging Roman Catholics to take part in public life in the Province ... the Government has, in fact, frequently extended invitations to prominent members of the Roman Catholic faith to serve on public bodies, or to attend public functions, but on quite a number of occasions these invitations, although attended by no embarrassing publicity, have been turned down by the persons concerned. All this has resulted in a situation in which the factor operative has not been discrimination, but the divisions in the community that followed from the decision of Nationalist Roman Catholics in 1921 not to support actively the new state of Northern Ireland.
>
> The Roman Catholic attitude has been eroded in recent years by a realisation that after four decades the Province's link with Britain is as strong as ever, and by the increasing recognition in Eire that there is a 'special relationship' with the United Kingdom that has rendered irrelevant the old Republican isolationism.
>
> The increasing evidence of a desire by prominent Ulster Roman Catholics to take a representative part in public life in the Province, has been recognized in liberal Unionist circles and while there will be no dramatic change in Government policy, it is understood that a more open acceptance of this desire will be a feature of future action.
>
> Captain O'Neill, Prime Minister, is himself believed to be sympathetic and his coming to visit a Roman Catholic school at

Ballymoney ... may be regarded as more than a straw in the wind of change that may shortly blow more strongly.[23]

Responsibility for achieving better community relations was firmly placed on catholics. Government concessions amounted to welcoming, on unionist terms, co-operation offered by conciliationist elements of the catholic middle class. In some respects it was an offer to accept the surrender of Irish nationalism with grace.

On 24 April O'Neill duly visited Lady of Lourdes Intermediate School, where he watched a hurling match.[24] The *News Letter*, despite frantic telephone calls to the editor made from the school by O'Neill's advisors,[25] published the next day a photograph of O'Neill striding below a highly visible crucifix in the company of a nun.[26] O'Neill, evidently not too keen on ramming home the symbolism of his visit, was horrified. He wrote later that: 'In such ways was co-operation made almost impossible. In such ways was reconciliation bound to fail.'[27]

O'Neill's minimal gesture towards catholics was quickly negated by an accumulation of traditional sectarian animosities towards the end of 1964. Northern Ireland seemed not to be advancing towards a new age of communal harmony, but actually retrogressing. The catalyst, as so often before, was a general election.

The Imperial General Election (as Westminster elections were known in Northern Ireland) of 1964 was to see a change of government in London for the first time in 13 years. In Ulster, however, it was the usual sectarian headcount. West Belfast Unionist Association had already been infiltrated by hard-right unionists sympathetic to the loyalist demagogue, Ian Paisley.[28] Patricia McLoughlin, sitting Unionist MP for Belfast West, announced her intention on 1 September not to defend her seat due to ill health. The nomination was secured by James Kilfedder, a London barrister, against the moderate, Katherine O'Brien.[29] Even if indirectly, the right had stitched up the Unionist nomination for West Belfast, Northern Ireland's most marginal seat.[30]

As the campaign gathered pace telephone calls of complaint flooded into the RUC concerning two flags in the window of the Republican headquarters off the catholic Falls Road, the tricolour and the starry plough.[31] Paisley announced his intention to march on the Divis Street headquarters and demanded that police remove the flag. Kilfedder sent a telegram to Brian McConnell, Minister of Home Affairs: 'Remove tricolour in Divis Street which is aimed to provoke and insult loyalists in West Belfast.'[32] McConnell ordered the RUC to remove the offending flags, explaining later that this was in response to the calls and 'feelings in adjacent [protestant] districts'.[33] Simultaneously he banned Paisley's march. The RUC visited the Republican headquarters on the morning of the 28th to find it locked and barricaded. Returning in the afternoon they broke in with pick-axes and crowbars and removed the flags.[34] Paisley went ahead with a 'protestant' rally outside City Hall, attracting over a thousand supporters, at which Kilfedder was present and welcomed from the platform.[35] Meanwhile one to two thousand people blocked the Falls Road, waved republican flags, sang rebel songs and hurled missiles at passing buses.[36]

For the two days following the flag seizure, there was relatively little trouble and only three were arrested.[37] The following Thursday, however, in an attempt at ordered protest, the tricolour was replaced in the window. Policemen smashed the door in and the flag was again removed. After haranguing their supporters the Republicans attempted, with a loud hailer, to persuade people off the streets. Their answer was a hail of stones and bricks that smashed the front windows of the headquarters. By 11 p.m. a crowd of four to five hundred blocked the road and the police moved in to disperse it. Within minutes Divis Street was a 'sea of glass' as bottles, iron gratings, stones, bricks and sticks were hurled at the RUC. For two hours a running battle was waged. Five RUC men were hospitalized and Constable Norman Laird, who suffered a fractured skull, was lucky to survive. It had been the worst night of rioting since 1935.[38] Clashes continued for three nights in a row, and at one point a crowd leader was seen to brandish a gun.[39] In total, 72 were arrested, 46 police officers injured, and 53 business premises, 14 police vehicles and 20 public transport vehicles were damaged or destroyed.[40] Half the arrested rioters were under 21.[41]

In a rare joint statement all main churches called for calm and order, as did the political parties, including the Republicans, and the trade union movement. O'Neill's comments, however, were less than ecumenical:

> During the IRA troubles of recent years the people of Northern Ireland retained a calm dignity in the face of violent provocation. To-day certain 'Republican' candidates, many of them with backgrounds in the IRA, an organisation illegal all over Ireland, north and south, now appear to be using a British general election to try and provoke disorder in Northern Ireland.[42]

At a time of heightened sectarian tension such blatant election-eering can hardly have been helpful.[43] The following weekend 1500 attended an inflammatory Paisley rally in the Ulster Hall.[44] The same day 2000 marched down the Falls Road behind the tricolour.[45] The Lord Mayor of Belfast, William Jenkins, in contrast to O'Neill, was more even-handed and blamed the 'extremists' on both sides. Professor Robert Corkery, ex-Moderator of the Presbyterian Church, condemned Paisley and his followers as 'brainless'.[46]

In Stormont, under considerable opposition criticism, O'Neill rebuked Paisley, but only mildly. He explained the twin aims of his administration so far – to advance Northern Ireland economically, and 'to build bridges between the two traditions within the community.' This phrase has since been seen as encapsulating O'Neill's policy.[47] Yet, after over 18 months as premier, this was the first time that O'Neill had stated reconciliation as official policy, and then only in reaction to serious sectarian tension for which Unionist electioneering was partially responsible.[48]

The Divis riot was only the lowest point of a seamy election campaign in West Belfast. The Unionists saw Labour as the main threat, fearing that William Boyd would split the protestant vote sufficiently to let Gerry Fitt (Republican Labour) or even Liam McMillan (Republican) win the seat.[49] Graffiti appeared in the Shankill Road linking the threats: 'Keep Labour and the IRA out'.[50] Paisley's Protestant Unionists actively supported Kilfedder.[51] They circulated an anti-Labour leaflet asking voters the question 'Do you want a Roman Catholic in your street?'[52]

Dubious election tactics were not limited to West Belfast however. A series of Republican rallies in Enniskillen, Dungannnon, Coalisland, Coleraine and Ballycastle, in an apparently co-ordinated campaign, were barracked and heckled by unionist crowds. Platforms speakers were stoned by mobs and often batoned by the RUC who moved in to seize tricolours.[53] In Fermanagh-South Tyrone the Unionists conducted a virulent campaign and Giles Fitzherbert, the Liberal candidate, complained that 'the political paraphernalia of Unionist Union Jackery is flauntly [sic] rampant.'[54] The Liberal candidate's car had its tyres slashed and, for fear of a retaliatory boycott, no local garage would repair the damage.[55] Election night proved a raucous affair. Fitzherbert, was forced to call a rally off in Ballinamallard after being pelted with eggs and tomatoes. This was excused by a Unionist spokesman who explained that he had 'made remarks that he might have known not to make in a 100 per cent Protestant area.'[56] A Liberal meeting in Fivemiletown was similarly attacked.[57]

The results went well for the Unionists and they won all twelve seats. Both Labour and the Republicans fell well short of their target, and the latter lost seven deposits.[58] James Kilfedder won the West Belfast seat with surprising ease, though his majority of 6659 was down 2177 on that of Patricia McLoughlin. The jubilant unionist crowd at the West Belfast count at Clarence Hall called out for Paisley and chaired him in triumph.[59] Northern Ireland Labour and Republican candidates were heckled and jostled in City Hall.[60]

Within days convincing evidence was produced of organized personation for the Unionist cause in West Belfast.[61] O'Neill refused to comment on any of these controversies and accused the opposition of 'sour grapes'.[62] When answering questions at a Royal Commonwealth function in London, he was challenged by the author Robert Harbinson to dissociate himself from Paisley and his election tactics. He replied weakly that Paisley was merely 'not to be commended'.[63]

O'Neill's subdued response to Paisleyism and disreputable election practices drew forth much disillusioned bitterness from assimilatory unionists.[64] Edward Gibson, Chairman of the Young Unionist Council, delivered an excoriating critique to Duncairn Unionist Association on 8 December:

> Right and wrong should still have a place in our thinking. There can be no justification for the behaviour of certain sections of our party at election times. It is wrong to personate votes, and it is wrong to build up animosity to secure votes. If our party is going to allow itself to be propped up with these artificial supports, it can only lead to our eventual downfall.[65]

Martin Wallace, deputy editor of the *Belfast Telegraph*, glumly noted that though 'the Prime Minister talks of building bridges … The only bridges being built are on the M.1. motorway.'[66]

By the end of 1964 Terence O'Neill has disillusioned many of his erstwhile liberal supporters. Yet the threat to his position came not from Ulster's intelligentsia, but the Parliamentary Unionist Party. O'Neill was not adept at governing through parliament or the party. His natural shyness inclined him towards authoritarianism. He had little enthusiasm for ideology and preferred the notion of enlightened rule by experts. On a visit to the United States in 1963 he visited a museum 'and saw the plans for a new Philadelphia. New vistas – the mall in front of Independence Hall entailing wholesale demolition. New blocks for business purposes. Removal of slums. Could a dictatorship do more? Could Belfast do a sixteenth of this without a riot?'[67] After retirement from Ulster politics, when in the House of Lords, O'Neill eschewed the neo-liberalism of Selsdon Man and the Thatcher/Reagan decade.[68] During the early 1970s he favoured a National Government, and at one point even a 'British De Gaulle', to deal with the economic crisis.[69] Whilst undoubtedly a democrat – he was acutely conscious of the precedent of appeasement and the rise of Nazism in Germany, something which contributed to his hostility towards Paisley[70] – O'Neill was inclined towards a technocratic, presidential, almost apolitical form of government. It boded ill for relations with his party.

From the outset O'Neill lacked legitimacy. Brookeborough had promised backbenchers in 1953 that his successor would be elected by the Parliamentary Party.[71] As it turned out O'Neill was selected by the Governor. In October 1963 an unsigned letter was delivered to 33 Unionist Members of Parliament at Stormont protesting at the lack of consultation in the party on O'Neill's appointment as Prime Minister.[72] It soon emerged that Edmund Warnock, a veteran MP now on the backbench, was the author.[73] Though he claimed that O'Neill himself was not being criticized it was an inauspicious beginning.

The seething discontent of the backbench in the final days of Brookeborough's premiership was slow to dissipate.[74] As a sign of a new start, Desmond Boal was readmitted into the Parliamentary Unionist Party and the Chief Whip began regularly to attend Cabinet meetings.[75] However, O'Neill's character was a greater impediment to sound relations. Personally shy and awkward, he had little inclination to mix with those with whom he had little in common, and to whom he certainly felt superior.[76] Despite urgings from his lieutenants, O'Neill rarely visited the Chief Whip's room in Stormont, where backbenchers tended to congregate.[77] Lord Brookeborough had always been careful to mix informally even with those backbenchers critical of his leadership. In Stormont O'Neill would dine only with his civil servants and even had a private WC built adjoining his office to avoid crossing through the Members' room.[78] David Bleakley, a Labour MP, noticed the gulf between O'Neill and his parliamentary rank and file.

I often sympathized with Unionist MPs who felt ignored by their leader and for whom he had little regard. A highly respected member of the Commons once said to me: 'Why is it that the PM when he passes me in the lobby always forgets my name – and, worse still, often says, "Good day Gerry",' confusing him with Republican Socialist MP Gerry Fitt (later Lord Fitt) then a Stormont MP![79]

O'Neill explained his twin aims as preserving the 'historic individuality of Ulster' and encouraging 'her progress as a development area integrally part of the British economy.'[80] Both these would certainly appeal to unionist opinion in principle, but their application in practice proved less favourable. For example, O'Neill liked to act as a roving ambassador for Northern Ireland, though his frequent trips abroad owed as much to his distaste for Stormont politics and his enthusiasm for meeting statesmen as they did to attracting foreign investment. In the first 18 months of his premiership he flew over 40,000 miles on public duties, equivalent almost to twice around the world. Two months after becoming Prime Minister he conducted an industrial tour of France. In September 1963 and March 1964 he toured North America. September 1964 saw him visit Europe, including Holland, Belgium, Germany, Luxembourg and France. All this was on top of regular trips to London, some 12 to 14 times a year, and promotional campaigns in north-east England, Manchester and Cardiff.[81] Such international jet setting was not always to the advantage of O'Neill's prestige at home. His visit to Philadelphia resulted in a letter of complaint from the local Ulster Society to Mayor Tate, which was gleefully reprinted by the nationalist *Irish News*:

We, former residents of Ulster, chose to ignore your slighting of Captain O'Neill during his recent visit until we contrasted the red carpet treatment accorded Mr. Lemass. The contrast of Mr. Lemass's thirty police motorcycle escort to Captain O'Neill's one red car; the two hundred police and plain clothes security force for the former to six police men for the Premier of Northern Ireland; your constant attendance to Lemass, to your total absence of any O'Neill function, all smack of rank discrimination. We consider this treatment an affront to Captain O'Neill and an insult to the Stormont Government and all the people that it represents. We shall advise the Northern Ireland Government to seek an apology.[82]

Equally troublesome were O'Neill's attempts to emphasize Ulster's historical identity. He was particularly attracted to the Scotch-Irish tradition and the American connection.[83] Thus he increased resources for the Ulster-American Folk Park, attended academic symposiums, encouraged the activities of the Ulster-Scot Historical Society and made US links a staple of the Government Information Service.[84] O'Neill's interest was undoubtedly genuine, as it continued long after his retirement from office.[85] More practically, however, he hoped also to attract American investment by highlighting ancestral links (an emulation of Southern Irish techniques) and politically to offset his aristocratic demeanour by rooting himself in an earthy Ulster Presbyterian tradition. Most problematic was his ambition to develop a unified Ulster identity that all could identify with. Given the strongly protestant flavour of Scotch-Irish tradition this was never likely to appeal to catholics.[86]

The salience of O'Neill's Scotch-Irish propaganda was dealt an embarrassing blow by his ignominious failure to bring President Kennedy to Northern Ireland. In April 1963, shortly after becoming Prime Minister, Terence O'Neill invited John F. Kennedy to come north during his planned visit to Ireland and open the Giant's Causeway.[87] Kennedy, keen to impress generally nationalist Irish American opinion, declined.[88] O'Neill's ham-fisted initiative had merely accentuated the humiliation for northern unionists at such a snub from a world leader, not to mention a wartime and NATO ally.[89] Even after Kennedy's assassination in November 1963 grassroots unionist opinion remained bitter. Belfast Corporation initially refused to approve 'John F. Kennedy' as a name for the new road through Turf Lodge and petitions were raised in Carrickfergus against a proposed 'Kennedy Drive' on the grounds that the President had 'insulted' Northern Ireland in turning down O'Neill's offer.[90] O'Neill, however, continued to identify with the myth of 'Camelot' and kept a portrait of JFK and Jackie over his fireplace.[91]

Most opposition to O'Neill from his own party, however, stemmed from his attempt to modernize the state. The very bulk of legislation initiated by O'Neill's reforming government put a strain on executive/legislature relations. Phelim O'Neill in July 1963 complained of the 'incredible' manner in which legislation was rushed through parliament. He noted that the House lacked etiquette, so that members made speeches without bothering to attend the rest of the debate or even the Minister's reply. Ministers, for their part, were contemptuous of ordinary MPs, behaved dictatorially and displayed an extraordinary reluctance to admit error.[92] Ministers, indeed, were often indifferent to their own backbenches. In February 1965 the New Town Bill provoked much controversy and four Unionist MPs refused to vote with the government. Despite this during the heated debate Brian Faulkner and Harry West, virtually ignoring proceedings, amused themselves by competing to aim paper darts through a grill.[93]

O'Neill's specific reforms, in upsetting vested interests, equally raised Unionist ire. Dr Robert Nixon (North Down) and David Little (West Down) led opposition to the New City plan within the Parliamentary Unionist Party, on the basis that it deprived rural and border constituencies of resources. It was probable that they expressed majority opinion on the Unionist backbenches.[94] Even in the Cabinet there were splits. Harry West, Minister of Agriculture, was especially worried that 'the New City would encourage accelerated depopulation of the western part of Northern Ireland.'[95] He later sharply criticized 'the economic and political consequences of the "growth towns" policy' in a 1966 Cabinet meeting.[96]

Attempts to rationalize local government structures also met with resistance. A resolution criticizing interference with the powers of County Councils was passed overwhelmingly – with only 20 out of about 200 delegates voting against – at the Unionist Party conference in April 1965.[97] The *Belfast Telegraph* complained that 'palpably necessary local government reform was rejected out of hand ... delegates seemed less interested in the benefits of local government itself than the maintenance of political control.'[98]

The government's policy of infrastructural modernization threatened to upset relations between the Belfast metropole and the localities. This was apparent both with the New City plan and, an issue with an even wider geographical scope to stir up dissent, railway rationalization. Condemnation from the areas principally affected, such as Portrush, Portstewart, Derry, Ballymena, Warrenpoint, Dungannon, Omagh and Newry, was immediate. All but Newry were Unionist-controlled councils (though the areas deprived were disproportionately catholic).[99]

The labour and trade union movement led a high profile resistance to the Benson Plan for railways, even if the leadership never intended to go to the wire. While many MPs were unwilling to antagonize their constituencies by wholeheartedly supporting the Benson proposals, few in private doubted their inevitability and even necessity.[100] In 1964, however, a resolution condemning the Benson Report was forwarded to the Unionist Party Annual Conference's first-ever open session.[101] It was proposed by North Londonderry Unionist Association and found the backing of eight other associations from counties Derry and Tyrone.[102] Though the financial reasons for rationalization could not be denied, John Hamill, proposing the anti-Benson motion, argued that the government should 'mothball' the railways in case expanded road traffic proved too dangerous. This hardly credible argument was bolstered by numerous appeals on behalf of outlying areas. Despite a 15 minute speech 'full of facts and tinged with emotion' from Bill Craig, the relevant minister, the motion was narrowly carried amongst the 700 delegates present after a 90-minute debate.[103] This was in spite of the absence of many rural delegates who had to leave before the vote to return home.

Naturally the government could not be expected to abandon such an important policy plank, on which its claims to be rationally expending resources provided by the British exchequer depended.[104] When the Executive Committee of the Party met there was outrage from several rural delegates who demanded that the conference decision be implemented. It was, according to one delegate, 'one of the liveliest [meetings] for a long time, with some strong words spoken on the transport question.'[105] In the end the vast majority saw no alternative to rail closures. But the Report had proved a bruising experience for O'Neill's first two years.

Similar was the controversy over planning powers. Initially the government's proposal for a central authority that would relieve local councils of arduous planning tasks was generally welcomed.[106] However as the implications of a loss of control over local patronage became more apparent resistance began to emerge from local government, led by the Belfast and Londonderry Corporations.[107] At the 1964 Unionist Party conference, Jack Roberts, vice-chairman of the party executive, condemned the idea of a central planning authority as 'outrageous'.[108]

On 3 July 1964 a Belfast meeting of mayors from 12 boroughs condemned the White Paper on planning.[109] As a sop to aggrieved local councils William Morgan was ejected from the Ministry of Health and Local Government and replaced by Bill Craig later that month. Craig immediately struck a conciliatory note.[110] Opposition was not easily mollified, however, and the Lord Mayor of Londonderry in the senate even blurted that the White Paper proposals 'would establish a form of fascism entirely foreign to our concept of government by the elected representatives of the people.'[111] A resolution sent to the 1965 Young Unionist conference condemned Stormont's 'dictatorial manner' in physical planning and its 'persistent encroachment on the powers and functions of County Councils.'[112] A resolution attacking undemocratic planning proposals was passed by 147 votes to 124 at the Unionist Party conference later that month.[113] Obstructed and whittled down, the bold reform plans fell into abeyance in favour of piecemeal legislation. Comprehensive reform of planning powers was eventually put on the long finger and was only completed in the 1970s.[114]

With railway rationalization having been largely conceded by 1965, the New City became a chronic cause of controversy. A bill was necessary to facilitate the buying out of land and the suspension of normal local government powers in favour of a planning commission. Owing to the technical difficulties of framing a measure specifically for the New City, a general New Towns Bill was published on 18 December 1964.[115] Active hostility to the project centred on the Armagh farmers who stood to lose their land and homes.[116]

The Ulster Farmers Union objected to a compulsory purchase clause in the New Towns Bill. This, they believed, conferred on the Minister of Development 'dictatorial powers to destroy the rights of individuals by depriving them of their homes and land'.[117] Unionist backbench opinion, while not going this far, reflected widespread unease at the centralization of planning power envisaged in the Bill and pressed for greater local authority input. Craig agreed to weaken the relevant clauses at a parliamentary party meeting and backbench approval was grudgingly conceded.[118] After a tumultuous debate the New Towns Bill, much amended, was passed on 24 February 1965. A total of six Unionists defied the whip.[119]

Unionist dissent was reflected in the contrasting attitudes of the two daily unionist papers, the *Belfast Telegraph* and the *News Letter*. The *News Letter* was less than enthusiastic about O'Neill's reforms and, by implication, his administration. On 27 February 1963 its editorial cast cold water on the just published Matthew Plan.[120] Matthew's projection that the annual rate of job creation would rise from 2000 to 10,000 per annum it described as 'desirable but probably utopian'. It expressed severe doubt over the New City plan.[121]

For the *News Letter* the resignation in August 1964 of the New City chief planner, Geoffrey Copcutt, was the final straw:

> Clearly the time has come for a reappraisal, not only of the new city idea, but of the whole thinking behind the Government's planning for the Province. ... If the Government is to have second thoughts on the subject, as now seems inevitable, Londonderry must at least come into the reckoning along with other towns which have strong claims.[122]

The *Belfast Telegraph*, in contrast, was vituperative against Copcutt.[123] This unusually sharp disagreement between the unionist dailies reflected a preference for Faulkner on the part of the *News Letter*, and for O'Neill on the part of the *Belfast Telegraph*.[124]

By 1966, however, the inevitability of the New City was generally accepted. The issue for unionists was now that of compensation for the 350 farmers on the New City site.[125] John Hewitt, a farmer who resisted compulsory purchase, became a *cause celèbre*. North Armagh Unionist Association fired off an angry telegram to the Prime Minister in his support:

> The Nazi methods used by the Ministry of Development of attempting to deprive a farmer in this area of his rightful interest in his property is not going to be tolerated by this Association. Far reaching consequences will result and no further support for the Craigavon project need be expected either from us or from those representing us on any local body.[126]

On 28 January 1966 Craig announced that £2 million was available to buy out the 200 farmers effected. This was a generous, indeed indulgent, package.[127]

O'Neill's modernization, therefore, was not without pain for traditional Unionist supporters. Of course it brought jobs and investment – though Brian Faulkner as Minister of Commerce got disproportionate credit for this – but railway cuts, the New City, and moves away from traditional sectarian rebel baiting worried many sections of the party and undermined O'Neill's position. As early as September 1963 strong rumours emerged that Faulkner was preparing to oust O'Neill in a palace coup.[128] The following month Warnock's letter criticizing O'Neill's method of selection as Prime Minister was leaked. Though ministers stayed above the fray it was reportedly the subject of much speculation in the lobbies.[129]

Almost from the outset tension between Faulkner and O'Neill was assumed. Brian Faulkner quickly won plaudits for his energy and efficiency as Minister of Commerce. The new civil service building – Dundonald House[130] – which housed his department, tended to remove Faulkner from the direct oversight of O'Neill and psychologically reinforced his autonomy. By August it was being said that 'Mr Faulkner... [is the]... solid man of the cabinet, while his Prime Minister is still finding his feet.'[131] Rumours of clashes between O'Neill and Faulkner abounded.[132]

In Cabinet Faulkner and O'Neill were often at odds, to the extent that the former appears to have been bloody-minded as much as principled. Faulkner opposed controversial anti-corruption measures in the Local Government Bill[133] and poured cold water on the Northern Ireland Economic Council, Ulster Weeks in Britain and the Wilson Plan, all key features of the O'Neill era.[134] When it appeared that he might be forced to give up his business directorships over O'Neill's code of conduct for government members, he threatened to resign.[135] He doggedly opposed any salary rise for Members of Parliament against unanimous Cabinet opinion.[136] On the question of funding the Roman Catholic Mater Infirmorum Hospital Faulkner was notably hard-line and successfully reduced O'Neill's scope for compromise on this long running source of controversy.[137] He was almost as obstructive in reaching a settlement with the Northern Ireland Committee of the Irish Congress of Trade Unions over recognition.

Nevertheless, Faulkner's dynamic performance as Minister of Commerce impressed assimilatory unionists and, particularly as he tended to stay above the fray of domestic politics in public, somewhat dimmed the memory of his previous career of sectarian populism.[138] He maintained a close connection with the Young Unionist movement and was willing to reflect their secular and liberal sentiments.[139]

In an after-dinner address to a Young Unionist school at Newcastle on 24 October 1964 Edward Gibson, the movement's chairman, expressed the disillusionment of assimilatory unionists with O'Neill's premiership in the aftermath of the squalid election campaign. Paisleyism, sectarianism and shady practices should be openly disavowed, he insisted. He charged O'Neill with failing to act on his rhetoric by rejuvenating the party.[140]

The following day the officers of the Young Unionist Council threatened to resign if Gibson did not retract his remarks or step down as chairman.[141] The *Belfast Telegraph* commented that Gibson's remarks had been mild and found the 'ultra-sensitivity of Unionists to self-criticism' as depressing as the conduct of the 1964 election to those hoping for a new unionism.[142] A compromise was reached when Gibson apologized for the embarrassment caused by his making the speech in the presence of visitors, but declined to retract his views.[143]

The episode was seen as being to Faulkner's advantage as much as to O'Neill's detriment. Gibson was known as a strong partisan of Faulkner and his criticism of O'Neill came at a time of renewed interest in the leadership question.[144] Faulkner denied a plot but was warm towards Gibson: 'Young Unionists must be allowed the greatest latitude for criticism and it is always better that criticism of this type should come from inside the party than from outside of it.'[145]

Later in Stormont Phelim O'Neill, Unionist MP for North Antrim, openly backed Gibson and referred to tensions within the Cabinet: 'One does from time to time hear rumours that perhaps the Government are not pulling as a team in a way that they should do.'[146] David Bleakley of the NILP, expanded on the lobby rumours of conflict in the Cabinet. Leadership, he observed, was the art of producing co-operation within a team:

> [The] Prime Minister ought to be studying very carefully whether he measures up to that ... [definition] ... It was rumoured ... that the team spirit is considerably strained inside the Government at the moment. ... I believe there is plenty of evidence available that there is in many branches of the Government a situation approaching civil war. ... one has only got to walk around the Lobbies and keep one's ears open to hear the kind of disputations that are taking place inside the [Civil] Service and inside Cabinet circles.[147]

A few days later Bleakley exposed a particular source of contention – the July Cabinet reshuffle. This, it seemed, had been carried through with minimum discussion and just before the parliamentary recess to frustrate a full examination. Even some Cabinet ministers heard of it first through the newspapers. It also caused considerable disruption to an unprepared civil service. The upgrading of Neill and Craig to senior ministers he believed to have been a ploy to create a buffer against Faulkner. Morgan's demotion from the Ministry of Health and Local Government was an obvious sop to critics of the New City and changes to planning legislation. The reshuffle was 'an attempt to prevent a palace revolution ... [and] ... above all else to appease outside and short-sighted critics of the Government.'[148] The *News Letter* confirmed that rumours of a Faulkner/O'Neill rivalry had been rife in the lobbies for quite some time.[149] O'Neill's performance under pressure was poor – he was visibly tense – and Faulkner was notable by his absence from the chamber.[150]

In the general mood of disaffection, the first criticisms of O'Neill's soft-soap on communal relations began to emerge. Desmond Boal, right-wing Unionist MP for Shankill and unofficial legal advisor to Paisley, expressed the suspicion many held of O'Neill's 'new image' for the province:

> People were sometimes afraid to use the word 'protestant', as if it is a dirty word. If one expresses his opinion dogmatically he is

immediately labelled an extremist or bigot. But if someone on the other side states their case strongly – that is not bigotry because that is not their belief and faith. In some queer way we accept that.

For good measure he went on to condemn liberalism as no more than 'anti-Unionism.' Significantly he congratulated Faulkner's exertions in the same breath.[151] Though this was a sharper speech than other mainstream unionists were prepared to make, it indicated a rising tide of concern. None were prepared to take up O'Neill's theme of building bridges.

Even though the NIC of ICTU had been recognized on 24 August 1964, the Northern Ireland Economic Council had yet to be convened by December. Ivan Neill, Minister of Finance,[152] proposed a replication of the British model in Northern Ireland. As Minister of Finance he would be chairman of a Cabinet Economic Steering Committee. Below this would be a Northern Ireland Advisory Council, headed again by Neill.[153] Such a structure would obviously make Neill the economic *supremo* and in effect demote Faulkner, who, up until now, had been the NIEC chairman in waiting.

In his own memorandum Faulkner argued that an exact replication of British regional structures was superfluous. Northern Ireland enjoyed a responsible regional government.[154] Though ostensibly finding common ground between both ministers, O'Neill clearly backed Faulkner and the retention of the NIEC. The rest of the Cabinet agreed, fearing the creation of an over-mighty Minister of Finance.[155] No doubt to the chagrin of O'Neill, Faulkner's authority had been greatly strengthened. Inaccurately, Neill's failed attempt to wrest overall control of the economy was seen as being inspired by an attempt by O'Neill to clip Faulkner's wings.[156]

The nationalist commentator, James Kelly, summed up the bind O'Neill now found himself in. Faulkner, he alleged, was 'winning hands down in the games of winning friends and influencing people'. From Dundonald House he was running a virtual 'shadow government', attracting investment, retaining the loyalty of unionist hard-liners while reaching out to moderates and modernizers such as Edward Gibson. Now, as a final straw,

Mr. Faulkner has been on television making sympathetic sounds in reply to Mr. Jack Lynch, his Dublin opposite number, who thinks there should be meetings between ministers on cross-border trade. In this situation, Mr. O'Neill is beginning to appear in the role of

Ramsey MacDonald – Prime Minister in name only, with a Baldwin breathing down his neck.[157]

O'Neill's strategy of equivocation and balancing between right and left within the party seemed only to generate hostility, confusion and disillusionment on all sides. Even the shiny new face of Ulster was dimming. It seemed possible that the charismatic and scheming Faulkner would construct an unholy alliance of disaffected groups from all wings to oust him. O'Neill desperately needed a new initiative to wrong-foot his rivals, garner public support and bind at least one section of the party to his chariot. The scene was set for his most dramatic scene-stealer in a premiership replete with gesture politics – the summit with Lemass.

5
'O'Neill Must Go!'

Seán Lemass, who became Taoiseach of the Irish Republic in 1958, recognized that the border would not be removed through bellicosity and non-recognition. Thus he spoke more generously of northern unionism and freely used the term 'Northern Ireland' rather than the provocative 'Six Counties'.[1] From 1961 high tariffs against northern goods were reduced on a piecemeal basis, though these were bilaterally negotiated with manufacturers rather than with Stormont.[2] Lemass regularly offered to meet the Northern premier. Brookeborough always refused, pending southern recognition of Northern Ireland's right to remain in the United Kingdom.[3] On 29 July 1963 Lemass publicly recognized that 'the Government and Parliament there exist with the support of the majority in the Six Counties area, artificial although that area is. We see it functioning within its powers ... within an all-Ireland constitution, for as long as it is desired to have them.' He concluded with a call for inter-governmental co-operation over matters where joint effort would be of benefit to both sides.[4]

Terence O'Neill responded to the Tralee speech only after a considerable lapse of time. He rejected Lemass' specific proposals and demanded full recognition: 'What a good thing it would be if this arid debate was brought to an end in a spirit of live and let live, allowing us to concentrate our respective energies upon the real tasks which face us in the sixties.' Somewhere in this supercilious rebuke was an invitation to treat. Lemass was a man with whom O'Neill could do business: 'Mr. Lemass deserves his reputation for realism. His remarks were certainly not without courage.'[5] Lemass recognized the gesture and immediately offered 'discussions at whatever level is likely to be most fruitful' and 'without political preconditions'.[6] O'Neill's reply was cautious but upbeat.[7] There was widespread speculation of talks between civil servants, if not the two premiers.[8]

It was not to be. During a tour of the United States the following month, Lemass made a number of more traditionalist anti-partition statements.[9] O'Neill's retort was frosty. He told a Young Unionist school in Newcastle that, while Lemass was a 'reasonable and sensible man', public statements on partition should cease.[10] On his return to Dublin Lemass wondered aloud why O'Neill was complaining. He had never concealed his hope that north-south co-operation would lead to formal reunification.[11] This was too much and O'Neill called a definite halt to megaphone diplomacy.[12]

From these exchanges it is clear that Northern Ireland feared an all-Ireland détente more than the Republic. Lemass could, and did, present any softening of relations as a move towards ending the animosities between 'Irishmen'. Ulster unionists, however, were acutely aware that Northern Ireland was not a sovereign state. It could not meet with its neighbour on a strictly equal basis nor it did not wish to appear as if it were paying homage to the island's natural centre of authority.[13] The alternative was to allow all relations with the Republic, an external power, to be dealt with by the United Kingdom. This, however, held its own dangers were the Republic and Britain to 'gang-up' on Northern Ireland. Truly, unionist Ulster's braggadocio concealed a fundamental insecurity rooted in its position as a double minority, within Ireland and within the United Kingdom. Their priority, thus, was to retain the greatest possible control over their own affairs commensurate with the maximum affirmation of Northern Ireland's status as an integral part of the United Kingdom. It was a difficult and ambiguous position to maintain.

Attitudes towards the southern government amongst sections of unionist opinion were softening, nonetheless.[14] Many felt Northern Ireland was sufficiently secure, and southern republicans sufficiently tamed, for a new foundation of friendship to be built. Significant was an interview with Lemass conducted by Ralph Bossence, chief political correspondent of the *News Letter*, in December 1963. Bossence was greatly impressed by the southern premier calling him 'shrewd, lively and well-informed. ... In an hour's talk with Mr. Lemass I formed an impression of a man who is tolerant, understanding of our point of view and anxious that bread and butter issues should be tackled by both Governments in their common interest.'[15]

Almost a year later Sean Lemass accepted an invitation to address, the following term, the Queen's University Literific Society, a student debating society.[16] In Stormont Harry Diamond, the Republican Labour MP, asked O'Neill why no courtesy meeting of the premiers was planned. O'Neill's response was as taciturn as any unionist traditionalist could hope: 'Courtesy must be reciprocal and Mr. Lemass does not encourage a meeting between us by his statements that the ultimate purpose of such a meeting would be to improve the prospects of ending partition.'[17] The *News Letter*, that most loyal of unionist dailies, responded with a highlighted page one editorial:

> ... is it a time to stand on ceremony? Are there not problems which involve both countries and which a meeting of two heads of state might solve? Several come to mind – tourism, transport and trade among them. ... In agreeing to talks Captain O'Neill would show the strength of his position. He would do well to think again.[18]

O'Neill, it seemed, was proving too conservative even for the unionist mainstream.

Brian Faulkner, generally looked on with favour by the *News Letter*, had already offered ministerial talks with his opposite number, Jack Lynch.[19] After the O'Neill/Lemass summit the *Financial Times* found it easy

> to detect the fingerprints of Mr. Brian Faulkner ... Like Lemass he is a pragmatist, and, as one of my Belfast friends put it, 'the very devil for business'; this has made him a hero for Belfast's home grown version of the Bow Group, which has been pressing rather harder for yesterday's meeting than O'Neill.[20]

Lemass's planned visit to Belfast, encouragement in the mainstream unionist press, and urgings from unionist radicals all brought pressure to bear. Faulkner's threat to by-pass O'Neill on the liberal flank, by involving himself in high-level North/South dialogue, virtually coerced O'Neill into taking an initiative.[21] O'Neill's decision to meet with Lemass was strongly motivated by a desire to out-manoeuvre Faulkner.[22]

The tale of the O'Neill/Lemass summit on 14 January 1964 has been often told. In great secrecy (to the extent that Ken Whitaker, who accompanied the Taoiseach, kept even his family in the dark as to his travel arrangements) Lemass drove north. Diplomatically improvising at the doors of Stormont Castle, O'Neill welcomed his guest 'to the north'. Both premiers were grimly aware of the political risks they were taking. Lemass betrayed his nerves with an initial taciturnity, O'Neill characteristically showed his by braying with laughter at the Taoiseach's mildest witticisms. The resulting photographs and television footage, however, conveyed a suitable atmosphere of *bonhomie*. An array of assembled journalists, awed by the historic encounter, were accommodatingly eulogistic. After a carefully bland communiqué, emphasizing that no political items had been discussed, a now more relaxed Lemass took his leave.

The summit was an idea long in gestation. O'Neill had since his accession intended to effect a cross-border meeting of premiers. Characteristically, meeting the southern civil servant Ken Whitaker (born in Rostrevor) at a meeting of the World Bank had inspired him, and it was through civil service contacts that the summit was arranged.[23] It was the timing that was significant. O'Neill wanted a publicity coup to out-manoeuvre Faulkner. The *Belfast Telegraph* indeed, saw the meeting primarily as a 'timely reassertion of his leadership'.[24] O'Neill failed to inform most of his Cabinet colleagues in advance of the meeting, despite the urgings of his Cabinet Secretary.[25] It is likely that he hoped to garner all the credit for the meeting to himself. He was appealing to public opinion against his unionist rivals.[26]

O'Neill's evident mistrust of his Cabinet only soured relations further.[27] Worse, O'Neill's hard-line rhetoric during the months of megaphone diplomacy with Lemass combined with the secrecy of the meeting was ill judged to assuage unionist fears. O'Neill had subordinated long-term strategic considerations to short-term political imperatives. Besides this, O'Neill seems to have relished the cloak-and-dagger orchestration of the summit.[28] Likewise, he lapped up the adulation of the press, both in Ireland and abroad.[29] He would often bid interviewers in his office to 'sit down on that chair, the one Lemass sat on.'[30]

Paisley and three colleagues were quick to react to the summit and, having circled Stormont in a Union Jack-bedecked car trailing a huge red ensign, delivered a letter of protest to O'Neill's assistant private secretary. Astutely criticizing O'Neill for having kept his Cabinet and backbenchers in the dark, it condemned his going back on previous commitments that there would be no meeting until Lemass recognized the northern state's legitimacy.[31]

At a meeting of Londonderry North Ward Unionist Association Desmond Boal, MP for Shankill Road, was the first Unionist to openly deprecate the summit. The secrecy in arranging the meeting, he held, implied guilty motives behind it.[32] O'Neill argued at first that Lemass had *de facto* recognized Northern Ireland's legitimacy by his visit.[33]

This was a spurious argument. After a period of discreet silence, Lemass made clear that '[as] regards the suggestion that my visit to Belfast involved recognition of the present constitutional status of the Northern Ireland Government, if by recognition is meant approval, I did not regard it as implying this, nor should it be so considered.'[34]

When O'Neill spoke in Stormont on the meeting, in a low-key, 'rather donnish' statement from which he raised his eyes only once,[35] he evinced a guarded justification:

> Our constitutional position is not in doubt; why should we continue to behave as if it were? Moreover, it seems to me in the spirit of the times to treat the border as nothing more – though, of course, as nothing less – than an ordinary frontier. Today, across virtually every all the frontiers of the world, friendly and co-operative exchanges take place, without any loss of prestige or sovereignty by either side. Why should we be the exception?[36]

Backbenchers put down a motion supporting the summit, if rather tepidly. Thirteen MPs immediately signed the motion, leaving seven unsigned.[37] The following day the Executive Committee of the Unionist Party backed the summit.[38] Unionist opinion was clearly rallying, despite liberal Unionist hopes of a showdown with the hard-liners.[39] All the emphasis, however, was negatively on the presumed *de facto* recognition conceded by Lemass.

Paisleyite agitation was still building. At a meeting in the Ulster Hall, attended by some thousand people Paisley announced that 'Captain O'Neill has forfeited the right to be our Prime Minister. ... He is a bridge builder he tells us. A traitor and a bridge are very much alike for they both go over to the other side.'[40] That this was finding an echo even in the ranks of the parliamentary party was made clear when O'Neill chided Unionist MPs who 'make speeches in this House which they think will be popular in their constituencies and make things awkward for people doing what they consider to be right'.[41]

Only Desmond Boal (Shankill) and Edmund Warnock (St Anne's) of the parliamentary party openly condemned the meeting. Boal quoted O'Neill's reply to Patrick Gormley in April 1963 that he would not meet Lemass until the South had recognized Northern Ireland's consti-tutional legitimacy. Though he was not against a summit in all circumstances, O'Neill's blasé disregard for his own pledge brought the constitutional principle into disrepute.[42] Warnock, for his part, criti-cized O'Neill's secrecy. Had he been in a Cabinet so bypassed, he would have resigned. O'Neill's unilateral decision had been 'an unwarrantable assumption of personal dictatorship.'[43] Such barbs, not without substance, struck home. However, the public popularity of the summit was reflected by the unwillingness of any Unionist MP actually to vote against the motion.[44]

Having seen out the Stormont debate, Terence O'Neill felt secure enough to make the inevitable return visit, this time with wives present, to meet Lemass in Dublin.[45] This meeting went off without a hitch. Years later, in 1973, Sean Lemass's widow, Kathleen Lemass, made a remarkable claim about this meeting:

> Sean explained to me that they [O'Neill and Lemass] wanted to convey the impression to the outside world that the talks were just about routine matters. In fact, both men wanted to see Ireland united. Their idea was to have several meetings at various levels between Government officials so that co-operation would begin, eventually leading to Irish unity.
>
> Sean normally disliked talking politics at home. But this one time he was really excited and in fact was brimming over with happiness. He told me he had great hopes that things would work out and that he and Captain O'Neill had found a lot of common ground and could talk to each other freely and sensibly without history spoiling things.
>
> Captain O'Neill seemed just as happy. On the day of his visit to Dublin he told me that his intention was to get Ireland united. ... Very few people have known until this day that both of those men wanted the unification of Ireland and I am convinced they could have achieved it.

O'Neill vehemently denied these claims, and pointed out verifiable inaccuracies in Mrs Lemass's account.[46]

It is at this date impossible to be certain of what to make of these allegations. Certainly they have the ring of wishful thinking, at least. However, there may have been a grain of truth. Terence O'Neill was prone to let the praise of his preferred constituencies – the liberal press, his civil servants and informed opinion outside Northern Ireland – go to his head. For example, from southern Irish quarters came the idea that the Council of Ireland be resurrected. The Council had been a provision in the 1921 Treaty intended by Britain as a vehicle with which to trundle Northern Ireland eventually into a united Ireland. Faced with northern hostility and southern indifference it had never come into being.[47]

Questioned on this in a lengthy interview for Irish radio O'Neill rejected it only on the grounds that the climate of opinion was 'not right ... I do not think we can really start running before we have started to walk.'[48]

In contrast to most unionists, for whom religion, culture and nationality were the corner stones of the Union,[49] O'Neill virtually never defended partition in any but economic terms.[50] This, surely, was the most negotiable of problems. O'Neill, indeed, considered himself not as an Ulster protestant, but as Anglo-Irish.[51] His sense of nationalism was redolent of pre-partition days, in which a loyalty to the British Crown subsumed, but did not obliterate, simultaneous loyalty to Ireland and the United Kingdom:

> It is very difficult to be Anglo-Irish. In the first place, if you have an Irish name you are romantically involved with Ireland even if you do not speak with an Irish accent. And yet you are brought up to believe that London is the capital of the *British Isles* and that the Monarch is the Head of your State.[52]

After his resignation O'Neill revealed that 'he was sure that one day, there would be a united Ireland', though not in his lifetime.[53] His hint in 1970 that he would 'let his name go forward as the next President of the Irish Republic' to follow De Valera attracted widespread, and incredulous, comment. The idea ran for two years with O'Neill obviously enthusiastic.[54] Given O'Neill's rather imperial distance from the passions on both sides of the border, the idea that O'Neill and Lemass had private discussions on such matters that could be construed as concerning the future reunification of Ireland under whatever dispensation is hardly outlandish. That there was ever any agreed model for Irish unity, never mind a mechanism, timetable or 'plot' of any kind, seems highly unlikely.

In practice, O'Neill was soon required to trim his sails very considerably. On 26 February a special meeting of the Grand Orange Lodge of Ireland was convened in Sandy Row Orange Hall to discuss the summit meetings.[55] A total of 120 delegates after a three and a half hour debate passed a unanimous vote of confidence in O'Neill.[56] Only later did it transpire that this came at the price of an assurance from O'Neill that no further talks would be held with the southern Taoiseach without prior consultation with the Cabinet.[57]

The practical fruits of cross-border co-operation were relatively limited.[58] It was Faulkner who proved to be the most enthusiastic to achieve something in this area. After meeting his opposite numbers civil service co-operation on electricity supply and tourism was launched.[59] When Harold Wilson suggested a meeting of the three premiers of the islands he was sharply rebuked by O'Neill.[60] The arch-ipelagic dimension could not be easily ignored however. From the beginning of the year talks had been underway between British and Irish civil servants on a Free Trade Agreement. Faulkner wanted to press for an accelerated reduction of tariffs between Northern Ireland and the Republic. For political reasons, Dublin had often offered such special concessions, but Stormont had insisted on being treated as an undifferentiated part of the United Kingdom.[61] 'Northern Ireland industries,' Faulkner now reported, 'were pressing strongly for a reduc-tion of the Irish tariff, and it would be extremely desirable to demonstrate that representations had been made on their behalf.' It was thus agreed that the Northern Ireland government would autho-rize the British Board of Trade to negotiate special concessions for the North, but not participate directly as a 'third party'.[62] Under pressure the Ministry of Commerce agreed to participate directly, but only as agents for the United Kingdom Board of Trade. Form was all.[63]

The Anglo-Irish trade pact was signed on 14 December 1965. Though invited, O'Neill, ever fearful of tri-partite arrangements, was absent from the signing ceremony.[64] Rolling tariff cuts were agreed until by July 1975 there would be free trade between the two states.[65] The deal seemed much to Ireland's advantage, but with a substantially weaker and protected economy, it would undergo the greater economic turbulence. As a special concession to Northern Ireland southern duties on its goods would either be abolished immediately or depreciate more rapidly.[66] This appears impressive, but it probably no more than compensated Northern Ireland for her loss of advantage in agricultural exports to the British market.[67]

Even in as innocent an area as tourist co-operation, the Stormont government trod with extreme caution, certainly more so than the Northern Ireland Tourist Board would have liked.[68] The publication of a mutually acceptable map of Ireland proved a time consuming problem.[69] Only in October 1965 did the Cabinet finally approve a draft.[70] The go-ahead for a complete brochure hung fire until September 1966.[71] Finance for a scholarly history of Ireland, already backed by the Republic, was summarily dismissed as it was a 'project over which the Government would have no control and whose end result might be unfavourably received in Northern Ireland.'[72]

The greatest achievement of North/South co-operation was in elec-tricity. Faulkner was keen to interconnect the two networks so that the

South would provide power to Fermanagh and South Tyrone.[73] Despite sustained opposition from Sir Knox Cunningham, the hard-right Westminster MP for South Antrim,[74] a deal was signed in October 1967 to connect the electricity grids.[75] Ironically IRA bombs finally put the interconnection out of action in 1971.

Certainly the summit with Lemass was the most memorable initiative of O'Neill's premiership. Though it added greatly to O'Neill's lustre as a liberal unionist, it elided the central dilemma of governing Northern Ireland: community relations.[76] Little strategic reasoning underlay the summit, besides an ambition to further goodwill and perhaps vague notions of resolving the border problem.

Rather than strike a concord with the southern Taoiseach, O'Neill's priority should have been to enter into direct dialogue with the representatives of the catholic community. A summit of O'Neill, Eddie McAteer (Nationalist leader) and Tom Boyd (for the NILP) to hammer out civil rights grievances was the real prize. No doubt unionist opposition would have been strong, particularly in the west of the province. In return for forgoing the doubtful advantages of gerrymandering, the restricted franchise and the near-monopoly of public appointments, however, they would have been in a strong position to insist on co-operative citizenship and perhaps even recognition of Northern Ireland's claim for self-determination. Certainly much moral advantage would have accrued to unionism. Indeed, such an internal, limited agreement implied fewer constitutional threats than open-ended contacts between North and South. An understanding on civic rights and duties between moderate unionism, the Labour movement and Liberal Party, and conciliatory nationalists, if need be validated by the electorate in a general election, would have stood fair chance of isolating the Unionist right. Instead O'Neill, fearful of Unionist backbench reaction, frittered away much capital on defending the ambiguous symbolism of his North/South rapprochement. Despite vindication at the polls in 1965, by 1967 the impetus of the summits had largely dissipated. In the absence of much practical cross-border co-operation, the sound and fury of O'Neill's initiative, whilst sowing copious seeds of mistrust in Ulster Unionist ranks, did little to salve community relations.

O'Neill's public relations coup with the summit did not still backbench discontent for long. In February the legitimacy of O'Neill's succession was again questioned and in March much of the party threatened to rebel over the location of the second university in Coleraine.[77]

Despite optimism that the serious cleavage apparent in the Cabinet at the end of 1964 had healed,[78] it actually came to a crisis point in April

1965 with the surprise resignation of the Minister of Finance, Ivan Neill. In October the previous year Neill had taken over as Leader of the House.[79] His high-handed behaviour in this post had annoyed both backbenchers and Cabinet colleagues. Neill clashed with the Chief Whip, Chichester-Clark, over their division of duties. When O'Neill came down on the side of Chichester-Clark, Neill, no doubt mindful of his humiliation in December 1964 over control of economic policy, offered his resignation. Having served so long in Cabinet, and holding such a senior position, he resented O'Neill's preference for seeking advice from civil servants rather than his ministers.[80] Admittedly a hard-working minister, Neill was uncharismatic and unpopular with MPs. Although he had reached the nominally second ranking post in the Cabinet, he was obviously over-shadowed by Faulkner and even Craig. Dispirited by poor prospects for further promotion, and defeated in his attempts to raise the authority of his Cabinet posts, Neill simply threw in the towel. O'Neill, eager to weld his lieutenant into firmer loyalty, offered the Ministry of Finance to Faulkner, who refused but did accept the position of Deputy Prime Minister. Herbert Kirk, formerly Minister of Education and a loyal ally of the Prime Minister, took over Finance.[81]

The Neill sacking was seized upon as a *casus belli* by the anti-O'Neill faction, despite the efforts taken to ensure Faulkner's loyalty. Edmund Warnock attacked O'Neill's North/South talks, the 'mishandling' of the university question and the 'inexplicable dismissal' of Neill. As the province appeared to be heading for a period of constitutional upset, he preferred 'to see another Prime Minister handle such a crisis.' Robert Nixon, MP for North Down, rang Glengall Street to demand O'Neill's dismissal and replacement by Faulkner. Ironically, he had been among the first to welcome the O'Neill/Lemass summit. His attitude reflected Unionist unease with O'Neill's leadership qualities:

> I am tremendously disturbed at the way things are going in Northern Ireland, and I told Unionist headquarters that I considered that the state of Unionism west of the Bann was appalling. Belfast, too, has gone, and Mr. Faulkner needs the time before the next election to bring Unionism together, especially in the city of Belfast and associations west of the Bann. ... Captain O'Neill has sacked Mr. Andrews, demoted Mr. Morgan and has now caused the sacking of Mr. Neill – his own picked team.[82]

Rumours held that as many as ten or twelve Unionist MPs supported Faulkner to replace O'Neill.[83]

A special meeting of the Parliamentary Unionist Party was called in April 1965 to 'clear the air.'[84] After a two-hour meeting a unanimous vote of confidence in O'Neill was passed. However, this was not before O'Neill gave 'certain assurances' on the constitution.[85] It was further agreed that no action would be taken against the rebel MPs. This was a grant of remarkable latitude for before the meeting Nixon had openly called, in effect, for a grassroots revolt of unionist associations.[86] A more ringing victory might have been expected over two such chronic malcontents as Nixon and Warnock. Evidently the parliamentary party concurred that O'Neill required reining in. It imposed on their leader considerable and onerous conditions.

Dr Nixon, one of the rebel MPs, failed to maintain discipline for long. In May he accused the government of caving in to pressure from a Unionist clique in Derry not to site the second university there. Eventually Nixon was expelled from the Parliamentary Unionist Party.[87] Nixon revealed that he had been 'most unhappy' since Andrews, the former Minister of Finance, had been 'sacked' by O'Neill and kicked upstairs as Leader of the Senate. He admitted having been at odds with the government for two years. A succession of issues – town planning, the New City, new industry, and the refusal to permit a public inquiry into planning – had all served to convince him of O'Neill's dictatorial tendencies. Derry had been the last straw.[88]

In 1966 opposition to O'Neill rapidly developed into a general loyalist reaction. For the first time bridge-building policies, rather than his reforms in the economy, government and infrastructure, became the focus of discontent. Central to this were the activities of the politico-religious agitator the Reverend Ian Paisley. Ian Paisley had first risen to prominence as an opponent of O'Neill's 'building-bridges' policy in 1963. Then he had protested against the flying of the Union flag at half-mast over Belfast City Hall in commiseration on the death of Pope John XXIII. He soon proved himself adept at turning out regular phalanxes of ultra-unionist protesters at short notice. Members of the Free Presbyterian Church, of which he was founder and moderator, formed a reliable core, but Paisley's soaring rhetoric and acute understanding of protestant insecurities ensured its regular complementation with wider layers. Though a sincere and evangelical Christian, he possessed sufficient strategic sense to construct organizations that could appeal to the intensely loyalist but devotionally indifferent protestant proletariat – the Ulster Constitution Defence Campaign (UCDC), the Ulster Protestant Volunteers and the Protestant Unionist Party. His populism appealed to protestant workers disgruntled by the decline of traditional industries in favour of new multinational companies and consequently the disruption of the sectarian labour market. Even Paisley's directly religious mission carried a political resonance. In campaigning against the ecumenical movement, as a Romeward trend in the mainstream protestant churches, Paisley articulated a widespread fear of sell-out to intolerant, expansionary international catholicism. It was no great difficulty to see in religious, cultural and political trends a cosmopolitan elite being seduced by the soft words of the catholic/nationalist nexus. Many might admit that Paisley's obsessive anti-catholicism and embrace of street politics were somewhat excessive, but this very excess ensured that Paisley was a bulwark. Better him than the effete appeasers at the helm of Unionism to guard against duplicitous catholic nationalism. Paisley was a rallying point of traditional segregatory unionism over the unknown perils of assimilatory strategies.

Paisley presented a unique problem for the authorities in Northern Ireland. Often a victim of the law, he used the courts as a tribunal and the prison cell as martyrdom. Yet, as the 1964 Divis Riot showed, his coat-trailing and provocative language could easily spark public disorder if unchecked. A relatively small number of determined militants, with the sympathy of a much broader layer, could draw the government into a self-defeating spiral of repression and retreat. Worse still, Paisley claimed, and could do so with some validity, the very traditions the Unionist Party was pledged, at least implicitly, to defend: the union with Britain, the protestant ethos of the state and the memory of past heroes.[89] By striking at Paisley the Unionist government seemed to strike at the very concepts of loyalist militancy, vigilance and anti-catholicism which were integral components of the Ulster Unionist heritage. Paisley would have been a formidable opponent for any Unionist Prime Minister. He was a nightmare for O'Neill.

Though Paisley spoke in more strident tones than the unionist mainstream, his message – that Roman Catholicism was intolerant, expansionist and undemocratic – was, at core, accepted by virtually all strands of unionism. Vatican II and the ecumenical movement were, for a small group, reasons to reconsider Roman Catholicism as a threat to liberty and the basis of partition, but even amongst liberals this was a minority opinion.[90] The *News Letter* in 1964 insisted that:

Whatever shade extremism takes it is outmoded and to be deplored but it exists here only because it can feed on the ambitions of the Roman Catholic Church. These have never been disguised. Always the purpose has been the establishment of an all-Ireland Roman

Catholic State. While that policy persists there can neither be compromise with it nor profitable co-operation with those who give it their support.[91]

Protestant Ulster was seen as a besieged bastion of liberty against catholic tyranny, whether it took a theocratic, fascist or communist guise.[92] It was easy to see political rapprochement between the communities and the ecumenical movement as an insidious weakening of unionist solidarity in the face of an undiminished catholic/nationalist threat.[93] Vatican II and conciliatory Irish nationalism raised as much fear of deception as hope for détente or assimilation on unionist terms.[94]

The irony was that while Paisley's specific policies might cause uneasiness, his very tunnel vision attracted those fearful of uncertainty and change. Thus a 1967 survey found that while 75 per cent were in favour of O'Neill's policies to improve community relations, 31 per cent (about 47 per cent of protestants) approved of Paisley.[95] A later poll showed that a third of protestants 'usually agreed' with Paisley. Terence O'Neill at the time commented that 'since nearly half of those who gave that answer favoured improved relations with the Republic, about two-thirds preferred me as Prime Minister, and the great majority favoured better relations between Protestant and Catholic, it is a little difficult to see what they usually agree about!'[96] Logically it was indeed a paradox, but it expressed a fundamental truth. O'Neill always preferred to appeal to the 'common-sense' of the electorate, as revealed to him by a liberal media, against the reactionary instincts of his own party. He failed to see that his own MPs, and even Paisley, more accurately reflected the protean amalgamation of pluralistic norms with communal identities, traditions and suspicions that characterized popular unionism.[97]

From an early stage Paisley appealed to a substantial section of the official unionist movement. His involvement in the Divis Street riots boosted his profile and, for a section, authority. Paisley's involvement in Kilfedder's West Belfast election victory heralded a strategy of infiltrating the Unionist Party. The O'Neill/Lemass summit added flesh to his accusations of appeasement and he launched a personalized and insistent 'O'Neill must go' campaign.[98] The events of 1966 massively expanded the cleric's opportunities.

In October 1963 work began on a new bridge across the river Lagan in Belfast.[99] As it neared completion, and in the aftermath of the 'Craigavon' controversy, there was much discussion about an appropriate name.[100] William Craig dismissed a leading news paper's suggestion that a name non-offensive to nationalists be chosen as 'sickening and... the sort of thing we must not allow to become prevalent.'[101] On Monday 14 January 1966 the Belfast Corporation Unionist Group caucus decided upon the name 'Carson Bridge' in preference to 'Somme Bridge'. However, a telephone call from the Governor, Lord Erskine, made it clear that the Queen, who was to open the development, would not wish to be mired in political controversy. He forcefully suggested 'Queen Elizabeth II Bridge' as an alternative. The Unionist caucus agreed but deplored the Governor's interference.[102] In a short but stormy session, the Belfast Corporation approved the name 'Queen Elizabeth II'.[103]

Pouncing on the issue, Ian Paisley addressed regular loyalist protest rallies of over 3000 in the Ulster Hall throughout February.[104] In March Edward Carson, an ex-Conservative MP at Westminster and son of the leader of the Ulster Unionists during the third Home Rule crisis, visited the province as a guest of Paisley. Carson was an eccentric, rather typical of the political innocents who tended to fall under Paisley's sway.[105] Now he emerged from obscurity to address a Paisleyite rally in the Ulster Hall.[106] Here he demanded the resignation of Lord Erskine and threatened the government with 'as much trouble as we can possibly give'.[107]

This was an ominous prelude to an election campaign for the Unionist Party. Harold Wilson's calling of a Westminster election in March 1966, to achieve a secure majority, was not in O'Neill's interests. Embarrassment for the Unionists came from an unusual direction. The Conservative Party manifesto devoted five paragraphs to Northern Ireland (the Labour Party's made no reference) and included a promise to allow the west of the province to 'share in growing prosperity'.[108] Nat Minford, Unionist MP for Antrim, complained with cause that this implied that the Stormont government was currently ignoring the west.[109] It was an unwelcome reminder that the locational policy controversies of 1965 had not gone unnoticed even by friendly eyes across the water. The Unionist election platform was parochial and uninspiring, seeking only special aid for Northern Ireland concerns such as the shipyard, aircraft factory, agriculture and the linen industry.[110]

On 16 March a long-feared bombshell hit unionism when it was announced that Edward Carson, backed by Paisley's UCDC, would stand against the liberal unionist Stratton Mills in North Belfast. He had the blessing of his mother, Lady Carson, vice-president of the Ulster Unionist Party. Carson was obviously contesting the seat out of personal pique for the offence done to his father's name. Rather than being a committed Paisleyite, he came across as rather petty and confused by Ulster politics. He opposed a 'nazi' state which discriminated against catholics, 'But I can't say I like Irish Roman Catholics very much. Loyalty to the Crown usually goes by religion.' Significantly, the greatest fear entertained by the Unionist machine appeared to be that if protestant Unionist activists were diverted to North Belfast it would prejudice Kilfedder's chance in West Belfast.[111] The Unionist reaction was testament not to Carson's real chance of success, but to the importance of the Paisleyites to official unionism in West Belfast.

It soon became clear, however, that Paisley and Carson would not easily split resilient Unionist unity. Lord Brookeborough personally telephoned Carson to dissuade him from standing. The North Belfast Unionist Associations – Clifton, Duncairn (Lord Carson's old seat), Shankill and Oldpark – all backed Stratton Mills.[112]

On 18 March O'Neill interrupted an engagement in England to attend an emergency meeting in Unionist headquarters. Paisley was threatening to field Independent candidates in all four Belfast constituencies unless an official Unionist seat was found for Carson. Showing little loyalty to Kilfedder, Paisley had Belfast West in mind. He demanded also the removal of Lord Erskine as Governor and the personal right to speak from Unionist platforms. O'Neill endorsed the decision, already taken by headquarters and a group of Westminster MPs (led by Robin Chichester-Clark, MP for Londonderry, and the Prime Minister's closest political friend), to reject the ultimatum. Over a tense weekend Paisley's next move was awaited. Carson's candidature was proving a liability, however, and, facing a lost deposit, Paisley blinked first. On the eve of the nominations deadline Edward Carson dropped out, protesting that he would not get a fair press. In fact, O'Neill had laid hands on a letter written by Carson years previously criticizing widespread gerrymandering in Northern Ireland. He had threatened to publicize this if Carson did not back down. Ian Paisley declined to stand in East Belfast.[113]

The *Belfast Telegraph* was only lukewarm at this partial victory: 'The Unionist Party, under the threat of a take-over of the popular base of its support, has stood firm. But it would have been a worthier victor if its leaders had spoken out and put the choice to the electorate openly and in black and white.'[114] Nevertheless, necessity had bound the party apparatus closer to O'Neill's bridge-building policy and put Paisley, for a while, beyond the Unionist pale.

James Kilfedder remained the bastion of hope for the anti-O'Neill right in the party, and he was the only Unionist candidate to attract Carson's endorsement.[115] As before, West Belfast promised to be the election's cockpit. After much bluster, the National Democratic Party was persuaded to step aside and give Gerry Fitt, Republican Labour Party MP at Stormont for Dock, a clear run. The NILP, which in 1964 had taken 12,500 of the anti-Unionist total of 30,000, declined to stand, owing to demoralization and the decay of its Woodvale branch.[116] Kilfedder promised to fight a clean, unemotional fight, but did not rule out accepting help from Paisley: 'I think Mr. Paisley is as much concerned as any Unionist with maintaining Ulster and the constitutional position. I think it would be doing him an injustice to say that he just attacks Roman Catholics.'[117]

Though he began as the underdog, and the NILP made no recommendation in favour of either of the candidates, Fitt pitched hard for the protestant Labour vote concentrated in the New Barnsley and Highfield estates.[118] The republican tag proved a millstone, however, and tempers ran high. The RUC excluded Fitt from canvassing protestant areas and on election day he had to recruit burly dock workers to man 'unionist' polling stations. Accusations of personation were freely made, reflecting the closeness of the battle expected to be decisive for many years to come.[119] Fitt won. He picked up a small slice of the protestant NILP vote but far more significant was the heavy polling in catholic areas.[120] Loyalist fears were only heightened.

The prospect of serious disorder around the 50th anniversary of the Easter Rising in 1966 spurred O'Neill into broaching head-on the question of community relations. Over the anniversary weekend Terence O'Neill delivered a considered address on 'The Ulster community' to a joint protestant and catholic conference at the inter-denominational Corrymeela Centre in Ballycastle. O'Neill boldly insisted that he would not shy away from 'frank speaking and an admission of differences of principle'. First he set out the problem:

> The Ulster community is a place in which two communities meet, the Irish Catholic tradition and the British Protestant tradition. ... By and large, these religious traditions are also synonymous with political views. This correspondence of religion and politics has, in the past, created certain peculiar frictions in our public affairs, and prevented us from mounting a united effort to surmount other social and economic problems.

He blamed the depth and perseverance of this division, as was usual from unionists all along the spectrum, on catholic insistence upon segregated education. More interestingly, he pointed out that 'political divisions become unusually sharp when the argument is not about means but ends. ... Here in Northern Ireland ... disagreement has been centred not around the activities of the state, but around its very existence.' Soft words, he declared, were insufficient to overcome this deep divide:

> I must say clearly that the constitutional position of Northern Ireland is not a matter on which there can be any compromise, now or in the future, and I must say so, too, that we have a right to call upon our citizens to support the Constitution. The whole basis of Constitutional government would be debased if the state were not to expect of its citizens at any rate the minimum duty of allegiance.

Though O'Neill defined the constitutional link with Britain as sacrosanct, the pill was sweetened by his minimalist definition of the Union, based upon economic advantage and the welfare state rather than nationality, race, religion or even culture. Continuing on this economistic track O'Neill posed a more flexible and hopeful future for the minority. His ambition as Prime Minister was to encourage everyone to participate in striving for social and economic achievements in which all would feel proud.[121]

O'Neill's speech can be regarded as significant because, on the one hand, it directly addressed the minority community and, in fair and measured tones, acknowledged their political and cultural inheritance. This contrasts with the widespread practice in unionist circles that equated Northern Ireland with only one section of its population – the loyalists. O'Neill's reduction of the Union to an economic boon offensive to none was an attempt to desensitize the issue of sovereignty and draw the sting of cultural subordination for catholics. By contrast traditional unionism linked the Union with a defence of the 'planter' tradition. The importance of the Corrymeela speech was in its direct communication with the 'Catholic Nationalist' minority and its optimism that both communities could unite in building the New Ulster. Its realism was in an appreciation of the intractability of the division. Its sop to unionist traditionalists was in its rejection of constitutional compromise and the failure to mention civil rights reform. It was an accurate snap-shot of O'Neillism through its current phase of evolution.

Hard on the heels of the election followed the 50th anniversary of the republican Dublin Easter Rising of 1916. Northern republicans intended to celebrate in style.[122] Both O'Neill and Cardinal Conway appealed for restraint.[123] Rumours circulated that 30,000 would arrive from Dublin to join celebrations in the North and the government was understandably anxious to reassure its unionist constituency. The Minister of Home Affairs, Brian McConnell, told Stormont: 'The events which are being celebrated do not commend themselves to the people of Northern Ireland as a whole. It is the duty of the Government to ensure that any celebrations are taking place within Northern Ireland do not offend our citizens.'[124] From Fermanagh County Grand Orange Lodge came a resolution, signed by Lord Brookeborough, requesting that the government ban all celebrations. Such sentiments were common in Orange circles. O'Neill refused on the grounds that British public opinion would neither understand nor accept such a drastic measure.[125]

On 4 April celebrations kicked off with an open-air pageant in Casement Park, attracting 7000.[126] The high-point was to be the actual anniversary on Sunday 17 April. As it approached, security was stepped up in border areas. Police stations were sandbagged and two re-opened at Whitecross and Clogher.[127] On 7 April a parliamentary ministerial statement informed the House that, since the release of intelligence on 7 December last that the IRA were planning a renewal of its military campaign, a Cabinet security committee, comprising O'Neill, Faulkner, Craig and McConnell, had been operating. The RUC and USC had been reinforced and liaison with the army stepped up. Police leave over Easter week was cancelled. The government's real fear was not the IRA's military capability, but that loyalist vigilantism might spark a sectarian conflagration.[128] As an earnest of the government's determination to render unnecessary loyalist pro-state violence, a traditional republican demonstration at the Loup, County Derry, was banned, though there was only one protestant house on the route of the procession.[129]

Army helicopters patrolled border areas as petty incidents of violence began to mount.[130] Though the Orange Order refused to organize a counter-demonstration on Sunday 17, the UCDC, supplemented by Paisley's newly formed Ulster Protestant Volunteers, had every such intention and the Cabinet security committee anxiously discussed ways to avoid a clash of parades.[131] To prevent an influx from the South, trains and buses were banned from crossing the border over the weekend and cars were to be searched. A security net was thrown round Belfast and police at the border were armed with Sterling machine-guns.[132]

As it turned out, all demonstrations passed off quite peacefully. Only a trickle crossed the border and the few Sinn Fein organized minibuses were allowed through. Of the 19 or so republican parades, all illegal as no permission from the RUC had been sought, that in Belfast was the largest. Tens of thousands participated, though numbers recorded vary wildly. There was no reported trouble at any republican event. Paisley's counter demonstration attracted 5000 and marched from Carlisle Circus to Bedford Street for a rally in the Ulster Hall. Paisley used the opportunity to launch a bellicose attack on the premier: 'We are prepared ... as a people to declare war on Captain Terence O'Neill. We will never cease until this Lundy is no longer Prime Minister.' Large crowds lined the route and a police barrier blocked egress into the catholic district at Castle Street. Catholics were assaulted at Carlisle Circus and it took police two hours to disperse the hostile crowd.[133]

By mobilizing broad resources of state power, but refusing to apply the law on illegal processions and flag flying as in October 1964, the Northern Ireland government had adroitly avoided a major law and order crisis. Nevertheless, permitting the commemorations, dominated by militant rather than constitutional nationalism, was unpopular with much Unionist opinion. Barry White of the *Belfast Telegraph* admitted that on this issue 'support for [Paisley's] vehement views may be fairly widespread.'[134] Though few Unionists had been willing to speak out during the high-pitch of crisis, at that year's Twelfth, George Currie, MP for Ards, openly stated that it had been a serious mistake to allow the 1916 commemoration to proceed and blamed the decision for a rise in loyalist unease.[135]

The Presbyterian Church of Ireland, impressed by Vatican II and cautiously willing to involve itself in the ecumenical movement, was, with remarkable candour, investigating and admitting to catholic charges of discrimination. In coming out in favour of civil rights reform it seemed to many unionists to combine the errors of both political and religious appeasement.[136] Early in June 1966 Paisley announced that he intended to march on and picket the Presbyterian General Assembly in Belfast to protest at its 'Romanising' tendencies. Part of the route led through Cromac Street, a strongly catholic area near the city centre. This was obvious coat-trailing. Even more offensive to Captain O'Neill was the implied threat to the dignity of VIPs attending the Assembly.[137]

Paisley's march went ahead and as nearly a thousand passed through Cromac Square they were attacked by 200 youths from the

Markets area. The engagement was brief, but led to a two-hour clash between catholic rioters and police. Paisley later lauded the fracas as a triumph: 'This is the first protestant march through the Markets area for thirty years. It is quite a victory'. The Paisleyites carried on to the General Assembly where the Governor, Lord Erskine, and his wife were severely jostled as they entered the hall. Badly shocked, Lady Erskine fell ill.[138]

Despite catholic aggression in Cromac Square, Paisley's relish in coat-trailing and, much more so, his barracking of state and religious dignitaries ensued that he attracted most criticism. The Grand Orange Lodge condemned the insult to the Queen's representative. Twelve Unionist backbenchers signed a motion deploring the 'provocation' of Paisley's march, the 'violence which ensued, the deliberate insults offered to Her Majesty's representative in Northern Ireland and the gross discourtesy to the General Assembly of the Presbyterian Church.'[139] Introducing the motion, which gave the government a blank cheque to take whatever actions it deemed necessary, Basil Kelly made it clear that Paisley's actions must be viewed in a UK context.

Does he [Paisley] not realize that Westminster and the British people will not take anything at all short of fair play from anyone within the United Kingdom? Does he not realize that ... if he goes too far, in Westminster, by a short Act of Parliament, they will undo our very existence?[140]

In a 20-minute speech Terence O'Neill insisted that 'What we have to make unmistakably clear today is: Who is to rule in Northern Ireland?' Paisley, he argued, was only playing the republican game and threatening to put Northern Ireland outside the pale of respectable British opinion. In a dramatic passage he likened protestant extremists to the Nazis.

To those who remember the thirties, the pattern is horribly familiar. The contempt for established authority; the crude unthinking intolerance; the emphasis upon monster processions and rallies; the appeal to a perverted form of patriotism: each and every one of these things has its parallel in the rise of the Nazis to power. A minority movement was able in the end to work its will, simply because most people were too apathetic or too intimidated to speak out. History must not be allowed to repeat itself in this small corner of the British Commonwealth.

Significantly he directed a shaft against fellow travellers in the unionist movement itself. 'I think it is also necessary for anyone in this House or outside it who may have some latent sympathy with extremism to consider very carefully indeed where he stands now and whither he may before long be led.'[141]

This was a clarion call for the liberal unionist establishment. The *Belfast Telegraph* acclaimed 'the brave words of the Prime Minister, who has said exactly what his well-wishing critics have been imploring him to say for eighteen months or more. Gone ... [are] the days of the 'tacit rebukes' and the careful substitution of 'extremism' for Paisleyism.'[142] The Parliamentary Unionist Party was less rapturous. Edmund Warnock admitted that there were 'thousands upon thousands of people of moderate views who are uneasy and anxious about certain recent trends. This uneasiness is in evidence in the constituencies and it is in evidence in the benches on which I sit. I understand it is not absent from the Cabinet'[143] Notably, O'Neill's Cabinet colleagues and the vast majority of Unionist backbenchers failed to contribute to the debate.

On 9 June the Minister of Home Affairs, Brian McConnell, dispatched by O'Neill, expressed regret on behalf of the government to a reproving General Assembly: 'I can assure you that the Government will take all possible steps to prevent a recurrence of such indignities to the head of this great church and his distinguished guests.' This was taken as an apology.[144] Brian Faulkner, with his customary skill and lack of Cabinet loyalty, a fortnight later condemned the assurance given to the Assembly that such a picket would never again be allowed as an 'unwarrantable interference with the rights of free speech and assembly.' He criticized Paisley for his anti-catholicism, the Cromac Square catholics for attacking a peaceful demonstration, and the Presbyterian General Assembly for dabbling in politics (by producing reports on discrimination) and then seeking immunity from the consequences. According to the *Belfast Telegraph*'s Barry White, these arguments accorded well with the majority of protestants.[145] It was a finely judged offering from a consummate politician.

Paisley was making the most of his notoriety and speaking to very many meetings, often attended by up to a thousand. He swore it as his 'duty to see that the reign of Captain O'Neill will be both short and stormy.'[146] Moderate unionist opinion, galvanized by O'Neill's broadside, responded with increasing intolerance and, perhaps, fear. The Morton Newspaper Group, which published six weekly local newspapers, including the *Lurgan Mail* and the *Portadown Times*, refused to carry advertisements for Paisleyite rallies.[147] Repression was popularly acclaimed by those more usually civil libertarian, and the NILP called for the full use, if necessary, of the Special Powers Act, Public Order Act and Flags and Emblems Act to suppress Paisleyite provocations.[148] O'Neill felt confident enough to sack Desmond Boal, MP for Shankill and a covert confidante and sympathizer of Paisley's, as Junior Counsel for the Attorney General, over his defence of the General Assembly Demonstration.[149]

In June 1966 the Ulster Volunteer Force came to sudden and fatal prominence. The UVF had been 're-formed' by a group of loyalist extremists – including Kilfedder's election agent – outraged by O'Neill's temporizing and particularly the loss of the Belfast West seat to a republican. Augustus Spence, a UVF leader, claimed that prominent Unionists urged the setting up of the group, but there is no good evidence for this claim.[150] Their strategy was to carry out operations that would be blamed on the IRA, thus undermining O'Neill's bridge-building. Sectarian enthusiasm, however, upset this coolly rational plan. In a desultory campaign three civilians, two of them catholic, were assassinated. That a conspiracy existed only became apparent with the killing of Peter Ward on Malvern Street on 26 June.[151]

Terence O'Neill rushed back from the Somme commemoration in France. In a voice 'charged with emotion', he announced to Stormont that he was banning the UVF under the Special Powers Act: 'The battle against these evil forces must be waged through-out the community; but it must begin here, in this House, today.'[152] For the first time a loyalist organization was proscribed under the Special Powers Act.

The following day O'Neill went further and linked Paisley to the new organization.[153] Indeed, Noel Doherty, ex-secretary of the UCDC and director of the Free Presbyterian Church's Puritan Printing Company, was convicted of conspiring to provide explosives to the UVF.[154] However, there was a distinct confusion of identities and organizations.[155] Certainly Paisley's condemnation of the assassinations was swift and firm.[156] Nevertheless, he was stirring a murky pool, and there was an interchange of membership amongst the various organizations of ultra-loyalism, as well as ideological mutual reinforcement.

Though the incident further blackened Paisley's name in mainstream opinion, he was still able to attract considerable support. On 1 July 1500 people, including eight Orange bands and the local Orange Lodge, attended a parade and open air meeting addressed by Paisley in Castlewellan. An army helicopter observed from overhead so seriously was Paisley's movement now taken.[157] The following day the *Belfast*

Telegraph announced that it was to carry no more adverts for 'extremist' rallies.[158]

Despite all the aggravation, Queen Elizabeth II visited Belfast to open the new Lagan bridge on 4 July. There was heavy security, the largest single operation since the war, and many known republicans were held under the Special Powers Act for the duration.[159] Nevertheless, two incidents marred the royal motorcade though the city. A deranged protestant chambermaid hurled a Guinness bottle at the royal car near the City Hall. More seriously, a catholic labourer, acting on impulse, dropped a concrete block onto the royal car from the fourth storey of offices under construction on Great Victoria Street.[160] The diplomatic fall-out of this was unexpected. O'Neill found Queen Elizabeth friendly but conscious of her position as a protestant monarch. A reference to improved community relations had been left out of her speech on her arrival. O'Neill now hoped to have a favourable reference made to his efforts in her departing message. O'Neill recorded:

> 'I see', she said, 'that he [Paisley] had ten thousand people listening to him last night.' ... 'The catholics in Northern Ireland do not like me,' she mused, 'what happens if the protestants also turn against me?' 'Well,' I replied, turning to the Duke, 'the Prime Minister is having a difficult time at the moment with his left wing [the CDU]. What is at stake is, quite literally, the constitutional position of Northern Ireland.' This seemed to impress the Duke – but not her unfortunately.

In the end she consented only to a bland statement. There was no endorsement of O'Neill's bridge-building policy. O'Neill lamented:

> The brick, which by this time the Queen knew had been thrown by a catholic, was enough to ensure that the farewell message was also muffed. The Queen, who in Ulster is more a symbol of protestantism than an ordinary monarch, had failed to use her position in a responsible manner. ... How can one drag Northern Ireland, kicking and screaming, into the second half of the twentieth century if single-handed, unaided even by one's Queen?[161]

On O'Neill's own initiative the motorcade had travelled through intensely loyalist Sandy Row. Cheering for the monarch was enthusiastic, but many booed O'Neill.

Rising discontent with ecumenism and political appeasement became clear in 1966's Twelfth of July Orange demonstration. The Twelfth had, throughout O'Neill's premiership, been a time for the expression of traditional protestantism and anti-catholicism.[162] Even Orangeism, however, seemed prepared to bless assimilatory experimentation. Speaking for the 1965 Twelfth (at which Lambeg drums were reintroduced for the first time in 27 years)[163] the Grand Master, George Clark, indicated considerable hope for greater understanding as a consequence of Vatican II.[164]

By 1966, however, Clark recognized that loyalist fundamentalism had strong support within Orangeism. He told Ireland's Grand Lodge on 8 June:

> I would be extremely dumb if I did not realize that there is a feeling that there is not enough militant people at the head of the Institution today. This dissatisfaction has given greater heart to a former member of our Institution, Mr. Paisley, and he has gathered around him a considerable number of militant Protestants who are perfectly entitled to their views. He has also gathered around him a considerable number of Orangemen who feel the same way.
>
> He has also carried out an active campaign against a brother Orangeman of considerable standing, the Prime Minister ... [If we] encouraged splinter groups... [we] would lose the right to have a voice in the Government.[165]

In 1966 the Order proposed for acclamation at all Twelfth rallies a stringently anti-ecumenical resolution. This viewed 'with the utmost concern the present trend towards one united Church, involving the surrender of our distinctive Protestant witness.' The political resolution, ostensibly in support of O'Neill, acidly urged him to defend the law and constitution with the same vigour as he promoted economic progress, and offered the aid of Orangemen in suppressing anti-government 'provocations'.[166] The imprint of Paisleyism was unmistakable. Protestant Church leaders vigorously protested at the implication that they were on a 'Romeward trend'.[167] Terence O'Neill declared he would not speak on the controversial anti-ecumenical or political resolutions at his local Cullybackey demonstration.[168]

Approximately 50,000 marchers turned out. The crowds were thought to be the largest ever and the speeches at all 19 fields were followed with unusual attention. In his speech O'Neill argued that the Union must be defended with modern methods and warned against a return to the sectarian violence of the 1930s, which would blacken Northern Ireland's reputation in Britain. Other Unionist speakers bent to the prevailing mood. Harry West at Irvinestown called for unity in defence of the constitution, a breach only having opened of late (in other words, under O'Neill). John Dobson, (West Down) at Gilford admitted that 'a large proportion of the Protestant population in Northern Ireland has certain misgivings as to the safety of our constitutional position, and in my opinion these misgivings are not unfounded.' Faulkner, though denouncing troublemakers, applauded the honest critic: 'The leaders of Church and State must be prepared to listen to such criticism, to refute it, or if necessary to learn from it.'[169]

Orchestrated heckling marred five of the 19 demonstrations. At the largest Finaghy rally, Herbert Kirk, Minister of Finance, proposed the motion of confidence in the government. As soon as he mentioned Terence O'Neill's name he was met with cries of 'Traitor', 'Put him out', 'He is a Lundy', 'O'Neill must go' and, one shout, 'We want Paisley'. No attempt was made by officials to regain order and the result of the vote, evidently close, was not announced.[170] At Derriaghy Paisley led cheers for Knox Cunningham and boos for Brian McConnell, the Minister of Home Affairs; Roy Bradford was jostled and kicked in Kilkeel; and in Ballynahinch Faulkner and especially Basil Kelly were taunted by *Protestant Telegraph* waving audience members. A small part of the Garvaghy crowd booed Chichester-Clark when he praised O'Neill; shouts in support of Paisley and Faulkner met the pro-government resolution in Armagh; and a Free Presbyterian minister led heckling in Coleraine.[171]

On 18 July Paisley was charged with a number of his lieutenants with unlawful assembly, relating to his picket of the Presbyterian General Assembly. One thousand protested outside the court.[172] Paisley and five others were each fined £30 and required to sign a 'good behaviour' pledge or serve three months in jail.[173] At a packed Ulster Hall rally, Paisley declared that all but one, who would remain at liberty to produce the *Protestant Telegraph*, would refuse to pay the fine. He announced too that 'with the help of God and the Protestants of Ulster' he would be elected as a Stormont MP.[174]

Once in Crumlin Road Gaol the martyrs attracted vigils of thousands for two nights running. On the third night the crowd rioted causing extensive damage to property, 20 people admitted to hospital (ironically in the catholic Mater) and 16 arrests. Water cannon was used for the first time in Northern Ireland. The following day a protest march to the city centre was planned. However the crowd of between 1500 and 2000 was confined to the Shankill Road by police order. The protest leaders lost control of their audience, who over-ran a police barrier at the Agnes Street junction. They were only blocked from entering the city centre at Peter's Hill and here another riot developed in which water cannon were again deployed.[175] Sporadic violence, often targeting catholic-owned property, continued over the weekend, outside the Crumlin Road Gaol, on the Old Lodge Road, in Sandy Row and even in the commercial city centre. A total of 41 arrests were made. On Monday Cabinet met in emergency session to consider the law and order crisis.[176]

A three-month ban on marches within a 15-mile radius of the centre of Belfast was imposed under the Public Order Act, but excluded were all traditional parades, by their nature mainly unionist. The RUC were authorized to disperse at will any gathering of more than three under the Special Powers Act.[177] In contrast to repressive legislation directed against the civil rights movement, this package was welcomed by Eddie McAteer, Gerry Fitt and Tom Boyd, leaders of the opposition.[178] The bout of violence petered to an end, but at the cost of an unprecedented restriction of loyalist rights to process. It was an uncomfortable situation for unionists to accept.

Soon it became clear that the almost continual crisis since the beginning of the year was causing stress within the Unionist Party. The quasi-official *Unionist* journal carried a series of articles reassuring readers on O'Neill's protestant antecedents and solidity on the constitution.[179] On 2 August Terence O'Neill issued a special statement to the Unionist Party, evidently a rejoinder to the propaganda of Paisley. O'Neill rejected 'any suggestion that the present Government is less than one hundred per cent firm on the constitutional issue. ... Ulster is not for sale, either now or in the future.' Very unusually for O'Neill, who normally treated the spheres of state and religious faith as quite separate, he acknowledged that many feared the English protestant church leaders were on a Romeward trend. Irish churches, he reassured loyalists, were independent and need not follow. He finished: 'We are a strong people firm in our principles. Why should we flee from false fears, to the embarrassment of our friends and the delight of our enemies.'[180] The chairman of the Ulster Unionist Council hailed the message, backhandedly, as 'removing all doubts' and called for party unity behind the Prime Minister.[181]

On 25 August 12 leading Unionists, representing the Ulster Unionist Council, Unionist Associations directly and the Parliamentary Unionist Party, met for three hours 'to discuss the present situation and how best to support the Prime Minister and Government.' The conference was called by the Chief Whip, James Chichester-Clark, 'in a response to the continual criticism of the Government from extreme Protestant organisations, including some members of the Orange Order. ... we must try and foresee what the opponents of the Government's policies may do next – and take precautions.' The possibility was even considered of calling on MPs and government ministers to back O'Neill more overtly. Though Senator John Drennan, chairman of the standing committee of the UUC, was present, of the Cabinet only Chichester-Clark attended and of backbenchers, only Nat Minford (Antrim) and John Dobson (West Down). It was a half-hearted but remarkably open attempt to rally a Prime Minister's party within Unionist ranks.[182]

This was the beginning of a 'back the government' group designed to combat extremism and organize moderate unionist opinion. O'Neill formally threw his weight behind the initiative.[183] The 'back the government' group met on 22 September to discuss further 'the best means of bringing the party together again'.[184] Present were MPs Nat Minford (Antrim) and Sam Magowan (Iveagh), Sir George Clark (Grand Master of the Orange Order, but representing Unionist Senators), Colonel George Liddle (vice-chairman of the UUC standing committee), James McCall (chairman of the UUC executive committee), William Beggs (vice-chairman of the executive), David McClelland (honoury secretary of the UUC) and Issac Hawthorne (deputy chief whip).[185] They attempted to persuade O'Neill to sack the Minister of Development, Bill Craig, who had aroused unionist ire over physical planning policy, especially the New City, and the Minister of Home Affairs, Brian McConnell, for his handling of public order since the Cromac Street riot. In this way, criticism of O'Neill from dissidents hostile to his 'progressive policies' would be deflected. O'Neill refused.[186] As they met that Sunday, however, it was clear the gravest threat to O'Neill's premiership so far was at hand.[187]

It emerged that a petition had been circulating amongst Unionist MPs for a number of days demanding the removal of Terence O'Neill, Brian Craig and Brian McConnell. A new leader, preferably Faulkner, was wanted to deal with the situation expected to arise after Paisley's release from prison. The petition was understood to state the central, if amorphous charge, that O'Neill had failed to unite the party and the unionist people behind him. It was an attempted indictment of his style and form of leadership.

In 1969 Sam Magowan (Iveagh) recalled being telephoned on 21 September 1966 by Desmond Boal and Austin Ardill, who pressed him to add his name to the petition. That night he visited Brian Faulkner on private business. There Boal and Ardill again confronted him. He went on: 'Mr Faulkner was in the room, but as soon as the matter was raised by Mr Boal and Mr Ardill, he left, saying he did not want anything to do with it.' Faulkner admitted that he had held audiences with the rebels three nights in succession:

> ... they wanted me to accept nomination for party leadership and to go before a party meeting. I told them what I also said on television and have repeated since: the important concern for the country is a united Parliamentary Party and I would only be prepared to be drafted the day that dissatisfaction could not be dissolved.

The following day he 'reported the dissatisfaction' of the backbenches to the Chief Whip, more, one suspects, in way of a threat than a friendly warning.[188]

Of 36 Unionist MPs at least 12 were believed to have signed the petition. As all appeared to have been backbenchers, this meant that over half the 22 Unionists MPs not in the government opposed O'Neill. Nine of the signatories can be named with reasonable certainty. It was known to have originated from the right wing, Desmond Boal (Shankill) and John Dobson (West Down) being its instigators. John Taylor (South Tyrone), irked by the government's reneging on a promise to extend a motorway to Dungannon in his constituency, also added his name. Edmund Warnock (Saint Anne's) openly declared his belief that O'Neill should go, as did Austin Ardill (Carrick). Walter Scott (Bloomfield), withdrew his name from the petition only at the last minute. William Kennedy (Cromac) was also numbered as a rebel. Robert Simpson (Mid-Antrim) admitted later that he supported the conspiracy, particularly so as to get rid of McConnell. Dr Robert Nixon (North Down) left early to avoid a vote of confidence in O'Neill in the climatic party meeting.

Another four, as rumoured at the time, very probably also added their names. It is highly unlikely that the extreme right-wingers John McQuade (Woodvale) and William Hinds (Willowfield) would have held aloof from any conspiracy to oust O'Neill.[189] Joe Burns (North Derry) also edges into this category. Dinah McNabb (North Armagh), who opposed government compensation policy in the New City area, was also a likely rebel. These 13 were almost certainly the signatories.[190] Another, Tom Lyons (North Tyrone), though chairman of Ways and Means, refused to commit himself to O'Neill at the outset.

On top of this, three Ministers, Brian Faulkner, Harry West[191] and, particularly, William Morgan, were implicated. Morgan (who was religiously evangelical)[192] resented his loss of responsibility for local government to the Ministry of Development. All were rumoured to be contemplating resignation.[193] In contrast those who rushed to O'Neill's defence were few, most opting for a non-committal silence.

Quite obviously O'Neill's government was on the ropes. How did it survive? First, O'Neill attested a convincing determination to crush what he saw as a disloyal and reactionary plot. He had been on holiday while the petition circulated but was alerted by an MP approached by the plotters and rushed back to condemn it immediately as a 'conspiracy':

> I have only this to say – I will fight this out; I believe that my policies represent the best safeguard to our constitutional position and our best hope for prosperity. I believe too that the people of Ulster support them. I do not intend to desert all those who have backed me. I fought for my country in time of war. I have fought to maintain our constitution in time of peace. There will be no surrender.[194]

It was clear that he would not go quietly and that he was prepared to appeal to the public against opposition in the party. Furthermore, by linking his own fall from power with the demise of progressive unionism, particularly at a time of intense pressure from the Paisleyite ultras, O'Neill was enormously raising the stakes. Opponents, seeing now that a quiet palace coup could not be effected, began to draw back from the brink.

Succour for O'Neill came from an unexpected direction – the Unionist Associations. By chance O'Neill had, as part of the 'back the government' initiative, summoned a meeting of 250 UA officers for 24 September.[195] This forum provided O'Neill with an excellent vantage from which to rally a fight-back. O'Neill was applauded for over a minute upon entering the conference and there repeated his determination not to retreat. He was given a solid vote of confidence.[196] Certain rebel MPs quickly came under some pressure as their Unionist Associations divided. The Aughnacloy branch in John Taylor's constituency repudiated his action, though the rest of South Tyrone UA supported the call for O'Neill to be replaced as Prime Minister.[197] Austin Ardill's constituency association in Carrick backed O'Neill, with the exception of Killyman branch.[198] West Down UA, John

Dobson's party, polled its 17 branches and found 14 in favour of O'Neill.[199] Before the crunch meeting of Unionist MPs O'Neill received messages of support from Ards and Iveagh Divisional Unionist Associations and the Spa branch of East Down UA.[200] Dr Robert Simpson admitted pro-O'Neill pressure from the Ballymena and Harryville branch of his Mid-Antrim UA.[201]

Though support for O'Neill was localized in Antrim and Down, an imitation of the terrain of 1959, the net balance of Unionist Association intervention in the 1966 leadership crisis was to O'Neill's advantage. Nevertheless, it was in the Parliamentary Unionist Party that the issue would be decided. Ever since Edward Carson, Unionism had been a movement that invested its obsession with unity in the figure of a strong and charismatic leader. Edmund Warnock summed up the central objection to O'Neill:

> When O'Neill succeeded Lord Brookeborough the Parliamentary Party was united and the constituency associations were working happily together, and the Orange Order was quietly doing its job. Today the Unionist Party is split, the constituency organisations are disturbed and the Orange Order is seriously dismayed. I don't want to see the Unionist Party destroyed, or the Orange Order destroyed – or damn near it – but I'm very much afraid that this may happen unless there is an immediate change.[202]

Brian Faulkner, the talented and hard-working Minister of Commerce, was widely canvassed as the alternative leader to Terence O'Neill.[203] Faulkner remained ambivalent, but his refusal to openly back O'Neill was obvious. He left for a ministerial trip to the United States, thus elevating himself above the fray.[204] Characteristically, Faulkner did not wish to expose himself to defeat, but nor did he do anything positive to back his Prime Minister. He was, in effect, signalling the availability of his services should the rebels succeed in toppling O'Neill.

Faulkner's unwillingness to get involved in dirty work must have annoyed the plotters, for they turned to Lord Brookeborough as possible caretaker Prime Minister. Brookeborough, on the onset of the crisis, had reasserted the traditional values of party unity, but in a way that precluded specific support for O'Neill.[205] He admitted that he had been asked to serve again as leader but, aged 78, he considered himself 'too old and too square. My only interest now is to do my best to try and save this unfortunate position.'[206]

As the rebels were unsure as to their leader, so too were they disparate on motives. The *Unionist*, which was in a position to know, listed six main areas of concern:

1. O'Neill's meeting with Lemass;
2. the scale of the Easter Rising commemoration parades in Belfast;
3. the imprisonment of Paisley;
4. persistent resentment in country areas at the scrapping of railways;
5. land troubles in the New City development area; and
6. the government's recognition of the Northern Ireland Committee of the Irish Congress of Trade Unions.[207]

There were a number of identifiable if over-lapping groups amongst the rebels. Certainly there was a right-wing core, unhappy with events such as the O'Neill/Lemass summit and the recognition of NIC-ICTU. Prominent amongst these were Ardill, Boal, Dobson, McQuade, Hinds and Jones. There were also congenital rebels on the left of the party who disliked O'Neill's rather autocratic style of leadership, especially Nixon, Simpson and Warnock (the latter now evolving rapidly to a liberal position on community relations questions). A swathe of MPs representing the west disliked primarily the government's developmental policy. Taylor and McNabb subscribed to this view. Harry West, a doubter in the Cabinet, was also disturbed by the prioritization of the New City to the detriment of agriculture.[208] Other rebels were waverers who were mainly concerned at the decline of the government's authority over the previous year and wanted to see a response, perhaps in the demotion of McConnell and Craig. Scott, Kennedy, Lyons and Simpson were in this category. Indeed, this view was maintained by many who remained loyal to the Prime Minister throughout. There was a growing number of malcontents who saw O'Neill as a barrier to their ambitions or who bore him a grudge for past slights, including Neill, Brookeborough and Faulkner.

This was not simply a clash of new unionism with Paisleyism, therefore. The revolt included committed progressives as well as reactionaries. For some it was a protest on principle, for others an expression of discontent over their exclusion from the pork barrel. The newer MPs were unhappy at the lack of consultation or input they enjoyed into government policy and decisions. The puritans of the Parliamentary Unionist Party strongly disapproved of some Cabinet Ministers well known for enjoying a drink, particularly Bill Craig. A hard core of chronic dissidents, Boal, Nixon, Warnock and Simpson, were prone to attack any government. Though few in number their eloquence in a party that lacked much rhetorical skill or intelligence was considerable.[209]

Though the Paisleyite phenomenon convinced many that O'Neill was failing to maintain the Unionist alliance unimpaired and was moving away too rapidly from traditional verities, it also created the dilemma of how to prevent intra-Unionist fighting rebounding to Paisley's advantage. Many of the rebels, far from being closet Paisleyites, believed that O'Neill should be replaced precisely because he was incapable of dealing with the Paisleyite threat.[210] The ever-voluble Warnock explained that 'if we had a more acceptable Prime Minister the extremist movement which has been so troublesome would have little to feed on and would subside.'[211] Barry White later reported that

> talking to the ... rebels, I detected a strong desire for the Government to escape from the bonds of Paisleyism. There has been a feeling that Paisley has been allowed to set the pace when he should have been forestalled. Many thought that Faulkner would have been the best man to cope with the difficult situation, and I found few who believed that this steely little man would become the tool of the extremists, as has been suggested since.'[212]

Of course it was the Prime Minister who nurtured this suggestion as part of a skilful fight-back. Though creating the potential for a wide-ranging alliance – and at time O'Neill seemed almost alone in his own party – the rebellion's confusion of motives allowed O'Neill to exploit its centrifugal tendencies. It was not difficult to paint his dismissal as a victory for the very movement most of the rebels were anxious to counter. In numerous television interviews he laboured the point that 'It would be a denial of government if we were to be dictated to by the mob in any way'. His removal would merely encourage 'a certain gentleman who has been carrying certain suggestions on his banner.' Paisley's championing of the 'O'Neill must go' slogan allowed the Prime Minister to tar all his opponents with the same brush. He was speaking no less than the truth, however, when he observed that a successful coup would leave the threat hanging over his successor of 'remember what happened to O'Neill.'[213]

O'Neill attacked the plotters on their weakest point – splitting ranks in the face of an enemy and facilitating a victory for vote losing, Britain-alienating extremism. At least in public he shifted the discussion from the substantive issues of law and order, resource allocation, planning policy and the exercise of marching rights. Not for the last time, he painted his own party as black reaction and allied himself with the moderation of the non-political 'reasonable majority'. He clearly saw his mandate from the party as subordinate to that from the public.[214]

On 27 September the decisive Parliamentary Unionist Party meeting was held: 33 MPs and 13 senators attended, close to a full turnout. One of the conspirators publicly took fright at the effectiveness of O'Neill's counter-attack and withdrew his name from the petition. The statement he issued is illuminating:

> It is now evident that in spite of explanations or arguments put forward by me as to my intentions, any more criticisms of the Prime Minister will be misconstrued and misinterpreted and taken as a condemnation of the forward policy of the Unionist Party which has been so strongly advocated by the Prime Minister and supported by me. If this misinterpretation is widely accepted, as I now believe it will be, damage may be caused to the recent image of a progressive Ulster which we have been so careful to promote... I wish to emphasise that my proposed action was never a suggestion of a move towards Paisleyism, nor towards the extremist element in the community... I also regret that because of the indirect pressure of this extremism, democratic decision within the Party is made more difficult.[215]

It is clear that this was the attitude of most rebels. Poorly led and facing a hostile press, public opinion and even Unionist Party structures, their morale had crashed.

The meeting lasted for six and a half hours, the longest since the establishment of the party. The controversial petition was never produced. A total of 37 speakers participated, 12 of whom were critical of O'Neill. Very many issues were raised, but the main points of criticism centred on the O'Neill/Lemass meeting, the Easter Rising celebrations, the closing of railway lines in Tyrone, the New City and planning powers. The Paisley problem was mentioned on numerous occasions. Only one MP, Desmond Boal, openly called on O'Neill to resign. Terence O'Neill, who wore the Red Hand tiepin of Lord Carson, as donated by the now-O'Neillite Edward Carson, replied at length.

In the initial vote of confidence Edmund Warnock abstained and John Taylor voted against. Desmond Boal and Robert Nixon absented themselves for the vote. Faulkner and John Dobson were not at the meeting. In the consultative vote of the Senators only John Barnhill abstained, primarily in protest at rail closures in Tyrone. A second vote of confidence was then taken to make it unanimous amongst the 29 MPs present. O'Neill afterwards denied that any concessions had been made, but confessed that government/backbench liaison was poor and refused to comment on future possible Cabinet changes. Nevertheless it was an ignominious collapse of the rebellion.[216]

The conspiracy against O'Neill failed for a number of reasons. It was gravely weakened by the lack of a declared candidate to challenge O'Neill's leadership, the failure of any Cabinet ministers to openly join it, the fortuitous timing of the constituency officers' meeting, the hostility of the press and O'Neill, successful identification of the revolt with Paisleyism.[217] The rebels lacked a central aim and, though O'Neill's grip of the constituency associations was not strong, they had done too little to counter the advantage of his incumbency with the rank and file. Ironically, and most importantly, Paisley's 'O'Neill must go' campaign made it impossible for the party to drop the pilot without seeming to change course. But the damage was done. If the episode showed the strategic weakness of the rebels, it equally revealed the structural weakness of O'Neill's position. He had fought virtually alone, with barely any support from his Cabinet colleagues. 'I got the impression this was a lonely fight', one reporter put to O'Neill. 'I try to lead myself', he replied rather bleakly, 'I am not one to sit around.'[218]

The events of 1966 encouraged a (not unreasonable) paranoia in O'Neill.[219] Aware that he was personally unpopular with his back-benchers, and fully reciprocating the sentiment, O'Neill was there-after always conscious of being under threat. Indeed, until he left office, he displayed prominently in his Cabinet room in Stormont Castle, as a melancholy joke, a plaque inscribed 'O'Neill must go'.[220] The year 1966 demonstrated that the fundamental problems of governing a deeply divided society remained. In later years O'Neill pinpointed the Easter Rising commemoration and the loyalist reaction as a turning point.[221] The tendency of militant Irish nation-alism and militant Ulster unionism mutually to reinforce in a spiral of escalating assertion had been vividly demonstrated. O'Neill knew enough to perceive his nemesis, if through a glass darkly, in the inexorable logic of communal antagonism.

Loyalist reaction pre-dated catholic mobilization in the civil rights movement. It was stirred by only a muted challenge from the minority community: the election of Gerry Fitt to Westminster and the Easter

Rising commemoration. Forced to tolerate a celebration of militant nationalism beyond the law, for fear of provoking the real thing, O'Neill violated the protestant unionist redoubt Northern Ireland symbolized. Thereafter, O'Neill believed, his influence with traditional loyalism was inexorably on the wane.[222] The failure of the government to assert forcefully the law and order of the majority, in particular to ban the Easter commemoration, and instead to deal with public order in a spirit of relative impartiality, shook the equanimity of many protestants. Such relaxation of punitive vigilance against the nationalist fifth column appeared premature. O'Neill might act as though Irish nationalism was definitively defeated and was no longer a threat deserving special measures, Unionist supporters were not so sure. Doubting the reliability of their own state, many now believed that its appeasing head was a liability.

6
From Civic Weeks to Civil Rights

In October 1966, in response to the coup attempt, Terence O'Neill reshuffled his Cabinet. The most obvious victim was Brian McConnell, demoted from Minister of Home Affairs to mere Minister of State in Development. Bill Craig was moved out of the Development super-ministry back into Home Affairs, a *de facto* demotion. The Ministers most implicated in the conspiracy, Brian Faulkner, William Morgan and Harry West, were left untouched. This was evidently a reshuffle to satiate the party rebels and both McConnell and Craig had reason to feel bitter.[1] On the other hand, O'Neill had not forgiven the rebels, and he refused to curry their favour.[2] O'Neill's failure to manage the party only built-up opposition to him on all sides.

O'Neill made a volatile enemy in Bill Craig. A leading Young Unionist before becoming MP for Larne in 1960, Craig was considered more Conservative than Unionist and joined the Orange Order only in 1958.[3] A solicitor since 1952 he was in the vanguard of a coterie of professions pushing their way into unionist politics. The 'eccentric diction and clipped mid-Atlantic accent' he sported marked him from the nasal drawls of unionism's traditional gentry leaders and the harsh Ulster inflection of the rank and file.[4] When appointed Minister of Home Affairs in April 1963, aged 34, the *News Letter* described him as 'moderate in his views and broad in his vision.'[5] Craig was an O'Neill acolyte and shared his passion for modernizing.[6] His inexperience, flamboyance and excitability, however, often created unnecessary ructions. An indifference to religious observance and liking for a drink offended many unionists. Prone to bursts of anger and depression, possibly due to a thyroid disorder, Craig's boyish charm easily gave way to truculence.[7]

In 1963 he attacked the trade unions for encouraging labour inflexibility.[8] When outraged engineering unions demanded a retraction,

Craig's response was undiplomatically robust: 'Far from apologising I would offer them this piece of advice: grow up, or failing that, for the good of all take a running jump off a great height.'[9] O'Neill attempted to defuse the matter by denying that Craig had used these words.[10] In fact, as Craig was forced to admit to parliament the following day, he had written the statement, only to forget having done so once his temper abated.[11] In the midst of the government's tussle with the ICTU Craig's *faux pas* was singularly ill timed. Similarly he announced himself keen to dispense with a railway system 'as obsolete as the stagecoach'.[12] Once again there was a storm of trade union protest, threatening a delicate rationalization of the network.[13] In 1965 he caused the government considerable embarrassment when he ridiculed the British Labour government's economic plans as 'theoretical nonsense'.[14]

Craig, however, was no traditionalist. Rather he espoused a militant assimilatory unionism. He wanted a progressive, inclusive unionism that concentrated on social and economic development. However, he eschewed palliatives and conciliationism in favour of aggressive triumphalism. More than anyone, Craig encapsulated the contradiction of assimilatory unionism. Craig seized upon its core hostility to irrational, backward Roman Catholicism and Irish nationalism with a frenetic fervour that ultimately propelled him to the right of the unionist spectrum.

Impressed by the Roman Catholic acceptance of 'religious liberty' after Vatican II, Craig openly supported the right of catholics to join the Unionist Party and even the Cabinet.[15] He was convinced that at heart the minority rejected political nationalism.[16] This is not to say that he had much time for cultural catholicism however. At an Orange rally in Letterbreen on 2 March 1964, he criticized 'the lack of family planning amongst the Roman Catholic community.' This, he implied, was the root cause of catholic disadvantage rather than discrimination.[17] The assimilatory unionist approach to community relations was predicated on the axiom that Irish nationalism was an outdated and declining force. Craig, with his usual outspokenness articulated this with, for the government, embarrassing belligerence. Irish nationalism was a 'poison' to be 'eradicated'.[18] He took the assimilatory unionist proposition that nationalism was on the wane and catholics could be won over to unionism, only to state it with provocative brashness.

Craig was exceptional amongst unionist leaders for the lengths to which he went in insisting upon the autonomy of Northern Ireland from Britain. He could be quite radical and imaginative in his willingness to reconceptualize constitutional structures. In August 1964 he suggested in Cabinet that the imperial contribution be abolished and Northern Ireland instead receive a block grant.[19] Eighteen months later he argued that parity with Britain on social services should be broken to deliver extra rates rebates in Belfast.[20] Significantly, in March 1966 he supported Rhodesia's declaration of UDI.[21]

For Craig, the 1966 conspiracy was a turning point. Demotion from his beloved Ministry of Development to Home Affairs embittered him. He told one civil servant, who found him worse the wear for drink, 'Well, if Faulkner can be a rebel I'll get to the right of Faulkner, so.'[22] It would be wrong, however, to see his subsequent evolution at odds with his earlier liberal reputation. He consistently held dear the assimilatory unionist self-image of superiority. His attitude to unionism's traditional enemies changed only from complacency to furious resistance.

Another result of the conspiracy was the establishment of a back-bench committee modelled on the British Conservative 1922 Committee.[23] This concerned itself with a wide range of policy matters including state support for the Mater hospital and the prospect of a further North/South meeting between premiers.[24] Most importantly, however, a sub-committee headed by Edmund Warnock drew up proposals for the future election of leaders by the Unionist MPs.[25]

A marked feature of 1967 was the developing penetration of the Unionist Party by Paisleyite supporters or sympathizers.[26] In the May local elections the Unionist candidate in Dock, Robin Bailie, dropped out when he realized that his fellow candidates – Frank Millar, Robert Fenton and Stanley Duff – were thinly disguised 'Protestant' candidates.[27] Millar responded by boldly declaring that he was 'an uncompromising Protestant opposed to the appeasement policies of Captain O'Neill.'[28] In an unusual and precedent setting stand, O'Neill openly repudiated Millar.[29] The election was a Unionist triumph with a 5.5 per cent swing in its favour. Millar was utterly defeated.[30] The result did much to secure O'Neill as an electorally popular leader for unionism. His brand of moderation seemed vindicated.

Paisleyism, in its more usual overt, picketing form, remained a reduced problem. The dangers to Terence O'Neill were highlighted in May 1968 when O'Neill addressed Woodvale Unionist Association. The 170 delegates gave him a vote of confidence, with only 12 dissenters. As he left the meeting in this intensely loyalist working-class area of Belfast, however, a crowd of 500 Paisleyites jeered him. Stones, bags of flour and eggs were thrown.[31] O'Neill was slightly injured, though as it was an eye wound it could have been serious. This generated much sympathy. Maghera Unionist Association sent a telegram to 'deplore the attack on you by rabble at Woodvale and offer you full support in keeping Ulster sane and British.'[32]

More important than Paisleyite violence and penetration at the grass roots, however, were the political constraints imposed on O'Neill by pressure from the mainstream right. A notable example was the difficulties he had in arranging a visit from Jack Lynch, who replaced Sean Lemass as Taoiseach in November 1966. Intemperate comments from southern politicians on civil rights and the national question ruled out an early meeting. O'Neill fired a 'friendly shot' across the border: 'If you want a meeting to take place, for God's sake stop talking about it.'[33] On Monday 11 December Lynch finally arrived at Stormont. The Cabinet this time had received prior notification over the weekend, and indeed had agreed to a new meeting some months previously.[34] Topics discussed included tourism, trade and electricity supply. Paisley, this time forewarned, picketed the event with a handful of others and hurled snowballs at Lynch's car. O'Neill, however, quickly announced a return visit to Dublin.[35]

The O'Neill/Lynch summit was accepted with relative passivity. Noticeable, however, was the length of time it took to arrange and the sensitivity of the premiers' plans to rhetorical spats.[36] The 1965 summit had been intended to normalize North/South relations and remove them from the arena of controversy. The events of 1966 quite obviously had scuppered that hope.

Clearly O'Neill was anxious to avoid giving the right, and particularly Paisley, issues around which to agitate. Such opportunities were bound to arise, however. One such was the invitation issued in January 1967 by the Irish Church Association to Dr John Moorman, Anglican Bishop of Ripon in England and a well-known ecumenicist, to address it on church unity. The Orange Order, aware of Moorman's stated belief that the Pope should head a reunited Christian church, decided to organize a protest.[37] To the relief of a nervous government the Dean of St Anne's Cathedral in Belfast, at which Moorman was to speak, cancelled the booking.[38] Moorman refused to address a private meeting and cancelled the engagement altogether.[39]

This was no unalloyed victory for the right, however. The Orange Grand Master, George Clark, was soon forced to react to widespread anger at what was seen as the Order's high-handed intolerance of free speech. He insisted that they had opposed only Moorman's use of the cathedral.[40] Liberal anger continued to grow and O'Neill became implicated when it became clear that the government had encouraged the Dean of St Anne's to cancel the engagement.[41] The Orange Order's image worsened when hard-liners demanded that the Church of Ireland hold 'Reformation services', especially for Orangemen, to appease for its transgression in inviting the Bishop of Ripon. This was too much and Dr F. J. Mitchell, Bishop of Down and Dromore, condemned this attempt 'to deprive the Church of freedom to act within her own domain.'[42]

The newly formed Paisleyite Orange Voice of Freedom planned to orchestrate anti-O'Neill heckling at 1967's Twelfth demonstrations.[43] Rather than address the field directly, Terence O'Neill issued a statement to Orangemen on the Eleventh Night. Only the loyalist people themselves, he warned, were capable of threatening the Union. Now secure, they no longer needed to 'dig up the long-dead bones of the unhappy and violent past. Our children ask of us not a handful of dust but a new world of opportunity.' The speeches themselves were markedly less political than in 1966, and while seven Cabinet ministers had spoken then only two did so this time: Faulkner in Derry and Captain Long in Dundonald. At Finaghy, the largest gathering, the Voice of Freedom distributed thousands of anti-O'Neill leaflets. When the resolution in support of O'Neill was voted on, having been proposed by a speaker who somehow managed to avoid referring directly to the Prime Minister, there was loud booing and it was not clear whether the motion was passed.[44]

The pro-O'Neill resolution was passed without incident at nine demonstrations. There were protests at Finaghy, Tandragee, Lisburn and Portglenone. At Enniskillen, Mourne and Kilkeel the resolution was completely omitted and at Fintona an amended resolution, excising any reference to O'Neill, was put and passed. The most serious disorder was at Coagh. Here George Forrest, Westminster MP for Mid-Ulster, was concussed and admitted to hospital with facial lacerations and abrasions. Flustered by heckling, Forrest had lunged for a chair. 'I was going to toss the chair at the cameraman', he explained, 'because I thought he was giving the hecklers, who were obviously supporters of the Rev. Ian Paisley, too much publicity.' Climbing from the stage he had been grabbed from behind and knocked unconscious.[45]

One Belfast march to Finaghy, led by the Prince Albert Temperance Lodge, stopped at Belfast jail to convey 'fraternal greetings' to the imprisoned UVF men – Gusty Spence and two others. Outside the walls the accordion flute band played 'No surrender' and 'The Protestant boys'.[46] John McQuade, MP for Woodvale and a member of the lodge, refused to comment on whether he had been present.[47]

Grassroots right-wing pressure on the government, therefore, continued unabated through 1967, if at a lower level than in 1966. A more serious crisis for O'Neill, and one that directly strengthened the organized forces arrayed against him in the party, was the dismissal of Harry West, Minister of Agriculture, in April 1967. The circumstances were complex but related directly to the question of ministerial professionalism and transparency which had blighted Brookeborough's dog days and on which O'Neill had attempted to set new standards.

West in 1964 had purchased from a cousin 90 acres of land in Fermanagh. As a minister he knew beforehand that Fermanagh County Council was likely to acquire part of it to develop the St Angelo Airport thereon. Suspicions that he was exploiting privileged information were inevitable. To protect the public interest O'Neill instructed him to sell the land required by Fermanagh County Council at a price independently set by the Commissioner of Valuation. West agreed, but then secretly appealed to the Lands Tribunal. O'Neill accepted that the Lands Tribunal valuation of £13,450 for 99 acres was more reasonable than the original Commissioner's estimate of £6500. This was not the point however:

> Government simply cannot be conducted unless a Prime Minister can expect, in a sensitive matter, greater candour than this from a colleague … the standards governing the conduct of Ministers are, and must be, more stringent than those which govern the conduct of private people. They must stand above suspicion.[48]

West's dismissal, as much as anything, represented a clash between O'Neill's almost puritanical, professional service ethic and the easy-going standards which had pertained at government level previously. Ministers were traditionally seen as part of their community and the idea that they might forgo the advantages of private citizenship to preserve public confidence was quite new. Indeed, ministerial government was only emerging tentatively from a cosy cocoon of short hours, life-long tenure, minimal effort, generous allowances for personal leisure and, often, clientelist relations with local unionist populations. Equally, it was symptomatic of the distance and mistrust that existed between O'Neill and his ministers. The St Angelo affair, which after all stretched over two and a half years during which most of the time O'Neill was kept in the dark, represented a signal break down of Cabinet government.

Harry West had long sat on the taciturn right of the Cabinet, refusing to enter into O'Neill's bridge-building rhetoric. In 1965, piqued at the Prime Minister's failure to forewarn the Cabinet of Lemmass's visit to Stormont, he had refused to meet the southern Taoiseach. He was a consistent doubter about the New City project and disliked the neglect of the west of the province. His worries about unionist insecurity in border areas inclined him against the reform of gerrymandered constituency boundaries or electoral reform. Closely allied to both Brookeborough and Faulkner, as well as being a firm Orangeman, he was personally and politically distant from O'Neill. Indeed, during the 1966 conspiracy he had been strongly identified with the plotters. Now he felt he was being victimized.[49]

A bluff farmer, Harry West best represented traditional unionism's sullen discontent in the face of O'Neillite innovation. His comment to the 1960 Twelfth demonstration at Lisbellaw, that 'the most serious problem facing Northern Ireland today from a political aspect is the Nationalist birth-rate', encapsulated brutally the counting of souls that underpinned all political calculations in Northern Ireland.[50] West's political instincts were segregatory. Though unable to 'put his finger on' the malaise he clearly opposed 'diluting' unionism to woo catholics as based upon 'foolish optimism'. Assimilatory unionism, he felt, threatened to divide unionists. It raised the possibility of an anti-unionist electoral majority, presumably of Nationalist, Labour and Liberal. 'If the Unionist Government ever goes out of power it will never get back in again,' warned West, 'The opposition will so manipulate things that it will be impossible for the Unionist Party to ever return to power.'[51]

Many suspected O'Neill of exacting vengeance on a recalcitrant colleague.[52] Indeed, while O'Neill made clear that he was sacking West for a breach of ministerial procedure and protocol, the broad-brush strokes of the case were bound to smack more of rank corruption to the public at large. Having done nothing forbidden a private citizen, West deeply resented any imputation against his morality. Particularly amongst rural Unionist MPs, who widely disliked government officiousness as an unfair barrier to profit, there was empathy with West's plight. Roy Lilley, the *Belfast Telegraph's* political commentator, observed that instead of a rational discussion of the matter there was 'a wave of emotional sympathy, springing up from Mr West's undoubted popularity ... an atmosphere of near hysteria.'[53]

Brian Faulkner, a close personal friend of West's, had implied that he might resign from the government and maintained that West was 'absolutely blameless'. At the Unionist Party's annual conference, which opened on 28 April, rumour ran riot that a new leadership crisis loomed. Supporters of O'Neill called for Faulkner to be dismissed while Ivan Neill, the former Minister of Finance now out of the Cabinet, hinted that he might be available as a new leader.[54]

Slowly support for O'Neill began to rally.[55] On 2 May West, flanked by Brookeborough, broke his silence to make his eagerly awaited resignation speech in Stormont. He set an extremely personal, bitter tone but failed to substantially contradict any of the facts laid out by O'Neill.[56] Following this statement the 66 Committee met and, by six votes to five, agreed that O'Neill had acted properly but that West had not been dishonest.[57]

Pressure now came onto Faulkner to conform, but still he refused to endorse O'Neill's leadership.[58] In Stormont Faulkner complained that West's reputation was being unfairly sullied; misjudgement was not the same as dishonesty. He explained that he had expressed these views to O'Neill. Had O'Neill asked for his resignation, he would have regretfully given it.[59] In the longer term West's dismissal seems to have convinced Faulkner that O'Neill could not maintain unity in the party and that he, in turn, would in due course be subject to a witch-hunt.[60]

Brian Faulkner was the most politically adept member of Terence O'Neill's Cabinet. Having managed his father's shirt factory during World War Two he had acquired valuable managerial skills but also the distaste of a unionist establishment in which evading military service was anathema. He plunged into Unionist Party politics in the 1940s, being a founder member of the Young Unionists and an important force in the modernization of the party's structures.[61] As an MP in the 1950s he was closely identified with militant anti-catholicism and Orange Order coat-trailing. During his stint as Minister for Home Affairs he oversaw the successful use of internment against the IRA and mounted a bravura defence of the indefensible when, against furious nationalist opposition, he piloted through parliament a bill consolidating electoral law. His father, a forceful personality, was 'fanatically ambitious' for his son to be premier.[62] Faulkner's ability and combativity was impressive, but hard-line rhetoric struck many as over-compensation for his war record and origins in 'trade'. Though popular with the rank and file he was passed over in favour of O'Neill in 1963 as 'inexperienced in the ways of the world', a snide comment both on his lack of military service overseas and his perceived lack of tact. His wife Lucy had been Brookeborough's secretary, and though she possessed a formidable political intelligence the marriage attracted

Lady Brookeborough's ire. From the beginning of his career he was convinced that his destiny was to be Prime Minister. Terence O'Neill, he felt, was an inferior who had pipped him to the post only because of his establishment connections.

Faulkner was greatly embittered by the succession of O'Neill, but he seems to have concluded that a change of public persona was required. Quickly he exchanged the reputation of a demagogue for that of a technocrat. His skill as Minister of Commerce was widely acknowledged by friend and foe alike.[63] In government Faulkner waged a low-key but unremitting struggle to undermine O'Neill and force him out.[64] A mixture of conviction and ambition restrained him from fully supporting O'Neill's attempt to 'build bridges' across the sectarian divide. If anyone gave theoretical rigour to segregatory unionist thinking, it was Faulkner.

The greatest strength of unionism and Orangeism, he believed, was its ability to unite all classes.[65] This, clearly, was his priority. Reconciliation between catholic and protestant could only come about if both communities remained discrete, sure of their own identity and even entrenched. Logically, therefore, he reviled an airy liberalism born of apoliticism: 'I am convinced that to be constructive mutual tolerance must come from mutual understanding of principles firmly held. Tolerance born of apathy, of a "couldn't care less" attitude, is a negative thing and good for nobody.'[66] Thus there was relatively little to be done to improve community relations in Faulkner's schema. Sectarian separation was natural and preferable to sectarian conflict or the blurring of identities.[67] This attitude of 'good walls make good neighbours' accorded well with majority unionist opinion.

Equally, he strongly believed that both Orangemen and Blackmen had not only a right but a duty to be involved in politics, specifically to have a direct input into the councils of the Unionist Party.[68] They were the core of resistance to a political Roman Catholic Church and conniving Irish nationalism.[69] The Orange Order's crucial role in the liberalization of society was ensuring that 'we do not move too fast.'[70]

Faulkner always protested his fealty to the policies of O'Neill's government. But he was canny enough, as the ever-potential alternative leader, to drop hints to disaffected Unionists that he understood their dilemma. Indeed, he was rather more assiduous at keeping his options open in this way than actively defending collective Cabinet decisions. Thus he played down the importance of achieving recognition of the Northern Ireland Committee of the Irish Congress of Trade Unions;[71] emphasized the need for a series of enlarged towns across the North, not just the New

City;[72] rejected the notion that by visiting Stormont Lemass had moved closer to recognition of the North's constitutional status;[73] opposed McConnell's apology on behalf of the government to the Presbyterian General Assembly;[74] and backed anti-ecumenical resolutions for the 1966 Twelfth.[75]

Faulkner was savagely critical of Paisley whose antics, he believed, distorted 'the true picture of a community with fundamentally different political and religious beliefs, which was nevertheless settling down to live together in greater harmony than ever before.' He admitted, however, that protestant fears of betrayal, if misguided, had real roots. They had been triggered by the summit with Lemass, heightened by cross-border trade discussions and the rise of ecumenism, and brought to a pitch by the 1916 Rising commemorations. As long as the protestant/catholic dichotomy remained as rigid and stable as that between the North and South of Ireland, all would remain well.[76]

Faulkner appealed to the rank and file majority who were unwilling to identity themselves with new-fangled assimilatory tendencies but who eschewed the reactionary label. He denied unsettling impressions of a new dawn in community relations and implied, moreover, that he sat in the Cabinet as a guarantor against a government sell-out.[77] Throughout the 1966 leadership crisis he refused to back O'Neill personally, rather stressing party unity and a policy *via media*. In the aftermath Terence O'Neill attempted to slake Faulkner's ambition by informing him that he intended to retire in September 1969 and would then support Faulkner as his successor. This seems to have been a highly secret, informal promise upon which Faulkner chose to place little reliance.[78]

Only after Harry West's dismissal in 1967 did Faulkner begin to endorse more overtly O'Neill's policy of building bridges, though still he made nods to the benefits of benign religious apartheid. In particular he cautiously accepted that the sectarian divide was being broken down and that the process could go further. He conceded that some time in the future the Unionist Party might receive widespread catholic support. Though couched in uncertain terms, this was a move away from his customary satisfaction at the rigidity of the communal divide and towards O'Neill's more dynamic concept of community relations.[79] Though he had made a concession to the long-term aspirations of assimilatory unionists, Faulkner was careful to hedge his bets and reiterated appreciation of mutually respectful segregation in the short term.[80]

It is likely that Faulkner's newly thoughtful approach was at least partly a response to the rising tempo of civil rights agitation. Referring obliquely to regular articles and editorials on civil rights deficiencies in Northern Ireland Faulkner advised a rational and guarded evaluation.[81] While by no means becoming a champion of widespread reform, Faulkner had subtly shifted the emphasis of his opinions over the years. From 1967 he began to consider seriously the long-term possibility of a crumbling of the sectarian divide – in unionism's favour of course – though he warned against precipitate action. By 1968 he even appeared to be preparing the ground for some concessions on reasoned civil rights cases.

Whilst in many respects an important victory for O'Neill the West episode seems to have exhausted the Prime Minister.[82] He must have been dispirited at the ubiquity of suspicion regarding his motives and rattled at the ease with which leadership plotting once again erupted. In Stormont on 3 May he carelessly quoted an unsubstantiated letter alleging that catholic priests were urging their congregations to discriminate against protestants. Spurred by a clerical outcry, and his genuinely held sense of fair play, he subsequently apologized. It was an embarrassing affair.[83]

The West affair crystallized an important source of opposition to Terence O'Neill in Fermanagh, a border area long resistant to his soothing words on community relations. Here a group around Lord Brookeborough, nicknamed the 'Fermanagh cabinet', expressed the 'not inconsiderable influence of the gentry element in Unionism.'[84] Many of its leading lights were closely related to each other.[85] Immediately West was dismissed the executive committee of the Fermanagh Unionist Association passed a motion of no confidence in O'Neill.[86] West announced his refusal to second a pro-O'Neill resolution at the Fermanagh Orange Twelfth demonstration. Officials of the County Lodge wanted the resolution withdrawn or re-drafted.[87] The officers of Fermanagh County Grand Lodge duly agreed to drop the offending resolution.[88]

Late in August 1967 Lord Brookeborough collapsed and was rushed to hospital suffering from a gastric haemorrhage.[89] Formal retirement from politics was now inevitable. His son, Captain John Brooke, had long been groomed to replace him.[90] When the crunch selection meeting came, however, Brooke faced stiff opposition and won by only 42 votes to 30.[91] Brooke's opponent for the nomination had been Fred Patterson, a prominent local Unionist. At a meeting of 70 protestant businessmen, held on 16 February 1968, Patterson agreed to contest the Lisnaskea seat as an independent opposed to the Brookeborough dynasty's control in Fermanagh.[92]

Brooke, aged 45, an old Etonian and captain in the 10th Hussars, had a personal following, largely due to the family name, but was generally considered brusque and arrogant. Brooke refused to give 'unequivocal support' to O'Neill, of whom Patterson was generally more supportive.[93] While Harry West, Lord Brookeborough, Brian Faulkner, John Taylor and Bill Craig enthusiastically canvassed for Brooke, Terence O'Neill was not invited to speak on any election platforms.[94]

On an 81 per cent poll John Brooke was victorious with 4428 votes, Fred Patterson polled 3270 and the Liberal candidate came third with 1104.[95] When Brooke took his seat in Stormont for the first time two stalwarts of the right, Desmond Boal and William Kennedy flanked him.[96] His Unionist Association, however, remained divided. Roy Kells, former chairman of the county's Young Unionist movement, was expelled from Fermanagh Unionist Association for canvassing in favour of Patterson during the election campaign.[97] In defiance of the Association, Lisnaskea Young Unionist branch re-elected him their chairman.[98] Subsequently the entire branch was expelled.[99]

At a standing committee of the Ulster Unionist Council on 10 May 1968, meanwhile, Harry West and John Brooke attacked Terence O'Neill for not personally backing Brooke in the by-election. O'Neill replied tartly that the vote of no confidence in him remained on Fermanagh Unionist Association's books.[100] Brooke widened his criticism from the Fermanagh issue and alleged a general unrest with O'Neill in Unionist ranks.[101] On 15 May Brooke and O'Neill, in the presence of McConnell (Chief Whip) and Burns (for the 66 Committee), met for a private 20 minute meeting to heal the breach. It was agreed to cordon the rift over O'Neill's failure to back Brooke in the by-election from the running sore of West's dismissal and the Fermanagh Unionist Association vote of no confidence. Brooke reserved the right of any MP to attack government policy. Such a ragged truce was hardly likely to hold.[102]

The Orange Order, a bastion of organized unionism, was also convulsed by a turbulent struggle between left and right. The Order had substantial representation on the party's leading bodies.[103] This relationship came under increasing scrutiny and pressure from the loyalist right, liberal unionist and nationalist quarters as O'Neillism shook up established configurations.

In July 1964 Captain L. P. S. Orr, MP for South Down and leader of the Parliamentary Unionist Party in Westminster, replaced Clark as

Imperial Grand Master (though Clark remained as Irish Grand Master).[104] In this capacity Orr, in replying to a toast, called on Orangemen to 'make sure delegates to the Unionist Party were able to represent the views of the institution, because it was vital for the safety of Ulster that they would never relax their grip on the Unionist Council.'[105] At the following year's Twelfth celebration he lauded Orange 'domination and control of the great Unionist Party ... It was created by Orangemen, and it should always be controlled by Orangemen as long as Ulster lasts.'[106] Catholic suspicions that an overtly anti-Roman Catholic organization controlled the governing party were reinforced. Given Paisleyite influence in the Order this was particularly disturbing.[107]

From early 1967 the Order was dogged by a controversy over the liberality of its membership criteria and its influence on MPs. In 1966 Phelim O'Neill, as part of a civic week in his North Antrim constituency, attended a Roman Catholic service. According to the Orange constitution members were required to 'avoid countenancing (by his presence or otherwise) any act or ceremony of Popish worship.'[108] By the early 1960s this in practice had been much relaxed, but the right were now keen to see a reassertion of ortho-doxy.[109] In June 1967 the County Antrim Grand Orange Lodge demanded that the MPs Phelim O'Neill and Nat Minford, another transgressor, present themselves to offer an explanation.[110] Minford turned up to explain his presence at the opening of a catholic school in Andersonstown and no further action was taken. Both Phelim O'Neill and Colonel Henry Cramsie, the Deputy Lieutenant for County Antrim who had accompanied him to the service, refused to attend. By a large majority, and amid much adverse publicity, the Antrim Lodge expelled them. This, however, would have to be ratified by the Grand Lodge of Ireland.[111]

Such obvious interference with the government's bridge-building policies exacerbated division within the Order.[112] Grand Master George Clark, despite his discouraging the admission of catholics into the Unionist Party in 1959, was actually quite strongly in favour of O'Neill's bridge-building.[113] In October 1967 Clark, aged 53 and Grand Master for ten years, announced his decision to resign. Though he cited pressure of work on his farm as a reason, unease with his rela-tive liberalism was more likely the cause.[114] The central committee of the Order recommended as a replacement John Bryans, Deputy Grand Master of Ireland and a senior figure in the Methodist Church. Given that Bryans was 81 years old, it is likely that the committee was parachuting in a non-controversial stopgap figurehead to avoid a bitter leadership struggle.[115]

Only on 11 June, with considerable secrecy, were Henry Cramsie and Phelim O'Neill finally expelled.[116] The seizure of power by a 'militant wing with a strong streak of puritanical authoritarianism' appeared to be confirmed.[117] An attempt to discuss the matter on the 66 Committee of backbench Unionist MPs was blocked by the acting chairman, Joe Burns, himself a Worshipful Master of an Orange Lodge.[118]

In an interview with the *Belfast Telegraph*, Imperial Grand Master L. P. S. Orr was anxious to rein back impressions of Orange extremism. He confirmed that 'It is quite possible for an Orangeman to attend, say, the funeral of an old friend or the wedding of a relative without of necessity "favouring" or "approving" the worship of the Church of Rome.'[119] Though the Phelim O'Neill episode undoubtedly represented a victory for the right, it was a fraught, drawn out and incomplete struggle. Liberal unionism had been driven back but only at the expense of some of the Orange Order's credibility in the wider community.[120]

PEP and Civic Weeks

Right-wing pressure did not bring an end to O'Neill's attempts to develop bridge-building. Indeed, he began to develop a theoretical framework for his approach. In October 1966 Terence O'Neill, addressing the annual conference of local authorities, called for 'a whole series of voluntarily organized community weeks held in all the larger centres of population in Northern Ireland to show our own people that "Ulster can make it", to convey the real significance of modern development to every part of the Province, and so emphasize the importance of individual effort and commitment.'[121] On 23 January 1967 he announced that Ulster Weeks, so far held in British cities, were to come to Northern Ireland. Belfast, Limavady, Downpatrick, Antrim, Newry, Coleraine, and Derry were all to have their own 'Civic Weeks'. The civic weeks movement would be co-ordinated by a new organization inelegantly titled, no doubt with an eye to the acronym, Programme to Enlist the People (PEP).[122]

The experience of local resistance to the government's plans to 'change the face of Ulster' – hostility to the New City, local government reform, town and country planning and so on – had convinced O'Neill that something was required to make ordinary people understand and appreciate the reforms enacted for their long-term benefit. He returned, yet again, to the theme of 'self-help'. If the citizen could be encouraged to participate in local events designed to highlight, encourage and explain social and economic progress, then he or she would comprehend the necessity for reform at the state-wide level. Such constructive activism, moreover, could help overcome sectarian divisions at grassroots level.[123]

Civic Weeks pre-dated O'Neill's formal initiative and to some extent were a genuine outgrowth of improving community relations in the 1960s. As early as 1965 Tandragee in County Armagh organized a civic week with events including a fancy dress parade, window dressing, professional wrestling, school sports, a donkey derby, a golf competition and a military band. Protestant and Roman Catholic churches organized a joint service. The organisers were the Unionist Urban District Council with much co-operation from the Roman Catholic Archbishop, T. D. Mayes. John Maginnis, the local Unionist MP, opened the festival and Terence O'Neill visited for a civic reception and a tour.[124] His visit to St James Primary was the first to a catholic school since Ballymoney.[125] The week was adjudged a great success.[126]

In 1966 a civic week was held in the mainly catholic town of Downpatrick. The local Trades Unions Council had first suggested it and the organizing committee was led by Lord Dunleath and Maurice Hayes, the catholic town clerk. The Nationalist leader of the Urban District Council, Eddie McGrady, welcomed O'Neill's visit to open proceedings. It was the first-ever visit of a Northern Ireland premier to the town. Dunleath praised the event as an example of 'constructive co-operation'.[127]

The following year O'Neill visited Ballynahinch, also in Down, where he watched a hockey match between protestant and catholic schools on convent grounds in the company of Sister Mary Jarleth. A Paisleyite demonstration was received badly by locals.[128] On 20 May 1967 O'Neill launched Belfast's civic week: 'Recently, in Newry and Ballynahinch, and now today in Belfast, I have sensed that latent pride which people have in "our town" – a pride which recognizes no religious or political or social boundaries.'[129] On 7 July PEP, the civic week co-ordinating body, held its first meeting.[130]

O'Neill was prone to grand theorizing on the ills of western society. PEP, in creating a sub-state mechanism for involving the alienated citizenry, he believed could contribute to British society in the late twentieth century. He suggested that the concept of civic weeks might be transplanted to Britain as a means to securing 'a greater involvement in national aims throughout the community'.[131] There was a regrettable tendency for individuals to abdicate responsibility to the state. Locally based, self-help activities could overcome this sense of anomie and revitalize civil society.[132] The drift towards nationalism in Scotland and Wales might even be arrested.[133] O'Neill was so taken with PEP that he wrote a pamphlet advocating its adoption throughout the United Kingdom, and had it published by the government.[134] In June 1968 he received a delegation of civic and commercial leaders from Leicester. He assured them that centralized government, appropriate only for a predominantly rural economy, must give way to devolution on the Northern Ireland model.[135] It all fitted snugly with O'Neill's enthusiasm for regional development.

In a major speech delivered to the Irish Association in February 1968, O'Neill endeavoured to explain the PEP approach to Northern Ireland's community relations problem. He admitted that civic life was dominated by denominationally segregated institutions, but wondered whether more co-operation was not possible in pursuit of common aims. Individuals and groups must make the effort and not wait on the government.

> People talk of building bridges as if it were a matter of a single crossing of the historic river of tradition and sentiment and loyalty which divides us. But the barrier represented by this great river is not one which can be nullified by a single bridge. Those who confront each other from the opposite banks must rather build their own bridges with their own materials and their own locations.

The 'opinions and prejudices of past generations cannot be abolished at the stroke of a pen'. His ability to soften old divisions by quasi-presidential fiat was limited.

> Action by words is an essential forerunner in difficult and contentious matters to action in deeds. And in many respects it is the only possible form of action. Tolerance and mutual respect cannot be the subject of legislation: they must stem from the minds and the consciences of individual men and women.

The telling phrase – 'action by words' – could serve as epitaph for O'Neill's policy of rhetoric in place of actual reform in the fraught field of community relations and civil rights.

O'Neill rejected 'a kind of reciprocal emasculation ... rather like trying to solve the colour problem by spraying everyone a pale shade of brown.' All citizens should be expected to support the constitution.

People, however, were less concerned with history or the sectarian divide than with practical social and economic problems. Herein lay the importance of the civic weeks and PEP.

> Whether one calls it Derry or Londonderry surely one wants one's native city to grow and prosper. In a better Ballynahinch there will be more opportunities for all its inhabitants. New industries for Newry mean new hope for all its people. It was hardly surprising that some of the most offensive picketing to which I have been subjected was in the context of a civic week, because the makers of mischief see in this upsurge of harmony a strong antidote to their policies of prejudice, division and malice.[136]

Civic weeks, O'Neill told a religiously mixed meeting of councillors, businessmen and local organizations in Newry in May 1967, could bring both communities together:

> Do we become obsessed about the things which divide us and about which we differ? Do we emphasize and exploit and almost glory in our divisions? Or do we accept them, realise that they are a fact of life which cannot be quickly changed, and then turn our backs as far as possible on those things to seek and pursue what can unite us all?

In the words of a World War Two song, people should 'accentuate the positive, eliminate the negative'.[137]

The *Observer* noticed that, 'strangely enough', civic weeks had become 'a main plank of social policy in the province'. Seven towns held civic weeks in 1966, 22 in 1967, 22 in 1968 and 17 in 1969. They were overwhelmingly middle-class affairs, organized primarily by Junior Chambers of Commerce. O'Neill confided that:

> An important aspect of the civic weeks though one that is not stressed too much for reasons of tact is to encourage the Catholic minority to become a more committed part of the community. To a large extent they have been non-joiners, either because half their loyalty is aimed at Dublin, or because the local Protestant majority have closed the door on them.[138]

PEP, thus, was a mechanism for the building of a civil society united in common endeavour and shared experience. PEP attempted to create a sub-state, sub-political arena in which both communities could engage without sacrifice or compromise. Theoretically shorn of political, sectarian or national implications and ceremony,[139] civic weeks promised a neutral zone based upon a common interest in social advancement and local fealty. O'Neill, thus, was offering no diminution in the protestant-unionist ethos of the state to win catholic allegiance. Nor was he offering to introduce British norms so that civil rights deficiencies would be eliminated. He believed that in due course, catholics would come to see with increasing clarity the benefits of the Union. The state, by virtue of its democratic mandate, could until then require their submission. To sweeten the pill, O'Neill offered catholics not a reformed and pluralistic Northern Ireland state, but the thin gruel of a PEP quasi-state.

O'Neill's attitude towards catholics has been characterized as that of a 'late nineteenth century paternalistic liberal.'[140] In fact the similarity of his thought to the 'constructive unionism' or 'progressive conservatism' of the 1880s–1900s is striking. Then too conservatives hoped to inculcate sturdy individualism based upon civic responsibility as a counter to the insidious collectivism of socialism, Irish nationalism and catholicism. O'Neill now hoped to harness it to undermine communalism.[141] Given his long family pedigree in politics it seems at least possible that O'Neill was consciously emulating his predecessors, from the 'Howth set' who advised Randolph Churchill, through Gerald and Arthur Balfour and George Wyndham, the Tory Chief Secretaries, to Lord Dunraven and Horace Plunkett.

O'Neill hoped that PEP and civic weeks would provide the focus for the 50th anniversary celebration of the foundation of the state in 1971. However his Chief Whip, Roy Bradford, pointed out that this was no ecumenical commemoration. Partition had been a unionist victory: 'Care must be taken not to frame a programme so bland and all-embracing that it appeared to turn its back on these associations.'[142] Clearly unionists were not enthused by PEP's inclusiveness.

On 27 September 1968 O'Neill made a speech to the last PEP committee meeting before the storm broke. Optimistically he pointed to the international hot summer of protest as a sign that over-centralization was no longer acceptable. The age of PEP was dawning.[143] Such hubris invited a fall. The civil rights movement exploded the idea that the PEP quasi-state could be a sufficient recompense for catholics alienated from the national life. On 20 June Austin Currie squatted in a house in Caledon, protesting at its misallocation to a protestant family. Charles Brett of the NILP commented ruefully:

'Captain O'Neill seeks participation by people in public life. In Caledon he has got it – and no wonder.'[144] A placard on the civil rights march from Coalisland to Dungannon on 26 August read: 'Ban O'Neill's PEP pill'.[145] One student placard on the Queen's students sit-down in Linen Hall street on 9 October ran: 'Civil rights, not civic weeks'.[146]

In the aftermath of Burntollet the Northern Ireland Civil Rights association (NICRA) threatened to urge the minority to withdraw from civic week events.[147] In ten points for a civil disobedience campaign, Radio Free Derry broadcast a vitriolic attacked on civic weeks.[148] Cardinal Conway disparaged the concept in an interview in March 1969:

> I think many Unionists underestimate the capacity of people to see when they are being fobbed off with words and gestures. Our people are not at all impressed, for example, when civic weeks and visits to Catholic schools seemed to be chalked up as much needed reform.[149]

In the fires of communal discord, the 'action by words' of civic weeks met an inevitable demise.

The Nationalist Party

Political nationalism was decrepit. The important catholic constituencies in Belfast had long been captured by various and fragmented labour nationalists, pushing mainstream Nationalism to the rural hinterland.[150] Of the nine Nationalist MPs in 1966 only three or four were considered competent parliamentary performers.[151] There was virtually no policy making apparatus or rank and file engagement.[152] Only in constituencies where it was sure to win did the party operate at all; about nine or ten out of 52.[153] The Nationalist Party was widely seen as being reactionary, outdated and increasingly irrelevant.[154] Its leader Eddie McAteer in earlier years had advocated a policy of complete non-co-operation with the state.[155] Avuncular and humorous he now gave the impression of having tired of the cut and thrust of political life. Hesitantly he decided upon a policy of limited accommodation to the state.

Pressure to replace a sterile policy of catholic representation and relentless anti-partitionism came from within the party, notably the brothers Patrick and Tom Gormley, MPs for Mid-Derry and Mid-Tyrone respectively, and a young product of Queen's University Belfast, Austin

Currie, elected for East Tyrone in 1964. In 1960 a pressure group determined to modernize nationalism politically and organizationally was established.[156] In April 1964 it met with members of the parliamentary party at a conference in Maghery, County Armagh.[157] The Nationalist leadership remained unimpressed. McAteer moodily commented that '[t]alk of a change of policy is all right for theorists.'[158]

A controversy in September 1964, however, seemed to signal a sea change in the leadership's policy. A Nationalist convention in Fermanagh/South Tyrone decided to give the Republican candidate a free run in the forthcoming United Kingdom general election. National Unity, a ginger group that advocated unity of the island by consent, led the torrent of condemnation of the Nationalist Party's political cowardice.[159]

Shortly afterwards the shaken Party published its first-ever policy document.[160] McAteer emphasized the importance of this initiative to the press with a startling admission: 'We are today stepping into the twentieth century.'[161] The party also strove to reunite the nationalist opposition to Unionism, approaching the Republican Labour Party, a force in Belfast working-class districts, and various one-man bands to discuss a merger. These foundered, as Belfast working-class catholic politics clashed with the rural conservatism of mainstream Nationalism, but an affiliated National Party was set up in the capital city so as to re-establish a foothold there.[162] Farcically this infant child rejected its parent within months to become the National Democratic Party.[163] McAteer worked tirelessly to heal the breach and reach out to other nationalist factions. Nationalist unity, he believed, 'would be the achievement of this half of the century.'[164]

After the O'Neill/Lemass summit in 1965 Dublin pressurized the Nationalists into becoming the official opposition at Stormont.[165] Nationalists, Lemass bluntly insisted, were as intransigent as the unionists and the conditions for reuniting Ireland would not be created by political means but through economic development in the South.[166] On 2 February 1965 brown paper covering the first word of 'Official Opposition' on the door of room 43 in Stormont was removed. The Unionist response, however, was ungenerous. Payment of McAteer as Leader of the Opposition would have signalled an appreciative welcome to the Nationalists as a legitimate official opposition.[167] Terence O'Neill, however, had long felt that the 'country areas' of the Unionist Party would react badly.[168] Other ministers were more sympathetic to the idea, but, in a rare alliance with Brian Faulkner, O'Neill prevailed.[169]

In June 1965 McAteer admitted that the party had been pursuing a deliberately low-key moderate policy for three years. He had to confess, however, that goodwill was not being reciprocated.[170] Following the 1965 general election, which greatly strengthened O'Neill's position, McAteer publicly offered him a compromise:

> We both have a great opportunity and in my view this is the moment for statesmanship. I am willing to meet Captain O'Neill in any form of confrontation with a view to a new deal. We have our ideal of a united Ireland and they have theirs, but in between there is a tremendous amount of agreement.[171]

To this potentially historic offer there was no Unionist response.

The first ever conference of the Nationalist Party was held on Sunday 22 May 1966. One hundred and twenty delegates heard McAteer outline the meagre results of the party's conciliationism. Despite his pessimism, McAteer insisted it was no time to 'hurl thunderbolts'. What was needed was 'a period of Cistercian-like quietness, so that the community might timidly mingle without raucous warning about hidden minefields.' Meanwhile the nationalist community must ignore the insults of the Unionists – 'wipe the spittle from our face' – and soldier on.[172] It was a homily on patient fortitude almost to the point of self-immolation.

There is no doubt that McAteer was aware that agitation on civil rights had the potential for sparking sectarian conflict. His preference was for quiet petitioning and conciliation.[173] This style of low-key persuasion and lobbying was closer to that adopted by the NILP than the radicalism of the emerging civil rights movement.[174] Capitalizing on a circumscribed ceremony due to the foot-and-mouth cattle epidemic, McAteer attended the 1967 state opening of parliament and Queen's Speech, the first time a Nationalist leader had done so.[175] From the beginning of February 1968 Nationalist MPs began attending prayers in Stormont.[176] The party offered no objection when Craig asked the House for a further £29,000 to fund a pay increase for the B Specials.[177] Discussions were under way about appointing a Roman Catholic chaplain for Stormont. As one veteran Nationalist sadly told McAteer: 'Ach, sure Eddie, there's hardly any such thing as politics now at all.'[178]

Strains were evident however. Speaking in Stormont on the banning of a Republican parade in May 1968, McAteer warned that he could 'smell sulphur in the air.'[179] Unusually, the speech was uninterrupted by a sober House.[180] To the party's annual conference on 23 June McAteer delivered his bleakest assessment yet:

> I detect a dangerous ground-swell of resentment among our people – a dangerous feeling of disillusionment that we are not really wanted here, and that there is no real desire for this much sought holy grail of community relations. I don't know what further efforts we can make. It is perfectly true that there are impatient ones among us who are thinking about going home and taking up pikes and so on. This is an understandable sort of reaction. But we must be realistic and try to remember that we are an entrapped minority here in the North of Ireland, and there is not much good in looking for help overseas, from America, or indeed, I regret to say, from our own fellow countrymen.[181]

It was clear, however, that the current policy of conciliation was becoming unendurable to the rank and file. Derry Alderman, James Hegarty, excoriated the present line:

> Nationalist efforts at co-operation had been spurned with arrogance, and conciliation and compromise had been interpreted as surrender. The Nationalist Party is now torn with doubt about its own role, and racked with divisions from within; and the nationally minded people are confused, disappointed and angry. The nationalist people want clear, uncompromising leadership. They have long since lost all belief in the efficacy of co-operation.[182]

The Nationalist Party was ideologically uncertain, in a strategic impasse and organizationally confused. Little wonder that its stock appeared to be plummeting amongst catholics, especially the younger generation. A 1968 poll found only 5 per cent of youth willing to vote for the party in Stormont elections, as against 17 per cent for the NILP and 28 per cent for the Unionists.[183]

Though the Party's tired anti-partitionism had disillusioned catholics it was not because they rejected nationalism *per se*. Rather catholics were embarrassed and annoyed because their representatives were handing over the advantage of eloquence and modernity to Unionists. The Party's rather pathetic conciliationism fared no better. By 1968 it was being regularly challenged by critics who counselled militant confrontation of the state around the emotive issue of civil rights. McAteer feared for the consequences but was powerless to prevent the transformation.

Civil rights

Discrimination and civil rights for catholic nationalists were chronic sources of bitterness and contention in Northern Ireland. What was new in the O'Neill years was the articulate propaganda of the minority. In 1963 a catholic agitation over housing allocation in Dungannon led to the formation of the middle-class-led Campaign for Social Justice (CSJ).[184] This aimed to force 'all the disturbing details of life here to the attention of the British and American people so that it can never be said that they were unaware of what was happening in Northern Ireland.'[185] Thus began a quasi-apolitical civil rights activism – a tentative contestation of the field of civic modernism O'Neill was so vigorously laying claim to.

The election of Wilson's Labour government, greeted enthusiastically in catholic areas,[186] posed a delicate problem for Unionists. Governing with no overall majority, Wilson's government was frustrated at their difficulty in passing core measures. When George Brown, Harold Wilson's deputy, visited Northern Ireland in May 1965, Faulkner hosted a dinner party in his honour. Speaking grandly on the need for economic growth, Faulkner assured his guest that 'We are with you up to the hilt.' 'Yes, up to the hilt in our back,' Brown growled, 'If it were not for your ... twelve MPs we would have a majority of fifteen.'[187] Unionist MPs at Westminster regularly voted with the Tories, while convention prevented Westminster from discussing Northern Ireland domestic affairs.

In March 1965 the *Sunday Times* published rumours that the British government were considering whether to curb the voting powers of Ulster MPs at Westminster. Despite public denials, Wilson was indeed considering such restrictions.[188] As it turned out, the March 1966 general election and Labour's much-increased majority removed immediate pressure to restrict the Northern Ireland MPs. Another factor was that Terence O'Neill encouraged a self-denying ordinance on the core of Unionist MPs who revelled in baiting the government. This could better be left to others, normally more capable, on the Conservative benches.[189]

Tension between the two governments focused more directly on the issue of discrimination. With the rise of the race relations question in Britain, British politics had become sensitized to the problem of discrimination.[190] Influenced by the CSJ's articulate and apparently non-partisan propaganda a number of British Labour backbenchers organized themselves into the Campaign for Democracy in Ulster

(CDU).[191] The election of Gerry Fitt, a plausible parliamentary performer who tailored his message for a British Labour audience, and the political and violent turmoil of 1966, both worked to the advantage of the CDU. By July 1966 it had 100 MPs in membership, many prominent, and more were to join.[192]

The quantitative extent of anti-catholic or anti-nationalist discrimination is hard to gauge, particularly as records were naturally not kept.[193] John Whyte's judgement is probably fairest: 'the picture is neither black nor white but a shade of grey. ... [But in the west of the province] the greyness of the picture ... changes to an ominous darkness.'[194] Catholics were certainly under-represented on statutory boards, while highly controversial appointees from the unionist tradition were not unusual.[195] More generally, the unionist ethos, which pervaded so much of official life in Northern Ireland, must have served to alienate many catholics. One young catholic graduate in 1965 explained,

> I had intended making a career in planning and applying to the Ministry of Development. I would have liked to have worked in the New City, but, when they called it Craigavon, I realized that a Catholic has no future in it. I'm going into teaching.'[196]

Nevertheless, there were strong grounds for unionists to contest many specific charges of discrimination. Allegations, however, were rarely answered in detail.[197] This may be explained by a reluctance to dignify unscrupulous opponents.[198] The Unionists were unwilling to engage with what they perceived as a politically motivated and essentially bogus Nationalist Party campaign on civil rights.'[199]

This only explains so much, however. Fundamentally most unionists did not believe their own assertion that protestant and loyalist security was not dependent on the tilting of the playing field against catholics.[200] Though few dared say so openly, the almost uniform understanding was that second-class citizenship for catholics was both necessary and morally justifiable. Above all, unionists were anxious not to upset delicate sectarian electoral geography by encouraging catholic social or spatial mobility. Job discrimination, for example, was widely accepted as a necessary evil.[201] Lord Brookeborough in 1969 referred to 'political difficulties' in easing discrimination: 'A man's religion is entirely his own affair. The point is, there are loyalists and disloyalists.'[202] The Reverend E. J. Ferguson argued in the quasi-official *Unionist* journal that:

Religious discrimination is deplorable but it is not indefensible ...
Employers and managements must be allowed to employ their own
discretion when making the appointment even though their choice
results in religious discrimination. The Apostolic injunction, 'Do
good unto all men, especially those who are of the household of
faith' suggests that we may sometimes discriminate in favour of
those nearest ourselves.[203]

The number of unionist appeals for sectarian solidarity around employment practices increased in the late 1950s and early 1960s. Undoubtedly
this reflected a rise in job insecurity and the arrival of new industries that
could not be relied upon automatically to favour the 'right sort'.[204]
American-owned firms, in particular, 'were not very amenable to advice
about recruitment of labour' as Ivan Neill, Minister for Labour and
National Insurance, complained in 1956.[205] Noting the introduction of
competitive examination into the civil service, D. G. Liddle, vice-
chairman of the Ulster Unionist Council, warned in January 1965 that
unless young unionists applied themselves to education 'in another ten
or fifteen year's time we will have lost control of all the executive
positions – Post Office, Civil Service and local government'.[206] It was not
job monopolization that unionists looked for, but adequate representation for 'their' workers, particularly in areas, such as Derry, where
catholics were in the majority. Discrimination was less winner takes all
than a means to preserve a perceived balance.[207] If they were to err,
however, it would inevitably be to the advantage of protestants.

The allocation of housing was a similarly contentious area. In
November 1963 the Unionist chairman of Enniskillen Housing
Committee said the Council would build houses for letting to the 'right
people' and make no apology about it. A Unionist council had no
obligation to 'cut a stick to beat itself'.[208] Unionists were ever watchful
on their electoral position and resentful of the Housing Trust's power to
upset it.[209] A statement from Middle Liberties Unionist Association in
Derry, handed to a Twelfth platform in 1967, read:

Discrimination against Protestants in Middle Liberties, where you
are now meeting. The Northern Ireland Housing Trust (Unionist
Government appointed) has made the following allocations in the
new estate to date – Roman Catholics 255, Protestants 23. As a
result the seat was thrown away at the last Rural District Council
election to non-Unionists. What do you really think of this? Please
tell the crowd.'[210]

For Unionists, accusations of discrimination in housing allocation mistook segregation for injustice.[211]

Equally, unionists were loath to stand against what was seen as legitimate hostility to the incursion of catholic culture and population into protestant areas. Attempts were made to prevent a catholic church being built on the Lisburn Road, a catholic youth club on the Ormeau Road and a catholic church, school and parochial house in Dundonald.[212] Well-defined sectarian boundaries should not be violated.

Gerrymandering[213] of electoral constituencies, while usually denied in public, was tacitly accepted as a necessary defence for 'border protestants' against nationalist domination.[214] Notoriously, Unionists asserted in private they could not afford the loss of prestige that would ensue if they lost control of Derry Corporation.[215] Similar considerations pertained elsewhere. Robert Campbell, the Unionist candidate in Bangor in February 1969 was quoted as supporting a delay in the revision of local government boundaries otherwise most of Armagh would be lost to the Unionist Party and that any revision should 'preserve Unionist autonomy.'[216] In 1967, when local councils were amalgamated, there was a fresh gerrymander in County Fermanagh.[217]

The Cabinet was well aware of the existence of anomalies in electoral districts.[218] Stormont constituency boundaries were not an apolitical matter, but to be discussed within the Unionist Party before amendment.[219] Reforms, such as the abolition of the university seats and the recasting of Belfast constituencies, were only approved on the basis that they would not be politically disadvantageous to the Unionist Party.[220] Similarly, Unionists feared that the concession of universal suffrage in local government elections, replacing a ratepayers' franchise that excluded some 250,000 people, disproportionately catholic and opposition supporters, would be 'traitorous to the loyalists of Tyrone, Fermanagh, Londonderry and Armagh.'[221] Unionists felt that so long as they stuck to the original 'bargain' implicit in devolution they had a right to defend their political interests. John Dobson, MP for West Down, rejected the 'argument ... that one should make a change to benefit one's political opponents. I can't see any Government at Westminster doing that.'[222] The Attorney General, Edward Jones, argued that Unionist Ulster had reached a covenant with Britain in the 1920 Government of Ireland Act that included guarantees for the minority. Unionists had no moral obligation to adopt any subsequent democratic reform in Britain, whether actual or, like votes at 18, likely, which would advance the disloyal and feckless catholic minority.[223]

Unionist attitudes to discrimination were fundamentally defensive rather than aggressive. The Stormont era was not, as has been depicted since, a period of rampant and triumphalistic unionist bigotry. Rather it was similar to later periods in its unionist attitudes: suspicious, defensive and ungenerous. In practice, almost all examples of discimination can be traced to a desire to preserve gerrymandered constituencies. Unionists feared to concede reform because it might in itself weaken the ramparts against Irish nationalism, or else open the way to further, more destructive, change. More fundamentally, to concede reform implied accepting the 50-year-old nationalist complaint that the Northern Ireland state was corrupt, oppressive and therefore illegitimate. Civil rights reforms could not be easily conceded because they were seen as being part of the armoury of Irish nationalism.[224]

What was most striking about the unionist response to accusations of discrimination was its inadequacy.[225] In the face of an increasingly sophisticated and substantiated civil rights campaign, Desmond Boal, in January 1965, warned that the Unionist Party was caving in to accusations of discrimination. 'When we heard the word at first we laughed, because we knew it was nonsense – but not now. We have heard it so much that we have come to believe it.'[226]

Some Unionists attempted to fight back more seriously. John Taylor addressed a conference of the National Conference of Civil Liberties in London on 13 March 1965. Here, in unprecedented detail, he defended the Unionist government's record. Taylor argued that Northern Irish politics were in a state of flux out of which new alignments and ideas were emerging. This was leading to improved community relations. Outside interference would 'only aggravate the problem'[227] He blamed the South's hostility to Northern Ireland, IRA attacks, Nationalist Party propaganda, and the Catholic Church's segregatory attitude for keeping alive old sectarian animosities. The mass of details and statistics Taylor adduced, while far short of the volume marshalled by the CSJ, was unusual for unionist propaganda. The only government discrimination he conceded was in favour of catholics in the Post Office (controlled from London) and in private business where, as he disingenuously put it, 'we all know catholic firms which do not employ protestants and vice versa.' The political landscape was changing and more of the minority accepting the material benefits of the Union. He concluded: 'In the society we see ahead there will be no place for second class citizens. But let me remind you, that being a first class citizen demands certain responsibilities to the State. Therein lies the challenge.'[228]

Thus, even in this most erudite retort to the civil rights propagandists, Taylor expressed the central dilemma that bedevilled unionist public relations. While keen to refute particular civil rights charges as unfounded, they persisted in believing and expressing, however obliquely, that treatment of the minority as second-class citizens was essentially justified by their lack of loyalty and the backwardness and illiberality of their catholic world-view. Catholics must change to earn first-class citizenship.

As the pitch of civil rights agitation continued to rise, unionists began to feel the pressure.[229] Some liberal unionists – Robin Bailie, Bob Cooper, Robert Nixon, Nat Minford, Robert Simpson, Phelim O'Neill – began to counsel timely reform.[230] Austin Ardill, MP for Carrick, claimed that, in the spring of 1966, he attempted to introduce comprehensive legislation to introduce universal suffrage in local elections, reorganize Derry to end minority control by Unionists, and remove legitimate grounds for complaint over gerrymandering and discrimination in general. The government, he claimed, rejected this as premature.[231] It seems that a party meeting on the 'Londonderry problem' was arranged. It was hoped to lessen the obvious iniquities of gerrymandering in the city whilst striving to maintain Unionist control.[232] However, the Maiden City's unionists remained obdurate against all O'Neill's urgings.[233] Most open, and most remarkable, was the valedictory campaign of the ageing Edmund Warnock. For years considered a right-winger, he turned the last of his political energies to persuading his fellow unionists that they had used their untrammelled power tyrannously and, in speech after speech, he urged conciliation.[234] Like Burke, whose advice that magnanimity 'is the most profitable policy' he echoed, Warnock's warning voice went unheeded.

The Unionist Party

Terence O'Neill's most important failure, perhaps, was in remoulding the Unionist Party itself. Upon becoming Unionist Party leader in 1963 he had hoped to 'create a Central Office on Conservative Party lines'.[235] On 10 April J. O. Bailie, 47 years old and with 21 years experience working in Unionist Party headquarters on Glengall Street, replaced the long-standing and hugely influential Billy Douglas as Secretary of the Ulster Unionist Council.[236] Six months later Harry Wallace, aged 36, was appointed assistant secretary.[237] Both Bailie and Wallace were young, media-conscious, moderates, very much in the

O'Neillite mould. Their brief was to reorganize the party so that it could win support back from the NILP and to strengthen links to the business community. The replacement of the old guard appealed tremendously to assimilationists as indicative of a new broom in the party, but Douglas' successors carried only a fraction of his influence and authority with the rank and file. The party could not easily be re-cast by bureaucratic fiat.[238]

It was hoped to attract outside talent directly into elected positions skipping the normal requirements of long-term active membership in the party.[239] Success in this direction was limited. Sir Cecil McKee complained that quality candidates were 'not the types to canvass the committee or apply to a "Wanted" advertisement.'[240] Those keen to move away from sectarian catchcrys were unlikely to endure kow-towing to Orange dominated constituency associations.[241] This was necessary for success – John Dobson won the unionist nomination for West Down partially because, in contrast to another contender, he agreed that catholics should not be admitted into the party.[242] The quality of MPs suffered. Of the 20 Unionist backbenchers in 1966, ten were regular attendees, five or six spoke regularly, and only three or four were judged competent.[243]

Assimilatory unionism seemed marginalized to a minority of intel-lectuals in the Young Unionist Movement. A group of ex-University Young Unionists, grouped around the Belfast Clifton branch, from 1960 acted as an unofficial Bow Group.[244] In October 1962 they published the first, and only, edition of a reformist political journal, *Review*. The key article in this was 'A United Ulster' by Robin Bailie. Bailie argued that Roman Catholicism, as it stood, was indeed inimical to democracy. He expressed the hope, however, that catholics might be ready to resist pressure from their Church and become loyal citi-zens. He insisted, thus, that anything likely to dissuade individual catholics from joining the Unionist Party, such as the link with the Orange Order, should be revised.[245] The magazine did not prosper, even in Young Unionist ranks.[246] Their influence quickly peaked in the Young Unionist Movement.

In January 1964 the County Down Committee of the Young Unionist Council agreed to establish a fund to encourage Young Unionists to stand for nominations in the forthcoming local elec-tions.[247] The political logic behind this was brazenly asserted by Edward Gibson, Young Unionist chairman: the old guard were out of touch, reactionary and simply not up to it. He even threatened to oppose sitting Unionists.[248] 'It is high time that many Young

Unionists set aside their personal political ambitions', he argued, 'and spoke their minds on subjects of importance, rather than try to curry favour by repeating outworn clichés that issue from many senior members.'[249] As never before, an attempt was being made to fashion the party's youth wing into a political pressure group. The scurrilous election tactics of October 1964 shocked Gibson into even greater criticism.[250] He accused O'Neill of reneging on his rhetoric in failing to rejuvenate the party.[251] Even within the Young Unionist Movement, however, Gibson was isolated.[252] In 1965, after the Young Unionists failed to officially approve O'Neill's summit with Lemass, Gibson and other assimilatory unionists resigned from the movement.[253] By 1969 it was in the van of anti-O'Neill opinion. *Review* intellectuals remained in the party, however, sustaining an effective critique of O'Neill's limitations, and made early and consistent calls for civil rights reform.[254]

Attempts to renew the adult party were equally fraught. Stratton Mills, liberal unionist Westminster MP for North Belfast, in 1964 warned that 'university graduates, schoolteachers, journalists, writers, television commentators' and others of the intelligentsia were under-represented in the party. He pointed to the work of R.A.B. Butler in making the Conservative Party 'intellectually respectable' in the immediate post-war years. Under O'Neill, the Unionist Party needed to attract those 'leaders of thought in the community who feel at present that they have no place in the party'.[255] O'Neill directly appealed for a body equivalent to the British Tory Bow Group to facilitate 'basic thinking and basic research at the political level into the basic problems of this day and age.'[256] The *Unionist*, though segregatory in instinct, also campaigned for a revivification of the party. It opposed particularly the monopolization of Unionist Association executive posts by aged timeservers.[257]

Nevertheless, despite the early shake-up of Glengall Street, it was clear that reform of the party lagged far behind O'Neill's reform of the administration and even policy.[258] Constituency associations enjoyed a high degree of autonomy and were not amenable to central direction.[259] From October 1965 Unionist Association officers were invited to forums at Glengall Street at which government ministers explained controversial policies.[260] In June 1966 the Unionist executive adopted a resolution calling for a review of party structures 'with a view to modernising and attracting youthful business and professional members.'[261] O'Neill, to the Ulster Unionist Council, had called for a newly scientific and business approach to organization, emulating the Scottish Conservative

Party.[262] The following year Glengall Street launched a drive to encourage passive supporters to become active unionists.[263] This developed into a reorganization of the Belfast party, principally to counter the NILP electoral threat.[264] William Beggs headed a committee charged with rearranging the fifteen divisional associations, improving finances, recruiting (especially young people), redrafting the standard Unionist Association (UA) rules, encouraging attractive annual programmes and developing public relations skills.[265]

Despite such efforts in February 1968 the *Belfast Telegraph* pointed out that the Unionist Associations had yet to be renewed by middle-class recruits. This created political difficulties for O'Neill: 'he has allied himself with the still rather embryonic liberal wing of the party, and has to do most of the bridge-building single-handed.'[266] Indeed, though middle-class elements keen to shift the party from its reliance on protestant support were certainly attracted into the party by O'Neill premiership, so too were traditionalists whose aggression and tenacity drove many moderates out of activity. From the mid-1960s most UAs seemed, on balance, to be actually drifting towards the right.[267] O'Neill, who had little interest in what he perceived as an uncongenial rank and file, preferred to work through the machinery of government and, particularly, the Cabinet Office.[268]

The election in 1965 failed to bring much new blood into the parliamentary party. Though the strongly assimilatory Roy Bradford was returned in Victoria (at the expense of David Bleakley, a unionist Labour MP) more typical was the return of aged stalwarts: Warnock (78), Brookeborough (77), McCoy (80), Stronge (71) and Lyons (69).[269] The assimilatory stream in unionism was failing to break through to high-profile public positions. O'Neill was aware of this atrophy. 'The trouble with these politicians is that their only contact [is] with certain members of the old Unionist Party clique in their constituency,' he maintained, ' and they are misled by them into thinking the people of Northern Ireland do not welcome the improvement in community relations and in our relations with the South.'[270] O'Neill, aristocratic of demeanour, detached from and critical of Ulster political traditions and almost openly scornful of his own party, was not the leader to re-educate the rank and file.[271]

The rearrangement of constituency boundaries in the Greater Belfast area, an administrative consequence of the abolition of the Queen's University seats in 1967, provided an impetus for reform which O'Neill and Glengall Street had signally failed to engineer. Four new seats were created: Newtownabbey, Larkfield, Bangor and

Laganvalley; and six were substantially altered: Carrick, South Antrim, Antrim, Bannside, North Down and Mid-Down. In the short term this forced an extension of the Belfast plan to create a reformed and expanded activist base.[272] In September 1968 the Prime Minister appointed Roy Bradford as Chief Whip with a specific remit to liase with and help modernize the Unionist Associations.[273] At the end of the month, on the initiative of O'Neill, a forum of 300 Unionist Association officers was organized to discuss a motion calling for an in-depth review of the organization, structure and financing of the party at local and central levels.[274]

More importantly, however, the creation of new seats, combined with the retirement of long-standing MPs – for example Robert Nixon and Edmund Warnock – gave unprecedented scope for new blood to be introduced into the Parliamentary Unionist Party. These seats were the middle-class, suburban, and comfortably protestant and unionist areas to which O'Neillism most appealed. Thus Robin Bailie, a 31-year-old Belfast lawyer and stalwart of the assimilatory *Review* group, was selected as Unionist candidate for the new seat of Newtownabbey.[275] Robert Babington, of an old Derry unionist family, but born and largely educated in Dublin, was selected by North Down UA. He too was a barrister.[276] Also a barrister, the 33 year old Richard Ferguson, was selected for South Antrim. Though an Orange Order member for ten years whose uncle had been Unionist MP for Enniskillen for 11 years, Ferguson was, like Bailie and Babington, notably liberal.[277]

There were signs at last, therefore, of an O'Neillite generation coming through in the Unionist Party to provide O'Neill with solid support from the backbenches. Educated, middle-class, urban and assimilatory, they were congenial to O'Neill both politically and personally. They offered, for the first time, an opportunity for O'Neill to develop a strategy that employed the Unionist apparatus rather than circumnavigated it through the civil service, media or plebiscitory elections. Events, however, overtook this evolutionary perspective.

As political and civil unrest intensified in Northern Ireland during 1966, Northern Ireland increasingly drew press attention.[278] The British government began casting a wary, and, for unionists, unwelcome eye on the Stormont administration.[279] Terence O'Neill had been aware for some time of the risk of British intervention. As unionist opposition to modernization grew, his earlier emphasis on selling Northern Ireland as a suitable area for investment developed into a crusade to preserve the province's political image.[280] This theme was constantly repeated throughout his struggle with Paisleyism in 1966.

On 2 August 1966 Harold Wilson formally summoned O'Neill to Downing Street.[281] The summit, on 5 August, lasted two hours. Present were Terence O'Neill, Harold Wilson and the Home Secretary, Roy Jenkins. After lunch Wilson explained that he was under 'irresistible' pressure from his backbenchers to ensure that reforms were forthcoming in Northern Ireland. 'It was necessary,' he insisted, 'that recent progress in Northern Ireland towards a more liberal atmosphere should continue and that a real effort be made to meet some of the grievances which had been expressed; otherwise Westminster would be forced to act.' O'Neill replied that the steps he had taken to 'bring about an atmosphere of reconciliation between opposing sections of the ... community' were 'a necessary pre-requisite to any concrete action' on reforms. The 1916 commemorations had produced a 'severe back-lash' amongst elements of the protestant community 'which made it politically impossible to make further moves at present'. Intervention by Westminster would be disastrous, merely re-creating a 1912 stand-off situation. Roy Jenkins warned that any pause would have to be temporary and if extremists took over or there was a 'return to unenlightened policies' the result would be 'Westminster "taking over"'. Wilson concluded with an acknowledgement of 'the changed atmosphere which Captain O'Neill had created since he assumed office and he thought it right in these circumstances to allow him to pursue his new policies without interference from London'.[282]

To his Cabinet Terence O'Neill emphasized that he had merely 'bought time'. Brian Faulkner, however, spoke for the Unionist majority. He 'wondered what practical action the United Kingdom Government and Parliament could really take. ... In any case the whole "discrimination" case had been greatly exaggerated, and at council level Nationalist local authorities were much the worse offenders.' O'Neill, though clearly in favour of substantive reform and supported by his Minister of Finance, Herbert Kirk, did not force the issue.[283]

A further summit, described by O'Neill as 'friendly' but with 'an underlying sense of pressure', was held on 12 January 1967. Wilson reiterated his previous arguments, pressing his points particularly on Faulkner who he suspected of plotting to isolate O'Neill. Convinced that Labour's animus sprang from partisan interventions from Unionist Members at Westminster, the Northern Ireland Cabinet agreed to rein the Imperial Parliamentary Party in.[284]

If anything, the recent street violence had probably dissuaded Wilson from intervening directly. The summits constituted a watershed, nevertheless. For the first time the British government had intervened directly in Northern Ireland affairs and made clear that they expected wide-ranging civil rights reform. The clock was ticking.

Run up to CRM, 1966–8

In practice O'Neill moved tentatively towards the amelioration of catholic grievances, and clearly had the intention of delivering more. But in deference to the unionist right, he simultaneously conducted a propaganda war denying the substance of civil rights charges. This step-by-step approach seems to have been fairly successful in minimizing unionist opposition and given a sufficient length of time might well have delivered all demanded reforms at little cost in unionist fragmentation. Negatively however, the approach politicized the civil rights question, disillusioned catholic opinion with the impression of governmental intransigence and stiffened unionist resolve that no sudden climb-down to civil rights demands was admissible. It set the scene for open conflict.

In September 1966 the NILP and the ICTU submitted a Joint Memorandum on Citizens Rights in Northern Ireland to the government. Having in August been warned by Harold Wilson that Westminster intervention was inevitable in the long run unless reforms were forthcoming, Terence O'Neill was concerned by this new development. 'As a former Minister of Finance,' he told his colleagues, 'he was very conscious of how easy it would be [for Whitehall] to turn the financial screw [on Stormont].'[285] Kirk reported, with sympathy, the opinions of a few backbenchers who 'were inclined to think that some concessions – no doubt of a minimal kind – might have to be given in response to the current pressures for change.'[286]

Consideration of the NILP's memorandum became the first major attempt to deal with civil rights grievances as a package by the Northern Ireland government.[287] Only concessions that would have 'no marked political effect' were accepted.[288] In the Queen's speech, and more so O'Neill's conciliatory gloss that followed, the reforms were announced. The business vote in Stormont elections (of little practical significance) was to be abandoned, the Queen's University seats abolished and redistributed, and a boundary commission in time was to re-examine all Stormont constituencies. Certain legal reforms were to be undertaken to facilitate the extension of state aid to the Mater Hospital.[289]

By chance the independent commission on Northern Ireland's Westminster constituency boundaries reported around this time. The four Belfast seats were extended in South Antrim and North Down.

The main political effects were to make West Belfast safe for Gerry Fitt, as it gained the 9000 extra voters, mainly catholics in Andersonstown and Ladybrook, from South Antrim. There was surprise all round at an outcome so far from a Unionist stitch-up.[290] Thus 1966, the year of crises, ended on an unexpectedly reformist note. The lack of reaction from Paisleyites or Unionist hard-liners suggested that their bluster and fury had been spent at least temporarily.[291] Catholic expectations, however, were rising fast, and the first great raft of civil rights reform was dismissed as woefully inadequate.

Reform continued at a low-key, almost subterranean, level. The question of state funding for the Mater Infirmorum Hospital was a long-running headache for the government.[292] Established in 1884 as a Roman Catholic-run institution it had remained outside the National Health Service in 1948. Though denominational hospitals were guaranteed protection of their 'religious character and associations' as part of the NHS in Britain, a promise to legislate similarly in Northern Ireland was not honoured. The Mater thus remained outside the state system, reliant on heroic fund-raising in the catholic community.[293] Due to its role as acute-centre for North Belfast, 25 per cent of in-patients and fully 85 per cent of out-patients were protestant. Public opinion in both communities overwhelmingly favoured state aid for the Mater.[294]

Early in 1964 the Cabinet began to consider a solution, but backbench opposition to funding a Roman Catholic institution bulked large.[295] Faulkner championed resistance to concession. O'Neill recognized that 'liberal Protestant opinion, notably amongst middle-class groups in Belfast' favoured state aid and that, as long as the present situation lasted, 'the grievance would be exploited to the utmost in Great Britain.' He was, however, unable to force through substantive reform against Faulkner's opposition.[296]

Probably to side-step Faulkner, O'Neill encouraged an independent departmental initiative and William Morgan, his Minister of Health, duly entered into talks with Roman Catholic Bishop Philbin. Much progress was made but, once again, Faulkner succeeded in blocking agreement in the Cabinet.[297] The Ministry unilaterally ended negotiations, to Philbin's fury.[298] O'Neill next attempted to press ahead with reform of the 1948 Act, to bring it into parity with British legislation, but was stymied by an intractable backbench.[299] The Health Services Bill promised in the 1965 Queen's Speech never came.

O'Neill's 'go softly' approach, evading set-piece battles with opponents of reform, eventually had some success in wearing down backbench opposition.[300] When a Health Services (Amendment) Bill was published in January 1967 a full Parliamentary Unionist Party meeting on the issue was convened.[301] This finally approved, in principle, state aid for the Mater on the basis of protection for its religious character to be negotiated with the catholic hierarchy.[302] On 20 September 1967 the Minister for Health for the first time formally met with Philbin to discuss state funding.[303] Though the atmosphere had improved and concrete steps taken, rank-and-file unionist opinion would allow no easy or rapid solution to the question. Negotiations outlasted O'Neill's premiership, and a deal was only agreed in 1971.[304]

Another partial breakthrough was in education, one of the thorniest question with which Unionist governments were periodically faced.[305] Education spending per head in Northern Ireland, at £69.40, was substantially lower than British levels, £95.40 in Scotland and £87.70 in England and Wales, but compared well to the Republic of Ireland's £26.60.[306] Substantial improvements were envisaged in a 1964 White Paper, which planned to reform the 11-plus exam after 1965, convert intermediates into secondaries, eliminate classes with over 40 pupils and close failing primaries.[307] The real problem, however, was in the voluntary, overwhelmingly Roman Catholic, sector. While one in 16 protestant primary school children went on to university, only one in 40 catholics did so. This could be explained by the lower socio-economic profile of catholics, but also the strains on the catholic school sector, which were certainly over-crowded, and arguably suffered from the impact of church control of teaching and management. A major problem in the catholic school sector was the lack of grammar schools. There were few catholic grammar schools for boys, none at all in Lurgan, Lisburn, Portadown, Bangor or Ballymena. Thus there were 1300 more girls in catholic grammars than boys.[308]

In 1966 the Roman Catholic Church applied for permission to establish a grammar school in Dundonald. Applications for Ballymena, Coleraine and Portadown were to follow. As the 1964 White Paper had envisaged the phasing out of grammars, however, the Minister of Education, William Fitzsimmons, was adamant that only new intermediaries should be permitted.[309] The Prime Minister was worried that 'refusal of consent would ... be characterized as discriminatory, and used to Northern Ireland's disadvantage at Westminster and elsewhere'.[310] O'Neill dealt with the problem by replacing Fitzsimmons with Captain Long as Minister of Education, who was happy to permit the grammar school to be built, as long as it gave assurances that it would turn intermediate if the entire state system did so.[311]

Inadequate finance, however, was the central problem for the catholic school system. Schemes were offered in which Local Education Authorities (LEAs) nominated two of every six on the school's management board ('four-and-two schools') in return for the state paying all heating, lighting, cleaning, maintenance and teachers' national insurance, and 65 per cent of building costs. Catholic suspicion of the sectarian intentions of local government, however, meant that only protestant voluntary schools took up the scheme. Catholic voluntary schools therefore received only a 75 per cent grant towards running costs, though the full 65 per cent for buildings. Teachers' pay was fully funded by the state.[312] Of 658 purely voluntary schools, 640 were catholic and only 18 protestant. Of 59 four-and-two schools (all of which were primary) 51 were protestant and only eight catholic.[313]

The Unionists made incessant propaganda use of segregated education. The *News Letter* in February 1966 remarked that 'the root causes of bigotry ... [is] Roman Catholic insistence on control of their own schools.'[314] Unionists were keen to occupy the moral high ground of secular rationalism and blame the Roman Catholic Church for perpetuating sectarian division. In reality, however, unionists were not enthusiastic about catholic schools accepting even the four-and-two system on the grounds of cost. Indeed, the Unionist inclination was towards cutting catholic voluntary schools adrift altogether.[315] The prospect of increased aid for voluntary schools in Britain, however, forced a re-think by Stormont.[316] O'Neill was clear that not to follow suit would be seen as 'discriminatory'. Led by Faulkner, his colleagues insisted that strings be attached as a 'first step towards breaking clerical control.'[317]

In October 1967 the government published a White Paper which proposed that voluntary schools outside the grammar school sector become 'maintained' schools, receiving 80 per cent building grants, up from 65 per cent. The government, too, would undertake to pay equipment and running costs. In return the management committee of maintained schools would be one third nominated by the LEA. Administration of the public funds, however, would be the sole responsibility of the LEA. Existing schools would not be required to join the system, but new voluntary schools would.[318] The catholic hierarchy at first reacted negatively, but evidence from the laity of widespread enthusiasm for a compromise soon forced a softening of their line.[319] The Unionist backbench 66 Committee backed the White Paper, though with only six MPs at the meeting.[320]

The biggest difficulty for catholics was the perceived sectarianism of the LEAs, on which sat few from their community. The ban on new voluntary schools also raised the prospect of a future general attack on catholic education through a unilaterally imposed change in the balance of school management committees.[321] Late in November, the White Paper was debated in Stormont. Robert Nixon, Unionist MP for North Down, during the debate effectively backed the Roman Catholic Church and, to the loud cheers of the opposition, called on the ministry to displace the LEAs entirely.[322] Phelim O'Neill (North Antrim) and Robert Porter (Queen's) also called for government flexibility.[323]

In the 1967 Queen's Speech, O'Neill attempted to reassure the hierarchy on what Cardinal Conway had identified as their greatest fear – the eventual forced integration of catholic schools:[324]

> It is no part of our philosophy to try to compress the whole of education into a single uniform mould whatever the views of those vitally interested – the parents. So I wish to make it very clear that although I regret some of these divisions and feel bound to point out their adverse effects as I see them, I recognize that they are an established fact which is unlikely to change in the foreseeable future. Nor will there be any pressure to compel or coerce those involved to bring about such a change.[325]

Renewed talks between the church and the ministry failed, however, and all suggestions submitted by the hierarchy were rejected.[326] The government was determined to stand by the integrity of local government against accusations of sectarian bias. It was prepared to forgo a fairly painless compromise, in which LEA representation would be replaced or diluted by ministry appointees, rather than hand the civil rights propagandists such a moral victory. All opposition amendments were therefore rejected, provoking the Unionist Robert Porter (Queen's) to accuse the government of letting 'common sense go by the board'. Phelim O'Neill (Mid-Antrim) even joined the opposition in voting for one amendment.[327] The Education Act was passed and was due to come into force on 1 April 1969.[328]

Behind closed doors, however, a less emotive solution was hammered out. On 24 May 1968 Captain Long told the Commons of a new deal based upon discussions between the hierarchy and the LEAs since March. In a detailed model agreement the LEA would provide equipment and pay for ancillary staff, but the four-and-two management committees would have rights of consultation and the authority to put in requests. The management committee would, of course, retain complete control of teaching appointments. These agreements were not binding, but would be backed by the ministry. The Roman Catholic bishops agreed to give the system a 'fair trial'.[329]

The Mater and education questions indicate that, even after 1966, O'Neill was pushing ahead with reform and meeting catholic grievances halfway. His achievements were real but have rarely counted in his favour, probably because, in reinforcing segregation, they went quite against liberal understandings of progress.[330] Nevertheless, they were recognizing contemporary social reality and dealt fairly with the minority. The difficulties O'Neill faced in pushing them by his own party and Cabinet were substantial. Progress, thus, was slow and, by necessity, little heralded. Any positive impact they might have had on community relations was thereby seriously diffused.

Such reform at a snail's pace attracted little attention; 1967 and 1968 were dominated by an intense political struggle over discrimination and civil rights. Civil rights activists powerfully urged the case for reform and British intervention. Unionists desperately battled to stem the tide. British public and political opinion were the increasingly discomfited spectators to the struggle. Gerry Fitt, elected to Westminster for West Belfast in April 1966, was immeasurably important in bringing the matter before a British audience. Breaking the convention that his maiden speech treat only of uncontroversial topics, Fitt lambasted discrimination in Northern Ireland and demanded British intervention.[331] Unionists were outraged. There was good cause for their concern. British ministers were reported as sympathetic to the CDU and sceptical about the rate of reform.[332]

The influence of the CDU called for a sustained Unionist counter-offensive. At the annual meeting of the Ulster Unionist Council Terence O'Neill launched a direct counter-blast to the CDU: his Campaign for Truth About Ulster.[333] There is little evidence of life in this rather crude riposte. The Unionist Party was weakened by a chronic shortage of funds.[334] Resolutions to the annual conference called for a Press Relations Officer to be appointed. James Chichester-Clark, replying for the leadership, protested that funds simply did not exist for a PRO. His appeal for the institution of a 'Defence of Ulster Fund' fell on deaf ears.[335]

On 15 April 1967 Stan Orme, Paul Rose and Dr Maurice Miller, three CDU MPs, visited Northern Ireland as Fitt's guests on a two-day fact finding tour.[336] The exercise drew forth contempt from the Unionists. Behind the sarcasm was an incredulous rage at the interference of know-nothing British wreckers, and a touch of despair at a propaganda battle being lost.[337] Unionists were convinced that Labour's interest in alleged malpractices in Ulster was in revenge for the NILP's trouncing in 1966 and a crude appeal to Irish immigrants in British constituencies.[338]

In his speech to the 1967 party conference, Terence O'Neill specifically replied to CDU allegations as part of his Truth About Ulster campaign. Critics should have 'the humility to appreciate that we in Northern Ireland live in a complex social and historical setting and can best be left to work out our own social problems for ourselves.'[339] This speech was the most sustained and detailed rebuttal of civil rights allegations from a Unionist leader. Its principal thrust, however, was to accuse civil rights propagandists of threatening improved community relations.

Much of the unwelcome attention focused on Northern Ireland in Westminster was due to the assiduous lobbying of Gerry Fitt. He had made many friends with Westminster backbenchers and ministers alike and was widely considered the most effective non-Unionist MP ever to be sent from Northern Ireland. Whilst he was careful to appear moderate and socialist rather than republican in Westminster, he was prone to express himself more forthrightly to home audiences.[340] In a rally organized by the Connolly Association in Trafalgar Square he warned that unless there was reform the day could 'arise when Irishmen would find it necessary to shoot brother-Irishmen.'[341] The Unionists were more than happy to expose Fitt as an extremist. O'Neill asked an Orange meeting in Cloughmills:

> What do these words mean? They seem to mean that if Mr Fitt and his friends cannot achieve their ends by constitutional methods they will use non-constitutional methods, not excluding the gun. That is a very grave suggestion. ... I am still waiting for Mr Paul Rose and his colleagues who are so interested in 'democracy in Ulster' to tell us their views about this apparent flirtation with the gun as a political weapon.[342]

Robin Chichester-Clark gleefully claimed that amongst his ex-allies at Westminster Fitt had been rumbled 'for the political bigot that he is.'[343] The Ulster Unionist Council circulated British Labour MPs with a copy of the Trafalgar speech.[344]

By the autumn of 1967 it appeared unionism had weathered the storm. The level of interest in the civil rights question had subsided considerably. In the CSJ's newsletter, Mrs Patricia McCluskey bemoaned Britain's trust in O'Neill.[345] The Unionists believed they had at last got the measure of Fitt.[346] Unionists saw both a threat and a tempting target in the civil rights radicals. Terence O'Neill differentiated the firebrands such as Fitt and Austin Currie from moderate nationalists in the mould of Eddie McAteer.[347] Many unionists saw the civil rights issue as the desperate last fling of a decaying Irish nationalism.[348]

O'Neill's appointment of William Craig to Home Affairs, ironically to quench one rebellion, added much fuel to the smouldering fire of the next. The wrong man for the post, Craig quickly became a lightening rod for catholic frustration and discontent.

Craig signalled from the outset that he intended to be a 'hard' Minister of Home Affairs.[349] His penchant for slip-ups did not desert him in his new post. Answering a question from Harry Diamond on catholic under-representation in the higher levels of the legal profession, he explained that 'No doubt there were social and educational reasons for this proportion.'[350] Naturally there was nationalist outrage at this slur on catholic professionalism and the Bar Council 'deplored' Craig's remark.[351] At first Craig refused to retract his statement, but facing a censure motion he apologized in the House.[352] Craig appears to have been prone to emotional instability and he was 'visibly moved' as he read his statement. When he sat down his colleague, William Long, put a consoling arm around the stricken minister.[353]

In March 1967 Stormont was put in uproar when, closing a debate on a opposition bill for a Northern Ireland ombudsman, Craig observed that: 'As a minister I am all too conscious of attempts by members to try and blackmail me into a course of action, based on friendship rather than the merits of the case. Honourable Members on both sides of the House know this to be true. You are guilty of it on the basis of the old pals' act.'[354] Whilst no doubt an admission with much truth to it, this was an impolitic accusation to throw so glibly at opposition MPs. An amused Austin Currie, Nationalist MP for East Tyrone, called out: 'You're in trouble again, boy.'[355] Vivian Simpson of the NILP stormed from the House. Eddie McAteer implied that the minister was speaking while drunk and called for his dismissal.[356] Yet again, Craig the following day was forced to apologize for the offence he had caused.[357] Four months later Craig was in hot water once more for comparing fraternal relations between the illegal UVF and some Orange lodges with the alliance of the Labour Party and trade unions.[358]

The year 1967 was the centenary of the Fenian rising and commemorations were planned in twelve centres.[359] Craig banned all but traditional Easter parades under the 1951 Public Order Act.[360] More

significantly he simultaneously banned the Republican Clubs organization as 'substantially the unlawful Sinn Fein organisation under
another label.'[361] This was a maladroit manoeuvre as the Clubs were
fairly broad based and peaceful.[362] Nor was the measure consistent.
The Republican Party, the cover name for Sinn Fein candidates in elections, was not proscribed although Republican Clubs were its
constituency associations.[363] The banning of a name – 'Republican
Club' – was both apparently repressive and difficult to enforce.

On 8 March 60 students met in Queen's University and established a
Republican Club in defiance of the order. As this Club was not connected
to the official republican movement, the idea was to highlight the
unfairness of banning an organization merely because of its name.
Indeed, according to Ciaran McKeown, the Student Union leader, there
were only about five Republicans in the university.[364] An *ad hoc* group,
made up of all campus political groups but the Unionists, organized a
march to the city hall and back. Placards and chants singled out Craig as
the principal culprit.[365] It was the first march of the civil rights era.

A similarly mismanaged prologue to the civil rights movement was the
banning, in April 1968, of a traditional republican parade in Armagh.
Though the route went through a wholly nationalist area, unsubstantiated threats from the Paisleyite Ulster Protestant Volunteers were
enough to persuade the acting Minister of Home Affairs, Captain Long,
to withdraw permission under the Public Order Act.[366] The march went
ahead nonetheless, with about 1000 participating and a heavy police
presence. In an early morning swoop the following day 12 members of
the organizing committee were arrested.[367] In protest several thousand
demonstrated the following Sunday.[368]

Speaking in Stormont on the ban, Eddie McAteer warned that should
government 'repression' continue 'there may well be a reaction which
all of us would deplore.'[369] Craig, however, unabashedly asserted that
the march was banned as much because it was politically offensive as
because of public order fears:

> as far as I am concerned ... it is not merely a matter of some group
> deciding to counter-demonstrate. ... Before a ban is placed upon
> such a procession one has got to decide whether or not there was a
> reasonable provocation.... . It is simply not judged on the basis of
> counter-demonstrations.[370]

The international wave of student and worker protest from Mexico to
France, Czechoslovakia to the USA, no doubt turned the attention of

activists to the strategy of direct action.[371] It is more accurate, however, to see this new turn as a response to the apparent bankruptcy of simple petitioning. The first landmark of the civil rights movement, appropriately, was organized in a spirit of frustrated outrage. On 18 June 1968 Austin Currie sent an urgent telegram to Terence O'Neill. He demanded the blocking, 'to prevent communal strife', of the allocation of a council house in Caledon to a 19-year-old female protestant, Miss Beatty, in preference to large catholic families on the waiting list. Instead, a catholic family of five, squatting next door, was violently evicted.[372] In Stormont John Taylor defended the allocation and dismissed objections as 'a political stunt from beginning to end ... a large number of Catholics in our community disapprove of it entirely.'[373] In a fury Currie stood at the bar of the House roaring 'It's all damned lies' and hurled his papers at the Unionist backbenches.[374] The next day Currie, with two others, squatted in Beatty's house.[375] After three hours Currie was escorted out by the RUC.[376] During a lengthy adjournment debate on the incident, during which Unionists gave no ground, Eddie McAteer wondered bitterly 'whether there is any bloody sense in our coming here at all.'[377] Only six months later did a Unionist publicly admit that the allocation had been 'stupid and indefensible'.[378]

Currie's action had shown the efficacy of direct action and the Nationalist Party's refusal to adopt similar methods left the way open for fringe civil rights groups. The CSJ and CDU, prominent up until now, were propagandist rather than activist organizations. For some time, however, the Republican movement had seen the potential for a civil rights campaign. In a November 1966 article in *Tuairisc*, produced by the Dublin Wolfe Tone Society, Thomas McGiolla, Sinn Fein president, proposed 'the establishment of civil rights committees in Northern Ireland'.[379] Rather than attempt to establish a mere front organization, however, Republicans encouraged the cohering of a genuine broad alliance. On 30 March 1966 a conference of over 80 representatives at the International Hotel in Belfast set up the Northern Ireland Civil Rights Association (NICRA), a 'non-political pressure group modelled on the National Council for Civil Liberties.' All political parties were represented, including Senator Nelson Elder for the Unionists.[380] Robin Cole, a member of the Queen's University Unionist Association, was quickly co-opted onto the committee.[381]

At first NICRA maintained a fairly low profile and, taking up the work of the CSJ, concentrated on producing evidence of abuses.[382] In March 1968 Robin Cole resigned from the body in protest against a speech delivered by the former chairman, Derek Peters, at NICRA's annual meeting. Comparing the Special Powers Act to South African repressive legislation, Cole believed, 'was unwarranted and unjustified … a deplorable return to a sophisticated form of gable wall politics.'[383] In August 1968 NICRA, inspired by Currie's sit-in, decided upon an American-style civil rights march from Coalisland to Dungannon.[384]

Two months previously, in defence of his ban on the Republican Clubs, Bill Craig in Stormont quoted at length a captured IRA policy document in which a policy of agitation over civil rights leading to armed insurgency was outlined.[385] In a speech in July he observed that known nationalist and republican cadres were participating in civil rights agitation. This was precisely the action envisaged by the IRA. He threatened firm measures: 'It is time the Nationalist people realised that if they do not accept the democratically elected Government of Northern Ireland, they cannot expect much consideration or generosity from those who do believe in it.'[386] Based upon probably accurate intelligence reports of republican infiltration of the civil rights movement, but lacking the empathy and imagination to divine the ground swell of genuine mass catholic outrage beneath it, Craig perceived a plot rather than a genuine movement of the minority. His response as Home Secretary would be one of repression rather than conciliation.

In Derry Gerry Fitt announced that all that could be done in Stormont and Westminster had been done: 'The days for talking have long since gone. The time for action has arrived. … If constitutional methods do not bring social justice – if they do not bring democracy to the North then I am quite prepared to go outside constitutional methods.'[387] A civil rights march from Coalisland to Dungannon was planned. The RUC barred the procession from Dungannon's town centre to avoid clashing with a Paisleyite counter-demonstration.[388] To the annoyance of elements of the 1500 strong crowd, the march leaders stopped at police lines where a sit-down protest took place. About 1000 counter-demonstrators sang 'The Sash' and 'Derry's Walls'.[389]

The speeches of Gerry Fitt and Austin Currie had been particularly hard hitting and anti-partitionist. Wilf Blackwood, a Liberal participant, reported that when the chairman had asked for the crowd to sing 'We shall overcome', a section had broken into 'A Soldier's Song': 'Many people joined in with great fervour. I feel that no further comment is required.'[390] For many unionists, the civil rights demonstrations from the outset bore the mark of Cain as an essentially nationalist movement.[391]

Derry next became the focus for agitation. The city had suffered an appalling economic and psychological blow in 1967 when the BSR factories closed. Unemployment had soared to 20.1 per cent. Though about a third of Industrial Development grants were channelled to the area in the late 1960s, and unemployment was halved again, the impression that Derry was being excluded from progress because of its catholic majority was not diminished.[392] Most observers thought the Derry people resigned and listless.[393] With an active and capable catholic leadership, however, the city was in reality ripe for revolt. On 27 August leftist activists in Derry – principally Eamon McCann – announced that they had invited NICRA to organize a march there. Their 'conscious, if unspoken, strategy was to provoke the police into over-reaction and thus spark off mass reaction against the authorities.'[394]

At the last minute the Apprentice Boys announced a parade along part of the same route to bring members of the Liverpool branch of the Murray Club into the city centre for an initiation ceremony.[395] This was claimed as a traditional procession, but senior Apprentice Boy sources admitted that normally initiates were ferried in by car. Nevertheless, Craig had his excuse to re-route the march outside the city centre, effectively keeping it corralled in the catholic quarter. His rationale was starkly partisan:

> The Apprentice Boys parade was an additional complication, but the Northern Ireland Civil Rights Association, despite its high-sounding name, is essentially a Republican Nationalist organisation. Quite contrary to normal practice, they proposed to move into an area which, by tradition, it has long been agreed they don't move into. ... there is no doubt that whether the Apprentice Boys were marching or not, we would have had to look at the public order aspect of a proposal that a nationalist element should go somewhere which would provoke extreme annoyance. ... The civil rights marchers will have plenty of room elsewhere. If they want to hold meetings it would be proper for them to have them in their own quarter.[396]

The Derry radicals announced that the ban would be defied.

The Derry march, of course, was attacked by the RUC and developed into two nights of rioting.[397] The 'hooligans' or 'street-fighters' as they were variously known, destined to drive catholic politics until at least 1970, had made their appearance. RUC brutality was exposed to the world's television and press.[398] But though the issues at stake seemed clear-cut in Britain, years of agitation and disputation had muddied the waters in Northern Ireland. Particularly from the end of 1966 the civil rights question had become thoroughly politicized and symbolic of the legitimacy or otherwise of the state. Faulkner argued:

> The phrase 'civil rights' has a positive, humanitarian ring about it. But when we plumb deeper we find that underneath this gloss is the same old Republicanism we know so well. The real objective behind this sort of exercise is to undermine, as much as possible, Ulster's constitutional position, by bringing the name of Northern Ireland into disrepute outside our borders.[399]

On the eve of the civil rights campaign about three-quarters of protestants felt there was no significant discrimination while three-quarters of catholics felt there was, though only a minority claimed any personal experience.[400] Contrary to British impressions, civil rights concerned less material grievances than communal attitudes toward the even-handedness, and implicitly the legitimacy, of the state. From the outset, it was a profoundly politicized and dangerously polarizing slogan. State violence, bestowed with partiality, ignited the conflagration.

7
Crossroads

Terence O'Neill was in Nottingham for an Ulster Week when news of the riots in Derry broke. At an impromptu press conference he was strangely fatalistic.[1] Such was the authentic, unscripted voice of O'Neill until his resignation in May 1969. Though he fought trenchantly to oppose the right wing of his party and maintain liberal standards in the face of deteriorating public order, O'Neill seemed resigned to the ultimate failure of his project from the outset.[2] Only constant urgings from British Ministers and his civil service cabal prevented his early retirement.[3]

While O'Neill tepidly backed his Minister of Home Affairs and the dubious conduct of the RUC, Craig was brazen in his own defence. Given the world-wide media coverage of RUC brutality, his unyielding posture, though appealing to unionists, was contemptible to virtually all others.[4] Support for Craig flooded in from the unionist rank and file.[5]

The Northern Ireland Civil Rights Association, meanwhile, had received invitations to organize further demonstrations in Armagh, Lurgan, Enniskillen, Newry, Dungannon and, again, Derry.[6] On 9 October, 1000 Queen's students staged a sit-down in Linen Hall Street, Belfast, after being barred from the City Hall area on the pretext of a Paisleyite counter demonstration.[7] The civil rights movement developed a tremendous forward momentum. For years Irish nationalism had been a declining, archaic force. Unionism, under O'Neill, had seized the mantle of modernism, liberalism and progressiveness. Catholics felt their old certitudes disintegrating and feared a loss of identity. Ironically, O'Neillism, which attempted to absorb them into a uniform, essentially unionist body politic, was much more corrosive to catholic communal self-respect that the hard-nosed repressiveness of old-style unionism. The catholic community, in many respects,

161

preferred to be feared and hated than to be patronized and dismissed.[8] The civil rights movement came as a festival of liberation and vengeance for the minority. A founder of the NDP triumphantly forsook conciliationism in favour of 'the extreme wing – the only position which is now defensible.'[9]

Suddenly catholics were vindicated in the eyes of the world, seeking modern rights against a Neanderthal, sectarian Unionist Party. Every dignified civil rights demonstration outraged unionist opinion, and catholics delighted in seeing their frustration. The civil rights movement, in the self-validation it afforded the minority, was much more than the sum of relatively minor civil rights reforms it demanded. It was a continuation, and intensification, of the communal struggle for the moral advantage. The sacrifice of a tangible if slow advance in community relations over the O'Neill years was a price considered well-worth paying.[10] As so often in Irish history, the lure of an heroic rising driven by a need to reinforce the traditions and identity of a beleaguered ethnicity outweighed 'rational' cost benefit evaluations of political strategies.[11]

John Taylor admitted that Unionists were being 'outdebated' by the civil rights propagandists: 'No one ... could close their eyes to the fact that only three Northern Ireland Cabinet members had contributed to the main political debate during the past three years.'[12] Assuming these to be O'Neill, Faulkner and Craig, this statement was incontestable. Suddenly in the full glare of world media scrutiny, the Unionists found themselves with few articulate defenders or developed and popular arguments.

In Stormont Terence O'Neill shied away from party political or controversial points and called for 'an interval of restraint in word and action'. Further disorder would inevitably mean 'on both sides a retreat into traditional attitudes and the slender bridges men of good-will have tried to build will tumble into a chasm. If these bridges should fall many years will pass before they could be built again.' Pointing to a recent poll, he insisted that the first concern of both protestant and catholic was not spurious deficiencies in civil rights, but material conditions:

> Here are our young people asking us for bread – for the houses, a decent prosperous life – and are we to offer them instead the stone of discord? For unless the province rapidly returns to sanity future progress is gravely at risk. I call above all for peace. The place for political argument is Parliament, not in the streets. Disorder is the way not to equal rights but an equal share of misery and despair.[13]

In a speech lengthily discussed by Glengall Street in advance, and intended to test protestant public opinion,[14] Roy Bradford, government Chief Whip, urged immediate action 'to clear our name of any allegations of injustice.' He regretted

> [t]he linking together, the lumping together of two separate and distinct issues – the social grievance which is real and largely affecting Catholics, and the political demand for changes in the franchize which has been largely whipped up and manufactured for party purposes.

Reform in social policy – an acceleration of the housing programme for example – should be prioritized. Universal suffrage in local government should await the planned overall review.[15]

Much Unionist ire attached itself to the media, as they saw themselves being out manoeuvred in the public image stakes.[16] Six resolutions submitted for the 1969 Unionist annual conference were concerned with improving party publicity.[17] Robin Chichester-Clark (Londonderry) and Stanley McMaster (East Belfast), Unionist MPs at Westminster, sent a telegram to the BBC complaining of bias in its reporting.[18] Bill Craig even implied censorship might be necessary.[19] The real problem, however, was the Unionists' own inarticulateness.[20] When Captain Orr praised the RUC as 'probably the finest and best police force in the world' Harold Wilson tartly replied: 'Up to now perhaps we have had to rely on the statements of himself and others on these matters, but since then we have had British television.'[21]

Immediately after the events of 5 October, O'Neill had warned his Cabinet that the line could not be held by repression alone and reforms were inevitable.[22] Pressure from Britain, he insisted, would now be irresistible. *Ad hoc* financial arrangements with the British exchequer meant that 'Her Majesty's Government do not have to do anything openly spectacular to make us feel the pinch; they merely have to be unwilling in the future to do any more exceptional things for us.' In a sharp reversal of Unionist self-deception he rhetorically asked his colleagues 'can any of us truthfully say in the confines of this room that the minority have no grievance calling for a remedy?' Hard-line resistance, the instinctive response of the unionist rank and file, would condemn them to 'govern[ing] Ulster by police power alone'. To preserve the partition settlement from interference from a vengeful Britain required immediate concessions: 'we may even in time have to make a bitter choice between losing Londonderry and losing Ulster.'[23] With this powerful and realistic statement O'Neill confronted his Cabinet as he had never attempted before. Yet this was not followed up with concrete proposals. Instead, he attempted to win his colleagues around merely to the principle of reform. Acutely aware of Faulkner's knee-jerk opposition to every proposal put by the Prime Minister, O'Neill left it to other ministers actually to propose specific options for reform.

Both Fulkner and Craig presented themselves as 'strong liberals' and spoke strongly against making concessions under 'duress'.[24] Whilst Faulkner, for example, on 15 October admitted that he had 'no dogmatic views on the franchize', his principal concern was to preserve the image of a 'strong government'.[25] It was to take a whole series of Cabinet meetings, plus pressure from Wilson, for O'Neill to break this resistance down

O'Neill, Faulkner and Craig met with Harold Wilson on 4 November. O'Neill had hoped to go armed with a programme of reform, but Faulkner, arguing that it would be wrong 'to give the impression of a concession wrung out of the Government by violence', successfully blocked this.[26] Not surprisingly, the meeting proved a roasting for the Stormont delegation. Wilson confirmed O'Neill's prognosis that pressure would be applied not through a constitutional stand-off but the squeezing of 'discretionary' subventions. There was a nuclear option however: were O'Neill to be ousted by hard-liners London 'would feel compelled to propose a radical course involving the complete liquidation of all financial arrangements with Northern Ireland'.[27]

The British Ministers pressed for universal suffrage in local government, a points system for the allocation of housing, an investigation into the events in Derry, abandonment of the Special Powers Act and the appointment of a parliamentary commissioner for administration (Ombudsman) in Northern Ireland. Prolonged delay would not be acceptable. O'Neill salved with honeyed words while Faulkner and Craig blustered, but with no positive proposals their hand was weak.[28]

The Stormont Cabinet were impressed by this dressing down, and O'Neill made bold enough to remind his colleagues that 'the maintenance of the overall constitutional position depended upon control at Stormont and not upon the control of certain local authorities in ways which were often difficult to justify'. Faulkner and Craig continued to balk at 'dictation as to how Northern Ireland should be governed'. O'Neill reacted heatedly and was backed by Roy Bradford who added that the 'Unionist Party existed to defend the Union, not to defy the British Government.'[29] The log-jam was finally broken by a typically indirect O'Neill's manoeuvre. A package of proposals was laid before the Cabinet by James Chichester-Clarke, but almost certainly at O'Neill's bidding.[30] Options considered and subsequently abandoned included an independent commission on the Derry disturbances, a speedy concession of government aid to the Mater, and an election or referendum on the issue of local government franchize. Faulkner's absence from two breakthrough Cabinet meetings undoubtedly facilitated progress.

The issue of 'one man one vote' in local government elections had emerged as the crunch issue for the entire Unionist Party. Just over half the backbenchers were adamant that no concession on the matter was permissible.[31] John Brooke expressed the talismanic significance of local government franchize: 'I would resist it to the very end. Not necessarily because of the franchize, but because it could lead to interference on a much wider scale.'[32] Nevertheless, the heart of the Unionist opposition lay in the fear that franchize reform would mean losing control to catholics and nationalists in certain areas. Members from the sensitive area west of the Bann, especially, were hostile to change. Not only would concessions immediately lose votes but, equally worrying in the longer term, the uncoupling of franchize from wealth would destroy the justification for gerrymandering.

Despite urgings from O'Neill the Cabinet refused to grasp the nettle of 'one man one vote'.[33] It informed Harold Wilson that immediate franchize reform was 'not possible in political terms ... [nor] acceptable to our Parliamentary Party or to the country'.[34] The government position remained that the matter would not be considered until the whole structure of local government had been reviewed – a process now expected to be completed by 1971.

Clandestine meetings of 'loyalists' were communicating to the government the rank and file's resistance to reform under pressure. In Craig they saw a champion in the Cabinet.[35] It was becoming clear, however, that the policy of repression he favoured was not viable. His attempt to ban all demonstrations in Derry collapsed on 16 November when 2000 staged a sit-down protest in the Diamond. This was only the first of a series of such incursions; 800 female factory workers and 200 dockers followed suit in the days following.[36] The Derry Citizens Action Committee was soon forced to attempt to stem a flood of unofficial and spontaneous demonstrations flouting Craig's prohibition with impunity.[37] The RUC secretly admitted that it was 'logistically impossible' to maintain the ban.[38] Under the glare of international publicity, the RUC felt unable to apply bare repression.[39] The Home

Minister's policy of coercion had humiliatingly failed. The imposition of a draconian but unenforceable order served only to bring lawful authority into contempt.[40]

On 21 November the Cabinet, after being in almost continual session for days, and no less than 15 fraught meetings, finally agreed a reform package.[41] O'Neill was clear-sighted about its chances of success. He

> congratulated his colleagues on the progress which had been made ... in the direction of reform but wondered whether the package, positive and concrete as it was, would be sufficient, in the absence of a commitment to alter the local government franchize, to satisfy the United Kingdom or to restrain the Civil Rights marchers.[42]

This was presented on 22 November to the Parliamentary Unionist Party, where it was bluntly questioned.[43] After four and a half hours, however, it was unanimously accepted. The five-point package was then unveiled in a three-page document.

The government rejected the truth or gravity of accusations levelled against it. It declared itself, however, determined to 'deal with any valid criticisms of administration, however marginal such criticisms may be'. A points system for housing allocations was to be adopted and an ombudsman appointed. Derry Corporation would be suspended and replaced by a commission, ostensibly to administer the Derry Area Plan along the same lines as the Craigavon Commission, but in reality to overcome objections to Unionist control of the Corporation through gerrymandering. The local government franchize would be examined after the review process was completed in late 1971. It was implied that one man one vote would be forthcoming, but in the context of a reformed rates system which would allow a continuing link between rateable values and constituency boundaries. Company votes would be abolished sooner. Finally, there would be discussions with the British government on withdrawing aspects of the Special Powers Act as soon as it could be done 'without undue hazard.' The government ended with a call 'for the support of all moderate-minded men and women, whatever their religious or political beliefs.'[44]

This was a significant but limited programme, the concessions of a points system and an ombudsman being the only U-turns.[45] Initially the civil rights movement was unimpressed. Like right-wing unionists, they had made a fetish of the local government franchize. The Derry

Citizens' Action Committee declared its determination to 'continue the struggle' until one man one vote was conceded.[46] NICRA rejected the five points as 'disappointing' and 'a surrender to the right wing of the Government party'.[47] Eddie McAteer was more sympathetic, acknowledging that 'after the flurry of political activity during the past few days ... any immediate move in this direction would have split the Unionist Party completely and precipitated a leadership crisis which Captain O'Neill could not have survived.'[48]

Bill Craig, in a press conference after the document's publication, immediately moved to put a strongly negative spin on its contents. It was up to him, as Minister of Home Affairs, to determine when the SPA could be safely changed. Until then 'there is no change whatsoever. We continue as before.' He later defended the ombudsman reform as a method of exposing false discrimination claims.[49] The Grand Orange Lodge of Ireland, in its first statement on the crisis, expressed concern at the influence of British pressure. It also explicitly demanded Craig's retention as Home Affairs Minister in response to a strong rumour that O'Neill intended to fire him.[50] The Unionist right bayed for repression now that the protest movement, it believed, had been deprived of legitimacy.[51] Such grudging attitudes only soured catholic opinion further. It seemed that the initiative had failed.

The situation deteriorated further with the Paisleyite occupation of Armagh. In reaction to a planned civil rights march, leaflets were distributed calling on 'every loyalist in Ulster' to assemble in Armagh 'to take control of the city'.[52] A thousand Paisleyites, egged on by another 2000, blocked Market Square on 30 November and refused police instructions to disperse. Many carried clubs and sticks and wore crash helmets. The 8000 civil rights marchers were thus stopped from entering the city centre for their planned rally.[53] As night fell, sporadic fighting broke out and 28 RUC and 12 civilians were injured. The government began to doubt the RUC's ability to contain the situation; one senior police officer warned that Northern Ireland stood at the brink of 'civil war'.[54] Civil rights opinion was outraged; NICRA planned a new series of marches and rallies.[55]

Craig's pandering to the right was making him increasingly unacceptable as a Minister of Home Affairs to the minority community. On 27 November he delivered a controversial speech in the Ulster Hall to a rally in support of the West Belfast Unionist candidate, Brian McRoberts. There was a fact some people were scared to talk about, he said, and that was 'the difference between our concept of democracy and that of a Roman Catholic country. ... Where you had a Roman

Catholic majority you had a lower standard of democracy.' He strongly implied that Northern Ireland should not consider itself dependent on Great Britain:

> If anything happened between us and Britain it would not follow that we would unite with the Irish Republic. ... Those affairs that are within our control will be controlled by us. Any interference will be met by a greater resolve that we have here tonight.'[56]

Such sentiments were not unusual in unionist ranks, even amongst those of an assimilatory bent. The baldness with which they were put, however, was considered unwise by unionist moderates. The speech certainly outraged catholic opinion, though perhaps causing little surprise. Of more concern to Terence O'Neill, was Craig's *obiter dicta* on relations with Britain. This was dangerous precisely because it threatened to chime with a substantial section of unionist opinion. Quite obviously the party was unhappy with the idea of Britain interfering with Northern Ireland's domestic affairs, relations with the republic of Ireland, or constitutional status.

Bill Craig had been for years outspoken on the need for and right of Northern Ireland to exercise autonomy. As early as 1964, he made a speech denying Northern Ireland's dependence on British money. O'Neill, without naming him, repudiated the suggestion.[57] In March 1967, reacting to rumours that Britain would apply financial pressure to force the pace of reform, Craig insisted that Stormont was sovereign on all transferred matters. He addressed section 75 of the 1920 Government of Ireland Act:

> It is not a section subtracting from or entitling any interference with the Parliament or Government of Northern Ireland. Let me sound a note of warning: that Ulster will fight and Ulster will be right, and that this sort of attack and interference would mobilize Ulster loyalists in the same way as attacks by bomb and bullet. ... Any suggestion to override a democratically elected Parliament in the name of democracy is the absurdity of all absurdities.[58]

Craig's conception of Northern Ireland's relationship was not merely defensive, but increasingly visionary. He proposed 'a federal system of government throughout the UK leaving only the big broad matters of foreign affairs and overall economics in central Parliament and Government.'[59] Early in 1969 he prepared a speech outlining his support for a devolution of powers along the lines of the West German federal system, incorporating the German mechanism for equalizing tax and expenditure between rich and poor areas. Only after consultation with O'Neill did he agree to water this down.[60]

The crisis from 5 October 1968 massively enlarged unionist fears of British intervention. Robin Bailie, Unionist candidate for Newtownabbey, deplored the developing 'UDI' tendency in the party.[61] Both Faulkner and Craig pandered to it.[62] In his first major speech since the crisis broke, delivered to the liberal Unionist Society, Terence O'Neill called for 'an end to talk about the United Kingdom as if it were some sort of hostile power. ... This is the great nation which has underwritten our march to progress over nearly half a century.' He emphasized that there was no political support in Britain for a reversal of the direction taken by the government since 1963.

> We cannot maintain Northern Ireland in a vacuum. We must in practice be part of the United Kingdom or part of the Irish Republic. Let us never forget that in rejecting the second course we necessarily adopted the first.[63]

O'Neill's first major speech since the Derry events, therefore, was not directed to the civil rights movement, but to the incipient opposition within his own party. The unionist attitude to Britain, not to the catholic minority, was the burning issue of the day.

Craig had reason to feel frustrated in his debate with O'Neill. 'I find it hard to excuse the Prime Minister,' he later complained, 'for he himself argued for a form of federal government in exactly the same terms I have used.'[64] Indeed, to British audiences in particular, Terence O'Neill was expansive on the potentials for constitutional innovation. He predicted

> ... regional parliaments all over Britain having a federal relationship with Westminster. When that is established I think it is possible that the South of Ireland Parliament will have an association with this federation. Maybe it will be a different kind of association from that enjoyed by the parliaments for the north east and north west but nevertheless the kind of association that would mean the British Isles becoming the British Isles again.[65]

It seems likely that O'Neill had such potentials in mind when he met with Lemass and Lynch. As so often, however, Craig enthusiastically seized an idea cautiously floated by O'Neill, and swung it about his head with passion and fury. O'Neill believed devolution all-round in the United Kingdom was sensible, but argued that the grand dominion-style titles and forms granted to Stormont only created a false image of Ulster sovereignty.[66] His model for devolution and, indeed, general outlook was Canada: he identified himself as a 'Progressive Conservative in the Canadian sense.'[67] Craig's modernizing theories, in contrast, were always rooted in the little-Ulster patriotism of protestant loyalism. He lacked O'Neill's caution and finesse, though he prevailed in terms of excitement and demagoguery.

Support for Craig in the Unionist Party, therefore, represented an anti-British government current of considerable concern to Terence O'Neill. Despite his failure to maintain public order as Minister of Home Affairs, and the debacle of the Derry march ban, Craig's hard-line utterances against marchers and outside interference reassured much of the rank and file. Since 5 October nearly every Unionist Association had passed a resolution backing Craig personally.[68]

In Stormont, on 4 December, O'Neill finally expressed an opinion on Craig's notorious Ulster Hall speech. An honest assimilatory unionist, he rejected 'not so much the contents' as the timing. Less gently, however, he raised the great unspoken of the state of Bill Craig's mental health. 'The Minister has been living through a period of considerable strain,' he said, 'I have noticed him fairly tired lately. I think we must bear this in mind when we consider the tone of some of his remarks.'[69] For Craig, who was seated behind the Prime Minister throughout, it must have been a terrible humiliation.

In an open act of defiance Craig repeated his speech word for word to a meeting in Clogher, where he shared the platform with John Taylor.[70] Craig, in a flurry of press interviews, which made clear his hard-right credentials, was quite obviously canvassing for power. It was in this context that Terence O'Neill announced that he would broadcast to the province, at 6 p.m., simultaneously on both television channels.[71]

Terence O'Neill faced a crisis in his own party. Craig was almost directly challenging his leadership, evidently with the support of many right-wing MPs and Unionist Associations. The five-point programme, meanwhile, had failed to still civil rights marches and agitation. His authority as Prime Minister was being inexorably chipped away. Yet it was clear that a substantial body of opinion was impressed by the scope of reforms conceded and supported for a period of tranquillity to allow them to work. O'Neill now hoped to tap this support.

Terence O'Neill's famous 'Crossroads' speech addressed three audiences. He enlisted public opinion to bring pressure to bear on all the main political representatives, particularly his own party: 'The issues are far too serious to be determined behind closed doors or left to noisy minorities. The time has come for the people as a whole to speak with a clear voice.' He returned to this theme in his closing peroration:

What kind of Ulster do you want? A happy and respected province in good standing with the rest of the United Kingdom? Or a place continually torn apart by riots and demonstrations and regarded by the rest of Britain as a political outcast? ... Please weigh well what is at stake and make your voice heard in whatever way you think best so that we may know your views of not a few but of many.

This appeal for active support from the silent majority was undoubtedly conscious and deliberate. However, it was by far the briefest section of the broadcast. More substantial was an appeal to the civil rights marchers. Their leaders he characterized as 'a minority of agitators, determined to subvert lawful authority' but he conceded that 'grievances real or imagined, had been piling up for years.' The November reforms, he promised, were genuine:

Perhaps you are not entirely satisfied; but this is a democracy and I ask you now with all sincerity to call your people off the streets and allow an atmosphere favourable to change develop. ... Your voice has been heard and clearly heard. Your duty now is to play your part in taking the heat out of the situation before blood is shed.

His final audience was the Unionist Party itself and this, in a broadcast to the entire community, was the largest single section. He explained the reforms undertaken so far and the rationale behind them:

As I saw it, if we were not prepared to face up to our problems, we would have to face increasing pressure both internally and from those who were seeking change, and externally from British public and parliamentary opinion which had been deeply disturbed by the events in Londonderry.

He explicitly addressed the question of the relationship with Britain: 'I know full well that Britain's financial and other support for Ulster so laboriously built up could no longer be guaranteed if we failed to press on which such a programme.' Defiance, O'Neill warned, would put the economic benefits of the Union at stake. The British government could and, if need be, would impose reform over Stormont's head.

O'Neill then launched into an extraordinarily virulent attack on those unionists who considered distancing the North from Britain; or rather a caricature of such.

> There are, I know today, so called loyalists who talk of indepen-
> dence from Britain – who seem to want a Protestant Sinn Fein. ...
> These people are not merely extremists. They are lunatics who
> would set the course along the road which could only lead at the
> end into an all-Ireland republic.

He warned that Ulster stood on the brink of chaos and ruled out simple repression as a solution. Order could only be restored on the basis of a moderate majority: 'We must be able to say to the moderates on both sides: 'Come with us into a new era of co-operation and leave the extremists to the law.'[72] O'Neill, despite his fondness for the medium, was a poor television performer. But in the highly charged political atmosphere it was a broadcast 'of appalling delivery but considerable power.'[73]

This speech is remembered as a statesmanlike appeal to warring communities, indeed as virtually the final appeal to sanity before the descent into chaos. Looked at in context, however, it was apparent that the broadcast was a much more party political, indeed factional, tactic. O'Neill, faced by leadership challenges, had appealed to the bar of public opinion before. In 1965 he had outflanked his opponents through the public relations spectacular of meeting Lemass. In 1966 he had invoked the spectre of a rampant Paisleyism to tar the back-benchers ranged against him. Now O'Neill was appealing to the public to support him against the right wing of unionism. In a struggle for survival O'Neill could be extremely ruthless, and his depiction of an extremist UDI tendency hardly did justice to Bill Craig or even Tom Lyons. Yet the aim was obvious. O'Neill, contemptuous of the unionist rank and file, was prepared to gamble on a presidential appeal to the people through a media he had long nurtured and thought he understood.

There can be no denying that the response he received was massive. Crucially, the Derry Citizens Action Committee, in a gesture of good-will, called a truce on marches until 18 January 1969.[74] The *Belfast Telegraph* printed special coupons for readers to send to O'Neill in his support. Support in general was 'mainly representative of the business and professional community throughout Northern Ireland.' Many signatories were doctors, lawyers, bankers, clergy and those in local government.[75] According to J.O. Bailie there was a rush to join the Unionist Party – mainly business and professional types.[76] In total about 125,000 wrote to support O'Neill, 77,836 on *Belfast Telegraph* coupons and 47,000 directly to Stormont. More than half came from Belfast.[77] The equivalent in Britain would have been almost seven million.[78] Early in 1969 it was announced that the names would be sifted by Glengall Street to allow Unionist Associations to target them for recruitment.[79]

On 10 December Terence O'Neill, riding high on the reaction to his broadcast, seized his opportunity and called a Parliamentary Unionist Party meeting for two days hence.[80] The following day Craig, after he had delivered a particularly defiant speech,[81] was sacked by Terence O'Neill. The reason given was Craig's 'attraction to ideas of a UDI nature'.[82]

On 12 December the Parliamentary Unionist Party met. Faulkner spoke to strongly criticize O'Neill's broadcast on the grounds that the party had already endorsed the five-point reform package. To appeal to the public over the head of the party was uncalled for. O'Neill was relaxed, buoyed by the response to his broadcast, and anxious to confront his opponents from a position of strength. At the end of a four- and-a-half-hour meeting, MPs were required to vote on a resolution personally endorsing O'Neill as 'leader of the Party and Prime Minister of Northern Ireland'. A second resolution repudiated any suggestion of UDI. Harry West (Enniskillen), Johnny McQuade (Woodvale), Desmond Boal (Shankill) and William Hinds (Willowfield) abstained on the first resolution, with John Brooke (Lisnaskea) reluctantly supporting it at the last minute. Other doubtfuls were John Dobson (West Down), John Taylor (South Tyrone), Albert Anderson (Londonderry) and Austin Ardill (Carrick). Craig left without voting. In all, 28 supported O'Neill. The split at Unionist Association level, however, was believed to be much wider.[83]

O'Neill, it seemed, had pulled off an enormously successful stroke, having stilled both dissent in unionist ranks and the civil rights agitation.[84] Rejoicing, however, was premature. Behind the broad support for O'Neill's moderation, even middle-class opinion was dangerously ambiguous.[85] Outside events could still shake unionist confidence in O'Neill's recipe for order. In the run up to O'Neill's broadcast, Alf McCreary of the *Belfast Telegraph* had sampled rank and file unionist opinion across Northern Ireland. He found them outraged by the breakdown in law enforcement and convinced that the civil rights movement was an IRA/republican front. O'Neill was losing support not due to his policies, but because of his perceived inability to preserve order. On the issue of one man, one vote, attitudes were hardening, especially near the border. Transfixed by the civil rights movement, most unionists simply did not pay much attention to the leadership contenders.[86] Traditional unionists were most distressed at their incapacity to retain the moral high-ground in public opinion despite what they perceived as the duplicitous nature of the civil rights movement. Increasingly they blamed the government for its poor public relations machinery:

> The Government was being comprehensively defeated in the propaganda war, was losing ground left, right and centre, and disorder was rampant. That is not an atmosphere in which a government can expect to receive a lot of support from its own party.[87]

Now the government itself had split between left and right. Not one of the five reforms announced in November were at issue, however. Rather, hard-line dissidents concentrated on amorphous problems: law and order, the inability of the Unionist leadership to project its case, pressure from the British government. The poverty of segregatory Unionists was that they had simply no alternative to O'Neill's strategic or even tactical decisions. Desperate to materialize the source of their angst, the supreme issue of contest became not any practical issue of policy, but the leadership of Captain Terence O'Neill. Unease with inclusive, secular and rationalist unionism was sublimated into personalized opposition to O'Neill for his aloofness from the party and 'the ordinary man in the street'.[88]

Respite for O'Neill over the Christmas holiday of 1968–9 came to an end at Burntollet Bridge. People's Democracy, a radical students civil rights organization rapidly metamorphosing into a revolutionary socialist cadre, proposed in December a four-day 'Long March' from Belfast to Derry in the new year. The socialist radicals argued that breaking the marching truce would expose the hollowness of O'Neill's concessions.[89] Major Ronald Bunting, leader of the Loyal Citizens of Ulster and Paisley's strong-arm henchman, warned the marchers to avoid 'loyalist areas, or be prepared to accept the consequences.'[90] Eddie McAteer openly expressed his concerns: 'I would rather they didn't march, but it is up to themselves. I think they are overplaying their hand at the present time. It is not good marching weather, in more senses than one.'[91]

Many nationalists besides left-wing radicals supported a march. They had enjoyed the discomfiture of unionism since 5 October 1968 and were loath to see it don the mantle of moderation at the cheap price of the November reforms and O'Neill's 'Crossroads' broadcast. For many nationalists there was a fear that 'the new found ecumenism ... would make Unionism palatable to Catholics'.[92] Precisely as was 5 October, the Long March was calculated to provoke and discredit Unionism. It was an all too successful bid for martyrdom.

It was with a forewarning of trouble to come that the marchers – 50 in all, half the number expected – set out from Belfast City Hall.[93] True to Bunting's promise, the march was continuously harassed. Following a night of violence in Maghera, where 1000 loyalists were thrice baton-charged by the RUC, the local Unionist MP, Captain Long, met for two hours with Bunting and Paisley in Stormont. Long called for the march to be left alone, so as to deprive 'the opponents of our country, both within and without, of further opportunity to besmirch its reputation.'[94] On television that night Long characterized the marchers as violent (one, allegedly, had thrown pepper into the eyes of an RUC man) and Paisley's followers as peaceful. The meeting with Paisley and Bunting he described as 'congenial'.[95]

On 4 January the marchers were seriously attacked at Burntollet Bridge. A well-organized ambush, marshalled by men with white arm-bands, swept into the virtually defenceless march while the RUC stood helpless or indifferent. Only by good fortune were there no fatalities. As the marchers straggled into Derry they were assaulted again, though less seriously, at Altnagelvin Hospital and Craigavon Hospital. Here 75 were hospitalized. Bloodied and footsore, the marchers were given a heroes' welcome by a crowd of 5000.[96] That night, and over the weekend, RUC crowd control in Derry degenerated into a veritable police riot. Order was only restored when the RUC were withdrawn from the nationalist Bogside area.[97]

On Sunday night Terence O'Neill issued a remarkable statement:

Enough is enough. We have heard sufficient for now about civil rights, let us hear about civic responsibility. ... The march to Londonderry planned by the so-called People's Democracy was from the outset a foolhardy and irresponsible undertaking. ... Some of the marchers and those who supported them in Londonderry itself have shown themselves to be mere hooligans ready to attack the police and others. And at various places people have attempted to take the law into their own hands in efforts to impede the march. ... Of course those who were responsible for this violence were playing into the hands of those who are encouraging the present agitation. Had this march been treated with silent contempt and allowed to proceed peaceably, the entire affair would have made little mark and no further damage of any sort would have been done to the good name of Ulster.

He warned that, unless the 'warring minorities rapidly return to their senses', the RUC would have to be reinforced with the Ulster Special Constabulary (B Specials) and the Public Order Act beefed up.[98] O'Neill's almost friendly advice to the Paisleyite ambushers contrasted with his vituperation against the civil rights marchers. He offered no reforms nor soft words, only the iron fist. The catholic minority were outraged at this lavish addition of insult to injury. The Derry Citizens Action Committee called off its truce.[99]

In December the People's Democracy had decided upon a march in Newry in January. Following the Burntollet events, this took on a new importance as an opportunity for catholics to express their anger. Though Bunting had called off his planned counter-demonstration an emergency Cabinet meeting decided to re-route the march.[100] A ten-person deputation from Newry, including three Protestant clergymen and two Unionist councillors, urged the Minister to allow the original route as long as there was no opposition. They were turned down. Louis Boyle, a member of Newry Young Unionists, condemned the decision as part of a deal with militant loyalism.[101] It is hard to avoid the conclusion that this decision was a deliberate provocation, designed to provoke violence from the civil rights demonstrators and so negate their propaganda coup garnered from the Burntollet/Derry episode.

The march was generally ill organized, the public address system breaking down during the crowd's stand-off at police lines. It is not surprising that violence did break out. Five police tenders were burned and one pushed into the canal. The RUC stood aside, refusing to call out the fire brigade or use their water cannons to douse the blaze. 'Police tactics were clearly to let the wreckers discredit the movement,' the journalist Barry White observed, 'and vandals were playing right into their hands.'[102] Austin Currie called for a new central civil rights organization to suppress the radicals.[103] On 17 January a planned civil rights demonstration was called off.[104]

Even now, however, it was clear that simple force could not restore order. The RUC were simply over-stretched.[105] O'Neill had to proceed with a judicious combination of concession and repression. A six-hour Cabinet meeting was held on 15 January.[106] Here O'Neill suggested that a commission be appointed to look into the background of the civil rights movement. This, in O'Neill's view, would inevitably propose the concession of universal suffrage in the local government franchize, thus getting the government off the hook of its pledge not to consider the matter before the end of 1971. Brian Faulkner argued that the concession should be made immediately on the government's own initiative, and the unionist rank and file be honestly persuaded of its merits. Other Ministers, well aware of backbench hostility and grassroots pressure, shied away from so openly breaking an oft-pledged commitment.[107] The government thus announced the establishment of an independent commission to inquire into the 'causes and nature' of the disturbances since 5 October 1968. This was accompanied by proposals to strengthen the Public Order Act.[108] A shaken populace accepted both with equanimity.[109]

Burntollet was not an irreversible turning point from which Northern Ireland descended into chaos. The riot in Newry threw the civil rights movement into a quagmire of self-doubt, and marching effectively ceased for over a month. In the public mind, the validity of O'Neill's 'Crossroads' appeal for a cooling of passions was largely, if not completely, restored. Burntollet did not destroy the government's credibility nor set the two communities at each other's throats. The crucial phase of disintegration came after Newry. The government's loss of authority stemmed not from the PD's misguided heroism in marching through a sectarian shatter-zone, but from the civil war which rapidly developed in the Unionist Party.

Numbed by the turmoil of events, unionists at first remained quiet. Most accepted that modernization was unavoidable and admitted that O'Neill projected a positive image in Britain, but they were unhappy, in an undefined way, with O'Neill 'uprooting that which is old and beautiful, and replacing it with something, which although new, is less enduring.'[110] On 20 January, the day before Stormont returned from its Christmas break, Craig announced his intention to campaign for O'Neill's removal.[111] Terence O'Neill met with representatives of the Orange Order the following day to bolster his position, but they refused to back him personally.[112]

Disaster struck O'Neill on 24 January when his Minister of Commerce, Brian Faulkner, suddenly announced his resignation. Any remnants of party unity were shattered and an immediate leadership crisis was unleashed. In his resignation letter Faulkner explained that he was unhappy with the establishment of an inquiry commission as a 'political manoeuvre and to some extent an abdication of authority'. To the surprise of most unionists, he advocated the immediate concession of universal suffrage in the local government franchize. The government's wavering between concession and repression he considered the worst of all worlds.[113] O'Neill's reply departed sharply with the formal protocol of such communications and revealed something of the depth of bitterness between the two men. Faulkner's position on the franchize confused the right of the party who heretofore saw him as the most widely acceptable party leader. In consequence no surge of unequivocal support for Faulkner developed amongst MPs or constituency associations.[114] On 25 January, however, William Morgan, a right-wing member of the Cabinet who had sat on the fence in 1966, resigned in solidarity. He believed it was time for a change of leadership.[115]

Two days later O'Neill ploughed on with a reshuffle of his Cabinet. The right wing of the Parliamentary Unionist Party, including John Brooke, had been approached by Roy Bradford to see if any would accept junior ministerial posts. All refused. Thus the reshuffle had a notably liberal bent. Robert Porter (Queen's), only in the government for three weeks, was promoted to Minister of Health and Social Services. Roy Bradford, formerly Chief Whip, took over Commerce. The Scottish judge, Lord Cameron, was appointed head of the commission to investigate recent unrest.[116] On 29 January O'Neill made John Andrews, leader of the Senate and a close ally, Deputy Prime Minister.[117]

On the night of 30 January Joe Burns resigned his post as a junior whip. A petition was handed to party secretary, Jim Bailie. It read

> We, the undersigned, being convinced that the disunity of the Parliamentary Party and constituency associations has reached grave proportions, and being dedicated to the principle that the progressive policies of the Unionist Party must be vigorously pursued by a united party, are satisfied that there must be a change of leader. We therefore call for a meeting of the Parliamentary Party in the House of Commons to consider the matter.

To this 13 backbenchers signed up: Desmond Boal (Shankill), John Brooke (Lisnaskea), Harry West (Enniskillen), Bill Craig (Larne), John Taylor (South Armagh), John Dobson (West Down), Tom Lyons (North

Tyrone), Albert Anderson (Londonderry City), Joe Burns (North Derry), Johnny McQuade (Woodvale), Austin Ardill (Carrick), William Hinds (Willowfield) and, though he retracted later in the night, Issac Hawthorne (Central Armagh). This was a much more unambiguously right-wing list than the 1966 equivalent. With Faulkner compromised over his 'sell-out' on the franchize and Craig considered too much of a loose cannon, William Morgan was the front runner as a successor.

The rebels strongly emphasized that they were not against existing policy. John Taylor argued that 'moderate policies were more likely to be welcomed in the Unionist Associations if the party had a new leader.' Tom Lyons identified the problem as O'Neill's tendency to work on his own and off the cuff: 'We strongly resent that in a Prime Minister. That is dictatorship and we do not like it.' O'Neill responded with a declaration that he would fight on. 'What they really seek,' he insisted, 'is a change of policy'.[118] The following day O'Neill met with the Cabinet, who put out a statement urging 'all Unionists in the country to examine closely the alternatives and to make their views known clearly to their associations and MPs.' It was an attempt to tap the mass support for O'Neill indicated by the response to his 'Crossroads' broadcast.[119]

On Saturday 1 February McQuade, West, Brooke, Craig, Anderson, Burns, Ardill, Dobson and Taylor caucused in a Portadown hotel. After the five-and-a-half-hour meeting Craig read to the press the rebels' 'manifesto'. He emphasized they had no dispute with government policy and reiterated support for the five-point reform programme. But without unity there could be no reassertion of order and thus no successful progressive policies.[120] The plotters' objections and ideas could be summarized in three points: party unity, strong government and collective Cabinet rule.

O'Neill would have preferred to channel his personal support amongst broad layers into the Unionist Party itself, and thus isolate and extirpate the hard-liners. However, his profound mistrust of the rank and file convinced him that change would be too slow. A general election, on the other hand, could mobilize popular support, renew his mandate, highlight the isolation of his opponents, and possibly even oust them in preference to more amenable MPs.[121] The 'Portadown Parliament', as it was quickly labelled, of rebel MPs gave O'Neill the *casus belli*. On 3 February a Stormont general election was called for 24 February 1969. The reason given was the rebels' failure to go through normal party procedures and, through the Portadown Parliament, taking 'the debate outside the Parliamentary Party to the country'.[122]

The electorate were being asked to adjudicate on an internal Unionist civil war.

Glengall Street made it clear that it would not impose candidates on Unionist Associations.[123] The inevitable result was a conflict within UAs over who would win the Unionist nomination, followed if necessary by electoral clashes between the party candidate and an Independent, either pro or anti-O'Neill. The 'crossroads' election drove a split down through the ranks of Unionism.[124]

Unionist Associations were evenly and bitterly split between pro-and anti-O'Neill factions in a broad swathe of constituencies. These ran from Londonderry in the north-west, across the north of the province, where County Antrim in particular was a shatter-zone, and curled around Lough Neagh into County Armagh. To the west of this band anti-O'Neillites dominated (Fermanagh and Tyrone), to the east pro-O'Neillites (Down). Belfast was also geographically divided with anti-O'Neill Unionist Associations in the north and west, pro-O'Neill Associations in the south and east.

Close run battles saw the most vicious intra-Unionist conflicts, particularly in North Londonderry and South Tyrone. Joe Burns (North Londonderry) and Bill Craig (Larne) were lucky not to be defeated. In Belfast pro-O'Neill candidates were elected in the large, leafy suburbs of south, east and much of north Belfast. Unionists elected in city centre constituencies tended to waver on the leadership issue. In the densely working-class constituencies of the west, St Anne's, Woodvale and Shankill, anti-O'Neill Unionists dominated. Despite this impression of domination in the city O'Neillite victories were not overwhelming, usually garnering between 55 and 60 per cent of the vote. Real O'Neillite strength was in the greater Belfast dormitory constituencies and north and west Down. Pro-O'Neill Unionists won over 65 per cent of the vote in North-Antrim, Mid-Antrim, Newtownabbey, South Antrim and North Down. Despite the closeness of selection contests, pro-O'Neill Unionists also overwhelmingly represented County Antrim. In the far south-west, in Fermanagh, anti-O'Neill Unionists romped home. Dynastic in-fighting led to senior Unionists rebelling against the 'Fermanagh cabinet' but their level of electoral support was derisory. For the rest of the province the picture was one of at least initial confusion. In counties Derry, Tyrone and Armagh six Unionists out of the ten returned fudged on the leadership issue. Joe Burns (North Londonderry), Albert Anderson (Londonderry City) and John Taylor (South Tyrone) clearly opposed O'Neill. Only Chichester-Clark in

South Londonderry, as a Cabinet minister, formally backed his Prime Minister but in practice avoided raising the issue. The Armagh MPs formed a *de facto* neutral bloc, but obviously tended against O'Neill. There was considerable support for O'Neill in the Derry seats, underpinned by cleavages based upon rival established Unionist families. A divide between east and west was apparent.

Notable is the congruence between electoral verdicts and votes cast in Unionist selection conventions. Liberal Unionists, following O'Neill's supercilious attitude to the rank and file, were convinced that the constituency Unionist organizations were far less progressive than were ordinary voters.[125] The support for O'Neill in the UAs, admittedly often less than whole-hearted, was little less than support in the unionist electorate. The unionist ranks, while hardly in the van of O'Neillism, were neither incorrigible reactionaries. The bastion of liberalism was obviously in urban areas, particularly greater Belfast (with the significant exception of working-class West Belfast, where protestants were cheek by jowl with catholics). The rural and sparsely populated western counties, where large catholic populations served as a continuous reminder of unionist insecurity, returned anti-O'Neill Unionists.

A total of 24 pro-O'Neill official Unionists were returned with 178,973 votes (32 per cent). Official anti-O'Neill Unionists returned 12 with 90,617 votes (16.2 per cent). Three pro-O'Neill Independents (Colonel Lloyd Hall-Thompson in Clifton, Tom Caldwell in Willowfield, both constituencies in Belfast, and Bertie McConnell in Bangor) were elected. Pro-O'Neill Independents in total won 72,120 votes (12.9 per cent). In three constituencies – Larne, North Londonderry and South Tyrone – pro-O'Neill Independents came within 8 per cent of the Unionist victor. Three sitting MPs, considered anti-O'Neill, had been de-selected by their UAs (Ardill in favour of Anne Dickson in Carrick, Belfast; Lyons in favour of William Fyffe in North Tyrone; and Hawthorne in favour of Herbert Whitten in Central Armagh). Morgan, forced to run as an unofficial Unionist in Clifton, was defeated at the polls by Hall-Thompson. Virtually all Unionists ranged against O'Neill strongly emphasized their support for 'progressive policies' and the November reforms. Most equivocated even on O'Neill's leadership. A few – William Hinds (Willowfield), James Stronge (Mid-Armagh) – endorsed O'Neill under pressure. In all 39 Unionist members had been returned, the largest number since 1921.

Pro-O'Neill Independents were well-heeled, often connected by blood or marriage, and drew upon markedly middle-class reserves of support. Colonel Lloyd Hall-Thompson stood as a pro-O'Neill

Independent Unionist in Clifton, Belfast. One of his rallies was described as a 'largely middle-class business and professional people's gathering.' Morgan's election workers, in contrast, 'looked younger and less prosperous, confirming the opinion that the Unionist Party in Belfast may be splitting along class lines.'[126] Tom Caldwell, who took up the challenge in Willowfield, had a 'plummy accent, redolent of Indian army days.'[127]

Anne Dickson in Carrick was the only pro-O'Neill Independent to have held elected office but even she would 'never have contemplated entering politics' in 'normal times', but felt she had to support Terence O'Neill.[128] Hugh Wilson, the pro-O'Neill Independent in Larne, was a surgeon and scion of a well-known local family.[129] In West Down A. W. [Bill] Buller, the pro-O'Neill Independent, was a substantial farmer.[130] Faulkner's pro-O'Neill opponent, who lived in Killyleagh Castle, was Lieutenant-Colonel Denys Rowan-Hamilton or 'the colonel, as his well-dressed and well-spoken band of enthusiastic supporters call him'.[131] He was a member of one of County Down's oldest 'blue-blooded' dynasties and was great nephew of the Countess of Clanwilliam.[132]

The Presbyterian cleric, Gerry Eakins, a well-known and popular manager of a spastic rehabilitation centre and holder of an OBE, ran as a pro-O'Neill Independent Unionist against Taylor in South Tyrone.[133] The core of Eakins' substantial support were moderate Unionist Party members, many of whom were ex-servicemen.[134] As many as 52 leading members of North Tyrone UA, including the Duke of Abercorn, opposed Tom Lyons' 'defection' from the Prime Minister.[135] A group of local businessmen met with James Stronge in Mid-Armagh, but were unable to extract from him a pledge of loyalty to O'Neill. They proceeded to nominate Irvine Magowan, formerly Permanent Secretary at the Minister of Agriculture, as an 'O'Neill Unionist'.[136] In North Londonderry James Barr, a Ballykelly farmer aged 33, had been approached by two separate groups requesting that he stand.[137] Barr, a substantial landowner of 2500 acres, stood as an Independent and quickly built-up an activist base including many Unionist Party members.[138] Peter Campbell, a 41-year-old former Royal Navy Commander, announced that he would stand as a 'Government Unionist' in Londonderry City.[139] He had no direct Derry links, lived in Belfast and, married to Lady Moyra, was brother-in-law of the Marquis of Hamilton (Westminster MP for Fermanagh and South Tyrone) and son-in-law of the Duke of Abercorn. Five members of the British Royal Family had attended his wedding.[140]

Even in the inauspicious unionism of Fermanagh and South Tyrone pro-O'Neill sentiment existed and was organized, though more due to rivalry between great family dynasties than a thirst for a 'New Ulster'. Pro-O'Neill sentiment was organized by Robert Grosvenor, the Duke of Westminster. He had served as Member of Parliament for the local Westminster constituency between 1955 and 1964.[141] Succeeding to the title on the death of his brother in 1967, he was a fabulously wealthy landowner, worth £60 million per annum. Early in February he announced the formation of a committee to oppose Harry West in Enniskillen and John Brooke in Lisnaskea.[142] Secretary of the committee was Dennis Archdale, of Castle Archdale, who until his resignation was vice-chairperson of Fermanagh Young Unionist Association.[143] Archdale ran as a pro-O'Neill 'Government Unionist' in Enniskillen.[144] During the election he enjoyed the support of the Duke of Westminster, the Earl of Erne (Colonel Michael Crichton) and Archdale Porter, a large farmer, all prominent members, still, of the Unionist Party.[145] John Brooke in Lisnaskea was opposed in the election by the independent 'Government Unionist', Major James Henderson, head of 'one of the best known families in the county'.[146] West identified the support for the 'Government Unionists' as being overwhelmingly middle class: 'mainly people found among the imports – people like teachers and the professional classes.'[147]

Much of the organization to promote pro-O'Neill candidates in the 'crossroads' election was based upon landed and gentry familial networks, many of whom had been mobilized by O'Neill's civic weeks. James Henderson (Lisnaskea), Peter Campbell (Londonderry) and Denys Rowan-Hamilton (Larne) were closely related to the Marquis of Hamilton. A prominent dissident in Larne UA, John McClintock, was related to Phelim O'Neill (North Antrim), James Chichester-Clark (South Derry) and of course Terence O'Neill (Bannside). Tom Caldwell (Willowfield) was a close friend of the Duke of Westminster. Richard Ferguson, of a well-established Fermanagh family and MP for South Antrim, was brother-in-law to Irvine Magowan, the pro-O'Neill Independent in Mid-Armagh.[148] Many of the Unionist Associations, in selecting candidates, split between branches located in prosperous areas, favouring O'Neillites, and working-class branches supporting anti-O'Neill candidates. The New Ulster movement, which backed pro-O'Neill candidates once they had emerged, was solidly middle class.[149]

The bourgeois and gentry profile of the pro-O'Neill independents was, in an increasingly populist age, something of an embarrassment.

Faulkner argued that pro-O'Neill activists across the province were without 'democratic mandate', attempting to influence the unionist rank and file and electorate by wielding their social 'authority'.[150] William Morgan continued this theme at a press conference. O'Neill's family had enjoyed power and privilege in Ulster for hundreds of years, he observed. 'They can claim the friendship of the landed gentry, and call upon the support of the belted earls and feudal dukes … this I think is where our trouble lies.'[151] O'Neill's unionists did appear, indeed, to represent the swan song of gentry political influence in Northern Ireland politics.

Why did unionist politics divide so sharply on these class lines? It has been suggested that working-class protestants feared losing their marginal privileges in employment while middle-class protestants, better set to withstand the amelioration of sectarian discrimination, were more concerned to pacify discontent with civil rights reform so as to return to profitable business.[152] In fact there is scant evidence that middle-class protestants were any more relaxed than their working-class counterparts at the prospect of the labour market being regulated. Polls found the middle class actually less inclined to accept the need for anti-discrimination legislation than the working class. Rose found that protestants in insecure employment, most likely to be anxious to defend sectarian employment norms, were no more politically ultra than those secure.[153] Indeed, the issue of alleged sectarian advantages for the protestant community barely came up in the election's intra-unionist debates.

Class divisions amongst protestants were politically important not for economistic reasons but because of relative cultural security. The middle class – practised in leadership, well educated, frequently travelled and culturally akin to cosmopolitan Britain[154] – were primarily concerned to appease Westminster and were confident that they could win catholic allegiance to the constitution. To achieve this they were willing to break up the pan-class protestant alliance. A strategic aim of O'Neillites in the election was to expel unionist ultras from the mainstream, even if they subsequently formed a viable political party.[155] Working-class protestants, socialized into insular communities replete with evangelical and communal markers archaic in British society,[156] were, understandably, less sure of their ability to influence British or catholic behaviour in their favour. For them protestant solidarity was strength. They resented and opposed the fragmentation of the pan-class alliance. Anti-O'Neill unionists saw O'Neill and the assimilatory unionists as the rebels.

In the east of the province, outside inner-city Belfast, society was more firmly modelled on contemporary Britain and with as yet a quiescent and proportionately smaller catholic population, the construction of a new unionist alliance taking in catholics and British opinion seemed viable. Thus the O'Neillite vote was here widespread across the classes. In areas where catholics lived in large numbers, it was obvious even to many of the middle class that they would not be so easily assimilated. The anti-O'Neill vote, in favour of protestant solidarity, was strong in the west of the province. Subsequently, after ten years of Troubles, middle-class optimism regarding their ability to defend unionist interests outside the stronghold of communal solidarity had dissipated. A person's location on the unionist political spectrum, thus, could no longer be reliably adduced from class, locality or denomination.[157] The socio-political basis of assimilatory unionism had temporarily collapsed under the pressure of civil conflict, though it was to develop again from the early 1980s.[158]

For some time the Unionist Party had been dropping tentative hints that it would welcome catholic support.[159] O'Neill explained his policy, with characteristic archaism, to the *Washington Post* in January 1969:

> What I have been trying to do is to persuade Catholics in Northern Ireland that they have a place within the United Kingdom. I have been succeeding, first with the professional class, and gradually with the artisans. I don't believe Catholics in Ulster want to be governed by the Republic of Ireland.[160]

Jack Maginnis, Westminster MP for Armagh, posed the problem baldly. Speaking to a pro-O'Neill Unionist rally he pointed out that 50 per cent of school children were 'of a faith other than that of his audience'. Unless they could attract the support of catholics 'the Unionists could exist only for another twenty years and the boat would sink.'[161] In private Unionists were blunter still. In 'the long run Roman Catholic votes must be secured if the constitutional position was to be maintained' insisted Roy Bradford.[162] O'Neillism was predicated on the assumption of unfavourable demography.

In practice, however, the party was loath to accept catholic involvement. The election in South Down reiterated this with devastating clarity. The Unionist Party did not intend to contest this seat, which was held by Michael Keogh of the Nationalist Party, but remarkably a meeting of 250, about half who were catholic, was held in the constituency demanding a pro-O'Neill Unionist candidate.[163]

Potentially an ideal candidate existed in Louis Boyle: catholic, Unionist Party member and brother of Kevin Boyle, the People's Democracy leader. When it became clear that there existed a demand for a pro-O'Neill Unionist in the constituency, Louis Boyle offered himself for nomination. His Young Unionist association backed him but the UA, from which he was excluded, decided not to contest the seat. Boyle was on the point of announcing his independent candidacy when he heard that Glengall Street was considering candidates and Boyle was on the shortlist. Rather than pick him, however, headquarters favoured James Kerr, a company director, former Belfast councillor and unsuccessful Unionist candidate in Woodvale in 1962. With heroic charity Boyle doubted whether Kerr's selection 'was an anti-Catholic decision', but he deplored the opportunity lost to attract catholic support.[164]

In fact, Kerr did not stand as a Unionist. South Down UA rejected his candidature on the pretext that there was insufficient time to call a full delegate meeting to ratify the selection. Kerr, in turn, refused to stand as a nominal Independent and seek Unionist ratification after nomination day.[165] Boyle, it seems, had been stitched up to prevent him declaring his candidacy in the Unionist interest before the close of nominations on 13 February. Instead no Unionist candidate stood, and the possibility of a pro-O'Neill MP for South Down being elected was let pass.[166] Three leading local Unionists, including two councillors, resigned from Newry UA in protest.[167] Captain Long, Minister of Home affairs, later admitted that the party 'might not be ready' for catholic candidates 'just yet'.[168] Finally concluding that the Unionist Party was 'still essentially based on a sectarian foundation', Boyle ultimately resigned.[169]

Unionist overtures to catholics, therefore, were purely rhetorical, but nonetheless unprecedented. The party's manifesto called for a 'a truly united community with common pride in shared achievements and a common determination to tackle outstanding problems'. Though the minority community was not mentioned explicitly, it was obviously intended for catholic as well as protestant consumption.[170] It was constrained, however, by the policy compromise embodied in the five-point programme, the post-Burntollet package of public order measures and the Cameron Commission. For 48 hours the manifesto launch was delayed as its framers attempted to make it sharp enough to discomfit the dissidents but not so liberal as to alienate support.[171] Though its language strained to go beyond the limits of acceptability to the right-wing rebels, the policy remained well within the sphere of what was already agreed.

O'Neill's problem, ironically, was that he could not sufficiently alienate, and thus expose, the rebel Unionists. From the outset, the rebels felt under pressure in their Unionist Associations and then from their constituency electorates. All were opposed by pro-O'Neill Independents. Their response was to declare themselves every bit as liberal as O'Neill, opposed only to his inadequacies as a Unionist leader.[172] Beyond that, the rebels needed only to make reassuring noises about the need for law and order to signal their reliability in the eyes of anxious loyalists. They had no incentive to expose themselves to hostile fire over policy differences with the government. O'Neill's last opportunity to expose segregatory unionists was to propose a radical reform in his manifesto, ideally one man one vote. To do so, however, would have threatened the unity of his own camp. The impressive, but essentially windy rhetoric of the manifesto was no alternative for a touchstone reform proposal. Indeed, with his explicit appeal for catholic support, Faulkner quickly trumped it.[173] William Fitzsimmons was forced to concede that all Unionist candidates had accepted the manifesto.[174] Roy Bradford scorned their short-term conversion to O'Neillism, but it reduced the choice before the electorate to the rather abstract alternatives of 'expediency and conviction.'[175]

Even this was disingenuous. The unionist right wing genuinely accepted all reforms conceded as well as the manifesto. The difference between factions was intangible, if highly significant. Joe Burns (North Derry) explained his faction's position to the *Belfast Telegraph*. He denied any disagreement at all over policy, or even O'Neill's personality. The only issue of contention was O'Neill's inability to unite the Unionist Party: 'It is leadership and leadership only.' He denied they were extremists, insisting that 'regardless of colour, race or creed each man deserves the same fair play. There is no difficulty about that.' Only once in the interview did Burns give glimpse to a fundamental difference of philosophy

> The party can be united again. There is no reason why not. If the Unionist Party is not united there is no hope for progressive policies, no hope for a happy Ulster. ... Captain O'Neill talks about uniting all Ulster, which is a marvellous thing. Nobody wants this more than I do, *but it is just not possible.*[176]

Assimilatory unionists wished and believed catholics, if generously treated, could be won to the Union; the traditionalists believed the minority to be irreducibly hostile to the state, and any reforms conceded were to appease British public opinion and stem disorder rather than to win catholic hearts and minds.

These were amorphous differences and difficult to explain to an electoral audience. With O'Neillism defined merely as inclusive rhetoric traditionalists found little difficulty in playing lip service to it while emphasizing order, resistance and the Union to reassure their core electorate. O'Neill was reduced to pleading with journalists and voters to probe the depth of his opponents' liberalism.[177]

Terence O'Neill was anxious for his Unionist opponents to suffer a rebuff at the polls – this, after all, was the whole point of his calling an election. He suffered a blow, therefore, when, on 8 February, Captain L.P.S. Orr, leader of the Westminster Parliamentary Unionist Party, declared that 'it would be quite wrong for anyone to vote for any splinter candidate.' Though Jim Bailie in Glengall Street was lending tacit support to pro-O'Neill independents, such a statement from a respected and largely neutral party leader as Orr could not easily be gainsaid.[178]

On 19 February Terence O'Neill for the first time canvassed openly for a non-party candidate, though Lloyd Hall-Thompson's opponent in Clifton, William Morgan, had been barred by the courts from standing as an official Ulster Unionist. The next day O'Neill issued a formal statement refusing to support Unionist candidates 'who have been progressive in public but reactionary in private.' He explicitly disowned the 'Portadown Parliament' rebels. There was a storm of protest from the dissident Unionist candidates. 'Some of us have always felt that the Prime Minister had not much use for the party,' Joe Burns observed accurately, 'We are pleased he has come out now and made this clear.'[179] Two days before polling day, O'Neill finally canvassed for pro-O'Neill candidates standing against the Unionist Party in Derry.

In the final days of the campaign, O'Neill's appeal to catholic voters became increasingly explicit.[180] The Nationalist Party had strongly hinted that their supporters should vote for the pro-O'Neill Unionist where no Nationalist was standing. Captain Long of the Unionist Party called on the Roman Catholic hierarchy to state openly that there was nothing wrong in catholics supporting the Unionist Party.[181] Roy Bradford predicted a large and unprecedented vote for government candidates.[182]

All opinion polls suggested that catholics were, indeed, prepared to vote for O'Neill in great numbers. One found that 91 per cent of catholics backed him as premier as against only 58 per cent of protestants.[183] No less than 45 per cent of catholics indicated that they would vote for pro-O'Neill candidates, as against only 20 per cent apiece for the Nationalist Party and NILP.[184] There were signs at ground level, however, of catholic disgruntlement at being taken for granted by triumphalistic moderate unionism: a Belfast street affirmed its 'right to be Irish and anti-Unionist'.[185] Predictions of an irresistible surge to the O'Neillites cast doubt on sections of the minority community fearful of having their vote for conciliation misrepresented as a vote for Unionism. In the end Unionists of whatever shade received 67.4 per cent of the vote. As it happened this was exactly the percentage of protestants of voting age revealed in the 1971 census.[186] Given the unprecedented range of unionist varieties to choose from it seems highly unlikely that protestant turn-out was significantly lower than that of catholics. Despite the intense worry that catholics were being lured to unionism, as expressed in the editorials and letter pages of the *Irish News*,[187] it seems that virtually no catholics were persuaded by O'Neill's assimilatory rhetoric to give their vote to Unionist candidates.[188]

This was partially due to the wide range of candidates thrown up in the ant-unionist election. The People's Democracy stood in a number of constituencies with the deliberate aim of drawing catholics away from pro-O'Neill candidates.[189] They fared surprisingly well, winning almost 5 per cent of the total vote. Fergus Woods came within an ace of ousting the Nationalist incumbent in South Down. A number of independents were propelled to prominence by the civil rights movement. John Hume defeated the weary Nationalist leader, Eddie McAteer, in Foyle. Paddy O'Hanlon, Paddy Devlin and Ivan Cooper[190] were elected after campaigning against the ineffective traditionalism of nationalist politics. Gormley and Richardson of the Nationalist Party joined McAteer in drinking from the bitter cup of defeat. Catholic voters had signalled their approval of a policy of combining flexibility on the border question with militant anti-unionism.

Roy Bradford predicted that in the public eye the general election would become reduced 'to the symbolic battle of Bannside.'[191] Bannside had been contested only twice before: in 1929 by the NILP and during the war by an Independent Unionist. Unionist officials had been confident that O'Neill would easily see Paisley off. Nevertheless the area was deeply religious and conservative. One of Paisley's Free Presbyterian churches was located in the constituency town Rasharkin.[192] Paisley ran a very effective, high-energy campaign.[193] In contrast Bannside UA, which had never contested a Stormont election under O'Neill, was anaemic.[194] Terence O'Neill's poor campaigning skills were a major hindrance. A reporter compared his technique with that of Bill Craig's:

> Terence O'Neill, cast by the world at large as the boy hero of Ulster, shifts uneasily, looks over his left shoulder, and tortures out a sentence or two. Bill Craig, billed as the starring heavy, suddenly illuminates and goes into the act essential to any serving politician. ...
>
> Mr O'Neill, facing the ordeal for the first time in his previously uncontested political career, seems to favour the factory visit, though he gets round to the door knocker as well. There is a curious air of embarrassment about the whole business, which spreads around him like some Old Testament plague. He is really much more at home with a policy than a person, as is evident from every encounter.
>
> 'My goodness.' He proclaims to the typing pool, 'it's nice and warm in here today. This is the right place to be today.' No one can fault it as an opening remark except that it is so generalized in thought and aim as to be almost incapable of response. So all it draws are those sort of smiles which ask where the nearest door is.
>
> In the sheds he is introduced to individual workers – the supervisors a bit too often – but seems unable to concentrate on the particular man or woman. Within seconds he has absorbed himself in the product or the machine. But chattering ironwork does not yet have the vote, and the man in charge of it does.
>
> ... as he stands saying goodbye to the factory manager a couple of hidden voices shout 'Up Paisley!' You know it is of little significance, but somehow you cannot imagine someone shouting 'Up O'Neill!' after Bill Craig.[195]

O'Neill deliberately avoided discussing politics while canvassing.[196] Perhaps this was as well, as his oratory, when not reading from a civil service crafted text, was awkward and ill judged. 'I don't want to be uncharitable,' he began when forced into a public speech in Dunloy, 'but I think that anyone who supports the other man would need to go into a mental institution, or something like that.'[197]

Michael Farrell, the People's Democracy candidate, managed to shear off many catholic votes which probably would have gone to O'Neill. He polled a creditable 2310 votes. In the end, O'Neill defeated Paisley by the relatively narrow margin of 1414.[198] Had the election campaign stretched another week, Paisley believed he would have ousted O'Neill.[199]

It was widely felt that O'Neill's savage attacks on his dissenting party colleagues, apparently at odds with his overall conciliationist message, had actually worked to the dissidents' advantage.[200] In the nine seats where there had been straight pro/anti-O'Neill Unionist fights it was official Unionist Party backing which proved crucial to the victor every time. O'Neill admitted that he had expected 'better results'. On the Bannside result and the failure of catholics to support him he was palpably bitter. 'Although there was Catholic support after my television broadcast', he admitted, 'it does not seem to have translated itself to the polling booths to the same extent. They are prepared to write letters of support but they are not reached the stage of putting an X against your name.'[201] His gamble had failed. As Richard Rose, the American political scientist, explained: 'building up or taking over a constituency organisation is done by methods very different from the television appeals he has favoured.'[202]

Terence O'Neill's 'dash for freedom'[203] in the 'crossroads' election had failed to come off, and in going so far in canvassing for Independents against Unionist Party candidates he had left himself dangerously exposed. At the first post-election Parliamentary Unionist Party ten anti-O'Neill MPs walked out, including two newly elected: Mitchell (North Armagh) and Laird (St Annes). Despite this when a vote of confidence was put only 23 (excluding O'Neill) out of 35 were in favour.[204] The steering committee of the Ulster Unionist Council met on 7 March. Three hundred delegates were in attendance, making it the largest in living memory. John Andrews, the Deputy Prime Minister, proposed a vote of confidence in O'Neill and Anne Dickson seconded.

The issue at stake was O'Neill's support for Independents in the election. In his speech O'Neill admitted that he had infringed the rules but asked 'What would you have done in my position?' Some delegates took this to be an 'apology'. In an important contribution Captain L.P.S. Orr, Westminster MP for South Down, reminded the audience that he had publicly called for all official candidates to be supported, but ended with a plea for reconciliation and support for O'Neill. The confidence motion was passed by 183 votes to 116, a majority of 67. The dissidents were temporarily stilled but O'Neill's position was unlikely to remain stable for long.[205]

Gerry Fitt best encapsulated the impact of the February 1969 election on the catholic minority when he stated:

The hard-line element in the Unionist ranks has been strengthened. But those who are the victims of the hard-line attitude are just not prepared to accept it any longer, and if it persists, there must be a direct confrontation – a head-on collision. It will be back to the streets again.[206]

The election had been particularly dangerous because, even more so than the Long March, it had mobilized catholic militancy and protestant reaction in the rural hinterland where atavistic sectarian passions were less bridled than in the east of the province.[207] This, rather than Burntollet, finally squandered the goodwill generated by the five-point reform programme and the 'Crossroads' broadcast. The Nationalist Party, who had responded to the civil rights movement more in fear than hope, was eclipsed in the election.[208] The success of militant civil rights candidates legitimized the methods of street politics. After a two-month lull civil rights marches were resumed.

The post-Newry caution of even the People's Democracy was now a thing of the past.[209] Attitudes hardened, and the Public Order Act, which had been generally welcomed in January, met with stiff opposition when re-introduced in March. With new clauses banning sit-down protests and occupations, the emphasis was seen to have switched from suppressing Paisleyite counter-demonstrations to suppressing civil rights protests. The new nationalist MPs conducted a tireless opposition to the bill in Stormont, amounting to a filibuster, in something of a parliamentary baptism of fire.[210]

The civil rights movement began to split as militant factions strained at the leash.[211] One man one vote and, despite an earlier welcome for its provisions, the Public Order Act were now the targets.[212] A succession of marches and rallies, often accompanied by counter-marches and violent clashes with the RUC, were organized during April weekends in a series of towns: Armagh, Belfast, Coalisland, Derry, Dungannon, Lisburn, Lurgan, Omagh, Portglenone and Toomebridge, to name but some. Communal tension was being screwed up to an unbearable pitch.

Terence O'Neill still hoped for an influx into party ranks to his advantage. He told the Ulster Unionist Council that:

All over the country thousands of people who never took the slightest interest in politics before want to join Unionist Associations and play their part. As a party, we should not merely accept this trend, but welcome it. We should take this historic opportunity to renew and strengthen the fabric of Unionism.[213]

Rank and file opinion, however, was moving away from O'Neill, not towards him.[214] O'Neill stood down as president of the UUC and was replaced by Deputy Prime Minister, John Andrews.[215] Despite this, a vote of confidence in O'Neill was only narrowly passed by 338 to 263, a slim majority of 75 out of 601. While O'Neill had won 61 per cent of the vote at the standing committee this had fallen in the UUC to only 56 per cent.[216] Overall, the meeting indicated a rapid right-wing take-over at grassroots level. Most vocal support for the Prime Minister, it was claimed, came from co-opted and Women's Unionist Associations delegates.[217]

The next battle was likely to be the election of the new executive committee. Both sides were concerned to mobilize at Unionist Association level for this, but while heretofore Association officials had generally remained loyal to the leadership, now it was clear that O'Neill's opponents were making much headway.[218] The struggle was shaping up into one over 'who will kick whom out of the party.'[219] The Young Unionist movement, which had only a few years previously sat on the left of the unionist movement, was now dominated by the ideas of its titular president, William Craig. The Young Unionist Council, on 24 March, passed a motion of no confidence in the Prime Minister.[220] Angered, O'Neill refused to attend the opening of the Young Unionist conference on 11 April.[221] Here resolutions were passed condemning weak and indecisive government, and calling for full use of the B Specials.[222] Seeing the writing on the wall, party headquarters at Glengall Street moved to sound out and reflect anti-O'Neill opinion.[223]

The government and Unionist Party seemed without direction and drifting helplessly in the aftermath of the 'crossroads' election. O'Neill was demoralized by the election result. His poor personal showing in Bannside became almost an obsession.[224] The party was deeply divided and wracked by internecine feuding at all levels. O'Neill was obviously a lame duck Prime Minister, but it was far from clear who should replace him. The civil rights movement, in contrast, though losing moderate adherents, was increasingly militant, well organized and ambitious. The contrast was highlighted and personalized by the by-election for the Westminster parliamentary seat of Mid-Ulster.

Though a marginal with a nominal catholic majority of 3000, Mid-Ulster had been held by a Unionist, George Forrest, until his death in December 1968.[225] As was fairly common in unionism his widow, Anna Forrest, was selected as the Unionist candidate to contest the seat.[226] With local nationalist opinion fearful of a split vote, the young and charismatic People's Democracy leader, Bernadette Devlin, was accepted as the Unity candidate.[227] In a secret deal, meanwhile, the Paisleyites put up no candidate to give the Unionists free run against Devlin.[228] This dramatic run-off between two females caught the media's rather sexist attention.[229]

Devlin's message was naive, if idealistic. 'If necessary we will take over the factories and run them for ourselves,' she advised. 'That way there will be no discrimination because there is no sectarianism in the heart of the ordinary working man that is not put there by a bigoted Unionist Party in order to keep itself in power.'[230] Forrest responded by attempting to split the catholic vote by labelling Devlin as a neo-communist and 'as much anti-Catholic as ... anti-Protestant.'[231] Forrest, however, had decided not to hold public meetings, severely limiting her capacity to mould the campaign.[232] She managed only a 'subdued effort almost to the point where it would appear to be token' and assiduously avoided the leadership issue.[233] Devlin's high-profile campaigning, often holding rallies in divided towns, inevitably attracted violent counter-demonstrations. There were strong rumours of plots to obstruct polling. Unionism, once more, was displaying an intolerant and undemocratic image.[234]

On a record 91.5 per cent turnout, Devlin was returned with a majority of 4211.[235] Forrest had held the Unionist vote, but Devlin had galvanized an enormous, overwhelmingly catholic, electorate revolt. The nature of the contest and the candidate ensured a transfixed and indulgent British audience. Devlin's maiden speech, delivered off-the-cuff on the rapidly deteriorating situation in Northern Ireland, was impassioned and articulate but darkly pessimistic and rather inflammatory. Nevertheless, the House rose to its feet in acclamation and senior parliamentarians hailed it as the best maiden speech since F.E. Smith's in 1906. Robin Chichester-Clark, responding for the Unionists, had 'seldom acquitted himself more effectively' but was eclipsed by the glamour of the newest Member of the House.[236]

On Saturday 19 April, as the province reacted to Devlin's momentous victory, the public order situation began to spin out of control. Sit-down demonstrations in Derry developed into running battles between catholic youths and the police. The RUC swept into the catholic Bogside and a ferocious resistance to this 'invasion' developed. Eventually the police were forced to withdraw. Fighting continued into Sunday and protests spread to Belfast. That night there was concerted petrol bombing of post offices. Even more seriously, the Silent Valley water reservoir, which supplied Belfast, was bombed. Water supplies to the city were more than halved. An electricity pylon near Loughgall in County

Armagh was also bombed. The RUC immediately blamed the IRA, though this was denied by republican sources. Direct British intervention seemed likely, particularly as the army was now required to guard key installations.[237]

Shaken by the escalation into crisis, O'Neill typically turned first for information and companionship to his civil servants, Harold Black and Ken Bloomfield. Politically, as he confided to Phelim O'Neill, he thought direct rule was now probably the only solution.[238] Nevertheless, when he summoned the Cabinet, which met for two-and-a-half-hours on 20 April, O'Neill used the immediate prospect of a *de facto* take-over of Stormont's functions by Westminster to force through concessions to stem catholic mobilization.[239] He secured the Cabinet's acceptance in principle of one man one vote in the local government franchize. Chichester-Clark and Captain Long had hitherto opposed such a concession, but now they appeared to 'bow to the general will'. The decision was immediately made public to prevent second thoughts.[240] O'Neill then threatened to resign if the party refused to accept the reform.[241] In Westminster the British Home Secretary, James Callaghan, delivered an ultimatum to the Parliamentary Unionist Party to accept one man one vote or face British intervention.[242]

On 23 April a joint meeting of Unionist MPs and senators accepted immediate concession of franchize reform by 28 votes to 22. Through personal pressure, O'Neill had managed to turn the votes of Senator Sam Rodgers and Joshua Cardwell (Pottinger). Faulkner criticized the decision as steamrollering 'the party in the country'.[243]

The final fatal blow came that night when James Chichester-Clark, Minister of Agriculture and widely believed to be O'Neill's preferred successor, announced his resignation from the Cabinet. He complained that the concession of one man one vote was ill-timed:

> I question firstly whether this concession at this time will stop the activity in the streets and secondly I fear that our supporters will lose all faith in the determination of the present Government ... I am not against the principle but the timing.

It was a weak excuse and seemed designed to reassure the assimilatory moderates while reaching out to the die-hards. It smacked of manoeuvring for the inevitable leadership contest.[244] To O'Neill's jaundiced eye it was a typical Chichester-Clark capitulation to his right-wing constituency and Orange pressure.[245] Chichester-Clark refused to align himself with the dissident MPs and declared himself to be, broadly speaking, still an O'Neillite.[246]

On 25 April, as bomb attacks and civil strife continued, the Unionist right called an emergency Ulster Unionist Council meeting to discuss universal suffrage.[247] In their first statement since 27 November, the Orange Order hinted that it was losing confidence in the government due to its 'yielding to threats ... [from] those whose aim it is to destroy the peace and prosperity of Northern Ireland'.[248] On Monday 28 April 1969, after hearing that he was about to lose the support of two MPs and thus, effectively, lose his majority, Terence O'Neill announced his resignation as leader of the Unionist Party.[249] He would resign as Prime Minister as soon as a replacement was elected.[250] That night about 14 MPs and Ministers, those loyal to O'Neill, attended a tea party to see the leader off. Significantly, Chichester-Clark was also in attendance.[251]

O'Neill had failed to translate his popular support, especially amongst the protestant middle classes, into organizational support within Unionist ranks. As he put it, with revealing class distinctions, 'While good men sleep and honest men play their golf and their bridge, these others, with unwavering zeal, are chipping away at the foundations of our democracy.'[252] Indeed, the middle class were conspicuously unwilling to engage in sustained political activity within official unionism.[253] A more fundamental problem, however, was the unrepresentativeness of liberal middle-class opinion. O'Neill failed to realize that his parliamentary party all too accurately reflected the mass of the protestant electorate – not died in the wool reactionary, by any means, but insecure, suspicious of the catholic community, desirous of firm leadership and anxious for solidarity against all interfering outsiders.

O'Neill's negativity for the future, hardly calculated to bolster his successor, permeated his farewell television broadcast:

> ... A few short weeks ago you, the people of Ulster, went to the polls. I called the election to afford you the chance to break the mould of sectarian politics once and for all. In many places, old fears, old prejudices and old loyalties were too strong. Yet I am not amongst those who say the election served no useful purpose. For it did allow me, with my colleagues, to proclaim a new declaration of principles which now binds every Unionist returned to parliament. It speaks in clear terms of justice and equality; it commits the party, in honour and in conscience, not merely to do nothing to enlarge

the divisions of our community, but to work positively to end them. You will be watching, as I will be, to see to it that these pledges are honoured.[254]

This sounded like a leader going not to the backbenches, but into opposition. O'Neill evidently believed that with his demise, Northern Ireland had lost its man of destiny and only possible saviour. That evening O'Neill and Jim Malley, his private secretary, visited the Newsboys Club off York Street. O'Neill recorded:

After presiding at the annual meeting we go upstairs for the enter-tainment. Just before taking my seat a large ex-naval chap comes up and, failing to speak, with tears in his eyes, he lifts up my right hand to his lips and kisses it – obviously he is a catholic. It is moving and it is a suitable exit.[255]

It was certainly an epilogue that said much of O'Neill.

The leadership contest that had been bubbling in the background was now in earnest. On 25 April O'Neill and his close supporters had held a contingency meeting to plan for a favourable succession. They agreed on John Andrews, Leader of the Senate and Deputy Prime Minister. On Sunday 27 April, however, Andrews declined to step into the breach, despite pressure from O'Neill individually, and a group of his supporters – Herbert Kirk, Roy Porter, William Fitzsimmons and Roy Bradford. Then 'in desperation' they turned to James Chichester-Clark.[256]

Chichester-Clark refused to say where he differed with Faulkner on policy but promised to continue the O'Neill line.[257] Faulkner had of late been making a concerted pitch for liberal support. He had called on Unionists to 'try to meet the wishes of the minority parties fairly'.[258] In an interview with Martin Wallace of the *Belfast Telegraph* he advocated a government based on all strands within the Unionist Party and stressed the need to accelerate the reform programme (most parliamentary time being taken up with the Public Order Bill). He also promised, however, to eschew O'Neillite rhetoric on community rela-tions in favour of practical economic progress.[259] Faulkner enjoyed the support of the unionist rank and file and, if a Belfast street poll was accurate, the general public.[260]

It was the Parliamentary Unionist Party that mattered however. Despite Faulkner's attempt to appeal to the liberals, the signatories of his nomination papers – Norman Laird (St Annes), John Taylor (South Tyrone), Harry West (Enniskillen) and Joe Burns (North Derry) –

revealed that he drew his core support from the anti-O'Neill right. In contrast, Chichester-Clark's papers were signed by Robert Simpson (Mid-Antrim) and Herbert Kirk (Windsor), both O'Neillite loyalists.[261] The contest could not have been closer. Chichester-Clark won 17 votes to Faulkner's 16 – O'Neill concluded that Captain Long and Nat Minford must have defected to Faulkner. John Brooke proposed that the decision be made unanimous and was seconded by Desmond Boal.[262] Terence O'Neill, who thereupon tendered his resignation as Prime Minister to Lord Grey, declared himself 'delighted' with the result. The new Prime Minister emerged 'looking flushed and tense'. Faulkner, in contrast, was jaunty and smiling and immediately proposed direct talks with the leaders of the civil rights movement.[263] The baton had been handed on to the more loyal colleague, but not the more capable.

It is quite probable, however, that Faulkner would have fared little better in the coming months. With remarkable rapidity O'Neill melted into the shadows of obscurity, but this only reflected the growing irrelevance of the Stormont political scene for protestants, and its total irrelevance for catholics. Any reforms now would clearly be conceded under duress. The idea that unionists, having harried and pulled down O'Neill, had any desire to build a 'New Ulster' genuinely inclusive of catholics seemed laughable. Violence had at last reached the powder keg of Belfast in the dying days of O'Neill's administration. A cycle of sectarian escalation was virtually unstoppable. Politics was now an affair of the streets, fed by suspicion, fear and a desperate, frenzied excitement. Both communities prepared for the showdown that came with shuddering force in the August riots. In doing so they cast barely a backward glance at the high hopes and expectations of the O'Neill years.

Conclusion

Unionism had traditionally been led by a social elite distant from the rank and file. The leaders had made up for this, however, by paying a populist attention to the opinions, attitudes and prejudices of their loyalist constituency. By the 1960s, however, the middle-class establishment had accepted a liberal consensus, which believed that battles over the border had been left in the past. Through catholic acceptance of the permanence of the partition settlement, old sectarian divisions would be healed. Terence O'Neill did not come to power on the back of this liberal consensus, but he was in sympathy with it. He won the leadership of his party because he was best placed, and placed himself, as the candidate to steal the NILP's technocratic, economically modernizing clothes. More substantially, he was willing to exploit the regional development climate current in Britain. This latter encouraged O'Neill to pursue an image-conscious strategy in which communal discord would be discarded in favour of progressive self-help and social solidarity as the predominant identity of Northern Ireland. A new, positive outlook would be all the better for attracting foreign investment and British subventions.

The government's radically reforming approach to the traditional power blocs in the unionist alliance – local government, Belfast corporation, the west of the province, farmers and so on – served to alienate a substantial section of the Unionist Associations and parliamentary party. This was not helped by O'Neill's aloof, even haughty, attitudes to his own party and colleagues. Challenged in particular by Faulkner, O'Neill was forced to accentuate his bridge-building policy so as to anchor a liberal faction of the party to his leadership. More importantly he appealed to a public opinion which he believed was substantially more liberal than official unionism. This in turn stirred up the traditionalists of the party in suspicious hostility to the emerging credo of

'O'Neillism'. More dramatically still, it aroused the inflammatory phenomenon of Paisleyism. For example, O'Neill met with Lemass in 1965, in great measure, to out-manoeuvre Faulkner, but in doing so aroused the enduring wariness of many unionists. Again, in 1966, O'Neill labelled his party opponents, opposed to his leadership on a wide range of grounds, as crypto-Paisleyites. In doing so he associated assimilatory unionism with his own person and demonized all those who stood against him. In his defence, however, few other unionists were prepared to join O'Neill even in his rhetorical bridge-building.

The very success of O'Neill's regionalist strategy in extracting funds from the exchequer encouraged the British government to play closer attention to the state where it was so freely expending resources. Political activists in the minority catholic community were keen to bring to their attention manifold civil rights grievances. Thus pressure built from Westminster for substantial reform. Terence O'Neill fobbed this off with further exercises in bridge-building and dire warnings of the perils of British involvement in Irish politics. Nevertheless, O'Neill was increasingly identified by unionist traditionalists as a creature of British pressure.

A recrudescence of sectarian disorder in 1966 accelerated the crystallization of an anti-O'Neillite, rather than simply anti-O'Neill, opposition within unionism. The disorder of that year further increased British concern, and added apocalyptic overtones to the civil rights debate which raged with increasing vigour through 1967. This only confirmed O'Neill in his belief that community grievances were not amenable to a legislative quick-fix. He developed instead his conception of civic self-help as a route to catholic incorporation into society. O'Neill was convinced that legal disabilities suffered by the minority were minor when compared to their 'second class citizenship' – a function both of their social and cultural inadequacy and of the majority's 'master-race' mentality.[1] During his premiership, O'Neill later recalled nostalgically,

> 'housing discrimination was breaking down and in many of the new estates catholics and protestants were living side by side. The catholics, astonished by the prosperity, thrift and hard work of their protestant neighbours, defied their priests and refused to have fourteen children.[2]

His priority, therefore, was to build on naturally improving community relations, draw catholics into full civic responsibility, and convince the protestants that they had nothing to fear in treating them, as equal fellow citizens. This strategy O'Neill was determined to preserve even if it meant extreme tactical caution in how far he was prepared to antagonize unionist opinion. Thus legislating for civil rights was not a priority. In the end, this simply built up catholic frustration and led to the civil rights explosion of 1968.

The Stormont era is sometimes looked upon as an era of protestant triumphalism. But, while Britain was often indifferent to the affairs of Northern Ireland, unionists were not indifferent to the opinion of Britain. They were acutely conscious of their precarious position at the edge of the Union. Unionists were anxious not to offend British standards of decency, violations of which they were well aware would be widely publicized by nationalists. Their fear of alienating the British government acted as a restraint on such corruption, patronage and discrimination such as might be expected in a one party state. On the other hand, acute awareness of the anti-constitutional sentiments of the catholic 'fifth column' put unionists on vigilant guard against minority 'infiltration' of the civil service, labour market and, crucially, electoral constituencies. Difficulties multiplied as British norms of decency evolved – most concretely with the concession of universal suffrage in local elections in 1949 – leaving unionists, who could not so lightly accept change, struggling in the wake. Thus discrimination occupied an agonizingly ambiguous position in the unionist worldview. Ambiguity was poor defence against the stark exaggerations of the civil rights movement and the Unionist community was left ideologically defenceless when the storm broke in 1968.

O'Neill, convinced that political actors on all sides in Northern Ireland were out of touch, had attempted to by-pass formal political structures – both the Unionist Party or the Nationalist Party – in favour of appealing directly to the populace. As Unionism began to fragment under the weight of its confusion over civil rights, O'Neill increasingly took recourse to presidential appeals, most notably in the 'crossroads' broadcast and 'crossroads' election. He under-estimated how closely the Unionist Party actually reflected popular protestant opinion. This meant that he consistently took inadequate measures to develop the besieged assimilatory tendency within the Unionist Party, a task he no doubt thought hopeless. He failed to realize that the dominant segregatory faction in the party was actually representative of much protestant opinion. O'Neill may have been a poor party leader, but he was constrained by the more fundamental reality that his support base was middle class and disinclined to political activism. Restructuring of the Unionist Party would always have been difficult, but O'Neill did little to try.

O'Neill was not completely lacking the political arts, however. He was not, as usually presented, simply parachuted into power on the strength of his social background, though this helped. Rather, he seized upon a crisis in unionist confidence to position himself as the best alternative to Brookeborough. Faulkner, embroiled in traditional unionist agitation was, for once, wrong-footed, the slight he perhaps found hardest to forgive. O'Neill continually manoeuvred against his many political opponents within the party in an un-ending battle. This did much to shape his image as a liberal and, in contradistinction, that of his opponents as reactionaries. Politics, for O'Neill as for any other practitioner, is the art of the possible. In the 1960s there was no consensus and precious little pressure for a reconsideration of the constitutional status quo. O'Neill was operating with a relatively circumscribed paradigm left to him by preceding Prime Ministers and past generations. Much is made of O'Neill distance from the Ulster mind-set but in fact he had an acute awareness of the fragility of communal peace in Northern Ireland and the hostility of protestants in general and the Unionist Party in particular to change. Thus he attempted to circumnavigate problems rather than run headlong into them. He recognized the need for reform in the field of civil rights, but saw too that unionists required cajoling if they were not to feel threatened by the loss of marginal privileges.

This leads on to the matter of O'Neill's motivation in the route he took. He has been described as a representative of non-sectarian international capital against local unionist capitalists,[3] a tool of Harold Wilson in a greater plan to bring about archipelagic reunification,[4] a technocratic modernizer striving to incorporate catholics for reasons of economic efficiency,[5] and an exponent of the modern British sense of identity in place of archaic Ulster-Britishness.[6] All actually have some basis, particularly if one considers his career chronologically. O'Neill was influenced by the attitudes of international businesspeople and politicians and eager to facilitate their investment. His initial liberalization was a conscious attempt to cater to the predilections of Anglo-American opinion in particular. Wilson did apply pressure for reform and all British politicians encouraged greater co-operation on the island of Ireland. Full catholic engagement in the economy, O'Neill hoped, would boost productivity and efficiency. Reform, he insisted repeatedly, could not be resisted if it accorded with British norms.

None of these are sufficient explanation in themselves. O'Neill listened to his civil servants and his press friends, to his gentry peer group and to British politicians. Though aware of the particularity of unionist politics, he imbibed and internalized the assimilatory assumptions of the establishment, as expressed by BBC Ulster and UTV, by the Anglican Church, and by the periodicals bought and read by the middle class. They preached in unison that religious disputation was out of date, civic nationalism was the basis of British citizenship, and economic and social advancement would ameliorate communal divisions. O'Neill thought seriously about these things, more seriously than is usually accepted, and attempted to develop a theory and practice in PEP and civic weeks. His lack of rapport with his own party forced him to rely disproportionately on the middle class assimilatory consensus. Kinship with civil servants, editors and gentlemen reinforced his assumptions and their unstinting support buttressed his sense of destiny. The origins of O'Neill's liberalism is perhaps best located in his weakness for flattery from those he admired. Not without cause did the king's discontented subjects grumble about the undue influence of his courtiers.

The irony was that, in destroying O'Neill, Ulster unionism opened an era, uninterrupted since, of *de facto* administration of Northern Ireland by the very liberal establishment they had so resented. The king had fallen but the courtiers, arrayed in the Northern Ireland Office, survived and prospered. There would be no returning to the hegemony of traditional Unionism.

Notes

Introduction

1 *Belfast Telegraph*, 26 January 1963.
2 Northern Ireland House of Commons (*Hansard*), vol. 71, 18 December 1968, c. 52.
3 Eamon Phoenix, *Northern nationalism: nationalist politics, partition and the catholic minority in Northern Ireland* (Belfast, 1994).
4 Patrick Buckland, *The factory of grievances: devolved government in Northern Ireland 1921–39* (Dublin, 1979).
5 Paul Arthur and Keith Jeffrey, *Northern Ireland since 1968* (Oxford, 1996, 1st ed. 1986) p. 6.
6 David Gordon, *The O'Neill years: Unionist politics 1963–1969* (Belfast, 1989) p. 9.
7 Lord O'Neill of the Maine, *The autobiography of Terence O'Neill, Prime Minister of Northern Ireland 1963–1969* (London, 1972) pp. 111, 137.
8 See, for example James Loughlin, *Ulster Unionism and British national identity since 1885* (London, 1995) p. 176. Fergal Cochrane, '"Meddling at the crossroads": the decline and fall of Terence O'Neill within the Unionist community', in Richard English and Graham Walker (eds) *Unionism in modern Ireland: new perspectives on politics and culture* (Dublin, 1996) pp. 148–9
9 In reviewing O'Neill's autobiography, T. E. Utley commented that it was 'unfair to him in that it conceals almost all of those amiable qualities (including a magnificent wit which depends largely though not wholly on mimicry) which makes him a delightful companion ...' *Daily Telegraph*, 9 November 1972, press cuttings, NIO files, Linen Hall Library, Belfast.

Chapter 1

1 From a radio broadcast, 4 May 1969. Cited in A. C. Hepburn, *The conflict of nationality in modern Ireland* (London, 1980) p. 182.
2 Report on the British Labour Party Conference, October 1966, 'Religious discrimination in Six Counties', Department of Foreign Affairs, National Archives Dublin, 98/3/24.
3 Ronan Fanning, '"The great enchantment": uses and abuses of modern Irish history', Ciran Brady (ed.), *Interpreting Irish history: the debate on historical revisionism 1938–1994* (Dublin, 1994) p. 153. See John Hume's 1964 comments on catholic youth, cited in Barry White, *John Hume: Statesman of the Troubles* (Belfast, 1984) p. 43.
4 Rex Cathcart, *The most contrary region: the BBC in Northern Ireland 1924–84* (Belfast, 1984) pp. 170–1, 201–2. C. E. B. Brett, *Long shadows cast before: nine lives in Ulster 1625–1977* (Edinburgh, 1978) p. 67. John Boyd, *The*

middle of my journey (Belfast, 1990) pp. 162–7, 185, 203–5.

5 Pamela Clayton, *Enemies and passing friends: settler ideologies in twentieth century Ulster* (London, 1996) p. 77.

6 *Belfast Telegraph*, 15 December 1967.

7 Jonathan Bardon, *A history of Ulster* (Belfast, 1992), p. 604. For details of the campaign, see J. Bowyer Bell, *The secret army: the IRA 1916–1979* (4th ed., Dublin, 1989) pp. 272–310.

8 *Round Table*, November 1958, p. 66.

9 The *Unionist*, March 1958.

10 The phrase was Terence O'Neill's.

11 *Belfast News Letter Annual Review 1960* (Belfast, 1961) p. 2.

12 Oliver P. Rafferty, *Catholicism in Ulster 1603–1983: an interpretative history* (London, 1994) p. 252. See also Andrew Boyd, 'United Ulstermen', *The Spectator*, 15 February 1963.

13 *Derry Journal*, 1 March 1966.

14 Timothy Pat Coogan, *Ireland since the rising* (Connecticut, 1966) p. 317.

15 *Belfast Telegraph*, 8 December 1967.

16 Ibid., 11 December 1967.

17 Richard Rose, *Governing without consensus: an Irish perspective* (London, 1971) p. 208.

18 *Irish News*, 18 April 1966.

19 *Irish News*, 30 May 1967, press cutting in 'Speeches by Mr. Fitt, MP', Cabinet secretariat papers, PRONI, CAB/9J/75.

20 Con Short, *The Ulster GAA story* (Ulster, 1984) p. 180.

21 Anthony P. Quinn, *Credit Unions in Ireland* (Dublin, 1994) p. 117.

22 Michael Viney, 'Journey North: The New Voices', *Irish Times*, 5 May 1964.

23 Rev. A. H. McElroy, 'The Liberal leaven in Northern Ireland', *New Ireland* (Belfast, 1964).

24 *Belfast Telegraph*, 8, 16 December 1967.

25 'People's Democracy: a discussion on strategy', *New Left Review*, no. 55 (May–June 1969) p. 6.

26 Speech by James Lennon, *Irish News*, 18 March 1964.

27 Editorial, *Derry Journal*, 20 March 1964.

28 Editorial, *Irish News*, 3 February 1966.

29 See Paddy Devlin's election manifesto for the Falls Road, Political ephemera, Linen Hall Library, Belfast.

30 This is in contrast to catholic pressure groups in the last years of direct rule in southern Ireland. See Senia Paseta, *Before the revolution: nationalism, social change and Ireland's catholic elite, 1879–1922* (Cork, 1999) Chapter 5.

31 There was a subsidiary feeling that, by stemming catholic emigration, civil rights might hasten a catholic numerical majority. The *Tablet*, 4 September 1965.

32 *Irish News*, 1 February 1969.

33 For Austin Currie's enthusiasm to topple the image of a 'New Ulster', see *Frontier Sentinel*, 22 August 1964.

34 Harold Jackson, 'Northern Ireland' in David McKie and Chris Cooke (eds) *The decade of disillusion: British politics in the sixties* (London, 1972) pp. 232–3. See also Patrick O'Farrell, *Ireland's English question: Anglo-Irish relations 1534–1970* (New York, 1971) p. 301.

35   *Belfast Telegraph*, 5 April 1963. See also Taylor in ibid., 13 January 1964.
     Literature on Unionist national (or otherwise) consciousness is volumi-
     nous. For notable contributions, see D. W. Miller, *Queen's rebels: Ulster
     loyalism in historical perspective* (Dublin, 1978). Jennifer Todd, 'Two tradi-
     tions in unionist political culture', in Tom Garvin and Michael Laver (eds),
     Irish political studies, vol. 2, 1987, pp. 1–26. Colin Coulter, 'The character of
     unionism', *Irish political Studies*, vol. 9, 1994, pp. 1–24. Fergal Cochrane,
     Unionist politics and the politics of unionism since the Anglo-Irish Agreement
     (Cork, 1997) pp. 35–87.
36   Frank Wright, 'Protestant ideology and politics in Ulster', *European Journal
     Sociology*, xiv (1973) p. 221. Cash uses the terms 'inclusive' and 'exclusive'.
     John Daniel Cash, *Identity, ideology and conflict: the structuration of politics in
     Northern Ireland* (Cambridge, 1996) pp. 80–90, 99–107, 123. 'Assimilatory'
     and 'segregatory', in my opinion, better conveys the societal and organic
     perspectives of these two trends. For stimulating discussion of the limita-
     tions of the various brands of unionism, under yet different labels, see
     Norman Porter, *Rethinking Unionism: an alternative vision for Northern Ireland*
     (Belfast, 1996).
37   With the single exception, significantly, of a catholic Unionist. Louis
     Boyle, 'Unionism at the crossroads', *Yearbook of the Conservative and
     Unionist Association of Queen's University Belfast 1967/8* (Belfast, 1967) pp.
     41–2, John Johnston papers, PRONI, D/3219/3/2. For the contrary, see the
     address delivered by strongly pro-O'Neill Harry Calvert, law lecturer and
     ex-member of the NILP. 'The workings of democracy', Unionist Society
     meeting, 29 January 1970, Records of the Unionist Society, minute book
     1962–71, PRONI, D/3292/A/3.
38   Norman Gibson, *Partition today – a protestant view* (Dublin, 1959) p. 7. Cf.
     Robin Bailie, 'A united Ulster', *Review: an Ulster political commentary*,
     October 1962. Editorials, *News Letter*, 24 January, 9 March 1964. John
     Brooke's speech recorded in *Belfast Telegraph*, 29 April 1964.
39   In reference to a speech by Joe Stewart M.P. *Unionist*, April 1960.
40   William Long, an Orange stalwart, expressed unionist self-identity with an
     illuminatingly complex and ambiguous metaphor 'The majority of our
     neighbours in the Republic might be described as the "charming girl next
     door". But we are already happily married to our beloved Commonwealth.
     We have no intention of becoming bigamists. ... [Any] Protestant who in
     1963 fails to glance over his shoulder at the persecution of his ancestors is
     a foolish man.' *News Letter*, 12 August 1963.
41   *News Letter*, 13 July 1968. Molyneaux later became leader of the Ulster
     Unionist Party.
42   Jennifer Todd, 'Unionist political thought 1920–72' in D. George Boyce,
     Robert Eccleshall and Vincent Geoghagan (eds), *Political thought in Ireland
     since the seventeenth century* (London & New York, 1993) p. 201.
43   *Northern Whig* quoted by James McSparran QC, Nationalist MP for Mourne,
     NIHC, vol. 41 (5 February 1957) col. 24.
44   *Round Table*, August 1956.
45   Terence O'Neill in *News Letter*, 28 January 1970, press cuttings, NIO files.
     J. A. Oliver, *Working at Stormont. The memoirs of John Andrew Oliver* (Dublin,
     1978) p. 77.

46 *Belfast News Letter* (2 November 1959) cited in Denis P. Barritt and Charles F. Carter, *The Northern Ireland problem. A study in group relations* (2nd edition, Oxford 1972) p. 47.

47 Barritt and Carter op. cit.

48 Letter from Sayers to Conolly Gage (6 August 1958) cited in Andrew Gailey, *Crying in the wilderness; Jack Sayers: a liberal editor in Ulster 1939–68* (Belfast, 1995) p. 51. See also *Round Table* (August 1958) cited p. 50. Letter from William Douglas, Secretary of the Ulster Unionist Party, to S. A. Walker, Conservative and Unionist Central Office, 16 April 1962, Conservative Party Archive, Area Service Files, Bodleian Library, Oxford, CCO 2/6/23.

49 Letters from Sayers to Conolly Gage (6 August 1958) and (11 November 1959) cited in Gailey, *Crying in the wilderness*, p. 51. See also *Round Table*, August 1958, p. 50.

50 Secretary's report, Unionist Society AGM, 2 April 1963, Records of the Unionist Society, minute book 1962–71, PRONI, D/3292/A/3.

51 There was much interest from the Republic's government in this initiative. 'Meeting Between Senator J. G. Lennon and Sir George Clark', Department of Foreign Affairs, National Archives, Dublin, 305/14/342.

52 *News Letter*, 20 August 1962, cutting in Ulster Unionist Council archive, press statements and newspaper cuttings (1962), PRONI, D 1327/21/27.

53 *News Letter*, 18 October 1962, in ibid.

54 *News Letter* in Ulster Unionist Archive, Press statements and newspaper cuttings, op. cit.

55 *News Letter*, 12 February 1962, in ibid.

56 *Belfast Telegraph*, 12 June 1964.

57 Ibid., 18 June 1963.

58 Ibid., 4, 12 July 1963.

59 *News Letter*, 17 December 1963, in Ulster Unionist Archive, Press statements and newspaper cuttings, op. cit.

60 *News Letter*, 10 September 1962, in ibid.

61 Barritt and Carter, *The Northern Ireland problem*, p. 62. Wilson, *Ulster under Home Rule*, p. 12. George Thayer, *The British political fringe: a profile* (London, 1965) pp. 219–20.

62 Barritt and Carter, *The Northern Ireland problem*, p. 71.

63 See Edward Gibson's critical speech to the Young Unionist Council. *News Letter*, 26 October 1964. Roy Bradford estimated the number of activists. *Belfast Telegraph*, 20 May 1966. Even amongst local government councillors standing as Unionists many were not active in the party. Minutes of a meeting of the Unionist Society, 8 December 1965, PRONI, D/3292/A/3.

64 Interview with Bob Cooper, 24 October 1996. Cf. Nancy Kinghan, *United we stood: the official history of the Ulster Women's Unionist Council 1911–1974* (Belfast, 1975) p. 79. Bill Craig's comments, *News Letter*, 6 December 1963. For the protestant middle class see the poem 'Coasters' (1969) in Alan Ward (ed.), *The selected John Hewitt* (Belfast, 1981) pp. 41–3.

65 For the importance of 'boundaries' in ethnic conflict, see Daniele Conversi, 'Reassessing current theories of nationalism: nationalism as boundary maintenance and creation', *Nationalism and Ethnic Politics*, vol. 1, no. 1 (London, Spring 1995) pp. 73–85.

Chapter 2

1 Paul Bew, *Ideology and the Irish Question: Ulster Unionism and Irish Nationalism 1912–1916* (Oxford, 1994), p. 29.
2 Lord O'Neill of the Maine, *The autobiography of Terence O'Neill, Prime Minister of Northern Ireland 1963–1969* (London, 1972) pp. 1–5.
3 Private information. O'Neill's mother was often abroad and his aunt, Sylvia O'Neill (later Rathcavan) did much to raise him. O'Neill, *Autobiography*, p. 18.
4 See letter from Harry J. MacMurrough-Kavanagh in the *Irish Press*, 2 January 1973 and *Irish Times*, 26 March 1963, press cuttings, NIO files. The *Unionist*, September 1966.
5 O'Neill, *Autobiography*, pp. 8–9.
6 Ibid., p. 14. In 1964 O'Neill told a newspaper that a brush with bandits in Ethiopia had been the tensest moment of his life. 'For...[O'Neill] ... surprisingly, the most exciting memories are those of childhood.' *Sunday Express*, 21 January 1964, press cuttings, Terence O'Neill papers, Lymington, Hampshire.
7 O'Neill, *Autobiography*, p. 17.
8 Ibid., pp. 17–8.
9 Ibid., p. 20.
10 Ibid., pp. 18, 21.
11 Ibid., p. 22. A 1700 drawing of the Whitaker family home, Pylewell, can be seen in Edward King, *Old times revisited in the borough and parish of Lymington* (Winchester 1976, 1900 ed., 1st ed. 1879) p. 160.
12 Desmond J. L. Fitzgerald, *History of the Irish Guards in the Second World War* (Aldershot, 1949) p. 366.
13 *News Letter*, 26 March 1963.
14 John Colville, *The fringes of power: Downing Street diaries 1939–55* (London, 1985) pp. 499–500.
15 O'Neill, *Autobiography*, pp. 23, 25. Fitzgerald, *History of the Irish Guards*, p. 512. *Daily Express*, 3 September 1964, press cuttings, O'Neill papers.
16 *News Letter*, 22 January 1968.
17 Ahoghill was riven with sectarian tension. This was pointed up by the wits' pun on de Gaulle's country retreat, Ahoghill Les Trois Églises. F. S. L. Lyons, *Culture and anarchy in Ireland 1890–1939* (Oxford, 1979) p. 113.
18 His wife, Jean O'Neill, participated in local organizations, such as the (exclusively Protestant) Women's Guild. The family had a home help, dogs, cats and horses. Mrs O'Neill's garden had a particular reputation for magnificence. She was, and is, a skilled horticulturist. *News Letter*, 27 March 1963.
19 O'Neill, *Autobiography*, pp. 25–6. O'Neill was not a religious bigot, however. He felt comfortable with English aristocratic recusants. Auberon Waugh, *Will this do? an auto biography* (London, 1991), p. 33.
20 Rose, *Governing without consensus*, p. 297.
21 *Irish Times*, 8 November 1972, press cuttings, NIO files, Linen Hall Library.
22 *Belfast Telegraph*, 25 April 1969.
23 Parliamentary debates: House of Lords *(Hansard)*, vol. 355, 12 December 1974, col. 1222.
24 Terence O'Neill, 'Ulster – the communication gap', *The Spectator*, 15 June 1974.

25 O'Neill, *Autobiography*, p. 31.
26 Martin Wallace, 'Profile – Terence O'Neill, *Belfast Telegraph*, 19 May 1961, press cuttings, O'Neill papers.
27 O'Neill, *Autobiography*, pp. 32–3.
28 John Cole, 'Ulster's last chance' (a review of Terence O'Neill's autobiography), *The Guardian*, 9 November 1972, press cuttings, NIO files. Ivan Neill, *Church and state* (Dunmurray, 1995) p. 52.
29 O'Neill, *Autobiography*, pp. 33–4.
30 'Northern Ireland Annual Review 1956', *Belfast News Letter*, 4 January 1957, p. 19.
31 O'Neill, *Autobiography*, p. 34.
32 Richard I. D. Harris, *Regional economic policy in Northern Ireland 1945–88* (Aldershot, 1991) p. 16.
33 Ibid., p. 16.
34 Report of the working group of officials, papers of the Cabinet Committee on Unemployment, PRONI, CAB/4A/38/20, pp. 17–18.
35 For example, the controversies in the 1950s over Orange processions through the Longstone Road, Annalong, and Dungiven. Andrew Boyd, *Brian Faulkner and the crisis of Ulster Unionism* (Tralee, 1972) pp. 12–13, 20–4.
36 Bowyer-Bell, p. 269.
37 'Memorandum by the Secretary of State', PRO, HO 284/61, p.4.
38 R.A.B. Butler, 'Memorandum to the Secretary of State', ibid.
39 'Draft paper for Economic Policy Committee; Unemployment policy in Northern Ireland', Memorandum by the Home Secretary, ibid.
40 *Ulster yearbook 1956*, Belfast, 1956, p. 120. Despite these wide terms of reference, the council considered its primary task to be 'to bring the facts about Northern Ireland to the knowledge of industrialists in the United Kingdom and abroad, notably the United States of America.', ibid.
41 Derek Birrell and Alan Murie, *Policy and government in Northern Ireland, lessons of devolution* (Dublin, 1980) pp. 15–18.
42 Arthur J. Green, *Devolution and public finances, Stormont from 1921 to 1972* (University of Strathclyde, 1979) p. 14.
43 'Industrial development in Northern Ireland', *Ulster yearbook 1962*, Belfast, 1962, p. xx.
44 In 1980 prices. Richard I. D. Harris, op. cit., p. 41.
45 Note on a ministerial meeting held on 4 May 1955 on the subject of unemployment in Northern Ireland, Cabinet secretariat papers, CAB/9F/188/9.
46 'Personal note from the Minister of Finance', n.d. [1958], papers of the Cabinet Employment Committee, PRONI, CAB/4A/38/29
47 Paul Bew, Peter Gibbon and Henry Patterson, *Northern Ireland 1921–1994: political forces and social classes* (London, 1995) p. 117.
48 *Second annual report of the Irish Congress of Trade Unions, 1959–60* (Dublin, 1960) p. 32. NIC minutes, 1 February 1961 and *Third annual report of the Irish Congress of Trade Unions, 1960–1* (Dublin, 1961) p. 36. Paul Bew, Peter Gibbon and Henry Patterson, op. cit., pp. 128, 131.
49 Sydney Elliott, *Northern Ireland parliamentary election results 1921–71* (Chichester, 1973).
50 NIHC, vol. 52, 20 June 1962, col. 62.
51 *Newsletter*, 11 February 1962.

52 *Round Table*, 1962, pp. 282–3.

53 Ibid., col. 29.

54 Edmund Warnock had called for his demotion and replacement by William Morris May. Ibid., vol. 46, 17 February 1960, cols. 236–8.

55 For example, NIHC, vol. 44, 20 May 1959, col. 1506.

56 Smiles was a political radical who, distrustful of socialism, espoused the benefits of initiative, individualism, hard work and active citizenship. His book, and later works, had an powerful and long-lasting influence on public opinion. As his son W. H. Smiles became managing director of the Belfast Rope Work Company, he had a particular resonance in Ulster. Samuel Smiles, *Self-help with illustrations of conduct and perseverance* (London, 1st ed. 1859, 2nd ed., with a centenary introduction by Professor Asa Briggs, 1958). Brian Walker, *Ulster politics: the formative years 1868–86* (Belfast, 1989) pp. 162–3, plate 3.

57 NIHC, vol. 48, 23 May 1961, c. 2193–4.

58 Boyd, *The middle of my journey*, pp. 102, 185.

59 Lord O'Neill of the Maine, op. cit., p. 36.

60 NIHC, vol. 52, 4 July 1962, cols. 433–5.

61 Harkness and Brookeborough appear to have got on well with each other. The two had worked closely together when Harkness had served as Brookeborough's secretary in both the Ministries of Agriculture and Commerce. See NIHC, vol. 49, 8 November 1961, cols. 757–8. Harkness was sceptical of the value of devolution and in 1969, after retirement, came out openly in favour of integration with the United Kingdom. Letter, *Sunday Telegraph*, 23 February 1969. O'Neill, in contrast, was an enthusiastic devolutionist.

62 Bloomfield, *Stormont in crisis*, 1994, p. 28.

63 John Cole, 'Introduction', in Terence O'Neill, *Ulster at the crossroads* (London, 1969) p. 21.

64 O'Neill, *Autobiography*, pp. 35, 38, 58, 62–3.

65 Oliver, *Working in Stormont* , Chapter 8, pp. 77–82.

66 See the remarks of Tom Boyd, leader of the Parliamentary Labour Party. NIHC, vol. 52, 3 July 1962, cols. 386, 388.

67 Harold Evans, *Downing Street diaries: the Macmillan years 1957–1963* (London, 1981), pp. 128–9.

68 'Report by officials on the proposals by the Northern Ireland Government for the relief of unemployment in Northern Ireland', no date (May 1961) in 'Hall Report', PRO, HO 284/63.

69 *Report of the joint working party on the economy of Northern Ireland*, Cmd 446 (Belfast: HMSO, 1962).

70 Ibid., paras 14, 17.

71 Pace, Bew, Gibbon and Patterson, *Northern Ireland 1921–1994*, pp. 131–2.

72 Cabinet conclusions, 7 March 1961, PRO, CAB 128.'Unemployment in Northern Ireland; memorandum by the Secretary of State for the Home Department', PRO, CAB 129/104. For the persistence of strategic interests in Northern Ireland until the end of the Cold War at least see Nicholas Watt, 'Thatcher gave approval for talks with IRA,' the *Guardian*, 16 October 1999.

73 R. J. Lawrence, *The government of Northern Ireland: public finance and public services 1921–1964* (Oxford, 1965) p. 101.

74 NIHC, vol. 52, 23 October 1962, c. 525, 698.
75 Ibid., col. 701, 703–4.
76 Ibid., col. 706.
77 Neill, *Church and state*, pp. 56, 58.
78 In June 1963 Field Marshal Viscount Alanbrooke, Brookeborough's influential uncle, died aged 79. *Newsletter*, 18 June 1963.
79 O'Neill, *Ulster at the crossroads*, p. 31.
80 Ibid., p. 32.
81 Ibid., pp. 33–5.
82 Ibid., pp. 35–6.
83 Ibid., p. 38.
84 Robert Millward, 'Industrial and commercial performance since 1950' in Roderick Floud and Donald McCloskey (eds), *The economic history of Britain since 1700, volume 3: 1939–1992*, Cambridge, 1994 (1st ed. 1981), pp. 59–60.
85 O'Neill, *Ulster at the crossroads*, p. 38.
86 Gordon Gillespie, 'The Ulster Liberal Party 1956–73', unpublished MSc thesis (Queen's University of Belfast, 1984) p. 25. Interview with Bob Cooper, 24 October 1996.
87 O'Neill, *Ulster at the crossroads*, p. 32.
88 Green, *Devolution and public finance*, p. 17.
89 Cabinet conclusions, 2 March 1960, PRONI, CAB/4/1120. The survey was expected to last two and a half years and cost £25,000.
90 It was discussed in Cabinet on 6 February 1963, though most consideration seems to have taken place within the various ministries. Attention centred on political implications. Cabinet conclusions, 6 February 1963, PRONI, CAB/4/1217. Memorandum submitted to the Cabinet by the Minister of Health and Local Government, 'Proposals for a new city at Lurgan-Portadown', ibid., CAB/4/1217/11.
91 Oliver, *Working at Stormont*, pp. 82–3.
92 Ibid. , p. 86.
93 The Matthew Plan was not even mentioned in O'Neill's autobiography.
94 *Belfast Telegraph*, 15 February 1963.
95 The company had insured boiler, electrical and mechanical plant in government buildings since 1922. Cabinet conclusions, 21 February 1963, PRONI, CAB/4/1219.
96 Edmund Warnock, Robert Nixon, Robert Simpson, Nat Minford, James Chichester-Clarke, Walter Scott, Fred McCoy, Phelim O'Neill and David Little. *Belfast Telegraph*, 23 February 1963.
97 See Edmund Warnock in *The Times*, 25 February 1963.
98 *Belfast Telegraph*, 25 February 1963.
99 Ibid.
100 For example, Jonathon Bardon, *A history of Ulster Belfast* (1992) p. 621.
101 *Belfast Telegraph*, 26 February 1963. Cabinet conclusions, 21 February 1963, PRONI, CAB/4/1219.
102 Ibid., 1 March 1963, 28 February 1963.
103 He was released on 13 March. *Belfast Telegraph*, 13 March 1963.
104 Interview with Rt Hon. Harry West, 15 December 1994.
105 'Change of Prime Minister – March 1963', a note by the Governor of

Northern Ireland made for Government House records, 29 March 1963, in file entitled, 'Resignation of Lord Brookeborough and the appointment of Captain Terence O'Neill as Prime Minister of Northern Ireland', Public Records Office, HO 284/57, p. 1.

106 Ibid. Harry West claims that Brookeborough had three candidates in mind and none of them was O'Neill: Jack Andrews (Minister of Commerce), Brian Faulkner (Minister of Home Affairs) and Bill Craig (Chief Whip). As still only a whip, however, Craig seems unlikely. Interview with Rt Hon. Harry West, 15 December 1994.

107 'Change of Prime Minister – March 1963', *op. cit.*, pp. 2–3.

108 W. A. Lewis, 'Northern Ireland Unionism 1963–1990: an examination of the liberal and conservative patterns within Unionism' (unpublished M. Phil., Trinity College Dublin, 1991), p. 24.

109 James Kelly, 'Cloak-and-dagger tactics behind the Unionist crisis', *Sunday Independent*, 25 September 1965, press cuttings, O'Neill papers.

110 Interview with Bob Cooper, 24 October 1996. Letter from Anne Callmont to Alice Ross, 23 April 1963, Records of North Antrim Women's Unionist Association, 1956–67, PRONI, D 2706/24.

111 'The peculiar nastiness of the British bourgeoisie is in shameless observances of status and obsession with spurious gentility.' 'The peculiarities of the English' (1965) in E. P. Thompson, *The poverty of theory and other essays* (London, 1978) p. 266.

112 Martin Wallace, *O'Neill*, loc. cit.

113 *Irish Times*, 26 March 1963, press cuttings, O'Neill papers. James Chichester Clarke and Phelim O'Neill at Stormont were related, as were the Westminster MPs for North Antrim (Henry Maitland Clark) and Londonderry (Robert Chichester-Clark). Robert Chichester-Clark was perhaps O'Neill's closest political friend.

114 Alvin Jackson, *Colonel Edward Saunderson: land and loyalty in Victorian Ireland* (Oxford, 1995) pp. 12, 19, 52, 66, 170, 186–7.

115 Information courtesy of Professor Peter Jupp.

116 For the persistence of gentry influence in Ulster politics, see David Cannadine, *The decline and fall of the British aristocracy* (New Haven, London, 1990) p. 672.

117 Interview with Rt Hon. Ivan Neill, 15 August 1995.

118 For example, O'Neill would consult regularly with Jack E. Sayers, editor of the *Belfast Telegraph*, over lunch at the Ulster Club. Gailey, *Crying in the wilderness*, p. 77.

119 The *Unionist*, August 1960.

120 *Irish Times*, 30 March 1963, press cuttings, O'Neill papers. *Belfast Telegraph*, 19 June 1962 cited in Andrew Gailey, *Crying in the wilderness*, p. 78.

121 The speech was delivered on 22 February 1963 to the Young Unionist Annual Conference in Portrush. A complete transcript was published in The *Unionist*, March 1963.

122 Ibid.

123 This celebrated phrase is customarily cited from O'Neill's first major speech to the Annual Meeting of the Ulster Unionist Council, 5 April 1963. O'Neill, *Ulster at the crossroads*, pp. 41–5.

124 The *Unionist*, March 1963.

125 Michael O'Sullivan, *Seán Lemass: a biography* (Dublin, 1994) pp. 139–42. Brian Farrell, *Seán Lemass* (Dublin, 1983) pp. 89–95.
126 *Irish Times*, 8 November 1972, press cuttings, NIO files.

Chapter 3

1 The *Unionist*, February 1965.
2 He was described at the time as 'one of the younger school of Unionist politicians, moderate in his views and broad in his outlook.' *News Letter*, 30 April 1963.
3 *Belfast Telegraph*., 26, 29 April 1963, *News Letter*, loc. cit.
4 *Belfast Telegraph*, 16, 17 May, 25 June 1963.
    1. The basic principle is that no minister should place himself in such a position that his private interest may conflict with his public duty. It follows that he should not engage in any activities which are incompatible, or which might interfere with the full and impartial discharge of his official duty.
    6. The application of these principles is the personal responsibility of each minister, but in any case of doubt the Prime Minister of the day must be the final judge. Ministers should, therefore, submit any such case to him for his direction.
    'Principles governing the retention of business interests by ministers', Cabinet conclusions, PRONI, CAB/4/1235/1.
5 Interview with Lord McConnell, 17 February 1995.
6 Interview of O'Neill by Ralph Bossence, *News Letter*, 8 June 1964.
7 'A passion for politics', interview of O'Neill by John Cole, *Guardian*, 9 November 1974, press cuttings, NIO files. His hobbies, largely given up by the 1960s, were genteel and invited little company. They included architecture, furniture, paintings, antique collecting, particularly Victorian Staffordshire figurines. He also tended a small plot of trees in his wife's considerable garden. Martin Wallace, 'Profile – Terence O'Neill, *Belfast Telegraph*, 19 May 1961, press cuttings, O'Neill papers. Information from Lady O'Neill.
8 Related to me while staying with Lady O'Neill at Lyle Cottage, Lymington, 24–28 August 1996.
9 Martin Wallace, 'Profile – Terence O'Neill, op. cit.
10 Cited in *Irish Times*, 30 March 1963, press cuttings, O'Neill papers.
11 O'Neill, *Autobiography*, pp. 35, 38, 58, 62–3.
12 Letter from O'Neill to Knox Cunningham, 17 April 1963, Prime Minister's Papers, PRO, PREM/11/4386.
13 *Irish Times*, 30 March 1963, ibid., 2 April 1963, press cuttings, O'Neill papers.
14 *Belfast Telegraph*, 28 March 1963.
15 *Northern Whig*, 30 March 1963, press cuttings, O'Neill papers.
16 Ken Bloomfield, *Stormont in crisis*, pp. 74–5. Interview with Rt Hon. Harry West, 15 December 1994. Cabinet conclusions, passim.
17 *Belfast Telegraph*, 22 July 1964. The Ministry of Development was finally established in January 1965.

18   Ibid., 21 January 1965.
19   O'Neill, *Autobiography*, p. 61.
20   *Belfast Telegraph*, 21 January 1965.
21   Ibid., 20 October 1964.
22   NIHC, vol. 44, 21 May 1959, c. 1569. Ibid., 2 December 1959, vol. 45, c. 1102. See also O'Neill's speech to the Edinburgh University Union, 1 May 1970, submitted to the Commission on the Constitution, Home Office, HO/221/161, PRO. In the mid 1960s O'Neill described himself as a 'Progressive Conservative in the Canadian sense.' Henry Kennedy, 'Politics in Northern Ireland', footnote, p. 59.
23   Interview with Lord McConnell, 17 February 1995.
24   *News Letter*, 22 February 1963. For the first time ever that work was curtailed at Stormont due to snowdrifts. Ibid., 7 February 1963.
25   Roy Lilley, 'Unionism today – looking forward at social issues', *Belfast Telegraph*, 21 October 1963.
26   See the discussion on linen industry subsidies, Cabinet conclusions, 29 March 1962, PRONI, CAB/4/1190/9. Faulkner successfully led the traditionalists.
27   Said Faulkner, following a review of the situation upon becoming Minister of Commerce, to his East Down Unionist Association. *Belfast Telegraph*, 29 July 1963.
28   Ibid., 19 November 1963.
29   'Economic plan for Northern Ireland (non-agenda item)', Cabinet conclusions, 21 October 1963, PRONI, CAB/4/1239/11, p. 4.
30   Ibid., pp. 4–5.
31   Ibid., p. 5.
32   Ibid.
33   Ibid., pp. 5–6.
34   See also 'Northern Ireland Economic Plan', Cabinet conclusions, 25 November 1964, PRONI, CAB/4/1279/8, p. 2. C. J. Bateman, 'Northern Ireland Economic Plan. Memorandum by the Secretary to the Cabinet', 20 November 1964, PRONI, CAB/4/1279/6, p. 3.
35   NIHC, vol. 55, 22 October 1963, c. 29–30.
36   [Wilson Report] *Economic Development in Northern Ireland*, Cmd 479 (Belfast, 1964).
37   Bew, Gibbon and Patterson, *Northern Ireland 1921–1994*, p. 136.
38   Thomas Wilson, 'First Economic Plan for Northern Ireland' in Michael Viney (ed.), *Seven seminars: an appraisal of regional planning in Ireland. Report on the 'Regional Planning Conference Ireland 1969' held in Belfast in March, 1969* (Dublin, 1969) pp. 15–17.
39   For Wilson's profound scepticism regarding the benefits of economic planning, see Wilson, *Ulster: conflict and consent*, pp. 91–2.
40   Ronnie Munck, *The Irish economy: results and prospects* (London, 1993) p. 59. Cf. Charles F. Carter, 'The Wilson Report: a further comment', *Studies: an Irish quarterly review of letters, philosophy and science* (Dublin, 1965) vol. LIV, pp. 183–6, p. 184. For the timidity of the second plan, covering 1970–5, see James Callaghan, *A house divided: the dilemma of Northern Ireland* (London, 1973) pp. 137–9.
41   *Belfast Telegraph*, 14 November 1963. Gavin McCrone, *Regional policy in*

Britain (London, 1969) pp. 121–9.

42 *News Letter*, 10 January 1963. *Belfast Telegraph*, 14 November 1963.

43 *Belfast Telegraph*, 5 December 1963. Cf. Ibid., 13 March 1964.

44 Alec Cairncross, *The British economy since 1945: economic policy and performance 1945–90* (Oxford, 1992) pp. 141–3.

45 *Belfast Telegraph*, ibid., 25 May 1964.

46 Ibid., 12 November 1964.

47 *News Letter*, 17 July 1963.

48 As the *News Letter* noted when O'Neill met Henry Brooke, the Home Secretary, in March 1964. *News Letter*, 13 March 1964.

49 Ibid., 6 July 1963.

50 Interview of Terence O'Neill by Ralph Bossence, ibid., 8 June 1964.

51 Ibid., 9 June 1964. The event was picketed by the Irish Workers' Group, the political nursery of many future People's Democracy leaders.

52 *Evening News*, 1 June 1965, *News Letter*, 1 June 1965, *Belfast Telegraph*, 14 June 1966, 17 July 1967.

53 'Ulster Weeks in Great Britain (non-agenda item)', Cabinet conclusions, 20 September 1963, PRONI, CAB/4/1238/20. The republic of Ireland had been organizing 'Irish Weeks' in Britain for some time. 'Ulster Weeks in Great Britain. Note for P.M. to speak at conclusion of Cabinet discussion on pre-release of White Papers, etc., to the Press', no date, PRONI, CAB/4/1238/7.

54 *News Letter*, 26 October, 17 November 1964.

55 Wilson, *Ulster: conflict and consent*, p. 84.

56 'Northern Ireland Economic Plan', Cabinet conclusions, PRONI, CAB/4/1283/3, p. 1.

57 See Marc Mulholland, '"One of the greatest hurdles ...": The recognition of the Northern Ireland Committee of the Irish Congress of trade unions 1963–4.', *Saothar*, 1997.

58 See the speech by Harold Binks, chairman of the NIC, to the annual Northern Ireland ICTU conference. *Report of the fourth annual conference of unions affiliated to ICTU in Northern Ireland*, 15 May 1963, NIC-ICTU papers. Report on Ulster Unionist Conference, *Belfast Telegraph*, 4 April 1963.

59 Cabinet conclusions, 17 April 1963, PRONI, CAB/4/1227, plus appended memorandum from the Minister of Finance.

60 Jack Macgougan, President of ICTU, announced it to the Vocational Teachers' Association Annual Conference in Athlone. *News Letter*, 18 April 1963.

61 'Unions move to end Economic Council deadlock', ibid., 3 October 1963.

62 David Gordon, *The O'Neill years: Unionist politics 1963–9* (Belfast, 1989) p. 15. The sensitivity of continuing negotiations was highlighted by the furious reactions to the leak on the part of NIC members. NIC minutes, 11 October 1963.

63 For details see: Minutes of a special meeting of the NIC, 24 May 1963; Minutes of a special meeting of the NIC, 10 June 1963; NIC minutes, 3 July 1963; Report of a special conference of unions affiliated to ICTU in Northern Ireland, 5 July 1963; *Belfast Telegraph*, 2 August 1963; Minutes of a special meeting of the NIC, 22 August 193; Appendix to Cabinet conclusions (correspondence between the Government and trade unions), 20 September 1963, PRONI, CAB/4/1238.

64 Cabinet conclusions, 20 September 1963, PRONI, CAB/4/1238; see also the appended memorandum by Herbert Kirk, 18 September 1963.
65 *Belfast Telegraph*, 23 September 1963.
66 W. D. Flackes, 'I.C.T.U. – the new relationship', ibid., 27 July 1964.
67 Herbert Kirk, 'Memorandum on the NIC of ICTU', 5 March 1964, PRONI, CAB/4/1259/8.
68 Cabinet conclusions, 11 March 1964, PRONI, CAB/4/1259/11.
69 *Belfast Telegraph*, 20 April 1964.
70 Ibid., 24 April 1964.
71 Ibid., 9 May 1964.
72 Reports of the working party on government/trade union relations, 15 May, 27 May & 4 June 1964. The draft as amended read:
The functions of the Northern Ireland Committee of the Irish Congress of Trade Unions shall be to implement, in respect to Northern Ireland, decisions of Annual and Special Delegate Conferences, and of the Executive Council, on matters of concern to affiliated organisations having membership in Northern Ireland, and to recommend to the Executive Council policy on matters of concern to affiliated organisations in Northern Ireland, *provided that*, subject to the requirements that decisions reached have due regard to the position of members outside Northern Ireland, *the Northern Ireland Committee shall* deal with matters relating to the internal, industrial, economic and political conditions of Northern Ireland and of direct concern to Northern Ireland members only, and *shall* implement its decisions and the decisions of the Northern Ireland Conference on such matters.
(Words italicized are those amended from the first draft).
73 Cabinet conclusions, 25 June 1964, CAB/4/1259/11.
74 *Belfast Telegraph*, 30 June 1964. O'Neill, *Autobiography*, p. 63. O'Neill also asserts that Faulkner argued that the decision on recognition be postponed. He may have been thinking of the 11 March Cabinet meeting. Faulkner admits that he was seen as a hard-liner on the recognition issue. Faulkner, *Memoirs of a statesman*, p. 30.
75 *Belfast Telegraph*, 28 July 1963.
76 Ibid., 24 August 1964; *The report of the NIC to the seventh annual conference of unions affiliated to the ICTU in Northern Ireland, 1965*, NIC-ICTU papers.
77 As an anonymous trade union leader told the *Belfast Telegraph*, 9 May 1964.
78 For example, the NEC banned the NIC from joining the National Association of British Manufacturers as a corporate member. NIC minutes, 3 March 1965.
79 Gordon, *The O'Neill years*, p. 19.
80 Faulkner, *Memoirs of a statesman*, p. 30. C. E. B. Brett, *Long shadows cast before*, p. 132.
81 According to Lord Blease, Faulkner became sympathetic to the trade unions through his shipyard connections as Minister of Commerce. Somewhat surprisingly Harry West, the Minister of Agriculture, was also sympathetic. Terry Cradden, *Trade unionism, socialism and partition: the labour movement in Northern Ireland 1939–53* (Belfast, 1993) p. 150. After recognition trade union relations with Faulkner markedly improved. Bleakley, *Faulkner*, pp. 58–9.

82 Sir Josiah Eccles, *Administration of the electricity supply service* (Belfast, HMSO, June 1963).

83 *Belfast Telegraph*, 21 November 1963.

84 Ibid., 30 October 1964. *A ten year programme for electricity supply* (Belfast, HMSO, 1965) Cmd 418.

85 *Belfast Telegraph*, 23 May 1963.

86 Terence O'Neill, as Minister of Finance, 'Ulster Transport Authority finances', Cabinet conclusions, 1 November 1961, PRONI, CAB/4/1176/13, pp. 1–2.

87 Henry Benson, *Northern Ireland railways* (Belfast, HMSO, 1963) Cmd 458.

88 NIHC, vol. 56, 13 February 1964, c. 613–25, 26 February 1964, c. 2777–80.

89 Ron Wiener, *The rape and plunder of the Shankill, community action: the Belfast experience* (privately published, 1976) pp. 49–52.

90 'Northern Ireland's Roads', 22 January 1964, Minutes of meeting between O'Neill and Home, 23 January 1964, Prime Minister's papers, PRO, PREM/11/4964.

91 'Progress report on the Economic Plan', Cabinet conclusions, 7 April 1966, PRONI, CAB/4/1328, p. 3.

92 Mark Arnold-Foster, 'The state of the nation – 5. Plans and whims in Ulster', *The Guardian*, n.d., press cuttings, O'Neill papers.

93 [Matthew Report] *Belfast regional survey and plan: recommendations and conclusions* (Belfast, HMSO, 1963) Cmd 451. The full plan was published on 13 April 1964.

94 *News Letter*, 6 April 1963.

95 Ibid., 9 May 1963.

96 The April jobless figures were down 5050 on the month and up 13 on the year. *News Letter*, 23 April 1963.

97 New City Design Group, *First report on the proposed New City, County Armagh* (Belfast, HMSO, 1964).

98 *Belfast Telegraph*, 9 December 1964.

99 'House of Commons motion on Belfast regional plan', memorandum from William J. Morgan, Minister of Health and Local Government, to the Cabinet, 25 April 1963, CAB/4/1229/6.

100 For example the Belfast Junior Chamber of Commerce in a lengthy report *Belfast Telegraph*, 19 October 1963.

101 William J. Morgan, Minister of Health and Local Government, 'Administration of town and country planning: draft White Paper', Cabinet conclusions, 11 December 1963, CAB/4/1247/9, p. 2.

102 *The administration of town and country planning in Northern Ireland*, HMSO, Cmd 465.

103 Liam O'Dowd, 'Regional policy', in Liam O'Dowd, Bill Rolston and Mike Tomilson (eds) *Northern Ireland: between civil rights and civil war* (London, 1980) p. 42.

104 Arthur Maltby, *The government of Northern Ireland 1922–72: a catalogue and breviate of parliamentary papers* (Dublin, 1974) pp. 138–43.

105 Martin Wallace, *Fifty years of self-government* (Newton Abbot, 1971) pp. 140–1.

106 William Craig, 'Local government re-organisation – memorandum submitted to the Cabinet by the Minister of Development', 15 October

1965, PRONI, CAB/4/1316/7.

107 'Local government re-organisation', Cabinet conclusions, 21 October 1965, PRONI, CAB/4/1316/10, pp. 1–2.

108 NIHC, vol. 67, 30 November 1967, c. 2432.

109 *The reshaping of local government: statement of aims* (Belfast, HMSO, 1967) Cmd 517. *The reshaping of local government: further proposals* (Belfast, HMSO, 1969) Cmd 530.

110 Oliver, *Working at Stormont*, pp. 89–90.

111 [Macrory Report] *Review body on local government in Northern Ireland* (Belfast, HMSO, 1970) Cmd 546.

112 J. L. O. Andrews and Ivan Neill, 'Lockwood Committee – joint memorandum by the Ministers of Finance and Education', 19 June 1964, PRONI, CAB/4/1270/6. 'Lockwood Committee', Cabinet conclusions, 25 June 1964, PRONI, CAB/4/1270/8, pp. 8–10. 'Lockwood Committee – second university and teacher training', Cabinet conclusions, 1 July 1964, PRONI, CAB/4/1271/11, pp. 3–4.

113 [Lockwood Report] *Higher education in Northern Ireland* (Belfast, HMSO, 1965) Cmd 475, pp. xi–xiv and *passim*.

114 Ibid. and Herbert Kirk, 'The Lockwood Report – memorandum by the Minister of Education', 11 December 1964, PRONI, CAB/4/1285/8.

115 'The Lockwood Report', Cabinet conclusions, 21 December 1964, PRONI, CAB/4/1286/7, pp. 2–5.

116 'The Lockwood Report', Cabinet conclusions, 6 January 1965, PRONI, CAB/4/1287/8, pp. 4–6.

117 *The Londonderry Sentinel*, 26 May 1965.

118 'Recommendations on agriculture faculty by Lockwood Committee', Cabinet conclusions, 9 March 1965, PRONI, CAB/4/1295/12, pp. 2–3. See also Harry West's memorandum, ibid., CAB/4/1295/9. A prominent civil servant remembers this 'one of the sharpest arguments' he could recall in the administration. John A. Oliver, 'The Stormont administration 1921–72', *Contemporary Record*, vol. 5, no. 1, 1991, pp. 71–104, p. 77. Brian Walker and Alf McCreary, *Degrees of excellence: the story of Queen's, Belfast 1845–1995* (Belfast, 1994), p. 121.

119 'Lockwood proposals for faculty of agriculture', Cabinet conclusions, 3 June 1965, PRONI, CAB/4/1308/7, pp. 4–5.

120 Harris, *Regional economic policy*, p. 33.

121 *Ulster: change and progress* (Belfast, 1970) UUC archive, PRONI, D/1327/20/4/16.

122 O'Neill called Belfast's housing record 'a public scandal'. Cabinet conclusions, 17 October 1968, PRONI, CAB/4/1408/19, p. 3. Cf. Dennis Kennedy, 'Religious houses', *Belfast Telegraph*, 25, 26, 27 November 1964. Barry White, 'Belfast's housing failure', ibid., 8, 9, 10, 11 March 1967. John Dinsmore, 'Too little living room in Derry' and 'An inexcusable delay', ibid., 27, 28 July 1967. Barry White, 'Building up. to a crisis', ibid., 5, 7, 8 March 1968. Alf McCreary, (on housing allocation), ibid., 25, 26, 27 September 1968.

123 Gerry Adams, *Before the dawn: an autobiography* (London, 1996) pp. 83–5, 88–9.

124 *Belfast Telegraph*, 30 April 1969. Wilson, *Ulster*, pp. 126–7.

125 A phrase he used many times, for example, NIHC, vol. 46, 9 February 1960, c. 28–9.
126 Later, of course, a renowned poet and Oxford scholar.
127 The *Unionist*, October 1965.
128 R. J. C. MacDermott, Chair of the Standtown Division of Victoria Unionist Association, reported in *Belfast Telegraph*, 22 February 1963. Cf. letter from Edmund Warnock to John Kerr, n.d. [1963], John Kerr papers, PRONI, D2022/1/44.
129 *Belfast Telegraph*, 19 October 1963.
130 NIHC, vol. 55, 22 October 1963, c. 7.
131 'Labour "thunder stolen"', *News Letter*, 23 October 1963.
132 O'Neill, *Autobiography*, p. 52.
133 The *Unionist*, December 1963.
134 Roy Lilley, 'Unionism today – the Glengall Street machine', *Belfast Telegraph*, 24 October 1963.
135 *Belfast Telegraph*, 1 October 1963.
136 Ibid., 28 March 1964. *News Letter*, 4, 6, 9 April 1964.
137 *Belfast Telegraph*, 6, 20, 24 February, 13, 25 March 1964.
138 Ibid., 18 April 1964. J. A. V. Graham, The consensus forming strategy of the Northern Ireland Labour Party, unpublished PhD thesis (Queen's University of Belfast, 1972) p. 138.
139 Roy Lilley, 'Unionism today – the socialist challenge', *Belfast Telegraph*, 23 October 1963.
140 *Belfast Telegraph*, 28 March 1964.
141 Ibid., 17 April 1964.
142 Ibid., 22 April 1964.
143 Betty Lowry and W. D. Flackes, 'The new middle class – part 5', ibid., 24 April 1964. Roy Lilley, 'Labour: the new foothold – and the future', ibid., 4 June 1964.
144 Ibid., 16 June 1964.
145 Papers of Miss N. Kinghan, PRONI, D 912/2A/6.
146 Patrick Lynch, 'Labour in the North', *Impact/Invictus: Irish Universities Left Review*, no. 1, May 1963.
147 J. A. V. Graham, 'The consensus forming strategy', pp. 110–11.
148 See the letter from Stewart Marshall McCauley, ex-assistant secretary of Bloomfield Divisional Labour Party in *Belfast Telegraph*, 1 February 1964.
149 See the comments of Paddy Wilson, admittedly a vehement anti-partitionist, at the NILP Annual Conference, ibid., 20 April 1965. J. A. V. Graham, 'The consensus forming strategy', footnote 2, p. 126. Paddy Devlin, *Straight left: an autobiography* (Belfast, 1993) p. 79.
150 J. A. V. Graham, 'The consensus forming strategy', pp. 142–72. Brett, *Long shadows cast before*, pp. 85–7, 128–9.
151 Barry White, 'Political diary', *Belfast Telegraph*, 18 June 1965.
152 Barry White, ibid., 13 October 1965.
153 *Belfast Telegraph*, 20 April 1965.
154 Speeches and statements, October 1965, PRONI, INF/3/3/53.
155 *Belfast Telegraph*, 22 October 1965. NIHC, vol. 61, 21 October 1965, c. 2415–44.
156 NIHC, vol. 61, 27 October 1965, c. 2549.

157 *Belfast Telegraph*, 27 October.
158 Ibid., 29 October 1965.
159 Ibid., 5 November 1965.
160 Speeches and statements, November 1965, PRONI, INF/3/3/54.
161 Ulster Unionist Council, *Forward Ulster to target to Ulster 1970* (Belfast, 1965), election ephemera deposited anonymously, PRONI, D. 230/2/10/1.
162 *Belfast Telegraph*, 23 November 1965.
163 Ibid., 22, 23, 24 November 1965. Interview with Rt Hon. David Bleakley, 27 August 1995.
164 Dennis Kennedy, 'Portrait of a premier face to face with the voters; the charmer who brings economics to the faithful', *Belfast Telegraph*, 24 November 1965.
165 Ibid., 11 November 1965. A reporter observed, however, that O'Neill canvassed Oldpark, Victoria, Willowfield, Pottinger, Duncairn, Woodvale and country areas with no armed guards in sight. Dennis Kennedy, 'Portrait of a premier face to face with the voters', *op. cit.* Ibid., 18, 20, 22 November, 3 December 1965.
166 Ibid., 19, 22 November 1965.
167 Ibid., 26 November 1965.
168 Ibid., 24 November 1965.
169 Emphasis in the original. 'Prime Minister answers *Telegraph* questions', ibid.
170 Dennis Kennedy, 'Portrait of a premier face to face with the voters', *op. cit.*
171 *Belfast Telegraph*, 25 November 1965.
172 Ibid., 26 November 1965.
173 Ibid. The *Unionist*, December 1965. Andrew Hamilton, 'Letter from Belfast; back to the old divisions', *Irish Times*, 1 December 1965. James T. Wolff, 'The Unionist Party; the 1965 "vote of confidence"', *Protestant Telegraph*, 30 March 1968.
174 *Belfast Telegraph*, 26 November 1965.
175 Ibid.
176 'Personal triumph for Prime Minister', ibid.
177 *Belfast Telegraph*, ibid.
178 Bloomfield, *Stormont in crisis*, p. 82.
179 Christopher Tugendhat, 'How the voting pattern varied', *Financial Times*, 17 October 1966. 'Press statements and newspaper cuttings', Ulster Unionist Council, PRONI, D 1327/21/29.
180 *Belfast Telegraph*, 1, 2 April 1966. The *Unionist*, April 1966.
181 David Bleakley, the ideal candidate, had left the country. *Sunday Independent*, 3 April 1963. Interview with Rt Hon. David Bleakley, 27 August 1995.
182 *Belfast Telegraph*, 24 March 1966.
183 Sir Alec Cairncross, *Managing the British economy in the 1960s: a treasury perspective* (Hampshire, 1966) pp. 141–58, 294. Roy Lilley, 'The face of change', *Belfast Telegraph*, 12 March 1968.
184 'Shorts Brothers and Harland Ltd.', memorandum by the Minister of Commerce, 26 November 1968, PRONI, CAB/4/1421/10. *Belfast Telegraph*, 18 December 1968.
185 'Harland and Wolff Ltd. – report by the Minister of Commerce', PRONI,

CAB/4/1339/2. 'Harland and Wolff Ltd.', Cabinet conclusions, 17 August 1966, PRONI, CAB/4/1339/4.'Harland and Wolff Ltd.', Cabinet conclusions, 24 August 1966, PRONI, CAB/4/1340/8. Brian Faulkner, 'Shipbuilding Industry (Loans) Bill – Cabinet memorandum by the Minister of Commerce', 22 September 1966, PRONI, CAB/4/1343.

186 *Belfast Telegraph*, 23 September 1966.

187 House of Lords (*Hansard*) vol. 362, 15 July 1975, c. 1242.

188 NIHC, vol. 66, 16 May 1967, c. 1204–23.

189 *Belfast Telegraph*, 24 August 1967.

190 Ibid., 6, 11, 12, 13 September 1967. *News Letter*, 14 September 1967. Cabinet conclusions, 14 September 1967, PRONI, CAB/4/1372, pp. 1–2.

191 'Economies in public expenditure', Cabinet conclusions, 18 January 1968, CAB/4/1382, pp. 1–5.

192 'Unemployment Situation', Cabinet memorandum by the Minister of Commerce, 31 August 1967; Cabinet conclusions, 6 September 1967, PRONI, CAB/4/1371, pp. 1–5.

193 'Unemployment', memorandum by the Minister of Commerce, 22 March 1968, PRONI, CAB/4/1392/5; Cabinet conclusions, 26 March 1968, ibid., CAB/4/1392/19, pp. 2–4.

194 'New city: formal steps', Cabinet conclusions, 6 July 1965, PRONI, CAB/4/1312/17, pp. 3–4.

195 NIHC, 6 July 1965, vol. 61, c. 1494.

196 *Belfast Telegraph*, 6 July 1965.

197 Ibid. For local catholic reaction to the name, see the *Armagh Observer*, 10 July 1965.

198 He suggested 'Clanrolla' or 'Lisnamintry', both local Irish names. Northern Ireland Senate (*Hansard*), 7 July 1965, c. 1309.

199 *Belfast Telegraph*, 10 July 1965.

200 Ibid., 12 July 1965.

201 Ibid., 19 August 1965.

202 Barry White, 'Political diary', ibid., 22 October 1966.

203 Table 2.16, Geoffrey Bell, *The protestants of Ulster* (London, 1976), p. 31.

204 *Belfast Telegraph*, 17 July 1963. The *Londonderry Sentinel*, 17 July 1963.

205 For a profile, see *News Letter*, 2 September 1963.

206 *Belfast Telegraph*, 20 August 1964. He issued a third statement on 24 August 1964.

207 Ibid., 14 August 1964. *News Letter*, 14 August 1964.

208 *News Letter*, ibid. See also *The Times*, 24 April 1967, press cuttings, NIO files.

209 *The Times*, 24 April 1967, press cuttings, NIO files.

210 *News Letter*, 24 July 1964.

211 *Church of Ireland Gazette*, vol. 1, no. 40, 31 July 1964.

212 Minutes of meeting between the Cabinet and Westminster MPs, 8 November 1963, 'Ulster party in Imperial House', Cabinet secretariat files, PRONI, CAB/9J/6/10.

213 Minutes of County Armagh Unionist Association, 1963, papers of J. W. Trueman.

214 New City Design Group, *First report on the proposed New City*, p. 50. *Craigavon New City, second report on the plan* (Belfast, HMSO, 1967) p. 51. Grants were targeted on migrants from Belfast though, ironically, most of

these turned out to be catholics fleeing communal violence. Had slum clearance and the urban motorway in Belfast proceeded as planned, many more of the displaced families available for re-location would have been protestant. Tim Blackman, 'Craigavon: the development and dismantling of Northern Ireland's new town; an example of capitalist planning and the management of disinvestment', *Capital and class*, no. 35, Summer 1987, pp. 123–4.

215 Coogan, *The Troubles*, p. 42.
216 *Belfast Telegraph*, 14, 28 August 1964.
217 'Northern Ireland Economic Plan: growth centres and population forecasts', cabinet conclusions, 1 December 1966, PRONI, CAB/4/1350/12, p. 4.
218 *Belfast Telegraph*, 10 December 1964.
219 Ibid., 3 February 1965.
220 Ibid., 13 February 1963.
221 Ibid., 30 January 1965. The *Derry Journal*, 29 January 1965.
222 *Belfast Telegraph*, 3 February 1965.
223 The *Derry Journal*, 9 February 1965.
224 The *Londonderry Sentinel*, 10 February 1965.
225 *Belfast Telegraph*, 15, 16 February 1965.
226 The *Derry Journal*, 19 February 1965.
227 Barry White, 'Political diary', *Belfast Telegraph*, 12 February 1965.
228 *Belfast Telegraph*, 17 February 1965. Cf. 'The new university: a call for statesmanship', letter from Edmund Warnock MP, ibid. 1 March 1965.
229 Speech by John Hume, 'University for Derry Campaign' papers, PRONI, D/2511/1/4A.
230 NIHC, vol. 59, 4 March 1965, c. 1465–9, 1468.
231 Ibid., c. 1554–9. *Belfast Telegraph*, 5 March 1965.
232 'Derry will press on in new spheres', letter from Mayor of Londonderry, Albert W. Anderson, ibid., 22 February 1965.
233 The *Londonderry Sentinel*, 3 March 1965.
234 *Belfast Telegraph*, 23 February 1965.
235 'Betrayed', letter from Ivan A. Cooper, ibid., 5 March 1965.
236 The *Londonderry Sentinel*, 12 May 1965. *Belfast Telegraph*, 8 May 1965.
237 *Belfast Telegraph*, 8 May 1965.
238 Ibid., 18, 19, 20 May 1965.
239 Ibid., 20 May 1965
240 NIHC, vol. 61, 26 May 1965, c. 42–3. For profiles of the seven accused, The *Londonderry Sentinel*, 2 June 1965.
241 NIHC, vol. 61, 26 May 1965, c. 103.
242 *Belfast Telegraph*, 27 May 1965.
243 Ibid., 31 May 1965.
244 Ibid., 1 June 1965.
245 Ibid. 22 June 1965.
246 Cabinet secretariat files, PRONI, CAB/9D/31/10.
247 *Belfast Telegraph*, 5 June 1965.
248 Ibid., 18 May 1966. The *Londonderry Sentinel*, 18 May 1966. The *Derry Journal*, 20 May 1966.
249 Victor Griffen, *Mark of protest: an autobiography* (Dublin, 1993) pp. 96–8.
250 Lockwood Report, p. 77, para. 215. F. V. Simpson of the NILP demanded a

ruling on whether this breached parliamentary privilege. NIHC, vol. 59, 10 February 1965, c. 504–7.

251 Lockwood Report, p. 79, para. 221. Sir Joseph Lockwood's attempt to put an innocent gloss on this in a television interview was considered to be uncomfortable and unconvincing. William Patrick, 'Coleraine preferred to Derry for new university', *Hibernia*, vol. 29, no. 3, March 1965.

252 'Lockwood Committee', Cabinet conclusions, 25 June 1964, PRONI, CAB/4/1270/8, p. 10.

253 For example, Liam O'Dowd, 'The crisis of regional strategy: ideology and the state in Northern Ireland', in Gareth Rees, Janet Bujra, Paul Littlewood, Howard Newby and Teresa L. Rees, *Political action and social identity: class, locality and ideology* (Hampshire, 1985) p. 151. O'Dowd's anti-capitalism essentially means that any planning decision taken outside the socialist utopia is discriminatory, which rather deflates the concept.

254 Harris, *Regional economic policy*, pp. 33, 52.

255 Government of Northern Ireland Economic Section, *Northern Ireland Economic Report on 1969* (Belfast: HMSO, 1970) p. 8.

256 Patrick Buckland, *A history of Northern Ireland* (Dublin, 1981) pp. 113–14.

257 N. F. R. Crafts, 'The golden age of economic growth in post-war Europe: why did Northern Ireland miss out?', *Irish Economic and Social History*, vol. XXII, 1995, pp. 5–26, p. 12.

258 Wilson quote, in minutes of 'Meeting at Downing Street on 4th November, 1968', CAB/4/1413/9.

259 Harris, *Regional economic policy*, p. 56.

260 Wiener, *The rape and plunder*, pp. 52–69. O'Dowd, 'Regional policy', p. 39.

261 Blackman, 'Craigavon: the development and dismantling of Northern Ireland's new town', p. 127.

262 Frank Gallager, 'Cleavages and consensus: Craigavon Borough Council 1973–81', unpublished MSc thesis (QUB, 1983), p. 1.

263 *Irish Press*, 24 January 1978, press cuttings, NIO files.

264 Paul Compton, *Demographic trends in Northern Ireland*, report 57 of the Northern Ireland Economic Council (Belfast, 1986) p. 101.

265 *Belfast Telegraph*, 26 March 1968.

266 Ibid., 30 October 1967.

267 'Inter-Exchequer Relation', memorandum by the Minister of Finance, 10 November 1967; Cabinet conclusions, 22 November 1967, CAB/4/1376, pp. 1–5.

268 NIHC, 28 March 1968, vol. 69, c. 270–2.

269 *Belfast Telegraph*, 8 April 1968.

270 NIHC, vol. 69, 1 May 1968, c. 821–7, 835–8, 838–44, 845–59, 864–6.

271 *Belfast Telegraph*, 5 June 1968.

272 'The Northern Ireland budget is a notoriously complicated document (when a Unionist MP who happens to be an accountant found a discrepancy of £10 million in the figures last year, it was suggested that this was due to the death of the only man in the Ministry of Finance who could understand the traditional way of cooking the figures).' The *Economist*, 13 May 1961.

273 O'Neill, *Autobiography*, pp. 103–4, House of Lords (*Hansard*), vol. 337, 5 December 1972, c. 188–9.

274 Harold Wilson, *The Labour Government 1964–1970: a personal record* (London, 1971) p. 270.

Chapter 4

1 John Cole, *As it seemed to me*, 18–19.
2 *Belfast Telegraph*, 26 March 1963.
3 NIHC, vol. 49, 4 July 1961, c. 340–3.
4 In a speech to the Annual Charter Day Dinner of Queen's University Association, *Belfast Telegraph*, 7 December 1963.
5 Roy Lilley, 'Unionism today – Looking forward at social issues', ibid., 21 October 1963.
6 A phrase he used in reference to the Matthew Report in a speech to the Annual General Meeting of Clifton Unionist Association, *Belfast Telegraph*, 15 November 1963.
7 *The Tyrone Constitution*, 20 December 1963.
8 *Belfast Telegraph*, 31 January 1964.
9 Ibid., 27 May 1963.
10 The phrase was James Craig's, Patrick Buckland, *Northern Ireland's first Prime Minister: James Craig, Lord Craigavon* (Dublin, 1980) p. 104. See also Patrick Buckland, *The factory of grievances: devolved government in Northern Ireland 1921–39* (Dublin, 1979) p. 17.
11 *News Letter*, 15 August 1963.
12 His itinerary included the Roman Catholic Church. Ballycastle Urban District Council put on a reception for the VIPs. Ibid., 24 August 1964.
13 *Belfast Telegraph*, 4 June 1963. *Irish Times*, 11 June 1963, press cuttings, O'Neill papers. Roy Lilley, 'Unionism today – widening the party's appeal', *Belfast Telegraph*, 22 October 1963.
14 *Belfast Telegraph*, Ibid., 18 December 1963
15 In forty-one major speeches and public statements delivered by O'Neill between 23 February 1963 and 4 April 1964 I found no such reference. *Belfast Telegraph, passim.*
16 The *Unionist*, February 1964.
17 *News Letter*, 14 February 1964. See also his interview with Mervyn Pauley, ibid., 18 January 1965.
18 *Belfast Telegraph*, 3 April 1964.
19 Ibid., 4 April 1963. Emphasis in the original.
20 *Irish Times*, 21 January 1964. See also Welsey Boyd, 'Bigotry still scrawls its ugly trail across North; disappointment with O'Neill's leadership', ibid., 29 January 1964, press cuttings, O'Neill papers.
21 *Belfast Telegraph*, 15 April 1964.
22 O'Neill may be referring to this in his autobiography when he writes: 'I took my first step in the direction of improving community relations... I visited a Catholic school in Ballymoney, County Antrim. And what was more, it emerged quite naturally as a result of my known wishes and attitudes.' O'Neill, *Autobiography*, p. 59.
23 *News Letter*, 17 April 1964.
24 *Belfast Telegraph*, 24 April 1964. *Irish News*, 25 April 1964.

25 Private information.

26 *News Letter*, 25 April 1964.

27 O'Neill, *Autobiography, op. cit.*

28 Ed Maloney and Andy Pollack, *Paisley* (Dublin, 1986) p. 101.

29 *News Letter*, 4, 5, 10, 16 September 1964. *Belfast Telegraph*, 8, 9 September 1964.

30 Kilfedder pandered to protestant sectarianism. Correspondence with Herbert Ditty, Honorary Secretary of the Ulster Loyalist Association, papers of Sir James Alex Kilfedder MP, PRONI, D/4127/1/2/1.

31 They had been up since 6 September without being noticed. Paisley is likely to have co-ordinated the calls. *Belfast Telegraph*, 26 September 1964.

32 Ibid., 28 September 1964.

33 *News Letter*, 29 September 1964. NIHC, vol. 57, 7 October 1964, c. 2893.

34 *Belfast Telegraph*, 29 September 1964. NIHC, vol. 57, 8 October 1964, c. 2894.

35 *Belfast Telegraph*, 30 September; NIHC, vol. 57, 7 October 1964, c. 2838.

36 *Belfast Telegraph*, 30 September 1964.

37 NIHC, vol. 57, 8 October 1964, c. 2894.

38 *Belfast Telegraph*, 1 October 1964. *Irish Times*, 3 October 1964.

39 *The Times*, 3 October 1964.

40 NIHC, vol. 57, 8 October 1964, c. 2896.

41 *Belfast Telegraph*, 13 October 1964.

42 Ibid.

43 See Ralph Bossence, 'As I see it', *News Letter*, 1 October 1964.

44 *Belfast Telegraph*, 5 October.

45 Ibid., 5 October 1964.

46 Northern Ireland Senate (*Hansard*), 7 October 1964, vol. 47, c. 1352 & 1370.

47 Denis Barritt, *Northern Ireland: a problem to every solution* (London, 1982) pp. 6–7.

48 NIHC, vol. 57, 7 October 1964, c. 2853.

49 *The Times*, 13 October 1964.

50 'Flag panic', letter, *Belfast Telegraph*, 29 October 1964.

51 'Paisley "not a Unionist Party member"', letter from Rev. Ian Paisley, Councillor James McCarroll and Alderman Albert Duff to the *Belfast Telegraph*, ibid.

52 NIHC, vol. 58, 29 October 1964, c. 202–3. See also leaflet in Papers of Councillor Mrs N. Laird, , 'Imperial election 1964 – West Belfast', PRONI, D 2669/4.

53 *Belfast Telegraph*, 12 October 1964.

54 'Liberal win will put Ulster on the map – McElroy', 'Election platform', ibid., 8 October 1964.

55 NIHC, vol. 58, 3 November 1964, c. 243–4.

56 *Belfast Telegraph*, 8 October 1964.

57 Northern Ireland Senate (*Hansard*), 15 October 1964, vol. 47, c. 1447–8. The *Fermanagh Herald*, 17 October 1964.

58 The *Unionist*, November 1964.

59 *Belfast Telegraph*, 16 October 1964.

60 Ibid., 16, 19 October 1964.

61 Ibid., 23 October 1964, 26 January 1965.
62 Ibid., 20 October 1964.
63 Percy Dymond, 'London letter', ibid., 13 November 1964.
64 *Belfast Telegraph*, 20 October 1964.
65 Ibid., 9 December 1964.
66 Ibid., 7 December 1964.
67 'Diary written on flight from Detroit to Minneapolis, North America September/October 1963', Monday October 12, O'Neill papers.
68 House of Lords (*Hansard*), vol. 315, 15 February 1971, c. 405; vol. 332, 5 July 1972, c. 1427; vol. 338, 5 February 1973, c. 917; vol. 339, 5 March 1973, cc. 902–3; vol. 348, 19 December 1973, c. 375; vol. 350, 13 March 1974, cc. 69–70; vol. 460, 11 February 1985, c. 70. For this reason he supported proportional representation, so as to strengthen the middle ground, and was a member of Conservative Action for Electoral Reform. Ibid., vol. 392, 9 June 1978, c. 77; vol. 398, 15 February 1979, c. 1424
69 Ibid., vol. 332, 5 July 1972, c. 1428; vol. 354, 30 October 1974, c. 118.
70 Letter to *The Times*, 10 November 1973, press cuttings, NIO papers.
71 'Change of Prime Minister – March 1963: supplementary note', in file entitled, 'Resignation of Lord Brookeborough and the appointment of Captain Terence O'Neill as Prime Minister of Northern Ireland', PRO, HO 284/57, p. 1. Minutes of a Parliamentary Unionist Party meeting cited by Edmund Warnock in *Belfast Telegraph*, 24 October 1963.
72 *Belfast Telegraph*, 23 October 1963.
73 His handwriting on the envelopes was recognized.
74 See Faulkner's speech to East Down Unionist association. *News Letter*, 29 July 1963.
75 Boal had been deprived of the whip for two years. His readmission was proposed by Dr. Robert Nixon and Nat Minford, both anti-Brookeborough rebels. *Belfast Telegraph*, 21 May 1963. Cabinet conclusions, 1963 ff. *passim*.
76 When the veteran Nationalist MP, Cahir Healy, resigned in 1965, O'Neill made the comment that 'In fact, curious though this may seem, I have learned more about Stormont from Mr. Healy than I have from any other Member of the House.' NIHC, vol. 61, 27 October 1965, c. 2549. Though perhaps exaggerated, this does indicate that O'Neill felt no great personal empathy with his own side.
77 Private information.
78 Interview with Harry West, 15 December 1994. Coralie Kinahan, *Behind every great man ... ?* (Templepatrick, n.d. [1997]) p. 303.
79 David Bleakley, *Peace in Ireland: two states, one people* (London, 1995) pp. 79–80. Cf. Hayes, *Minority verdict*, p. 65.
80 Interview in *The Times*, 31 May 1965.
81 *News Letter*, 16 September 1964.
82 *Irish News*, 19 October 1963, press cuttings, O'Neill papers.
83 See his 1963 Twelfth speech, *News Letter*, 13 July 1963. The *Unionist*, August 1963.
84 *Ulster Commentary*, no. 236, September 1965. *Belfast Telegraph*, 24 September 1965. Dennis Kennedy, 'Putting the "Scotch-Irish" image to work for politics and trade', *Hibernia*, vol. 29, nos 9, 10, October 1965.
85 Brian Faulkner's father was more sceptical. "What's he bloody talking

about? ... Sure his bloody ancestors drove them out of Ulster." Kelly, *Bonfires on the hillside*, p. 181.

86 Gailey, *Crying in the wilderness*, pp. 96–7.

87 O'Neill, *Autobiography*, pp. 47–9; *Belfast Telegraph*, 30 April 1963. For correspondence between O'Neill and Kennedy, see Arthur Mitchell, *JFK and his Irish heritage* (Dublin, 1993) p. 130.

88 *Belfast Telegraph*, 1 May 1963. Perhaps he agreed with Samuel Johnson: 'BOSWELL. "Is not the Giant's-causeway worth seeing?" JOHNSON. "Worth seeing? yes; but not worth going to see."' James Boswell, *The life of Samuel Johnson* (London, 1949) vol. 2, p. 291.

89 The *Unionist*, June 1963.

90 *Belfast Telegraph*, 21 January, 4 February 1964. *News Letter*, 3 February 1964.

91 Timothy Patrick Coogan, *Ireland since the rising* (Connecticut, 1966) p. 316. Portraits of the martyred president were a staple in Irish catholic homes.

92 NIHC, vol. 54, 2 July 1963, c. 2087–94.

93 Barry White, 'Political diary', *Belfast Telegraph*, 2 April 1965.

94 Nixon alleged that 'there was probably a majority in the House who thought that this was not the proper site or a solution of the problem Professor Matthew posed.' *News Letter*, 6 February 1964. Ibid., 30 April 1964. The Lib-Lab opposition generally supported the project, though with some reservations, while the Nationalists opposed it.

95 'The New City', Cabinet conclusions, PRONI, CAB/4/1280/11, p. 5. West later claimed that he always opposed the New City scheme as it was a diversion of necessary funds from agriculture. Interview, 20 March 1995.

96 Economic Plan', Cabinet conclusions, 15 June 1966, PRONI, CAB/4/1334/23, p. 5.

97 *Belfast Telegraph*, 30 April 1965.

98 Ibid., 1 May 1965.

99 Ibid., 17 July 1963. *News Letter*, 17 July 1963.

100 Roy Lilley, 'Political diary', *Belfast Telegraph*, 15 November 1963.

101 Following a resolution passed at the 1963 Annual Conference calling for a reorganization of the event to make it 'of greater value and interest' the Executive Committee agreed to certain changes. The Annual Conference was moved to April, separating it from the Annual Meeting of the Ulster Unionist Council in March; of the three sessions one was open to the press; the platform, including the Cabinet, would face the hall; resolutions were streamlined; and the venue was moved from the Wellington Hall to the more illustrious Ulster Hall. Ironically these changes designed to modernize the party's image in the new media age only accentuated the embarrassment of delegate revolts. Agenda of the Annual Conference of the Ulster Unionist Council, Friday 8 May 1964, UUC papers, PRONI, D 1327/9/23, p. 9

102 *Belfast Telegraph*, 21 April 1964.

103 *Belfast Telegraph*, op. cit. The motion was only carried very narrowly on a show of hands and was disputed. The Chairman, David McClelland, refused a ballot. *News Letter*, 9 May 1964.

104 'The Prime Minister... pointed out that the Treasury might look again at the roads programme if the Government failed to deal with the railway situation, and the Minister of Finance agreed.' 'Transport policy', Cabinet

conclusions, 12 February 1964, PRONI, CAB/4/1256/11, p. 5.
105 *Belfast Telegraph*, 3 July 1964.
106 *Belfast Telegraph*, 25 March 1964. The White Paper was welcomed by one Major Bunting, then spokesperson of the Rate Payers' Association, but later to be the chief lieutenant of Paisley. *News Letter*, 25 March 1964.
107 *Belfast Telegraph*, 27 April and 5 May 1964.
108 Ibid., 8 May 1964.
109 Ibid., 3 July 1964.
110 Ibid., 23 July 1964.
111 Northern Ireland Senate (*Hansard*), 27 October 1964, vol. 48, c. 10.
112 *Belfast Telegraph*, 13 April 1965.
113 Ibid., 30 April 1965.
114 Liam O'Dowd, 'Regional policy', p. 42.
115 *Belfast Telegraph*, 18 December 1964.
116 The *Portadown News and County Armagh Advertiser*, 14 August 1964. A protest committee met on 14 August, *Belfast Telegraph*, 15 August 1964.
117 *Farmweek*, 5 January 1965.
118 *Belfast Telegraph*, 15, 17 February 1965.
119 NIHC, vol. 59, 24 February 1965, c. 1067–70 and vol. 60, 1 April 1965, c. 751–2.
120 *News Letter*, 26, 27 February 1963.
121 Ibid., 20 April 1964.
122 Ibid., 14 August 1964.
123 *Belfast Telegraph*, 14 August 1964.
124 Andrew Boyd, 'The Copcutt controversy', *Irish Times*, 1 September 1964, press cuttings, O'Neill papers.
125 *Irish Times*, 17 December 1965, ibid.
126 *News Letter*, 2 September 1966. *Irish News*, 20 September 1966.
127 Ibid., 28 January 1966. *Farmweek*, 1 February 1966.
128 Roy Lilley, 'When two and two make five', *Belfast Telegraph*, 5 September 1963.
129 Roy Lilley, 'Political diary', *Belfast Telegraph*, 25 October 1963.
130 It opened in April 1963. *Northern Whig*, 20 April 1963.
131 *Irish Times*, 10 August 1963, press cuttings, O'Neill papers.
132 They were carried in the *Sunday Times, Sunday Telegraph, Observer* and *Irish Times*. *The Impartial Reporter and Farmers' Journal*, 5 September 1963.
133 'Local Government (Members and Officers) Bill', Cabinet conclusions, 2 May 1963, PRONI, CAB/4/1229/8, p. 2.
134 'Proposed Economic Council', Cabinet conclusions, 9 May 1963, PRONI. CAB/4/1230/11, p. 1; 'Ulster Weeks in Great Britain', Cabinet conclusions, 20 September 1963, PRONI, CAB/4/1238/20, p. 6; '"Ulster Weeks" in Great Britain', Cabinet conclusions, 21 May 1964, PRONI, CAB/4/1267/8, p. 2.
135 'Ministers' private interests – code of principles', Cabinet conclusions, 25 June 1963, CAB/4/1235/1, pp. 1–2.
136 For example, 'Salaries etc. of ministers and Members of Parliament', Cabinet conclusions, CAB/4/1246/10, p. 4.
137 'Mater Infirmorum Hospital', Cabinet conclusions, 22 January 1964, PRONI, CAB/4/1253/9, pp. 1–3. 'National Health Service – Position of Mater Infirmorum Hospital', Cabinet conclusions, 28 May 1964, PRONI,

CAB/4/1268/11, pp. 4–5, 7.
138 For which see Boyd, *Faulkner*, pp. 20–47.
139 *Belfast Telegraph*, 21 September 1964.
140 Ibid., 26 October 1964. *News Letter*, 26 October 1964.
141 *Belfast Telegraph*, 26 October 1964.
142 Ibid., 30 October 1964.
143 Ibid., 5 November 1964.
144 In 1969, in honour of Faulkner's 'courageous stand' in resigning from the government over local government universal suffrage, Gibson and his wife named their baby son Brian. Ibid., 27 January 1969.
145 Ibid., 26 October 1964.
146 NIHC, vol. 58, 29 October 1964, c. 194.
147 Ibid. , c. 196–203, 198–9.
148 NIHC, vol. 58, 4 November 1964, c. 336–40.
149 *News Letter*, 6 November 1964.
150 Roy Lilley, 'Political diary', *Belfast Telegraph*, 6 November 1964.
151 Ibid., 24 November 1964.
152 On 29 October he had also been confirmed as Leader of the House, relieving O'Neill of this responsibility. *Belfast Telegraph*, 29 October 1964.
153 Ivan Neill, 'Arrangement for the co-ordination of economic and physical development policies. Memorandum by the Minister of Finance.', 27 November 1964, Cabinet conclusions, CAB/4/1282/2.
154 Brian Faulkner, 'Arrangement for the co-ordination of economic and physical development policies. Memorandum by the Minister of Commerce.', 30 November 1964, Cabinet conclusions, PRONI, CAB/4/1282/1.
155 'Arrangement for the co-ordination of economic and physical development policies', Cabinet conclusions, 10 December 1964, PRONI, CAB/4/1282/3, pp. 1–3.
156 *Sunday Press*, 13 December 1964, press cuttings, O'Neill papers.
157 James Kelly, 'I say: let everybody see Stormont on telly', *Sunday Independent*, 13 December 1964, ibid.

Chapter 5

1 'Six Counties – Use of names 'Ulster' and 'Northern Ireland', Department of the Taoiseach, National Archives, Dublin, S 1957/63. For a rather economistic analysis of Lemass's motives, see Henry Patterson, 'Seán Lemass and the Ulster question, 1959–65', *Journal of Contemporary History*, 1999, vol. 34, no. 1, pp. 145–59.
2 'Social and Economic Co-operation between the 26 and 6 Counties', Department of the Taoiseach, National Archives, Dublin, 97/6/57.
3 *Round Table*, 1958–62, *passim*. He claimed later that a meeting had been considered, but deemed impossible due to the IRA campaign. *Belfast Telegraph*, 23 January 1965.
4 Speech draft in 'Partition: Government Policy 1963', Department of the Taoiseach, S 9361 K/63, National Archives, Dublin. Lemass made a similar speech to the Oxford Union as early as October 1959. Ian McAllister, *The Northern Ireland Social Democratic and Labour Party: political opposition in a*

divided society (London, 1977), p. 18.

5   Speeches and statements , September 1963, PRONI, INF/3/3/29.
6   *Belfast Telegraph*, 13 September 1963.
7   Speeches and statements , op. cit.
8   *Belfast Telegraph*, 16 September 1963.
9   Ibid., 15, 18 October 1963. Speech draft in 'Partition: Government Policy 1963' op. cit.
10 Speeches and statements , September 1963, PRONI, INF/3/3/30.
11 *Belfast Telegraph*, 19 October 1963.
12 *Ballymena Observer and County Antrim Advertiser*, 8 November 1963. 'Aspects of relations with the Irish Republic', Aide-Memoire by O'Neill, 22 November 1963, Prime Minister's papers, PRO, PREM/11/4964.
13 The unionist Liberal, Robin Bailie, described the widespread fear that a summit would be 'a sort of latter day Niall of the Nine Hostages coming to pay homage to the High King of Ireland'. 'Finding a basis for North-South co-operation', *New Ireland*, 1964.
14 There was, however, little evidence of overwhelming business pressure for rapprochement. It is notable that the first meeting of leaders of the three principal Chambers of Commerce in Ireland, Belfast, Cork and Dublin, took place after the O'Neill/ Lemass summit. The example to business was set by the political sphere and not vise versa. *News Letter*, 24 September 1965.
15 *News Letter*, 19 December 1963.
16 *Belfast Telegraph*, 3 November 1964.
17 NIHC, vol. 58, 18 November 1964, c. 688.
18 *News Letter*, 20 November 1964.
19 In response to Lynch's proposal for a trade committee made up of senior officials from North and South. *Irish Times*, 15 December 1964. Cf. Brian Faulkner, 'Cabinet memorandum by the Minister of Commerce – co-operation with the Irish Republic: tourist publicity', 8 January 1965, PRONI, CAB/4/1289/5.
20 *Financial Times*, 15 January 1965. A nationalist journalist wrote later that 'Faulkner, in a surprise switch, was one of the first to make overtures on cross border co-operation and was actually preparing for a visit to Dublin when Mr. O'Neill staged his dramatic meeting with Lemass.' James Kelly, 'Cloak-and-dagger tactics behind the Unionist crisis', *Sunday Independent*, 25 September 1966. Press cuttings, O'Neill papers.
21 O'Neill decided on a meeting with Lemass at the earliest in mid-December, at the latest in early January. By either reckoning, O'Neill would have been aware of Lemass's visit to Queen's, The *News Letter's* attitude and Faulkner's intentions. Barry White, 'The day Lemass came to Stormont', *Belfast Telegraph*, n.d. [1975], press cuttings, NIO files. Lord O'Neill of the Maine, *The autobiography of Terence O'Neill* (London, 1972) p. 68.
22 'Another important reason for Mr. O'Neill's initiative probably was the rivalry between himself and the Minister of Commerce, Mr. Faulkner. Mr. Faulkner has made no secret of his ambition for the premiership and has been emerging more and more as a champion of better relations with the South.... With Mr. O'Neill being pushed into the background it began to look as if Mr. Faulkner's bid for the premiership could not be long delayed.

Today, Mr. O'Neill is firmly in control and Mr. Faulkner has faded into the background... Mr. O'Neill is now leading enlightened opinion in the North-East.' *Irish Independent*, 18 January 1965, press cuttings, O'Neill papers.

23 O'Neill, *Autiobiography*, pp. 68–73. Gray, *The Irish answer*, pp. 380–1.
24 *Belfast Telegraph*, 15 January 1965.
25 Barry White, 'The day Lemass came to Stormont', loc. cit. *Belfast Telegraph*, 5 February 1965. Brian McConnell, Home Affairs Minister, was informed shortly before Lemass crossed the border as he was responsible for security. Interview with Lord Brian McConnell, 17 February 1995.
26 NIHC, vol. 59, 19 January 1965, c. 15. A survey found one quarter of protestants, however, opposed to the summit. *Belfast Telegraph*, 2 July 1966.
27 Interview with Rt Hon. Harry West, 15 December 1994.
28 *Belfast Telegraph*, 4 February 1965.
29 Press cuttings, O'Neill papers.
30 Cal McCrystal, *Reflections on a quiet rebel* (Harmondsworth, 1997) p. 250.
31 *Belfast Telegraph*, 15 January 1965.
32 Ibid.
33 Ibid.
34 Public debates, Dáil Eireann, 10 February 1965, vol. 214, c. 3.
35 *Irish Times*, 20 January 1965.
36 NIHC, vol. 59, 19 January 1965, c. 14–5.
37 *Belfast Telegraph*, 22 January 1965. The signatories were Dr Robert Simpson (Mid-Antrim), Phelim O'Neill (North Antrim), Samuel Magowan (Iveagh), Ian McClure (Queen's University), Joseph Burns (North Derry), David Little (West Down), William Kennedy (Cromac), William Hinds (Willowfield), Alec Hunter (Carrick), Bessie Maconachie (Queen's University), Issac Hawthorne (Central Armagh).
38 *Belfast Telegraph*, 23 January 1965.
39 Barry White, 'Political diary', ibid., 22 January 1965.
40 *Belfast Telegraph*, 22 January 1965.
41 NIHC, vol. 59, 3 February 1965, c. 319.
42 Ibid., c. 283–94.
43 Ibid., c. 251–7, 254.
44 Ibid., c. 319–20.
45 *Belfast Telegraph*, 9 February 1965.
46 *Sunday People*, 4 November 1973, press cuttings, NIO files.
47 David Harkness, *Northern Ireland since 1920* (Dublin, 1983) p. 5.
48 Transcript, 18 February 1965, Department of Foreign Affairs, National Archives, Dublin, 96/3/15.
49 John Whyte, *Interpreting Northern Ireland* (Oxford, 1990) p. 149.
50 For example, see O'Neill cited in *Irish Independent*, 9 October 1963. O'Neill, *Crossroads, passim*.
51 He bracketed himself, sometimes, with strange company. 'The rebel Countess, Countess Markowitz, was, like the noble Earl, Lord Longford, and myself, of impeccable Anglo-Irish descent.' House of Lords (*Hansard*) vol. 337, 5 December 1972, c. 189. Only 2 per cent of Ulster protestants considered themselves to be Anglo-Irish. Rose, *Governing without consensus*, p. 208.

52 Terence O'Neill, 'A spectator's notebook', *Spectator*, 22 June 1977, my emphasis.

53 *Irish Times*, 14 October 1972. *Belfast Telegraph*, 7 November 1972, *Irish News*, 9 November 1972, press cuttings, NIO files.

54 *Interplay*, November 1970, *Belfast Telegraph*, 7 November 1970, *Sunday Independent*, 8 November 1970, *Sunday News*, 8 November 1970, The *Observer*, 8 November 1970, *News Letter*, 8 November 1970, *Irish News*, 9 November 1970, *Irish Press*, 12 January 1971, *News of the World*, 22 October 1972, The *Guardian*, 8 November 1972, *Daily Mail*, 8 November 1972, *Irish Press*, 8 November 1972, press cuttings, NIO files.

55 *Belfast Telegraph*, 24 February 1965.

56 *News Letter*, 27 February 1965. The *Unionist*, March 1965.

57 *Belfast Telegraph*, 9 April 1965.

58 There were, however, 'a few hectic weeks' of highly symbolic cross-border meetings and conciliatory rhetoric following the summit. Fergal Tobin, *The best of decades: Ireland in the 1960s* (Dublin, 1996), p. 128.

59 *Belfast Telegraph*, 4 February, 2 April 1965. NIHC, vol. 59, 10 March, c. 1742.

60 The *Guardian*, 18 March 1965. NIHC, vol. 60, 18 March 1965.

61 'Cross-border trade', Cabinet conclusions, 14 April 1965, PRONI, CAB/4/1300/12, p. 8.

62 'Anglo-Irish trade', Cabinet conclusions, 29 June 1965, PRONI, CAB/4/1311/9, p. 4.

63 'Anglo-Irish trade: preferential treatment for Northern Ireland industries', Cabinet conclusions, 11 August 1965, PRONI, CAB/4/1313/11, pp. 6–7.

64 *Belfast Telegraph*, 23 December 1965. Harold Wilson had caused Unionist shudders when he suggested a meeting of the three premiers on the islands. The *Guardian*, 18 March 1965.

65 *Free trade agreement and related agreements, exchanges of letters and understandings, laid by the Government before each House of the Oireachtas* (Dublin, 1965).

66 NIHC, vol. 62, 16 December 1965, c. 19.

67 Dr Robert Simpson (Mid-Antrim) and Phelim O'Neill (North Antrim) were so enraged at the repercussions on Northern Ireland farming that they lobbied for the dismissal of Harry West, Minister of Agriculture. *Sunday Press*, 29 January 1967, press cuttings, O'Neill papers.

68 'Co-operation on tourist development', Cabinet conclusions, 3 June 1965, PRONI, CAB/4/1308/7, pp. 1–3.

69 'Joint North/South tourist literature', Cabinet conclusions, 11 August 1965, PRONI, CAB/4/1313/11, pp. 7–8.

70 'Co-operation with the Irish Republic: joint tourist literature', Cabinet conclusions, 7 October 1965, PRONI, CAB/4/1315/12, pp. 3–4.

71 'Joint tourist publicity', Cabinet conclusions, 15 September 1966, PRONI, CAB/4/1342/13.

72 'Projected history of Ireland', Cabinet conclusions, 11 August 1965, PRONI, CAB/4/1313/11, p. 6.

73 'Electricity (Supply) Bill', Cabinet conclusions, 15 June 1966, PRONI, CAB/4/1334/pp. 4–5.

74 That the Republic's end of the link-up was in Maynooth he considered

particularly ominous. See, for example, *Belfast Telegraph*, 8 May 1965.

75 *Electricity in Ireland: report of the Joint-Committee on Cooperation in Electricity Supply* (Belfast, HMSO, March 1966). *Belfast Telegraph*, 5 October 1967. O'Neill, *Autobiography*, p. 75.

76 Conor Cruise O'Brien, *States of Ireland* (Frogmore, 1974, 1st ed. 1972) pp. 140–1.

77 *Belfast Telegraph*, 4, 26 February 1965.

78 Barry White, 'O'Neill 100 weeks later', *Belfast Telegraph*, 4 March 1965.

79 *Belfast Telegraph*, 29 October 1964.

80 Interview with Lord McConnell, 17 February 1995. Private information. Interview with Rt Hon. Ivan Neill, 15 August 1995.

81 *Belfast Telegraph*, 3 April 1965.

82 Ibid., 6 April 1965.

83 Ibid.

84 Ibid., 7 April 1965.

85 Ibid., 9 April 1965.

86 Ibid., 8 April 1965.

87 Ibid., 20 May 1965.

88 Ibid., 28 October 1965.

89 Alvin Jackson, 'Unionist myths 1912–1985', *Past and present: a journal of historical studies*, no. 136, August 1992, pp. 164–85, pp. 168–9.

90 The clearest example of ecumenically influenced thinking was expressed, significantly, by a catholic Unionist. Louis Boyle, 'Unionism at the crossroads', *Yearbook of the Conservative and Unionist Association of Queen's University Belfast 1967/8* (Belfast, 1967) pp. 41–2, John Johnston papers, PRONI, D/3219/3/2. For the contrary, see the address delivered by Harry Calvert, law lecturer and ex-member of the NILP. 'The workings of democracy', Unionist Society meeting, 29 January 1970, Records of the Unionist Society, minute book 1962–71, PRONI, D/3292/A/3.

91 *News Letter*, 9 March 1964.

92 The *Unionist*, September 1959, January 1969.

93 Ibid., November 1965.

94 M. W. Dewar, John Brown, S. E. Long, *Orangeism: a new historical appreciation* (Belfast, 1967) p. 190.

95 *Belfast Telegraph*, 13 July 1967.

96 Interview with Roy Lilley, 'Capt. O'Neill on this fascinating document', ibid., 18 December 1967.

97 The comments of Andrew Harris, an 18-year-old shipyard worker and Orangeman, are illustrative: 'I'm labour-minded I suppose. O'Neill seems so remote. He sits up there like a figurehead. I'm all for the meetings with Lynch if they are really for the good of both sides. As for Paisley, I wouldn't say I am a follower exactly but I agree with a lot of his points. I don't like the way he goes on about Roman Catholics all the time – some of my best friends are Roman Catholics – but I do agree with him wanting to keep things as they are in Northern Ireland. I can't see that there will ever be a united Ireland. I think there will soon be a Paisley party here.' Suzanne Lowry, 'Seeing life from a shop and a shipyard', ibid., 29 February 1968.

98 A journalist has suggested that MI5 had a hand in the 'O'Neill must go' campaign as part of a long-term plot to facilitate British withdrawal from

Northern Ireland. Chris Moore, *The Kincora scandal: political cover-up and intrigue in Northern Ireland* (Dublin, 1996) pp. 38, 232–5.

99 *Belfast Telegraph*, 10 October 1963.
100 Throughout January 1966 there were regularly over twelve letters on the subject published daily in the *Belfast Telegraph*.
101 Ibid., 3 January 1966.
102 *Irish Times*, 22 February 1966. Memorandum, 18 February 1966, 'Northern Ireland; royal matters – general; naming of bridge in Northern Ireland "Queen Elizabeth II Bridge"', PRONI, HO 5/149.
103 *Belfast Telegraph*, 1 March 1966.
104 *Irish Times*, 1 March 1966, press cuttings, O'Neill papers.
105 Biographical details in *Belfast Telegraph*, 16 March 1966.
106 Ibid., 1 March 1966.
107 Ibid.
108 'Action not words: the new Conservative programme' in F. W. S. Craig (ed.), *British general election manifestos 1959–1987* (Dartmouth, 1990) p. 79.
109 *Belfast Telegraph*, 10 March 1966.
110 Ibid.
111 Ibid., 16 March 1966.
112 Ibid., 17 March 1966.
113 Ibid., 22 March. The *Belfast Telegraph* leaked this story to scotch rumours of a deal. It was keen to mark the victory for O'Neill and, by doing so, widen the division with the Paisleyites. Letter from Jack Sayers to Connolly Gage, cited in Gailey, *Crying in the wilderness*, p. 100. *Belfast Telegraph*, 21 March 1966. Maloney and Pollack, *Paisley*, p. 129.
114 *Belfast Telegraph*, 21 March 1966.
115 Ibid., 22 March 1966.
116 Ibid., 9, 10, 11, 14 March 1966.
117 Ibid., 15 March 1966.
118 The bookmakers gave his odds as 7 to 4 against, *Belfast Telegraph*, 14 March 1966. Ibid., 28, 29 March 1966.
119 Ibid., 31 March 1966.
120 Cornelius O'Leary, 'Belfast West', D. E. Butler and Anthony King (eds), *The British general election of 1966* (London, 1966) p. 258.
121 O'Neill, *Ulster at the crossroads*, pp. 113–16.
122 *Irish News*, 3 January 1966,
123 Tobin, *The best of decades*, p. 145.
124 NIHC, vol. 62, 2 March 1966, c. 1539.
125 *Protestant Telegraph*, 28 May 1966. 'Commemoration of the 1916 rebellion', Cabinet secretariat files, PRONI, CAB/9B/299/1.
126 *Irish News*, 4 April 1966.
127 *Belfast Telegraph*, 23 March 1966.
128 Ibid., 7 April 1966. For Government concerns about IRA activity, Prime Minister's Papers, PREM/13/980, PRO.
129 Ibid., 7 April 1966. *The Mid-Ulster Mail*, 9 April 1966.
130 *Belfast Telegraph*, 8 April 1966.
131 Ibid., 13, 14, 15 April 1966.
132 Ibid., 15, 16 April 1966.
133 Ibid., 18 April 1966. *Irish News*, 18 April 1966.

134 Barry White, 'Political diary', *Belfast Telegraph*, 22 April 1966.
135 *Belfast Telegraph*, 12 July 1966.
136 'Presbyterian Church in Ireland', Department of the Taoiseach, National Archives, Dublin, 96/6/721. *Belfast Telegraph*, 10 June 1965, *Irish Times*, 24 May 1966. Irish Independent, 10 June 1967.
137 NIHC, vol. 64, 7 June 1966, c. 29.
138 *Belfast Telegraph*, 7une 1966
139 Ibid., 10 June 1966.
140 NIHC, vol. 64, 15 June 1966, c. 301.
141 Ibid., c. 307–13.
142 'Political diary', *Belfast Telegraph*, 17 June 1966.
143 NIHC, vol. 64, 15 June 1966, c. 336–7.
144 Copy of speech in 'Disturbances in Belfast, June 1966', PRONI, CAB/9B/300/1. *News Letter*, 10 June 1966. Lord McConnell insists that he was misrepresented. Interview with Lord McConnell, 17 February 1995.
145 *Belfast Telegraph*, 24 June 1966.
146 Ibid., 16 June 1966.
147 Ibid., 17 June 1966. The *Protestant Telegraph*, 2 July 1966.
148 *Belfast Telegraph*, 18 June 1966.
149 Ibid., 18 June 1966. He had come under pressure from Jack Sayers, editor of the *Belfast Telegraph*, to do this. Letter from Sayers to Harold Black, Cabinet Secretary, in 'O'Neill – Lemass meeting 1965', NIO files.
150 For the lurid rumours current at the time see the leaflet, 'The Truth about the UVF and the Ward and Scullion murders', 97/6/57, Department of the Taoiseach, National Archives, Dublin.
151 David Boulton, *The UVF: an anatomy of loyalist rebellion* (Dublin, 1973) pp. 34–61. Steve Bruce, *The red hand: protestant paramilitaries in Northern Ireland* (Oxford, 1992) pp. 24–6. Maloney and Pollack, *Paisley*, pp. 135–42.
152 NIHC, vol. 64, 28 June 1966, c. 778. *Belfast Telegraph*, 28 June 1966.
153 NIHC, vol. 64, 29 June 1966, c. 820–1.
154 *Belfast Telegraph*, 19 October 1966.
155 For a confusion between the UVF and Ulster Protestant Volunteers, see NIHC, vol. 64, 30 June 1966, c. 1026.
156 *Belfast Telegraph*, 29 June 1966.
157 Ibid., 2 July 1966.
158 Ibid.
159 *Daily Mirror*, 4 July 1966, press cuttings, O'Neill papers.
160 *Irish Times*, 5 July 1966. *Belfast Telegraph*, 4 July 1966.
161 Terence O'Neill, 'The Queen's visit', July 1966, O'Neill papers.
162 Cf. *Belfast Telegraph*, 13 July 1964.
163 Ibid., 12 July 1965.
164 Ibid.
165 Ibid., 8 June 1966. Cf. Ibid., 12 July 1966. Paisley had left the Orange Order in September 1962. Maloney and Pollack, *Paisley*, p. 54.
166 *Belfast Telegraph*, 12 July 1966.
167 Ibid., 7, 8 July 1966.
168 Ibid., 11 July 1966.
169 Ibid., 12 July 1966
170 Ibid.

171 Ibid., 13 July 1966.
172 Ibid., 18 July 1966.
173 Ibid., 19 July 1966.
174 Ibid., 20 July 1966.
175 Ibid., 23 July 1966.
176 Ibid., 25 July 1966.
177 'The recent disturbances in Belfast', Cabinet conclusions, 25 July 1966, PRONI, CAB/4/1336/2.
178 *Belfast Telegraph*, 26 July 1966.
179 The *Unionist*, September 1966.
180 *Belfast Telegraph*, 3 August 1966.
181 Ibid.
182 Ibid., 26 August 1966.
183 *Belfast Telegraph*, 6 September 1966.
184 Ibid., 21 September 1966.
185 *News Letter*, 23 September 1966.
186 James Kelly, 'Cloak-and-dagger tactics behind Unionist crisis', *Sunday Independent*, 25 September 1966, press cuttings, O'Neill papers.
187 *Belfast Telegraph*, 23 September 1966.
188 Ibid., 11 February 1969.
189 McQuade was a product of the quasi-Paisleyite Court Ward Unionist Association and admitted that he won his council seat from the NILP by fighting the election 'on Protestantism', ibid., 1 June 1966. William Hinds (with William Kennedy) had attended in 1964 a rally addressed by Paisley condemning O'Neill's visit to a catholic school in Ballymoney, ibid., 27 April 1964.
190 Though estimates of the number of signatories vary, John Taylor admitted that he had signed and his had been the last and thirteenth name on the list. Ibid., 26 September 1966.
191 West, it seems, accompanied a rebel delegation to meet Faulkner at his home. Bleakley, *Faulkner*, p. 72. He had advised Faulkner to stay his hand for a month. Gailey, *Crying in the wilderness*, p. 113.
192 'The failure of our people to attend public worship regularly in our churches, with the consequent falling-off in habit of our personal bible reading and prayer, are the direct causes of the tragically unsatisfactory state of our national life.' From Morgan's Twelfth speech at Finaghy, *Belfast Telegraph*, 12 July 1963.
193 This estimate of rebel names and numbers is derived from the *Belfast Telegraph*, 24, 26, 27, 28 September 1966. *Irish Times*, 26 September 1966.
194 *Belfast Telegraph*, 24 September 1966.
195 Claud Gordon, 'Welcoming back the Paisleyites', *Sunday Press*, 25 September 1966, press cuttings, O'Neill papers.
196 *Belfast Telegraph*, 24 September 1966.
197 Ibid.
198 Ibid., 26 September 1966.
199 Ibid., 27 September 1966.
200 Ibid.
201 Ibid., 28 September 1966.
202 Ibid., 26 September 1966.

203 Ibid.
204 Ibid., 24 September 1966.
205 Ibid.
206 Ibid., 26 September 1966.
207 The *Unionist*, October 1966.
208 Interview with Rt Hon. Harry West, 15 December 1994.
209 Barry White, 'But what will happen when Parliament resumes?', *Belfast Telegraph*, 29 September 1966. J. H. Whyte, 'Intra-Unionist disputes in the Northern Ireland House of Commons, 1921–72', *Economic and Social Review*, vol. 5, no. 1, October 1973, p. 103.
210 Anonymous backbencher in *Belfast Telegraph*, 24 September 1966.
211 Ibid., 26 September 1966.
212 Barry White, 'But what will happen when Parliament resumes?', *loc. cit.*
213 *Belfast Telegraph*, 26 September 1966.
214 Ibid., 27 September 1966.
215 Walter Scott's statement, Ibid.
216 Ibid., 28, 29 September 1966.
217 One liberal supporter, Peter Montgomery, president of the Arts Council and a Fermanagh aristocrat, wrote to O'Neill expressing his delight at the Prime Minister's 'resounding victory over the powers of darkness.' Letter to Terence O'Neill, 29 September 1966, Papers of Peter Montgomery, PRONI, D 627/A/2/193.
218 *Belfast Telegraph*, 28 September 1966.
219 From this time he had added police protection due to threats of assassination from loyalists.
220 Profile and interview with Michael Mills, 'Removing the balance of hatred', *Irish Press*, 27 March 1967, press cuttings, O'Neill papers.
221 Transcript of interview with Lord O'Neill for *This Week – Five long years*, BBC radio, July 1974, O'Neill papers.
222 Terence O'Neill cited in Conor Cruise O'Brien, *Ancestral voices: religion and nationalism in Ireland* (Dublin, 1994) p. 150.

Chapter 6

1 *Belfast Telegraph*, 8 October 1966. *Sunday Press*, 9 October 1966.
2 Van Voris, *Violence in Ulster*, p. 47.
3 Dennis Kennedy, 'Northern Ireland's future premier', *Hibernia*, February 1966.
4 Michael McKeown, 'William Craig', Ibid., 12 December 1968.
5 *News Letter*, 30 April 1963.
6 Bloomfield, *Stormont in crisis*, pp. 73, 74, 85–6.
7 Michael McKeown, 'The life and hard times of William Craig', *Hibernia*, 28 August 1970.
8 *Belfast Telegraph*, 30 May 1963.
9 Ibid., 1 June 1963.
10 NIHC, vol. 54, 4 June 1963, c. 1230, 1245–6.
11 Ibid., 5 June 1963, cols 1250–1.
12 *Belfast Telegraph*, 30 November 1963.

13 Ibid., 3 December 1963.
14 See above.
15 *Irish Times*, 17 January 1966. See also his debate with Brian Lenihan, a southern minister, in Larne, *Irish News*, 7 December 1965.
16 *Belfast Telegraph*, 19 January 1966.
17 Ibid., 3 March 1964.
18 Ibid., 3 January 1966. The *Portadown News and County Armagh Advertiser*, 7 January 1966.
19 'Inter-exchequer relations', Cabinet conclusions, 26 August 1964, PRONI, CAB/4/1272/7.
20 'Rebate on rates', Cabinet conclusions, 27 January 1966, PRONI, CAB/4/1322/15, pp. 2–3.
21 *Belfast Telegraph*, 29 March 1966.
22 Van Voris, *Violence in Ulster*, pp. 45, 48
23 *Belfast Telegraph*, 11 October 1966.
24 Ibid., 24 January, 22 February 1967.
25 Ibid., 8 February 1967.
26 *Sunday Press*, 24 October 1965 & 12 May 1966. Barry White, 'The road ahead for Capt. O'Neill', *Belfast Telegraph*, 22 July 1966.
27 *Belfast Telegraph*, 4, 8 May 1967.
28 Ibid., 11 May 1967.
29 Ibid., 12 May 1967.
30 The *Unionist*, July 1967. After the onset of the Troubles, however, Millar used his notoriety from this episode in a successful bid to be elected. Jonathon Bardon, *Belfast: an illustrated history* (Belfast, 1982) p. 281.
31 *Belfast Telegraph*, 21 May 1968.
32 Ibid., 22 May 1968.
33 Ibid., 13 December 1966, 5, 9 January 1967. Public debates, Dáil Eireann, 8 February 1967, vol. 226, c. 788. *Belfast Telegraph*, 17 February 1967. NIHC, vol. 65, 22 February 1967, c. 1436.
34 *Irish Times*, 12 December 1967, press cuttings, NIO files.
35 *Belfast Telegraph*, 12, 14 December 1967. Cabinet conclusions, 9 January 1968, PRONI, CAB/4/1381. For details of the meeting, see 'Meeting of Captain O'Neill and Taoiseach', 96/6/23, National Archives, Dublin.
36 Roy Lilley, 'Today's O'Neill-Lynch meeting – the background', *Belfast Telegraph*, 11 December 1967.
37 *Belfast Telegraph.*, 28 January 1967.
38 Ibid., 30 January 1967.
39 Ibid., 2 February 1967.
40 Ibid., 3 February 1967.
41 NIHC, vol. 65, 7 February 1967, c. 900–1, 14 February 1967, c. 1131. Maloney and Pollack, *Paisley*, p. 156.
42 *Belfast Telegraph*, 10 February 1967.
43 Ibid., 14 June 1967.
44 Ibid., 12 July 1967.
45 Ibid., 13, 14 July 1967. *Protestant Telegraph*, 22 July 1967.
46 *Belfast Telegraph*, 13 July 1967.
47 Ibid., 14 July 1967.
48 Ibid., 25 April 1967. NIHC, vol. 66, 26 April 1967, c. 640–8, 646–7

(O'Neill), 2 May 1967, 817–35 (West's reply), 839–41 (O'Neill's reply), 858–69 (Jones).
49 Interview with Rt Hon Harry West, 15 December 1994.
50 The *Unionist*, August 1960.
51 *Impartial reporter and Farmers' Journal* 13 July 1967, *Belfast Telegraph* 29 June 1968, 4 January 1969.
52 NIHC, vol. 66, 26 April 1966, c. 648–50 (Diamond), 651 (Gormley), 651–2 (Nixon), 652 (Murnaghan).
53 *Belfast Telegraph*, 28 April 1967.
54 Ibid., 27 April 1967.
55 Ibid., 29 April 1967.
56 NIHC, vol. 66, 2 May 1967, c. 817–35.
57 *Belfast Telegraph*, 10 May 1967.
58 Ibid., 3 May 1967.
59 NIHC, vol. 66, 2 May 1967, c. 841–2.
60 Bleakley, *Faulkner*, p. 74.
61 Brian Faulkner, *Memoirs of a statesman* (London, 1978) p. 15.
62 Letter to the author from Mr Kenneth Darwin, 4 June 1998.
63 For example, 'Nationalist MP praises Faulkner', *Belfast Telegraph*, 21 March 1968.
64 Interview with Rt, Hon. Harry West, 15 December 1994.
65 *The Londonderry Sentinel*, 30 January 1963. See his Twelfth speech, *Belfast Telegraph*, 12 July 1963. Also 'Orange barrier to reds', ibid., 7 February 1968.
66 Ibid., 12 July 1964.
67 Faulkner's 1965 Twelfth speech, ibid., 12 July 1965.
68 For example see, ibid., 29 August 1964.
69 Ibid., 7 August 1965, 22 June 1968
70 Ibid., 10 February 1968.
71 To the Unionist annual conference. Ibid., 9 May 1964.
72 Ibid., 11 December 1964.
73 Ibid., 2 March 1965.
74 Ibid., 24 June 1966.
75 Ibid., 9 July 1966.
76 Ibid.
77 Ibid., 27 August 1966.
78 O'Neill, *Autobiography*, p. 86. Faulkner, *Memoirs*, p. 41. Hayes, *Minority verdict*, p. 65. Bloomfield, *Stormont in crisis*, p. 85.
79 *Belfast Telegraph*, 8 May, 12 July 1967.
80 Ibid., 8 July 1967.
81 Ibid., 31 July 1967.
82 'Premier O'Neill's position', *Sunday Independent*, 7 May 1967, press cuttings, O'Neill papers.
83 NIHC, 3 May 1967, c. 896–7. Ibid., 4 May 1967, c. 967. Ibid., 9 May 1967, c. 1014.
84 *Irish Times*, 28 April 1967, press cuttings, O'Neill papers.
85 Letter from L. O. Fleming to Terence O'Neill, 19 May 1967, O'Neill papers.
86 *Belfast Telegraph*, 27 April 1967. *Impartial Reporter and Farmers' Journal*, 4 May 1967.

87 *Belfast Telegraph,* 7 July 1967.
88 Ibid., 11 July 1967.
89 *Belfast Telegraph,* 29 August 1967.
90 Ibid., 15 December 1967.
91 Ibid., 12 February 1968.
92 Ibid., 17 February 1968. *Impartial Reporter and Farmers' Journal,* 22 February 1968.
93 *Belfast Telegraph,* 15 March 1968.
94 Ibid., 18, 19, 20, 21 March 1968.
95 *Impartial Reporter and Farmers' Journal,* 28 March 1968.
96 *Belfast Telegraph,* 28 March 1968.
97 *Impartial Reporter and Farmers' Journal,* 4 April 1968.
98 *Belfast Telegraph,* 14 May 1968.
99 Ibid., 16 September 1968.
100 Ibid., 10 May 1968.
101 Ibid., 13 May 1968.
102 Ibid., 16 May 1968.
103 Harbinson, The *Ulster Unionist Party,* p. 40.
104 *Belfast Telegraph,* 10 July 1964.
105 Ibid., 9 December 1964.
106 Ibid., 12, 13 July 1965.
107 On 10 August 1966 a new pressure group sympathetic to Paisley, the Orange Voice of Freedom, met in Ulster Hall. Major Ronald Bunting was a spokesman. Ibid., 11, 23 August 1966.
108 'The qualifications of an Orangeman', Billy Kennedy (ed.) *Steadfast for faith and freedom: 200 years of Orangeism* (Belfast, 1995) p. 3.
109 *Belfast Telegraph,* 16 February 1967. The Catholic Church, it should be said, only allowed its adherents to attend protestant services in late 1966. Tobin, *The best of decades,* p. 193.
110 *Belfast Telegraph,* 9 June 1967.
111 Ibid., 15 June 1967.
112 Ibid., 4 July 1967.
113 Ibid., 29 June 1964.
114 Ibid., 6 October 1967. Roy Lilley, 'Political diary', ibid., 14 June 1968.
115 Ibid., 25 October 1967.
116 Ibid., 12, 13 June 1968.
117 Roy Lilley, 'Political diary', loc. cit.
118 *Belfast Telegraph,* 2 July 1968.
119 Interview by Roy Lilley, 'Where is the Orange Order marching to now?', ibid., 9 July 1968.
120 See the defensive article in the *Unionist,* July 1968.
121 *News Letter,* 16 January 1967, press cuttings, O'Neill papers.
122 *Belfast Telegraph,* 23 January 1967.
123 *Irish Times,* 11 April 1967, press cuttings, O'Neill papers.
124 *News Letter,* 28 April 1965, ibid.
125 Ibid., 5 May 1965.
126 *Portadown Times,* 14 May 1965.
127 *Belfast Telegraph,* 20 April 1966. *Sunday Press,* 1 May 1966, *Sunday Independent,* 1 May 1966, press cuttings, O'Neill papers. Hayes, *Minority*

verdict, pp. 67–8.

128 *Belfast Telegraph,* 16 May 1967. *Down Recorder,* 19 May 1967. *Protestant Telegraph,* 27 May 1967.

129 *Belfast Telegraph,* 22 May 1967. The *Unionist,* June 1967.

130 *Belfast Telegraph,* 7 July 1967.

131 Ibid., 13 September 1967.

132 Speech to Irish Rotary Clubs conference. *Coleraine Chronicle,* 7 October 1967.

133 Speech opening an Ulster Week in Manchester. *Belfast Telegraph,* 4 March 1968.

134 Terence O'Neill, *Putting PEP into the local community* (Belfast, HMSO, n.d. [1967]).

135 *Belfast Telegraph,* 17 June 1968.

136 Speeches and statements, February 1968, PRONI, INF/3/3/81.

137 *Newry Reporter,* 11 May 1967.

138 Roy Perrott, 'Bodysnatchers and babies at Ballynahinch', The *Observer,* 26 May 1968. *Belfast Telegraph,* 17 April 1969.

139 Though in reality cultural programmes for civic weeks were steadfastly British in tone and they were often the occasion for recruitment to HM's armed forces.

140 Wichert, *Northern Ireland since 1945,* p. 86.

141 Roy Foster, 'To the northern counties station: Lord Randolph Churchill and the Orange card' in Roy Foster, *Paddy and Mr Punch: connections in Irish and English history* (1993) pp. 233–49. Andrew Gailey, *Ireland and the death of kindness: the experience of constructive unionism 1890–1905* (Cork, 1987) pp. 14–19. Gailey, *Crying in the wilderness,* p. x.

142 Eric Montgomery, 'Memorandum by the Director of Information on Fiftieth Anniversary Celebrations', 1 May 1968, PRONI, CAB/4/1399/4. 'Northern Ireland Jubilee, 1971', Cabinet conclusions, 3 October 1968, CAB/4/1404/2, p. 4.

143 Speeches and statements, September 1968, PRONI, INF/3/3/88.

144 *Belfast Telegraph,* 24 June 1968.

145 Ibid., 26 August 1968.

146 Ibid., 9 October 1968.

147 Ibid., 3 January 1969.

148 Paul Arthur, *The People's Democracy 1968–1973* (Belfast, 1974) appendix F, p. 125.

149 *Belfast Telegraph,* 28 March 1969.

150 Ibid., 5 February 1965. In 1963 the anti-partitionists on Belfast City Council were represented by Independents, the Republican Labour Party and Independent Labour. In 1965 they were joined by the National Democratic Party.

151 *Belfast Telegraph,* 14 October 1966.

152 Ibid., 14 August 1965.

153 Michael Grant, 'A Nationalist voter takes a look at the Party', *Hibernia,* vol. 27, no. 2, February 1963.

154 See Edmund Warnock's speech, *Belfast Telegraph,* 16 January 1963.

155 Eddie McAteer, *Irish action: new thoughts on an old subject* (Ballyshannon, 1948).

156 Barry White, 'The new nationalism – part 1', *Belfast Telegraph*, 8 February 1968.
157 Ian McAllister, *The Northern Ireland Social Democratic and Labour Party: political opposition in a divided society* (London, 1977), p. 19.
158 *Belfast Telegraph*, 23 June 1964.
159 Ibid., 2 September 1964.
160 *Irish News*, 21 November 1964. A copy is in 'Six County Nationalist Party', Department of Foreign Affairs, National Archives, Dublin, 305/14/360.
161 *Belfast Telegraph*, 20 November 1964.
162 Ibid., 14, 16 November, 7 December 1964, 27, 28 January, 5, 8 February 1965.
163 Ibid. 21 June 1965.
164 Ibid., 17 January 1967.
165 Ibid., 22 January 1965.
166 See McAteer's account cited in Frank Curran, *Derry: countdown to disaster* (Dublin, 1986), pp. 37–8.
167 This had been offered in the late 1950s, when the Nationalist Party last considered becoming the official opposition. It had been turned down, however, partially because McAteer threatened to resign from the party. Interview with Lord McConnell, 7 February 1995. Frank Curran, *Derry*, p. 17.
168 'Report from salaries committee: notice of motion (non-agenda item)', Cabinet conclusions, 7 November 1963, CAB/4/1243/9, p. 6. 'Payment of salaries to Official Opposition', Cabinet conclusions, 21 May 1965, PRONI, CAB/4/1306, pp. 5–6.
169 'Ministerial and Other Offices Bill', Cabinet conclusions, 16 January 1964, PRONI, CAB/4/1252/11, p. 2.
170 *Belfast Telegraph*, 18 June 1965. The *Derry Journal*, 18 June 1965.
171 *Sunday Independent*, 5 December 1965, press cuttings, O'Neill papers.
172 *Belfast Telegraph*, 23 May 1966. *Irish News*, 23 May 1966.
173 See his response to the Labour Lawyers survey on civil rights. *Belfast Telegraph*, 8 August 1967. Brendan Lynn, *Holding the ground: the Nationalist Party in Northern Ireland 1945–72* (Aldershot, 1997) pp. 202–3, 206–7.
174 Brett, *Long shadows cast before*, pp. 133–6.
175 *Belfast Telegraph*, 19 December 1967.
176 Barry White, 'The new nationalism – part 1', ibid., 8 February 1968.
177 NIHC, vol. 68, 14 February 1968, c. 1270.
178 John Wallace, 'Political diary', *Belfast Telegraph*, 16 February 1968.
179 NIHC, vol. 69, 7 May 1968, c. 918–20.
180 Roy Lilley, 'Political diary', *Belfast Telegraph*, 10 May 1968.
181 *Irish News*, 24 June 1968.
182 Ibid.
183 *Belfast Telegraph*, 17 October 1968.
184 Conn McCluskey, *Up off their knees: a commentary on the civil rights movement in Northern Ireland* (Republic of Ireland, 1989) pp. 15–19.
185 *Belfast Telegraph*, 17 January 1964.
186 Jonathan Moore, 'The Labour Party and Northern Ireland in the 1960s', Eamonn Hughes (ed.), *Culture and politics in Northern Ireland 1960–1990* (Milton Keynes, 1991) p. 71.
187 James Kelly, 'Quiet Coleraine doesn't know what's coming its way soon',

Sunday Independent, 30 May 1965, press cuttings, O'Neill papers.

188 *Belfast Telegraph*, 29 March 1965. *Sunday Times*, 28 March 1965. *London Evening Standard*, 29 March 1965. Department of the Prime Minister, PREM/13/1663, PRO.

189 *Belfast Telegraph*, 27 April 1966.

190 Thus Labour orientated activists in Northern Ireland often presented civil rights in this context. For example, see Northern Ireland Society of Labour Lawyers, *Discrimination – pride for prejudice* (Belfast, 1969) pp. 5–12.

191 Paul Rose, *Backbencher's dilemma* (London, 1981) p. 178.

192 *Belfast Telegraph*, 1 July 1966. Geoffrey Bell, *Troublesome business: the Labour Party and the Irish question* (London, 1982) p. 104.

193 The colloquial term for confidentiality was 'in lodge', a reference to the ubiquity of informal fixing through the Orange Order. Editorial, *Derry Journal*, 24 July 1963. For an admission of the prevalence of discrimination, see editorial, *News Letter*, 16 August 1965. Perhaps the most blatant form of discrimination was sexual, against married women. 'Operation of the Marriage Bar in the Civil Service of Northern Ireland', memorandum by the Minister of Finance, 29 March 1968, PRONI, CAB/4/1393/5.

194 John Whyte, 'How much discrimination was there under Stormont 1921–68?', pp. 1–35 in Tom Gallagher and James O'Connell (eds) *Contemporary Irish studies* (Manchester, 1983), pp. 30–1. O'Neill agreed with this picture of a east/west divide. Transcript of interview with Lord O'Neill of the Maine, 'This week: Five long years', O'Neill papers.

195 Brookeborough blocked the appointment of a catholic judge to the High Court in favour of a senior Unionist. Basil McIvor, *Hope deferred: experiences of an Irish unionist* (Belfast, 1998) p. 37. See also *Belfast Telegraph*, 1 November 1963.

196 Dennis Kennedy, 'Catholic education–teaching is a safe, frustrating job', *Belfast Telegraph*, 27 July 1965.

197 One senior Derry unionist admits they were 'lax and lazy' in countering civil rights charges. Paul Kingsley, *Londonderry revisited: a loyalist analysis of the civil rights controversy* (Belfast, 1989) p. 144.

198 See *Belfast Telegraph*, 12 June 1963.

199 Resolutions to the 1964 annual conference, papers of the Ulster Unionist Council, PRONI, D 1327/9/23.

200 For a good summary of protestant attitudes, cf. Griffen, *Mark of protest*, pp. 90–3.

201 For open support for discrimination see comment of Robert Babington, later an O'Neillite MP, *Newsletter*, 6 March 1961, cited in Farrell, *Northern Ireland*, p. 227. See also Senator Barnhill, also an O'Neill loyalist, in *Belfast Telegraph*, 9 January 1964, The *Derry Journal*, 10 January 1964, Letter to the *Belfast Telegraph*, 12 February 1969. Stanley Revels, a Newry JP, was defended by a junior minister when he advocated discrimination: the *Newry Telegraph*, 30 May 1964, *Newry Reporter*, 4 June 1964, NIHC, vol. 57, 9 June 1964, c. 1778. See comment of Albert Anderson, MP for Londonderry: *Belfast Telegraph*, 10 December 1968. For evidence of system-atic discrimination practised by Unionist Trade Union Alliance, an official party body, see Letters, *Belfast Telegraph*, 20, 30 July 1963. Discrimination was most blatant in private employment. To take one example, Sirocco

Engineering Works, abutting the catholic Seaforde Street in Belfast, employed less than five catholics out of 1500 employees. *Irish Press*, 28 May 1966. Discrimination also had deep roots even in central government, however. For insider information, see G. C. Duggan, 'Northern Patterns of Discrimination', *Irish Times*, 4 May 1967.

202 *Belfast Telegraph*, 18 February 1969.

203 Rev. E. J. Ferguson, 'Religious discrimination in Northern Ireland', the *Unionist*, August 1967.

204 As Terence O'Neill found. Parliamentary debates (*Hansard*), House of Lords, vol. 362, 15 July 1975, cols 1242–3 and vol. 411, 17 July 1980, cols 1979–80.

205 Cabinet conclusions, PRONI, CAB/4/1023/14, p. 4.

206 *Belfast Telegraph*, 16 January 1965.

207 Formal arrangements to this end were made with Du Pont in Derry for example. Interview with Bob Cooper, 24 October 1996. Cabinet conclusions, 19 November 1957, PRONI, CAB/4/1052, p. 4.

208 C. E. B. Brett, 'Religious discrimination in Northern Ireland', the *Guardian*, 3 March 1964. *Belfast Telegraph*, 19 November 1963. Dennis Kennedy, 'Religious houses–part one', ibid., 25 November 1964. NIHC, vol. 55, 19 November 1963, c. 945.

209 John Mitchell, Registration Officer of the Londonderry and Foyle Unionist Association, was recommended for a political honour in the following terms: 'His work for Unionism and the loyalist cause in Londonderry has been quite invaluable. It would, I think, be an education for anyone to see the organisation he has built up. At any one time he can tell you the position in any of our areas. Only the other day I rang him up and asked him the up-to-date local government position in the Middle Liberties. The reply was immediate – a majority of four (814–811). Every house that is advertised for sale in the area is noted by him and the details kept …' Letter to Brian Faulkner, 8 September 1959, 'Political honours, 1960, Queen's Birthday and New Year', Ulster Unionist Council, PRONI, D. 1327/11/1/50.

210 The *Londonderry Sentinel*, 19 July 1967.

211 Speech by Harry West, *Impartial Reporter and Farmers' Journal*, 3 December 1964. There was also a feeling, however, that protestants should not have forced upon them feckless and dirty catholics as neighbours. See comments of William Kennedy, MP for Cromac. *Belfast Telegraph*, 19 March 1968. NIHC, vol. 69, 20 March 1968, c. 57–8. Belfast Corporation refused to censure Kennedy, who was a councillor. *Belfast Telegraph*, 28 March 1968.

212 *Belfast Telegraph*, 7, 12 November 1966, 4 July, 29 September 1967. *Protestant Telegraph*, 19 November 1966. Editorial, *Derry Journal*, 22 November 1966.

213 'Gerrymander – to 'manipulate the boundaries of (a constituency etc.) so as to give undue influence to some party or class.' *The concise Oxford dictionary of current English* (Oxford, 1990).

214 For a subtly damming report, produced confidentially by civil servants, see 'Franchise' n.d. [October 1968], PRONI, CAB/4/1411/2.

215 C. E. B. Brett, 'Discrimination in Northern Ireland; religious apartheid', the *Guardian*, 4 March 1964. *Belfast Telegraph*, 17 January 1966. Londonderry

Junior Chamber of Commerce, *Thoughts on the boundary extension* (1966). *Belfast Telegraph*, 18 May 1966. The *Londonderry Sentinel*, 18 May 1966. Griffen, *Mark of protest*, p. 96. Derry's gerrymander in the early years of the state had been confidentially justified to Unionist MPs as an emergency and temporary measure. Letter from Edmund Warnock to Terence O'Neill, 13 November 1968, PRONI, CAB/4/1414/5.

216 The resignation letter of Noel J. Ince, Secretary of Ballyholme Unionist Men's Branch, cited in *Belfast Telegraph*, 14 February 1969. The *County Down Spectator and Ulster Standard*, 21 February 1969.

217 *Irish News*, 23 December 1966. The *Fermanagh Herald*, 31 December 1966.

218 'Census of population', Cabinet conclusions, 30 January 1964, CAB/4/1254/8, p. 3.

219 'Constituency boundaries', Cabinet conclusions, 4 November 1964, PRONI, CAB/4/1277/18, p. 1.

220 'Constituency boundaries' (confidential annex), Cabinet conclusions, 2 June 1965, PRONI, CAB/4/1307/12, pp. 1–4. 'Queen's Speech', Cabinet conclusions, 28 October 1965, PRONI, CAB/4/1318/17, p. 7. R.W.B. McConnell, 'Memorandum for the Cabinet by the Minister of Home Affairs on constituency boundaries', 28 February 1968, annex, PRONI, CAB/4/1327/13. 'Constituency boundaries', Cabinet conclusions, 10 March 1966, PRONI, CAB/4/1327/16, p. 3. 'Constituency boundaries', Cabinet conclusions, 6 December 1966, PRONI, CAB/4/1351/6, pp. 3–5.

221 A resolution to the Young Unionist annual conference, 1969. Cited in *Belfast Telegraph*, 4 April 1969.

222 See Tom Lyons MP on universal suffrage. Barry White, 'Who are the reformers?', ibid., 26 October 1968.

223 Edward W. Jones, '"Citizens rights" – proposals by the Northern Ireland Labour Party – memorandum by the Attorney General', 28 October 1966, PRONI, CAB/4/1347/5. Cabinet conclusions, 29 January 1967, PRONI, CAB/4/1352, p. 3.

224 Interview with Rt Hon. Harry West, 15 December 1994. For a similar point of view, from a senior civil servant of the time, see Oliver, 'The Stormont administration 1921–72' p. 87.

225 See, for example, *Belfast Telegraph*, 28, 29 January 1964. The *Londonderry Sentinel*, 29 January, 1 February 1964.

226 *Belfast Telegraph*, 15 January 1965.

227 Ibid., 13 March 1965.

228 John D. Taylor, BSc, 'Charges of discrimination', the *Unionist*, May 1965.

229 See Henry Clark's comments, *Belfast Telegraph*, 12 July 1965.

230 Ibid., 22 April, 18 December 1965, 18 October, 12 November 1966, 26 October 1967. NIHC, vol. 67, 1 November 1967, c. 1274. Ibid., vol. 64, 3 November 1966, c. 2137.

231 *Carrickfergus Advertiser and East Antrim Gazette*, 13 February 1969. Interview with Austin Ardill, 10 August 1998.

232 *Sunday Press*, 25 September 1966, press cuttings, O'Neill papers.

233 Bloomfield, *Stormont in crisis*, pp. 99–100.

234 NIHC, 22 March 1967, vol. 66, c. 327–33. *Belfast Telegraph*, 28 June 1967. Edmund Warnock, 'The power to be generous', *Belfast Telegraph*, 8 November 1967. NIHC, 21 May 1968, vol. 69, c. 1342–3. Ibid., 16 October

1968, vol. 70, c. 1035. Edmund Warnock, letter, 'Moderation our most powerful political weapon – Mr Warnock', *Belfast Telegraph*, 11 November 1968. Remarkably for a politician he seems to have been struck with remorse at his government's mistreatment of the catholic minority. See his letters to O'Neill, 12 and 13 November 1968, PRONI, CAB/4/1414/5.

235 [Jack Sayers], *Round Table*, May 1963, p. 275.

236 *Belfast Telegraph*, 9 March 1963. *News Letter*, 10 April 1963. The *Unionist*, May 1963. Douglas died, aged sixty-nine, in 1965. *Belfast Telegraph*, 25 August 1965. Bob Cooper describes Douglas, with Lady Brookeborough, as 'the power behind the throne during the Brookeborough era'. Interview with Bob Cooper, 24 October 1996.

237 *Belfast Telegraph*, 27 August 1963.

238 Interview with Bob Cooper, 24 October 1996.

239 Roy Lilley, 'Unionism today – the Glengall Street machine', *Belfast Telegraph*, 24 October 1963.

240 *News Letter*, 7 September 1964.

241 Ralph Bossence, 'As I see it; the "shackles" that bind Ulster's Prime Minister', *News Letter*, 2 November 1964.

242 Barry White, 'Political diary – a tactical mistake?', *Belfast Telegraph*, 11 June 1965.

243 *Belfast Telegraph*, 14 October 1966.

244 Leading personalities were Robin Bailie solicitor, Robert Cooper, a law graduate and personnel officer, John Hutchinson, an art teacher and John Fairleigh, also a law graduate. The Bow Group was a liberal 'think tank' in the British Conservative Party.

245 Robin Bailie, 'A united Ulster', *loc. cit.*

246 Copies were burnt at a Young Unionist beach bonfire during a Summer school. *News Letter*, 22 October 1962.

247 Ibid., 31 January 1964.

248 *News Letter*, 5 February 1964.

249 *Belfast Telegraph*, 26 February 1964. Cf. ibid., 5 March 1964.

250 Ibid., 26 October 1964.

251 *News Letter*, 26 October 1964.

252 Robert Cooper, 'The Young Unionists', *Focus: a monthly journal*, December 1964, vol. Viii, no. 12, p. 274.

253 *Belfast Telegraph*, 2, 9, 10, 18 February 1965.

254 See their retrospective statement. Ibid., 4 December 1968. For the fate of the *Review* ginger group, cf. Rosita Sweetman, *On our knees: Ireland 1972* (London, 1972) pp. 240–1.

255 Stratton Mills, 'Forward – the Ulster eggheads!', *Belfast Telegraph*, 4 March 1964. For similar points, see Robin Bailie's speech, ibid., 29 April 1965; Brian Roberts' (a Unionist candidate for South Armagh) speech, ibid., 11 November 1964, Roy Bradford's article, 'The questions Unionists are asking about party organisation – and some purely personal answers', ibid., 20 May 1966.

256 *News Letter*, 21 February 1964.

257 The *Unionist*, April 1965. Interview with Reginald Empey, 7 December 1995.

258 Martin Wallace, 'Speaking my mind', *Belfast Telegraph*, 21 January 1965;

Barry White, 'The face of Unionism: how is it changing?', ibid., 29 April 1965.

259 Ian McAllister and Sarah Nelson, 'Modern developments in the Northern Ireland party system', *Parliamentary Affairs*, vol. 32, no. 3 (Oxford, 1979) pp. 283, 285. See Martin Smyth's comments cited in David Hume, *The Ulster Unionist Party 1972–1992: a political movement in an era of conflict of change* (Belfast, 1996) p. 147.

260 *Belfast Telegraph*, 17 June, 9 October 1965.

261 Agenda of the Annual Conference of the Ulster Unionist Council, Friday 23 April 1967, UUC papers, PRONI, D 1327/9/26, p. 18.

262 The *Unionist*, July 1966.

263 Ibid., August 1967.

264 *Belfast Telegraph*, 30 September 1967.

265 The *Unionist*, November 1967, January, February 1968.

266 *Belfast Telegraph*, 29 February 1968.

267 This is the opinion of Lady Faulkner, cited in Amy Miracle, 'A liberal in spite of himself: Terence O'Neill and moderate Unionist politics', unpublished MSc thesis (QUB, 1987) p. 25.

268 Roy Lilley, 'The face of change – can the party match the pace of its leader?', *Belfast Telegraph*, 15 March 1968.

269 *Irish Times*, 2 November 1965, press cuttings, O'Neill papers.

270 Interview with Michael Mills, 'Removing the balance of hatred', *Irish Press*, 27 March 1968, ibid.

271 For O'Neill's aloofness, see Donald S. Connery, *The Irish* (London, 1968) pp. 236–7.

272 The *Unionist*, February 1968.

273 *Belfast Telegraph*, 3 September 1968.

274 The *Unionist*, September 1968. *Belfast Telegraph*, 26 September 1968.

275 The *Unionist*, June 1968.

276 Ibid., July 1968.

277 Ibid., October 1968. Interview with Rt Hon. Basil McIvor, 3 November 1995.

278 Notably in 'John Bull's political slum', by Cal McCrystal, *Sunday Times*, 3 July 1966.

279 See Harold Wilson's reply to a question from Gerry Fitt. WHC, vol. 729, 26 May 1966, c. 721–2.

280 See his speech to the 1966 Unionist conference. Speeches and statements, April 1966, PRONI, INF/3/3/58. See also Terence O'Neill, 'Our surest shield is our good name'. *Ulster Unionist Council Yearbook 1967* (Belfast, 1966) p. 9.

281 *Belfast Telegraph*, 2 August 1966.

282 Harold Black, 'Discussions at Downing Street on 5th August, 1966 – note on main points raised – based on recollections after the meeting', PRONI, CAB/4/1338/2.

283 'Discussions at Downing Street, 5th August, 1966', supplementary Cabinet conclusions, 9 August 1966, PRONI, CAB/4/1338/3.

284 'Meeting at 10 Downing Street on 12th January, 1967' (minutes), Cabinet conclusions, PRONI, 29 January 1967. 'Taoiseach's meeting with the British Prime Minister', 14 February 1968, Department of Foreign Affairs, National Archives, Dublin, 98/217.

285 'Memorandum on 'citizens' rights' by NI Labour Party and others', Cabinet conclusions, 19 October 1966, PRONI, CAB/4/1344/15, p. 2.
286 Ibid., 27 October 1966, PRONI, CAB/4/1345/8, p. 3.
287 Though publicly the memorandum was scornfully dismissed. Brett, *Long shadows cast before*, p. 134.
288 William Craig, 'Memorandum to the Cabinet by the Minister of Home Affairs on the Northern Ireland Labour document on "civil rights"', 4 November 1966, PRONI, CAB/4/1347/8. 'Memorandum on "citizens' rights" by NI Labour Party and others', Cabinet conclusions, 10 November 1966, PRONI, CAB/4/1347/11, pp. 1–4.
289 NIHC, vol. 65, 13 December 1966, c. 4–10, 32–45.
290 *Belfast Telegraph*, 16 December 1966. Indeed, the Unionists submitted most objections during the public review stage. Ibid., 13 January 1967.
291 Sir Knox Cunningham, MP for South Antrim, lobbied against the abolition of the university seats, but discreetly. Letters from Knox Cunningham to Douglas Savoury and Bessie Maconachie (19 November 1966). Correspondence with MPs at Westminster 1942–65, papers of Professor Sir Douglas Savoury, PRONI, D 3015/1a/6/1/1–100.
292 Henry Kennedy, 'Politics in Northern Ireland', pp. 140–52.
293 Barry White, 'Mater Hospital – the price of catholic loyalty', *Belfast Telegraph*, 2 February 1967.
294 81 per cent of Unionist supporters, 69 per cent of Nationalist supporters. *Belfast Telegraph*, 14 December 1967.
295 William Morgan, 'Mater Infirmorum Hospital – memorandum to the Cabinet submitted by the Minister of Health and Local Government', 1 January 1964, PRONI, CAB/4/1253/8.
296 'Mater Infirmorum Hospital', Cabinet conclusions, 22 January 1964, PRONI, CAB/4/1253/9, pp. 1–3. *Belfast Telegraph*, 5 February 1964.
297 'National Health Service – Position of Mater Infirmorum Hospital', Cabinet conclusions, 28 May 1964, PRONI, CAB/4/1268/11, pp. 2–3. W. J. Morgan, 'National Health Service – Position of Mater Infirmorum Hospital – memorandum to the Cabinet by the Minister of Health and Local Government', 21 May 1964, PRONI, CAB/4/1268/9.
298 *Belfast Telegraph*, 29 April 1965.
299 'Mater Infirmorum Hospital', Cabinet conclusions, 27 January 1965, PRONI, CAB/4/1290/14, p. 2. Ibid., 24 February 1965, PRONI, CAB/4/1293/10, pp. 1–2. NIHC, vol. 59, 5 March 1965, c. 1726–30. NIHC, vol. 59, 5 May 1965, c. 1283–5. Memorandum, CAB/4/1310/10. 'Mater Infirmorum Hospital', Cabinet conclusions, 23 June 1965, CAB/4/1310/ 14, p. 4.
300 'Mater Infirmorum Hospital', Cabinet conclusions, 6 July 1965, PRONI, CAB/4/1312/17, p. 2.
301 Barry White, 'Mater hospital – how the impasse came about', *Belfast Telegraph*, 1 February 1967. *Belfast Telegraph*, 17 January 1967.
302 Ibid., 7 February 1967.
303 Ibid., 19, 20 September 1967.
304 Ian Budge and Cornelius O'Leary, *Belfast: approach to crisis: a study of Belfast politics 1913–1970* (London, 1973), p. 161.
305 Donald Harman Akenson, *Education and enmity: the control of schooling in Northern Ireland 1920–50* (Newtown Abbot).

306 *Belfast Telegraph,* 17 January 1967.

307 *Educational development in Northern Ireland* (Belfast: HMSO, 1964) Cmd 470.

308 Dennis Kennedy, 'Catholic education 1 – what impedes the flow to grammar schools?', *Belfast Telegraph,* 26 July 1965.

309 'Memorandum by the Minister of Education – policy in relation to the establishment of new grammar schools', 25 August 1966, PRONI, CAB/4/1341/8.

310 'Establishment of a new grammar school', Cabinet conclusions, 1 September 1966, PRONI, CAB/4/1341/14, pp. 1–2.

311 'Policy in relation to establishment of new grammar schools', Cabinet conclusions, 19 October 1966, PRONI, CAB/4/1344/15, pp. 3–4. Ibid., Cabinet conclusions, 2 November 1966, PRONI, CAB/4/1346, p. 6

312 Dennis Kennedy, 'Catholic education', *Belfast Telegraph,* 26, 27, 28 July 1965.

313 W. K. Fitzsimmons, 'Redundancy payments to teachers – memorandum by the Minister of Education', 16 September 1965, PRONI, CAB/4/1314/9.

314 *News Letter,* 11 February 1966.

315 See comments of William Craig, 'Redundancy payments to teachers', Cabinet conclusions, 23 September 1965, PRONI, CAB/4/1314/12, pp. 1–2.

316 'Grants to voluntary schools and local authorities', Cabinet conclusions, 6 December 1966, PRONI, CAB/4/1351/6, pp. 3–5.

317 Cabinet conclusions, PRONI, CAB/4/1354, pp. 2, 3.

318 *Local education authorities and voluntary schools* (Belfast: HMSO, 1967) Cmd 513.

319 *Belfast Telegraph,* 19, 20 October 1967.

320 Ibid., 25 October 1967.

321 Ibid., 2, 8, 16 November 1967.

322 NIHC, vol. 67, 29 November 1967, c. 2356. *Belfast Telegraph,* 28 November 1967.

323 NIHC, vol. 67, 29 November 1967, c. 2356.

324 *Belfast Telegraph,* 2 December 1967.

325 NIHC, vol. 68, 19 December 1967, c. 36.

326 *Belfast Telegraph,* 5 February 1967.

327 NIHC, vol. 68, 8 February 1968, c. 1092 (O'Neill), 7 February 1967, c. 872 (Porter).

328 *Belfast Telegraph,* 26 March 1968.

329 Ibid., 23 May 1968. As a quid pro quo protestant churches were secretly, and probably unconstitutionally, guaranteed representation on the Management Committees of new state schools. Cabinet conclusions, PRONI, CAB/4/1352.

330 For example, see F. S. L. Lyons, *Ireland since the famine* (London, 1973, 1st ed. 1971) p. 743.

331 WHC, vol. 727, 25 April 1966, c. 437–46.

332 *New Statesman,* 26 January 1967.

333 The *Unionist,* March 1967.

334 The *Unionist,* September 1965. Interview with Lord Brian McConnell, 17 February 1995.

335 *Belfast Telegraph,* 28 April 1967. Agenda of the Annual Conference of the Ulster Unionist Council, Friday 30 April 1965, UUC papers, PRONI, D 1327/9/24, p. 6.

336 Their report, slight in content, can be found in 'Religious discrimination in Six Counties', Department of Foreign Affairs, National Archives, Dublin, 98/3/24.
337 *Belfast Telegraph*, 18 April 1967.
338 For example, see the speech by Westminster MP for South Belfast, Rafton Pounder, to a Young Conservative rally. Ibid., 17 June 1967.
339 'Speech by the Prime Minister, Captain the Rt Hon. Terence O'Neill, D.L., M.P., at the annual conference of the Ulster Unionist Conference, in the Ulster Hall, Belfast, on the evening of Friday, April 28, 1967', UUC papers, PRONI, D 1327/9/26. For a reply from Paul Rose of the CDU, see *Belfast Telegraph*, 16 June 1967.
340 Pat Walsh, *From civil rights to national war: Northern Ireland catholic politics 1964–1974* (Belfast, 1989) pp. 24–35.
341 *Belfast Telegraph*, 19 June 1967.
342 Ibid., 1 July 1967.
343 Ibid., 12 July 1967.
344 Percy Dymond, 'Ulster letter from London', ibid., 21 July 1967.
345 *CSJ Newsletter*, September 1967.
346 WHC, vol. 751, 25 October 1967, c. 1675–7.
347 The *Unionist*, November 1967.
348 See Roy Bradford's speech in Loughgall. *Belfast Telegraph*, 1 July 1967.
349 Ibid., 8 October 1966.
350 NIHC, vol. 64, 17 November 1966, c. 2454.
351 *Belfast Telegraph*, 22 November 1966.
352 NIHC, vol. 64, 23 November 1966, c. 2799–800.
353 *Belfast Telegraph*, 24 November 1966.
354 NIHC, vol. 65, 7 March 1967, c. 1790–6.
355 *Belfast Telegraph*, 8 March 1967.
356 NIHC, vol. 65, 7 March 1967, c. 1790–6.
357 Ibid., 8 March 1967, c. 1807–8.
358 *Belfast Telegraph*, 20, 21, 24, 25, 26 July 1967.
359 Ibid., 6 March 1967.
360 The nationalist response to this was muted. Roy Lilley, 'Political diary', ibid., 10 March 1967.
361 NIHC, vol. 65, 7 March 1967, c. 1764.
362 Barry White, 'Republican Clubs: how they see themselves', *Belfast Telegraph*, 28 May 1968.
363 *Belfast Telegraph*, 22 March 1967.
364 *Student life*, no. 1, November 1966.
365 *Belfast Telegraph*, 10 March 1967.
366 Ibid., 13 April 1968. *Armagh Guardian*, 18 April 1968. The *Armagh Observer*, 20 April 1968.
367 *Belfast Telegraph*, 13 April 1968.
368 The *Armagh Observer*, 27 April 1968.
369 NIHC, vol. 69, 7 May 1968, c. 918–20.
370 Ibid., c. 926.
371 David Caute, *Sixty-eight: the year of the barricades* (London, 1988). Michael Farrell (ed.), *Twenty years on* (Dingle, 1988) pp. 11–22.
372 *Belfast Telegraph*, 18, 19 June 1968.

373 NIHC, vol. 70, 19 June 1968, c. 390.
374 *Belfast Telegraph*, 20 June 1968.
375 Ibid.
376 Ibid., 21 June 1968. The *Dungannon Observer*, 22 June 1968.
377 NIHC, vol. 70, 20 June 1968, c. 461–2
378 According to Roy Bradford. *Belfast Telegraph*, 12 December 1968.
379 *Tuairisc*, November 1966.
380 *Belfast Telegraph*, 30 March 1967.
381 Ibid., 7 February 1967.
382 For example, a document on the operations of Special Branch against opposition political parties. Ibid., 7 September 1967.
383 Ibid., 7 March 1968.
384 Ibid., 14 August 1968.
385 NIHC, vol. 70, 13 June 1968, c. 190–5.
386 *Belfast Telegraph*, 8 July 1968. The *Unionist*, September 1968.
387 *Belfast Telegraph*, 22 July 1968. Stratton Mills posted a copy of the speech to Harold Wilson.
388 Ibid., 24 August 1968.
389 Ibid., 26 August 1968.
390 Wilf Blackwood, 'Disorder at Dungannon' (letter), ibid., 29 August 1968. The catholic nationalist hymns, 'A nation once again' and 'Faith of our fathers' were also sung. Bernadette Devlin, *The price of my soul* (London, 1969) pp. 91, 93–4.
391 Barry White, 'The march of civil rights', *Belfast Telegraph*, 11 October 1968. This impression would have been reinforced in government circles by the extremely prejudiced police report 'Civil Rights march from Coalisland to Dungannon on Saturday 24th August, 1968', PRONI, CAB/9b/205/7.
392 *Ulster: change and progress* (February 1970), Ulster Unionist Council, PRONI, D. 1327/20/4/16, p. 15. 'Brief on "economic progress in North-West Ulster"', n.d. [1968], PRONI, CAB/4/1411/4.
393 Cal McCrystal, 'Gloomy Londonderry Air', *Sunday Times*, 23 October 1966; Barry White, 'At the end of the day it's really down to us', *Belfast Telegraph*, 9 January 1999.
394 Eamonn McCann, *War and an Irish town* (London, 1993 [1st ed. 1974]), p. 91.
395 *Belfast Telegraph*, 3 October 1968.
396 Ibid., 4 October 1968.
397 Coogan, *The Troubles*, pp. 61–2.
398 The report by the three CDU observers present noted that a woman of about sixty 'who was hysterical on the pavement after having been hosed down by water-cannon' had her spectacles removed by a police man with one hand while 'he hit her over the head with his baton with the other.' *Belfast Telegraph*, 10 October 1968.
399 Ibid., 16 September 1968.
400 Rose, *Governing without consensus*, pp. 271–2

Chapter 7

1   There were rumours in September 1968 that O'Neill, who seemed to visit abroad at any excuse, was keen to quit as Prime Minister and constrained to remain only by Harold Wilson. James Kelly, 'Does O'Neill want to quit?', *Sunday Independent*, 22 September 1968, press cuttings, O'Neill papers. *Belfast Telegraph*, 7 October 1968.
2   Bloomfield, *Stormont in crisis*, p. 98.
3   O'Neill, *Autobiography*, pp. 102–3, 112–13, 122. Bloomfield, *Stormont in crisis*, p. 106.
4   *Belfast Telegraph*, 7 October 1968, ibid. Goulding denied being in Derry, but other Sinn Fein leaders, including Thomas MacGiolla, were.
5   Ibid., 7, 8 October 1968.
6   Ibid., 8 October 1968.
7   Ciaran McKeown, *The passion of peace* (Belfast, 1984) pp. 49–52.
8   Thus Thomas McGiolla, leader of the republican movement, preferred the 'Irish', 'plain-talking' Craig to the 'English' and 'condescending' O'Neill. *Belfast Telegraph*, 7 February 1969.
9   Ibid., 16 October 1968.
10   '... it seems now that the Catholic minority in Northern Ireland at large, if it is to retain any self-respect, will have to run the risk of wrecking the new moderation and seek justice more vociferously.' Seamus Heaney, 'Old Derry's walls', The *Listener*, 24 October 1968, p. 522.
11   For the mood of empowerment and moral superiority in catholic areas see Bernadette Devlin, *The price of my soul* (London, 1969) p. 143; McCann, *War and an Irish town*, pp. 103, 105; Adams, *Before the dawn*, pp. 91–2; Devlin, *Straight left*, p. 91.
12   *Belfast Telegraph*, 9 October 1968.
13   NIHC, vol. 70, 15 October 1967, c. 1003–4.
14   Fergus Pyle, 'Silent Unionists being heard; aftermath of Derry', *Irish Times*, 29 October 1968.
15   *Belfast Telegraph*, 26 October 1968.
16   The *Unionist*, October 1968, February 1969. *News Letter*, 9 October 1968. Political leaders on all sides recognized that television and press were crucial determinants in the conflict influencing directly British government intentions. R. S. P. Elliott and John Hickie, *Ulster: a case study in conflict theory* (London, 1971) p. 129.
17   Agenda of the Annual Conference of the Ulster Unionist Council, Friday 25 April 1969, UUC papers, PRONI, D 1327/9/27, pp. 5–17.
18   *Belfast Telegraph*, 8 October 1968.
19   NIHC, vol. 70, 16 October 1968, c. 1074.
20   Ibid., 4 December 1968, c. 2229.
21   WHC, vol. 770, 22 October 1968, c. 1089. Wilson, *Labour Government*, p. 671.
22   'Disturbances in Londonderry', Cabinet conclusions, 8 October 1968, PRONI, CAB/4/1405/10, pp. 1–2.
23   'Memorandum by the Prime Minister', 14 October 1968, PRONI, CAB/4/1406, pp. 2, 3.
24   Fergus Pyle, 'Silent Unionists being heard', *op. cit.*
25   'Political aspects of recent events', Cabinet conclusions, 23 October 1968,

PRONI, CAB/4/1409/11, p. 3. Terence O'Neill, *Autobiography*, appendix II, pp. 150–4.

26 'Memorandum by the Prime Minister', 28 October 1968, PRONI, CAB/4/1411. 'Company Vote at Local Government Elections', Cabinet conclusions, 31 October 1968, CAB/4/1412/23, p. 2.

27 For the benefit of Unionist backbenchers, but in even more ominously vague terms, Wilson publicly repeated this the following day in Parliament. WHC, vol. 772, 5 November 1968, col. 690.

28 'Meeting at Downing Street on 4th November, 1968', PRONI, CAB/4/1413/9, quotes from pp. 1 & 2. WHC, vol. 772, 5 November 1968, c. 688–9. Alf McCreary, 'Fifty days–Northern Ireland's political revolution; pressure from No. 10 ... and a warning from O'Neill', *Belfast Telegraph*, 2 December 1968. Wilson, *Labour Government*, p. 672. Callaghan, *A house divided*, p. 10.

29 'Downing Street Discussions', Cabinet conclusions, 7 November 1968, PRONI, CAB/4/1413/22, p. 4.

30 'The political situation', Cabinet conclusions, 14 November 1968, PRONI, CAB/4/1414/15, pp. 2–5. O'Neill, *Autobiography*, p. 106. Bloomfield, *Stormont in crisis*, p. 99.

31 *Belfast Telegraph*, 23, 24 & 30 October 1968. *Irish Times*, 24 October 1968, press cuttings, O'Neill papers. Barry White 'Who are the reformers?' *Belfast Telegraph*, 26 October 1968.

32 *Belfast Telegraph*, 31 October 1968.

33 'The political situation', Cabinet conclusions, 20 November 1968, PRONI, CAB/4/1418/11, pp. 2–4. Only Bradford and Andrews took O'Neill's part

34 'Second draft: reply to Mr. Wilson', [n.d., December 1968], PRONI, CAB/4/1423/7.

35 *Protestant Telegraph*, 16 November 1968.

36 *Belfast Telegraph*, 16, 18 November 1968.

37 Ibid., 20 November 1968

38 'The maintenance of law and order in Londonderry', Cabinet conclusions, 20 November 1968, PRONI, CAB/4/1418/11, pp. 1–2.

39 Cf. instructions of Detective Inspector Ross McGimpsey, in *Belfast Telegraph*, 18 November 1968:

I wish Non Commissioned Officers to impress on all men under their command that a very critical audience of press, radio and television persons will have their sights focused on them and that the dignity, firmness and tact of our police force must be clearly evident.

40 Terence O'Neill was later critical of Craig on this score:

Mr Craig had his chance to show what he could do as Minister of Home Affairs. He chose to impose an absolutely meaningless and quite unenforceable ban in Londonderry, which was defied day after day and sometimes several times a day. I do not think that was a period which increased respect for the law, particularly when you had a minister calling for calm on one hand and making inflammatory speeches on the other.

Ibid., 15 February 1969.

41 *Belfast Telegraph*, 21 November 1968.

42 'Political situation', Cabinet conclusions, 21 November 1968, PRONI,

CAB/4/1419/26, p. 3.

43 *Belfast Telegraph, loc. cit.*

44 Ibid., 23 November 1968.

45 Sir Edmund Compton, the British Ombudsman, pointed out that his Northern Ireland counter-part, lacking jurisdiction over local authorities, statutory bodies, Crown appointments and the police, would be toothless. 'Meeting at the Home Office on 19th November, 1968, PRONI, CAB/4/1419/15. This proved to be the case.

46 *Belfast Telegraph, loc. cit.*

47 Ibid., 25 November 1968.

48 Ibid., 23 November 1968.

49 Ibid., 23, 30 November 1968.

50 Ibid., 23 November 1968. *Protestant Telegraph*, 30 November 1968.

51 *Belfast Telegraph*, 3 December 1968.

52 Ibid., 25 November 1968.

53 Ibid., 30 November, 2 December 1968.

54 *The Times*, 2 December 1968. Cabinet conclusions, 2, 5 December 1968, PRONI, CAB/4/1422/11, CAB/4/1423/18.

55 *Belfast Telegraph*, 2 December 1968.

56 Ibid., 29 November 1968.

57 The *Unionist*, January, February 1966.

58 *Belfast Telegraph*, 24 March 1968. The *Unionist*, April 1968.

59 *Belfast Telegraph*, 30 September 1967.

60 *Irish Times*, 12 December 1968, press cuttings, O'Neill papers.

61 *Belfast Telegraph*, 18 October 1968. UDI referred to Unilateral Declaration of Independence, an echo of the refusal by Rhodesia's whites to accept Britain's dictation.

62 Ibid. 23 October 1968.

63 The *Unionist*, November 1968.

64 *Belfast Telegraph*, 21 February 1969.

65 *Daily Mail*, 2 January 1969. See also *Irish Times and Belfast Telegraph*, 2 January 1969

66 Parliamentary debates (*Hansard*) of the House of Lords, vol. 339, 29 March 1972, cols 1075–80, vol. 344, 24 July 1973, cols 661–6, col. 664.

67 Henry Kennedy, 'Politics in Northern Ireland', p. 59.

68 *Belfast Telegraph*, 3 December 1968.

69 NIHC, vol. 70, 4 December 1968, c. 2181–4.

70 *Belfast Telegraph*, 5 December 1968.

71 Ibid., 9 December 1968.

72 O'Neill, *Ulster at the crossroads*, pp. 140–6.

73 The *Listener*, 19 December 1968.

74 *Belfast Telegraph*, 10 December 1968.

75 Ibid., 11 December 1968. Even pro-O'Neill badges were produced. Miscellaneous election ephemera, anonymous donor, PRONI, D/2966/31.

76 *Belfast Telegraph*, 14 December 1968.

77 Ibid., 16, 18 December 1968. By way of indirect comparison, 25,500 signed a civil rights/Human Rights Year petition in Derry alone on one day, 10 December 1968. Ibid., 11 December 1968.

78 *Daily Mail*, 31 January 1969, press cuttings, O'Neill papers.

79 *Belfast Telegraph*, 27 January 1968.
80 Ibid., 10 December 1968.
81 Ibid., 11 December 1968.
82 Letters, ibid.
83 Ibid., 12, 13 December 1968.
84 *Financial Times*, 11 December 1968.
85 *News of the World*, 15 December 1968, press cuttings, O'Neill papers.
86 Alf McCreary, 'The grass roots', *Belfast Telegraph*, 11 December 1968.
87 Interview with Reginald Empey, 7 December 1995.
88 For example, see Ann Purdy, *Molyneaux: the long view* (Antrim, 1989) pp. 48–9.
89 Farrell, *Northern Ireland*, p. 249.
90 *Belfast Telegraph*, 21 December 1968.
91 Ibid., 31 December 1968.
92 *Irish News*, 30 December 1968.
93 *Belfast Telegraph*, 1 January 1969.
94 Ibid., 3 January 1969.
95 Ibid., 4 January 1969.
96 Ibid. Barry White, 'Battle of Burntollet bridge', 'People's Democracy marchers tell their own story', ibid., 5 January 1969.
97 [Cameron Report] *Disturbances in Northern Ireland: report of the commission appointed by the Governor of Northern Ireland* (Belfast: HMSO, 1969) Cmd 535, p. 73, para. 177.
98 Speeches and statements, January 1969, PRONI, INF/3/3/92.
99 *Belfast Telegraph*, 7 January 1969.
100 Ibid., 10 January 1969. The planned route was traditional and the 'loyalist' area to be sealed off barely inhabited.
101 Ibid., 11 January 1969.
102 Ibid., 13 January 1969.
103 Ibid., 16 January 1969.
104 Ibid., 17 January 1969.
105 Chris Ryder, *The RUC: a force under fire* (London, 1989) pp. 107–8.
106 *Belfast Telegraph*, 15 January 1969.
107 O'Neill, *Autobiography*, appendix II, pp. 150–4. *News Letter*, 9 January 1969.
108 *Belfast Telegraph*, 16 January 1969.
109 Ibid., 17 January 1969.
110 William J. Wilson, 'What price progress?', The *Unionist*, January 1968. This article expresses well the segregatory mainstream, which The *Unionist* itself encapsulated.
111 *Belfast Telegraph*, 20 January 1969.
112 Ibid., 21 January 1969.
113 O'Neill, *Autobiography*, appendix II, pp. 150–4.
114 *Belfast Telegraph*, 25, 27 January 1969.
115 Ibid., 27 January 1969.
116 Ibid., 6 February 1969.
117 Ibid., 29 January 1969.
118 Ibid., 31 January 1969.
119 Speeches and statements, January 1969, PRONI, INF/3/3/92.
120 *Belfast Telegraph*, 4 February 1969.

121 An O'Neill advisor remembered that 'he tried to … bring in the outsiders, the people who really didn't take any part in politics at all, and with a small nucleus from the Unionist Party build up a new climate of opinion.', Van Voris, *Violence in Ulster*, p. 108.
122 *Belfast Telegraph*, 4 February 1969.
123 Ibid., 4 February.
124 This survey is based upon: *Belfast Telegraph, News Letter, City Week, Times, Irish Times, Northern Constitution, Ballymena Observer and County Antrim Advertiser, Lisburn Herald, Ulster Star, East Antrim Times, Newtownards Chronicle and County Down Observer, Banbridge Chronicle, Down Recorder, County Down Spectator and Ulster Standard, Newtownards Spectator and Donaghadee Review*, the *Outlook , Tyrone Constitution, Dungannon News and Tyrone Courier, Portadown News and County Down Advertiser, Mid-Ulster Mail, Armagh Observer, Armagh Guardian, Lurgan Mail, Londonderry Sentinel*, the *Unionist, Fermanagh News and West Ulster Observer, Impartial Reporter and Farmers' Journal*. Sydney Elliott, *Northern Ireland parliamentary election results* (Chichester, 1973) pp. 35–86. Cornelius O'Leary, 'The Northern Ireland general election (1969)', F. A. Hermens (ed.) *Verfassung und verfassungwarkslicheit* (Verlag, 1969). F. W. Boal & R. H. Buchanan, 'The 1969 Northern Ireland election', *Irish Geography*, vol. vi, no. 1 (Dublin, 1969) pp. 78–84. Miracle, 'A liberal in spite of himself', pp. 34–51. Robin Bailie, 'Progress in parliament – not on the streets', *Belfast Telegraph*, 13 March 1969.
125 See remarks of Phelim O'Neill as recorded in J. C. Beckett's diary, 16 January 1969, Papers of J. C. Beckett, PRONI, D/4126/A/1/23.
126 *Belfast Telegraph*, 21 February 1969.
127 Ibid., 14 March 1969.
128 *The Times*, 17 February 1969, press cuttings, O'Neill papers.
129 *East Antrim Times*, 13 February 1969.
130 Ibid., 14, 21, February 1969. The *Outlook*, 21 February 1969.
131 *Belfast Telegraph*, 22 February 1969.
132 *Down Recorder*, 14, 21 February 1969. The *Newtownards Chronicle and County Down Observer*, 20 February 1969.
133 *Tyrone Constitution*, 14 February 1969. Vera E. Nevin, *I am an Irish dimension (a prod's-eye-view of Northern Ireland)*, (Ulster Educational Press, 1986), p. 14.
134 One such was Ken Maginnis, later a Unionist Westminster MP for Fermanagh-South Tyrone. Nevin, *I am an Irish dimension*, p. 24; Ken Maginnis, 'Why I switched support' (letter), *Dungannon News and Tyrone Courier*, 19 February 1969.
135 *Belfast Telegraph*, 5 February 1969.
136 Ibid., 12 February 1969.
137 Ibid., 11 February 1969.
138 *Northern Constitution*, 22 February 1969.
139 *Belfast Telegraph*, ibid. For a detailed account of the split in Derry unionism, Niall Ó Dochartaigh, *From civil rights to armalites: Derry and the birth of the Irish Troubles* (Cork, 1997) pp. 70–89.
140 *Belfast Telegraph*, 4 February 1969. The *Londonderry Sentinel*, 5, 12 February 1969.

141 *News Letter*, 1 February 1969. The *Impartial Reporter and Farmers' Journal*, 6 February 1969. *Belfast Telegraph*, 3 February 1963.

142 The *Impartial Reporter and Farmers' Journal*, 6 February 1969.

143 *Belfast Telegraph*, 8 February 1969.

144 Ibid., 11 February 1969.

145 Ibid., 6 May 1969.

146 Ibid., 12, 21 February 1969.

147 Ibid., 21 February 1969.

148 The *Unionist*, October 1968.

149 P. H. McMillan, 'The New Ulster Movement and the formation of the Alliance Party of Northern Ireland', unpublished MSc thesis (QUB, 1984) pp. 1–12.

150 *Belfast Telegraph*, 13 February 1969.

151 Ibid., 17 February 1969.

152 Ó Dochartaigh, *From civil rights to armalites*, pp. 85–9. Patrick Buckland, *A history of Northern Ireland* (Dublin, 1981) pp. 127–8.

153 Rose, *Governing without consensus*, p. 298. See also *Belfast Telegraph*, 13 December 1967.

154 W. D. Flackes and Betty Lowry, 'The middle class', *Belfast Telegraph*, 20, 21, 22, 23, 24 April 1964.

155 When asked whether the election might lead to a formal split in the Unionist Party, O'Neill sounded unconcerned: 'One seldom achieves absolute unanimity in any sphere, and least of all in politics. I shall be quite content if the outcome is a better balanced reflection of what I believe to be the real mood of the country.' O'Neill interviewed by Roy Lilley, *Belfast Telegraph*, 5 February 1969.

156 G. W. Target, *Unholy smoke* (London, 1969) p. 14. David Bleakley, *Young Ulster and religion in the sixties* (Belfast, n.d [1964]) pp. 103–7. Steve Bruce, *God save Ulster! The religion and politics of Paisleyism* (Oxford, 1986) pp. 262–5. Sabbatarianism was markedly stronger in working class than middle class districts in Belfast. In a mini referendum conducted by Belfast City Council in 1968 to gauge opinion on whether play centres should be opened on Sundays, out of twenty-one areas only Hemsworth Street, Eastland Street (both off the Shankill Road), the Donegall Road and Castleton (off North Queen Street) voted against, if narrowly. All were solidly working class. Haymarket, Willowbank and Beechfield Street, middle class areas, were overwhelming in support of opening. *Belfast Telegraph*, 26 June 1968. There were marked class differences on whether Northern Ireland's social laws – particularly on Sunday drinking – should be brought into line with Britain's. The working class was more conservative than the middle class. *Belfast Telegraph*, 9 December 1967.

157 Ian McAllister, 'Class, region, denomination, and protestant politics in Ulster', *Working Papers in Sociology* (Canberra, 1982) pp. 9–10.

158 For a good narrative of this process, though without the categories here presented, see David Hume, *The Ulster Unionist Party 1972–1992: a political movement in a era of conflict of change* (Belfast, 1996) pp. 74–105.

159 For example, see O'Neill's speech to Carrick UA, the *Unionist*, February 1968.

160 *Washington Post*, 21 January 1969, press cuttings, O'Neill papers.

161 *Portadown News and County Armagh Advertiser*, 21 February 1969.
162 Cabinet conclusions, 20 November 1968, PRONI, CAB/4/1418/11, p. 3. For Bradford's public comments see *Belfast Telegraph*, 12 December 1968.
163 *Belfast Telegraph*, 11 February 1969.
164 Ibid., 12 February 1969.
165 Ibid., 13 February 1969.
166 Gordon, *The O'Neill years*, p. 148.
167 The *Newry Telegraph*, 15 February 1969.
168 *Belfast Telegraph*, 19 February 1969.
169 John Darby, 'The historical background', John Darby (ed.), *Northern Ireland: the background to the conflict* (Belfast, 1983) p. 26. Cf. John Biggs-Davison and George Chowdharay-Best, *The cross of St Patrick: the catholic unionist tradition in Ireland* (Buckinghamshire, 1984) pp. 377–9.
170 Ulster Unionist Party, *Ulster at the crossroads* (Belfast, 1969), Nancy Kinghan papers, PRONI, D/912/2A/15.
171 *Sunday Times*, 9 February 1969.
172 Cf. Desmond Boal's election address, John Laird papers, Political Collection, Linen Hall Library.
173 *Down Recorder*, 15 February 1969.
174 *Belfast Telegraph*, 18 February 1969.
175 Ibid., 17 February 1969.
176 Ibid., 20 February 1969. My emphasis.
177 Ibid., 21 February 1969.
178 Bailie passed election material to the Independents through intermediaries still in the party such as Robert Cooper. Interview with Bob Cooper, 24 October 1996. *Belfast Telegraph*, 8 February 1968.
179 Speeches and statements, February 1969, PRONI, INF/3/3/93. *Belfast Telegraph*, 20 February 1969.
180 *Belfast Telegraph*, 21 February 1969.
181 Ibid., 19 February 1969.
182 Ibid., 22 February 1969.
183 Ibid., 13 February 1969.
184 *The Times*, 13 February 1969.
185 *News Letter*, 20 February 1969. *Belfast Telegraph*, ibid.
186 Paul Compton, 'The demographic background', in David Watt (ed.), *The constitution of Northern Ireland: problems and prospects* (London, 1981) p. 89.
187 *Irish News*, 3–25 February 1969 *passim*. For a near hysterical attack on 'turncoats' see editorial of 25 February.
188 About 5 per cent of catholics claimed to support the Unionist Party before the civil rights movement. Rose, *Governing without consensus*, p. 235.
189 See the comments of Michael Farrell in 'People's Democracy: a discussion on strategy', *New Left Review*, no. 55, May–June 1969, p. 15.
190 Cooper was a protestant and ex-Young Unionist activist, who only a few years previously had brazenly defended anti-catholic discrimination. He told a Young Unionist conference that 'employers could not be blamed if they preferred to employ people with Unionist affiliations on the grounds that they received more loyal support from them.' *News Letter*, 2 March 1964.
191 *Belfast Telegraph*, 17 February 1969.

192 *News Letter*, 6 February 1969, press cuttings, O'Neill papers.
193 *Belfast Telegraph*, 19 February 1969.
194 Ibid., 1 May 1969.
195 Harold Jackson, 'O'Neill stands aloof from Craig's banter', *The Times*, 18 February 1969, press cuttings, O'Neill papers.
196 *News Letter*, 18 February 1969. *Ballymena Observer and County Antrim Advertiser*, 20 February 1969.
197 *Daily Mirror*, 19 February 1969, press cuttings, O'Neill papers.
198 Elliott, *Election results*, p. 52.
199 *Belfast Telegraph*, 25 February 1969.
200 *Irish Times*, 27 February 1969, press cuttings, O'Neill papers.
201 *Belfast Telegraph*, 25 February 1969.
202 Richard Rose, 'Why the election settled nothing', *Belfast Telegraph*, 6 March 1969.
203 The phrase is Harold Wilson's. Wilson, *Labour Government*, p. 674.
204 *Belfast Telegraph*, 28 February 1969.
205 Ibid., 7, 8 March 1969.
206 Ibid., 8 March 1969.
207 Bernadette Devlin thanked O'Neill 'for affording us the platform of the election to spread the civil rights movement as far as possible through Northern Ireland in the shortest possible time.' *Northern Constitution*, 1 March 1969.
208 For Nationalist uneasiness about the civil rights movement, see a civil servant's record of a conversation with McAteer, 'Civil Rights Campaign in Northern Ireland dating from August, 1968', PRONI, CAB/9b/205/7. 'Informal discussions with Mr. R. O'Connor', Cabinet conclusions, 15 November 1968, PRONI, CAB/4/1415/11, pp. 3–4.
209 PD had attempted to develop. a strategy less likely to give rise to sectarian tension. Bob Purdie, *Politics in the streets: the origins of the civil rights movement in Northern Ireland* (Belfast, 1990) p. 242.
210 McAllister, *The Northern Ireland Social Democratic and Labour Party*, pp. 27–9.
211 Fred Heatley, 'The civil rights story – the NICRA split', *Fortnight*, 10 May 1974, no. 83, pp. 13–14.
212 *Belfast Telegraph*, 19 March 1969.
213 Ibid., 31 March 1969.
214 A bomb attack on an electricity sub-station outside Belfast, carried out by loyalist agent provocateurs, helped the process along. O'Neill, *Autobiography*, p. 122.
215 *News Letter*, 2 April 1969.
216 *Belfast Telegraph*, 31 March 1969.
217 *Irish Times*, 1 April 1969, press cuttings, O'Neill papers.
218 *Belfast Telegraph*, 1 April 1969.
219 *Irish Times*, 2 April 1969.
220 *Belfast Telegraph*, 24 March 1969.
221 Ibid., 11 April 1969.
222 *Sunday Press*, 13 April 1969, press cuttings, O'Neill papers.
223 McIvor, *Hope deferred*, pp. 52–3.
224 Private information.
225 *Belfast Telegraph*, 11 December 1968.

226 Ibid., 7 February 1969.
227 Michael Farrell in *Belfast Telegraph*, 14 March 1969. Ibid., 19 March, 2 April 1969. Devlin, *The price of my soul*, pp. 159–69.
228 *Belfast Telegraph*, 15 May 1969.
229 Ibid., 2 April 1969.
230 Ibid., 8 April 1969.
231 Ibid. 8, 10 April 1969.
232 Ibid., 1 April 1969.
233 Martin Wallace, 'Dynamo Devlin drives unusual chariot around Mid-Ulster area', ibid., 15 April 1969.
234 *Belfast Telegraph* 15, 16, 17 April 1969.
235 Ibid., 18 April 1969.
236 WHC, vol. 782, 22 April 1969, c. 281–8. Percy Dymond, 'MPs hail Bernadette's speech as 'the best since 1906', *Belfast Telegraph*, 23 April 1969.
237 *Belfast Telegraph*, 21 April 1969. The Sunday Times Insight Team, *Ulster* (Middlesex, 1972) pp. 74–8. The British government was inclined to believe the IRA's denial of responsibility. WHC, vol. 782, 22 April 1969, c. 319–21.
238 Terence O'Neill, Diary of the last days, written 6–8 May 1969, O'Neill papers.
239 Callaghan, *A house divided*, p. 25.
240 O'Neill, Diary, O'Neill papers.
241 *Belfast Telegraph*, 22 April 1969.
242 WHC, vol. 782, 22 April 1969, c. 322.
243 *Belfast Telegraph*, 24 April 1969.
244 Ibid., 23, 24 April 1969. O'Neill, Diary, O'Neill papers.
245 O'Neill, Diary, O'Neill papers.
246 *Irish Times*, 24 April 1969, press cuttings, O'Neill papers.
247 *Belfast Telegraph*, 25 April 1969.
248 Ibid.
249 *Irish Times*, 8 November 1972, press cuttings, NIO files.
250 *Belfast Telegraph*, 28 April 1969.
251 *Irish Independent*, 30 October 1969, press cuttings, O'Neill papers.
252 *Belfast Telegraph*, 30 April 1969.
253 Interview with Richard Ferguson, QC, 27 March 1996.
254 Speeches and statements, April 1969, PRONI, INF/3/3/95.
255 O'Neill, Diary, O'Neill papers.
256 O'Neill, Diary, O'Neill papers. *Belfast Telegraph*, 29 April 1969.
257 *Belfast Telegraph*, 30 April 1969.
258 Ibid., 21 April 1969.
259 Ibid., 26 April 1969.
260 Ibid., 29 April 1969.
261 Ibid., 30 April 1969/.
262 O'Neill, Diary, O'Neill papers.
263 *Belfast Telegraph*, 1 May 1969.

Conclusion

1 O'Neill, *Autobiography*, p. 87. Speech to Leinster Society of Chartered Accountants, Dublin, 24 November 1977, O'Neill papers.
2 Letter to Jock Colville, 29 July 1976, ibid.
3 For example, Belinda Probert, *Beyond orange and green: the Northern Ireland crisis in a new perspective* (London, 1978) p. 79. Michael Farrell, *Northern Ireland: the orange state* (London 1980 [1st ed. 1976]) p. 238.
4 Some believe that Wilson wished to smooth the way to a free trade deal with the Republic, itself part of a long-term scheme to reunify Ireland in close association with Britain. Versions of this had a considerable appeal for those of a conspiratorial beut in both unionist and nationalist circles. The earliest example on the unionist side I have found is a speech delivered by Sir Knox Cunningham, Unionist MP for South Antrim, cited in *Belfast Telegraph*, 9 October 1965. Republicans developed a similar theory. Henry Pattterson, *The politics of illusion: republicanism and socialism in modern Ireland* (London, 1989) pp. 89–91, 99–100. It has found an echo in academic literature. Cf. Frank Wright's (excellent) *Northern Ireland: a comparative perspective* (Dublin, 1987) p. 189.
5 Sabine Wichert, *Northern Ireland since 1945* (Essex, 1991) p. 90.
6 James Loughlin, *Ulster Unionism and British national identity since 1885* (London, 1995) pp. 174–84.

Bibliography

Newspapers

Armagh Guardian
Ballymena Observer and County Antrim Advertiser
Belfast News Letter Annual Review
Carrickfergus Advertiser and East Antrim Gazette
Church of Ireland Gazette
Coleraine Chronicle
County Down Spectator and Ulster Standard
Daily Express
Daily Telegraph
Derry Standard
Dungannon News and Tyrone Courier
Dungannon Observer, The
East Antrim Times
Farmweek
Fermanagh News and West Ulster Observer
Fortnight
Guardian
Impact / Invictus: Irish Universities Left Review
Impartial Reporter and Farmers' Journal
Irish Independent
Irish Press
Leader, The
Listener, The
London Evening Standard
Londonderry Sentinel
Lurgan Mail
Mourne Observer
New Statesman
Newry Telegraph
Belfast News Letter (until 1963: thereafter News Letter)
Newtownards Chronicle and County Down Observer
Newtownards Spectator and Donaghadee Review
Northern Whig
Newry Telegraph
Observer, The
Portadown News and County Armagh Advertiser
Protestant Telegraph
Review: an Ulster political commentary
Spectator, The
Sunday Independent

Armagh Observer
Banbridge Chronicle
Belfast Telegraph
Catholic Herald
City Week

Daily Mail
Daily Mirror
Derry Journal
Down Recorder

Economist
Evening News
Fermanagh Herald
Financial Times
Constabulary Gazette
Hibernian

Interplay
Irish News
Larne Times
Lisburn Herald
Liverpool Post

Mid-Ulster Mail
New Ireland
Newry Reporter
News of the World

Northern Constitution
Newry Reporter
Northern Constitution
Outlook
Portadown Times

Round Table
Sunday Express
Sunday News

Sunday Press
Sunday Telegraph
Strabane Weekly News
Tablet
Tuairisc
Tyrone Constitution
Ulster Gazette and Armagh Standard
Unionist

Sunday Times

Student life
The Times

Ulster Star
Washington Post.

Government publications and papers

Report of the joint working party on the economy of Northern Ireland, Cmd 446 (Belfast: HMSO, 1962).

[Matthew Report] *Belfast regional survey and plan: recommendations and conclusions* (Belfast, HMSO, 1963) Cmd 451.

Henry Benson, *Northern Ireland railways* (Belfast, HMSO, 1963) Cmd 458.

Sir Josiah Eccles, *Administration of the electricity supply service* (Belfast, HMSO, June 1963).

The administration of town and country planning in Northern Ireland (Belfast, HMSO, 1964) Cmd 465.

Educational development in Northern Ireland (Belfast: HMSO, 1964) cmd. 470.

New City Design Group, *First report on the proposed New City, County Armagh* (Belfast, HMSO, 1964).

Craigavon new city, second report on the plan (Belfast, HMSO, 1967).

[Lockwood Report] *Higher education in Northern Ireland* (Belfast, HMSO, 1965) Cmd 475.

A ten year programme for electricity supply (Belfast, HMSO, 1965) Cmd 478.

[Wilson Report] *Economic Development in Northern Ireland*, Cmd 479 (Belfast, 1964).

Electricity in Ireland: report of the Joint-Committee on Co-operation in Electricity Supply (Belfast, HMSO, March 1966).

Local education authorities and voluntary schools (Belfast: HMSO, 1967) Cmd 513.

The reshaping of local government: statement of aims (Belfast, HMSO, 1967) Cmd 517.

The reshaping of local government: further proposals (Belfast, HMSO, 1969) Cmd 530.

[Cameron Report] *Disturbances in Northern Ireland: report of the commission appointed by the Governor of Northern Ireland* (Belfast: HMSO, 1969) Cmd 535.

[Macrory Report] *Review body on local government in Northern Ireland* (Belfast, HMSO, 1970) Cmd 546.

Government of Northern Ireland Economic Section, *Northern Ireland Economic Report on 1969* (Belfast: HMSO, 1970).

Paul Compton, *Demographic trends in Northern Ireland*, report 57 of the Northern Ireland Economic Council (Belfast, 1986).

Prime Minister's papers (Public Records Office, Kew).

Cabinet conclusions (Public Records Office, Kew).

Home Office papers (Public Records Office, Kew).

Cabinet conclusions (Public Records Office, Northern Ireland).

Cabinet committee on unemployment papers (Public Records Office, Northern Ireland).
Cabinet secretariat files (Public Records Office, Northern Ireland).
Home Affairs papers (Public Records Office, Northern Ireland).
Government Information Service (Public Records Office, Northern Ireland).
Northern Ireland Information Service, *Facts and Figures*.
Northern Ireland Information Service, *Ulster: change and progress* (February 1970)
Northern Ireland Information Service, *Ulster Commentary*, 1960–9.
Northern Ireland Information Service, *Ulster Yearbook, 1960–9.*
Parliamentary debates: Northern Ireland House of Commons (*Hansard*).
Parliamentary debates: Northern Ireland Senate (*Hansard*).
Parliamentary debates: House of Lords (*Hansard*).
Public Debates, Dáil Eireann, Republic of Ireland.
Free trade agreement and related agreements: exchanges of letters and understandings, laid by the Government before each House of the Oireachtas (Dublin, 1965).
Department of the Taoiseach papers, National Archives, Dublin.
Department of Foreign Affairs papers, National Archives Dublin.

Private papers

Papers of J. C. Beckett (Public Records Office, Northern Ireland).
Election ephemera deposited anonymously (Public Records Office, Northern Ireland).
Election ephemera, deposited anonymously (Public Records Office, Northern Ireland).
Montgomery Hyde papers (Public Records Office, Northern Ireland).
John Johnston papers (Public Records Office, Northern Ireland).
John Kerr papers (Public Records Office, Northern Ireland).
Papers of Sir James Alex Kilfedder MP (Public Records Office, Northern Ireland).
Papers of Miss N. Kinghan (Public Records Office, Northern Ireland).
Papers of Councillor Mrs N. Laird (Public Records Office, Northern Ireland).
Papers of John Laird (Political Collection, Linen Hall Library).
Papers of Mary McNeill (Institute of Irish Studies, Queen's University of Belfast).
Papers of Peter Montgomery (Public Records Office, Northern Ireland).
Papers of Sam Napier (Public Records Office, Northern Ireland).
Papers of North Antrim Women's Unionist Association, 1956–67 (Public Records Office, Northern Ireland).
Papers of the Northern Ireland Committee of the Irish Congress of Trade Unions (Lord William Blease).
Northern Ireland Office files (Linen Hall Library, Belfast).
Papers of Lord O'Neill of the Maine (Lymington, Hampshire).
Papers of Professor Sir Douglas Savoury (Public Records Office, Northern Ireland).
Papers of J. W. Trueman (Portadown, Armagh).
Ulster Unionist Council archive (Public Records Office, Northern Ireland).
Unionist Society papers (Public Records Office, Northern Ireland).

'University for Derry Campaign' papers (Public Records Office, Northern Ireland).
Political ephemera, Linen Hall Library, Belfast.
Conservative Party Archive, Bodleian Library, Oxford.

Contemporary newspaper articles

Bailie, Robin, 'A united Ulster', *Review: an Ulster political commentary*, October 1962.
Bailie, Robin, 'Finding a basis for North-South co-operation', *New Ireland*, 1964.
Bailie, Robin, 'Progress in parliament – not on the streets', *Belfast Telegraph*, 13 March 1969.
Bossence, Ralph, Interview with Terence O'Neill, *News Letter*, 8 June 1964.
Bossence, Ralph, 'The shackles that bind Ulster's Prime Minister', *News Letter*, 2 November 1964.
Boyd, Andrew, 'United Ulstermen', *Spectator*, 15 February 1963.
Boyd, Andrew, 'The Copcutt controversy', *Irish Times*, 1 September 1964.
Boyd, Welsey, 'Bigotry still scrawls its ugly trail across North; disappointment with O'Neill's leadership' *Irish Times*, 29 January 1964.
Boyle, Louis, 'Unionism at the crossroads', *Yearbook of the Conservative and Unionist Association of Queen's University Belfast 1967 / 8* (Belfast, 1967).
Bradford, Bradford, 'The questions Unionists are asking about party organisation – and some purely personal answers', *Belfast Telegraph*, 20 May 1966.
Brett, C. E. B., 'Religious discrimination in Northern Ireland', the *Guardian*, 3 March 1964.
Brett, C. E. B., 'Discrimination in Northern Ireland. Religious apartheid', the *Guardian*, 4 March 1964.
Brett, C. E. B., 'Discrimination in Northern Ireland; oranges and lemons', the *Guardian*, 5 March 1964.
Dinsmore, John, 'Too little living room in Derry' and 'An inexcusable delay', *Belfast Telegraph*, 27, 28 July 1967.
Duggan, G. C., 'Northern Patterns of Discrimination', *Irish Times*, 4 May 1967.
Dymond, Percy, 'MPs hail Bernadette's speech as "the best since 1906"', *Belfast Telegraph*, 23 April 1969.
Farrell, Michael, *et al*, 'People's Democracy: a discussion on strategy', *New Left Review*, no. 55 (May–June 1969).
Flackes, W. D. and Lowry, Betty, 'The middle class', *Belfast Telegraph*, 20, 21, 22, 23, 24 April 1964.
Flackes, W. D., 'Challenges facing the new city council', *Belfast Telegraph*, 24 May 1964.
Flackes, W. D., 'I.C.T.U. – the new relationship', *Belfast Telegraph*, 27 July 1964.
Gordon, Claud, 'Welcoming back the Paisleyites', *Sunday Press*, 25 September 1966.
Grant, Michael, 'A Nationalist voter takes a look at the Party', *Hibernia*, vol. 27, no. 2, February 1963.
Hamilton, Andrew, 'Letter from Belfast; back to the old divisions', *Irish Times*, 1 December 1965.
Heaney, Seamus, 'Old Derry's walls', *The Listener*, 24 October 1968.

Heatley, Fred, 'The civil rights story – the NICRA split', *Fortnight*, 10 May 1974, no. 83.

Insight, 'John Bull's political slum', *Sunday Times*, 3 July 1966.

Jackson, Harold, 'O'Neill stands aloof from Craig's banter', *The Times*, 18 February 1969.

Kelly, James, 'I say: let everybody see Stormont on telly', *Sunday Independent*, 13 December 1964.

Kelly, James, 'Quiet Coleraine doesn't know what's coming its way soon', *Sunday Independent*, 30 May 1965.

Kelly, James, 'Cloak-and-dagger tactics behind the Unionist crisis', *Sunday Independent*, 25 September 1966.

Kelly, James, 'Does O'Neill want to quit?', *Sunday Independent*, 22 September 1968.

Kennedy, Dennis, 'Religious houses', *Belfast Telegraph*, 25, 26, 27 November 1964.

Kennedy, Dennis, 'Catholic education', *Belfast Telegraph*, 26, 27, 28 July 1965.

Kennedy, Dennis, 'Putting the "Scotch-Irish" image to work for politics and trade', *Hibernia*, vol. 29, nos 9, 10, October 1965.

Kennedy, Dennis, 'Portrait of a premier face to face with the voters; the charmer who brings economics to the faithful', *Belfast Telegraph*, 24 November 1965.

Kennedy, Dennis, 'Northern Ireland's future premier', *Hibernia*, vol. 30, no. 2, February 1966.

Lilley, Roy, 'When two and two make five', *Belfast Telegraph*, 5 September 1963.

Lilley, Roy, 'Unionism today', *Belfast Telegraph*, 21, 22, 23 24 October 1963.

Lilley, Roy, 'Labour: the new foothold – and the future', *Belfast Telegraph*, 4 June 1964.

Lilley, Roy, 'Today's O'Neill-Lynch meeting – the background', *Belfast Telegraph*, 11 December 1967.

Lilley, Roy, 'The face of change', *Belfast Telegraph*, 12, 15 March 1968.

Lilley, Roy, 'Where is the Orange Order marching to now?', *Belfast Telegraph*, 9 July 1968.

Lowry, Betty and Flackes, W. D., 'The new middle class ', *Belfast Telegraph*, 20, 21, 22, 23, 24 April 1964.

Lowry, Suzanne, 'Seeing life from a shop and a shipyard', *Belfast Telegraph*, 29 February 1968.

Lynch, Patrick, 'Labour in the North', *Impact / Invictus: Irish Universities Left Review*, no. 1, May 1963.

McCreary, Alf (on housing allocation), *Belfast Telegraph*, 25, 26, 27 September 1968.

McCreary, Alf, 'Fifty days – Northern Ireland's political revolution; pressure from No. 10 ... and a warning from O'Neill', *Belfast Telegraph*, 2 December 1968.

McCreary, Alf, 'The grass roots', *Belfast Telegraph*, 11 December 1968.

[McCrystal, Cal.], 'John Bull's political slum', *Sunday Times*, 3 July 1966.

McCrystal, Cal, 'Gloomy Londonderry Air', *Sunday Times*, 23 October 1966.

McElroy, Rev. A. H., 'The Liberal leaven in Northern Ireland', *New Ireland*, 1964.

McKeown, Michael, 'William Craig', *Hibernia*, 12 December 1968.

McKeown, Michael, 'The life and hard times of William Craig', *Hibernia*, 28 August 1970.

McNeill, Mary A., 'A Northern Protestant view', *Hibernian*, September 1958.
Mills, Michael, 'Removing the balance of hatred', *Irish Press*, 27 March 1967.
Mills, Stratton, 'Forward – the Ulster eggheads!', *Belfast Telegraph*, 4 March 1964.
O'Neill, Terence, 'A spectator's notebook', the *Spectator*, 22 June 1977.
Patrick, William, 'Coleraine preferred to Derry for new university', *Hibernia*, vol. 29, no. 3, March 1965.
Perrott, Roy, 'Bodysnatchers and babies at Ballynahinch', *Observer*, 26 May 1968.
Pyle, Fergus, 'Silent Unionists being heard; aftermath of Derry', *Irish Times*, 29 October 1968.
Rose, Richard, 'Why the election settled nothing', *Belfast Telegraph*, 6 March 1969.
Taylor, John D., 'Charges of discrimination', the *Unionist*, May 1965.
Tugendhat, Christopher, 'How the voting patter varied', *Financial Times*, 17 October 1966.
Viney, Michael, 'Journey North: The New Voices', *Irish Times*, 5 May 1964.
Wallace, Martin, 'Profile – Terence O'Neill, *Belfast Telegraph*, 19 May 1961.
Wallace, Martin, 'Dynamo Devlin drives unusual chariot around Mid-Ulster area', *Belfast Telegraph*, 15 April 1969.
Warnock, Edmund, 'The power to be generous', *Belfast Telegraph*, 8 November 1967.
White, Barry, 'O'Neill 100 weeks later', *Belfast Telegraph*, 4 March 1965.
White, Barry, 'The face of Unionism: how is it changing?', *Belfast Telegraph*, 29 April 1965.
White, Barry, 'The road ahead for Capt. O'Neill', *Belfast Telegraph*, 22 July 1966.
White, Barry, 'Mater Hospital', *Belfast Telegraph*, 1, 2 February 1967.
White, Barry, 'Belfast's housing failure', *Belfast Telegraph*, 8, 9, 10, 11 March 1967.
White, Barry, 'The new nationalism – part 1', *Belfast Telegraph*, 8 February 1968.
White, Barry, 'Building up to a crisis', *Belfast Telegraph*, 5, 7, 8 March 1968.
White, Barry, 'Republican Clubs: how they see themselves', *Belfast Telegraph*, 28 May 1968.
White, Barry, 'The march of civil rights', *Belfast Telegraph*, 11 October 1968.
White, Barry, 'Who are the reformers?', *Belfast Telegraph*, 26 October 1968.
White, Barry, 'Battle of Burntollet bridge', *Belfast Telegraph*, 5 January 1969.
White, Barry, 'The day Lemass came to Stormont', *Belfast Telegraph*, n.d. [1975].
Wilson, William J., 'What price progress?', the *Unionist*, January 1968.
Wolff, James, T., 'The Unionist Party; the 1965 "vote of confidence"', *Protestant Telegraph*, 30 March 1968.

Books, articles and pamphlets

Primary works (contemporary or memoirs)

Adams, Gerry, *Before the dawn: an autobiography* (London, Heinemann, 1996).
Arthur, Paul, *The People's Democracy 1968–1973* (Belfast, Blackstaff Press, 1974).
Barritt, Denis, *Northern Ireland: a problem to every solution* (London, Quaker Peace and Service, 1982).

Barritt, Denis P., and Carter, Charles F., *The Northern Ireland problem: a study in group relations* (2nd edition, Oxford, Oxford University Press, 1972).

Belfast News Letter, 'Northern Ireland Annual Review 1956'.

Bleakley, David, 'The Northern Ireland trade union movement', *Journal of the Statistical and Social Inquiry of Ireland* (1953–4) vol. XX.

Bleakley, David, *Young Ulster and religion in the sixties* (Belfast, Church of Ireland Members, n.d [1964]).

Bleakley, David, *Faulkner: conflict and consent in Irish politics* (Oxford, Mowbray, 1974).

Bleakley, David, *Peace in Ireland: two states, one people* (London, Mowbray, 1995).

Bloomfield, Ken, *Stormont in crisis: a memoir* (Belfast, Blackstaff Press, 1994).

Boal, F. W. & Buchanan, R. H., 'The 1969 Northern Ireland election', *Irish Geography*, vol. vi, no. 1 (Dublin, 1969).

Boyd, John, *The middle of my journey* (Belfast, Blackstaff Press, 1990).

Brett, C. E. B., *Long Shadows cast before: nine lives in Ulster 1625–1977* (Edinburgh, J. Bartholomew,1978) p. 132.

Callaghan, James, *A house divided: the dilemma of Northern Ireland* (London, Collins, 1973).

Carter, Charles F., 'The Wilson Report: a further comment', *Studies: an Irish quarterly review of letters: philosophy and science* (Dublin, 1965) vol. LIV.

Cole, John, *As it seemed to me: political memoirs* (London, Weidenfeld and Nicolson, 1995).

Colville, John, *The fringes of power: Downing Street diaries 1939–55* (London, Hodder and Stoughton, 1985).

Connery, Donald, S., *The Irish* (London, Eyre and Spaltiswoode, 1968).

Coogan, Timothy Pat, *Ireland since the Rising* (Connecticut, Greenwood, 1966).

Curran, Frank, *Derry: countdown to disaster* (Dublin, Gill and Macmillan, 1986).

Devlin, Bernadette, *The price of my soul* (London, Deutsch, 1969).

Devlin, Paddy, *Straight left: an autobiography* (Belfast, Blackstaff Press, 1993).

Dewar, M. W., Brown, John, Long, S. E., *Orangeism: a new historical appreciation* (Belfast, Grand Orange Lodge of Ireland, 1967).

Evans, Harold, *Downing Street diaries: the Macmillan years 1957–1963* (London, Hodder and Stoughton, 1981).

Farrell, Michael (ed.), *Twenty years on* (Dingle, Brandon, 1988).

Faulkner, Brian, *Memoirs of a statesman* (London, Weidenfeld and Nicolson, 1978).

Fitzgerald, Desmond J. L., *History of the Irish Guards in the Second World War* (Aldershot, Gale and Polden, 1949).

Gibson, Norman, *Partition today – a protestant view* (Dublin, Tvairim, 1959).

Gray, Tony, *The Irish answer: an anatomy of modern Ireland* (London, Heinemann, 1966).

Green, Arthur J., *Devolution and public finances: Stormont from 1921 to 1972* (University of Strathclyde, 1979).

Griffen, Victor, *Mark of protest: an autobiography* (Dublin, Gill and Macmillan, 1993).

Hayes, Maurice, *Minority verdict: experiences of a catholic public servant* (Belfast, Blackstaff Press, 1995).

Hepburn, A. C., *The conflict of nationality in modern Ireland* (London, Edward

Arnold, 1980).

ICTU, *Second annual report of the Irish Congress of Trade Unions, 1959–60* (Dublin, ICTU, 1960).

ICTU, *Third annual report of the Irish Congress of Trade Unions, 1960–1* (Dublin, ICTU, 1961).

Isles, K. S. and Cuthbert, N., *An economic survey of Northern Ireland* (Belfast, HMSO, 1957).

Jackson, Harold, 'Northern Ireland' in David McKie and Chris Cooke (eds) *The decade of disillusion: British politics in the sixties* (London, Macmillan, 1972).

Kelly, James, *Bonfires on the hillside: an eyewitness account of political upheaval in Northern Ireland* (Belfast, Fountain Publishing, 1995).

Kinahan, Coralie, *Behind every great man ...?* (Templepatrick, Privately published, n.d. [1997]).

Kinghan, Nancy, *United we stood: the official history of the Ulster Women's Unionist Council 1911–1974* (Belfast, The Appletree Press, 1975).

Londonderry Junior Chamber of Commerce, *Thoughts on the boundary extension* (Derry, 1966).

McAteer, Eddie, *Irish action: new thoughts on an old subject* (Ballyshannon, Donegal Democrat, 1948).

McCann, Eamonn, *War and an Irish town* (London, Pluto Press, 1993 [1st ed. 1974]).

McCluskey, Conn, *Up off their knees: a commentary on the civil rights movement in Northern Ireland* (Republic of Ireland, privately published, 1989).

McCrystal, Cal, *Reflections on a quiet rebel* (Harmondsworth, Michael Joseph, 1997).

McIvor, Basil, *Hope deferred: experiences of an Irish unionist* (Belfast, Blackstaff Press, 1998).

McKeown, Ciaran, *The passion of peace* (Belfast, Blackstaff Press, 1984).

Mitchell, Arthur, *JFK and his Irish heritage* (Dublin, 1993).

Mulholland, Marc, *A calendar of material kept in the Public Records Office of Northern Ireland relating to the annual conferences of the Northern Ireland Labour Party, 1958–1963, plus one special conference of the party, 1962* (unpublished, 1994).

Neill, Ivan, *Church and state* (Dunmurray, Renewal Publications, 1995).

Nevin, Vera E., *I am an Irish Dimension (a prod's-eye-view of Northern Ireland)*, (Ulster Educational Press, 1986).

Northern Ireland Society of Labour Lawyers, *Discrimination – pride for prejudice* (Belfast, 1969).

O'Brien, Cruise, Conor, *Ancestral voices: religion and nationalism in Ireland* (Dublin, Poolbey, 1994).

O'Leary, Cornelius, 'Belfast West', D. E. Butler and Anthony King (eds), *The British general election of 1966* (London, Macmillan, 1966).

O'Leary, Cornelius, 'The Northern Ireland general election (1969)', F. A. Hermens (ed.) *Verfassung und verfassungwarkslicheit* (Verlag, 1969).

Oliver J. A., *Working at Stormont: the memoirs of John Andrew Oliver* (Dublin, Institute of Public Administration, 1978).

Oliver, John A., 'The Stormont administration 1921–72', *Contemporary Record*, vol. 5, no. 1, 1991.

O'Neill, Terence, *Putting PEP into the local community* (Belfast, HMSO, n.d.

[1967]).

O'Neill, Terence, *Ulster at the crossroads* (London, Faber and Faber, 1969).

O'Neill, Terence, *The autobiography of Terence O'Neill: Prime Minister of Northern Ireland 1963–1969* (London, Hart Davis, 1972).

Rose, Paul, *Backbencher's dilemma* (London, Muller, 1981).

Sweetman, Rosita, *On our knees: Ireland 1972* (London, Pan Books, 1972).

Target, G. W., *Unholy smoke* (London, Hodder and Stougton, 1969).

Thayer, George, *The British political fringe: a profile* (London, A. Bland, 1965).

Ulster Unionist Council, *Yearbook*, 1960–9.

Ulster Unionist Party, *Forward Ulster to target to Ulster 1970* (Belfast, Ulster Unionist Council (UUC), 1965)

Ulster Unionist Party, *Ulster at the crossroads* (Belfast, UUC, 1969).

Van Voris, W. H., *Violence in Ulster: an oral documentary* (Amherst, University of Massachusetts Press, 1975).

Walmsley, Albert J., *It was like this your worship* (Northern Ireland, privately published, 1988).

White, Barry, 'At the end of the day it's really down to us', *Belfast Telegraph*, 9 January 1999.

Wilson, Harold, *The Labour Government 1964–1970, a personal record* (London, Weidenfeld and Nicolson, 1971).

Wilson, Thomas (ed.), *Ulster under home rule* (Oxford, Oxford University Press, 1955).

Wilson, Thomas, 'First Economic Plan for Northern Ireland' in Michael Viney (ed.), *Seven seminars: A appraisal of regional planning in Ireland. Report on the 'Regional Planning Conference Ireland 1969' held in Belfast in March, 1969* (Dublin, An Faras Forbartha, 1969).

Wilson, Thomas, *Ulster: conflict and consent* (Oxford, Basil Blackwell, 1989).

Yearbook of the Conservative and Unionist Association of Queen's University Belfast 1967 / 8 (Belfast, UUC, 1967).

Secondary works

Akenson, Donald Harman, *Education and enmity: the control of schooling in Northern Ireland 1920–50* (Newtown Abbot, David and Charles, 1973).

Arthur, Paul and Jeffrey, Keith, *Northern Ireland since 1968* (Oxford, Blackwell, 1996 [1st ed. 1986]).

Bardon, Jonathan, *Belfast: an illustrated history* (Belfast, Blackstaff Press, 1982).

Bardon, Jonathan, *A history of Ulster* (Belfast, Blackstaff, 1992).

Bowyer Bell, J., *The secret army: the IRA 1916–1979* (4th ed., Dublin, Academy Press, 1989).

Boyd, Andrew, *Brian Faulkner and the crisis of Ulster Unionism* (Tralee, Anvil Books, 1972).

Bell, Geoffrey, *The protestants of Ulster* (London, Pluto Press, 1976).

Bell, Geoffrey, *Troublesome business: the Labour Party and the Irish question* (London, Pluto Press, 1982).

Bew, Paul, *Ideology and the Irish Question: Ulster Unionism and Irish Nationalism 1912–1916* (Oxford, Clarendon Press, 1994).

Bew, Paul and Patterson, Henry, *Sean Lemass and the making of modern Ireland 1946–1966* (Dublin, Gill and Macmillan, 1982).

Bew, Paul, Gibbon, Peter and Patterson, Henry, *Northern Ireland 1921–1994: political forces and social classes* (London, Serif, 1995).

Birrell, Derek and Murie, Alan, *Policy and government in Northern Ireland: lessons of devolution* (Dublin, Gill and Macmillan, 1980).

Birrell, W. D., 'Local government councillors in Northern Ireland', Studies in public policy (University of Strathclyde, 1983).

Blackman, Tim, 'Craigavon: the development and dismantling of Northern Ireland's new town; an example of capitalist planning and the management of disinvestment', *Capital and class*, no. 35, Summer 1987.

Boswell, James, *The life of Samuel Johnson* (London, 1949) vol. 2.

Boulton, David, *The UVF: an anatomy of loyalist rebellion* (Dublin, Torc Books, 1973).

Bruce, Steve, *God save Ulster! The religion and politics of Paisleyism* (Oxford, Clarendon, 1986).

Bruce, Steve, *The red hand: protestant paramilitaries in Northern Ireland* (Oxford, Oxford University Press, 1992).

Buckland, Patrick, *The factory of grievances: devolved government in Northern Ireland 1921–39* (Dublin, Gill and Macmillan, 1979).

Buckland, Patrick, *Northern Ireland's first Prime Minister: James Craig, Lord Craigavon* (Dublin, Gill and Macmillan, 1980).

Buckland, Patrick, *A history of Northern Ireland* (Dublin, Gill and Macmillan, 1981).

Budge, Ian and O'Leary, Cornelius, *Belfast: approach to crisis, a study of Belfast politics 1913–1970* (London, Macmillan, 1973).

Cairncross, Alec, *The British economy since 1945: economic policy and performance 1945–90* (Oxford, Blackwell, 1992).

Cairncross, Sir Alec, *Managing the British economy in the 1960s: a Treasury perspective* (Hampshire, Macmillan, 1966).

Cannadine, David, *The decline and fall of the British aristocracy* (New Haven, London, Yale University Press, 1990).

Cash, John, Daniel, *Identity, ideology and conflict: the structuration of politics in Northern Ireland* (Cambridge, Cambridge University Press, 1996).

Cathcart, Rex, *The most contrary region: the BBC in Northern Ireland 1924–84* (Belfast, Blackstaff Press, 1984).

Caute, David, *Sixty-eight: the year of the barricades* (London, Hamish Hamilton, 1988).

Clayton, Pamela, *Enemies and passing friends: settler ideologies in Twentieth Century Ulster* (London, Pluto Press, 1996).

Cochrane, Fergal, '"Meddling at the crossroads": the decline and fall of Terence O'Neill within the Unionist community', in Richard English and Graham Walker (eds) *Unionism in modern Ireland: new perspectives on politics and culture* (Dublin, Macmillan, 1996).

Cochrane, Fergal, *Unionist politics and the politics of unionism since the Anglo-Irish Agreement* (Cork, Cork University Press, 1997).

Compton, Paul, 'The demographic background', in David Watt (ed.), *The constitution of Northern Ireland: problems and prospects* (London, Heinemann, 1981).

Conversi, Daniele, 'Reassessing current theories of nationalism: nationalism as boundary maintenance and creation', *Nationalism and Ethnic Politics*, vol. 1, no. 1 (London, Spring 1995).

Coogan, Tim Pat, *The Troubles: Ireland's ordeal 1966–1995 and the search for peace* (London, Arrow, 1995).

Coulter, Colin, 'The character of unionism', *Irish Political Studies*, vol. 9, 1994.

Cradden, Terry, *Trade unionism, socialism and partition: the labour movement in Northern Ireland 1939–53* (Belfast, December, 1993).

Crafts, N. F. R., 'The golden age of economic growth in post-war Europe: why did Northern Ireland miss out?', *Irish Economic and Social History*, vol. XXII, 1995.

Craig, F. W. S. (ed.), *British general election manifestos 1959–1987* (Aldershot, Dartmouth, 1990).

Darby, John, 'The historical background', John Darby (ed.), *Northern Ireland: the background to the conflict* (Belfast, Appletree Press, 1983).

Edwards, Owen Dudley, *The sins of our fathers* (Dublin, Gill and Macmillan, 1970).

Elliott, R. S. P. and Hickie, John, *Ulster: a case study in conflict theory* (London, Longman, 1971).

Elliott, Sydney, *Northern Ireland parliamentary election results 1921–71* (Chichester, Political Reference Books, 1973).

Fanning, Ronan, '"The great enchantment": uses and abuses of modern Irish history', Ciaran Brady (ed.), *Interpreting Irish history: the debate on historical revisionism 1938–1994* (Dublin, Irish Academ Press, 1994).

Farrell, Brian, *Sean Lemass* (Dublin, Gill and Macmillan, 1983).

Farrell, Michael, *Northern Ireland: the orange state* (London, Pluto Press, 1980 [1st ed. 1976]).

Foster, Roy, 'To the northern counties station: Lord Randolph Churchill and the Orange card' in Roy Foster, *Paddy and Mr Punch: connections in Irish and English history* (London, Penguin Press, 1993).

Gailey, Andrew, *Ireland and the death of kindness: the experience of constructive unionism 1890–1905* (Cork, Cork University Press, 1987).

Gailey, Andrew, *Crying in the wilderness; Jack Sayers: a liberal editor in Ulster 1939–68* (Belfast, Institute of Irish Studies, 1995).

Gordon, David, *The O'Neill years: Unionist politics 1963–1969* (Belfast, Athol Books, 1989).

Greer, Alan, *Rural politics in Northern Ireland: policy networks and agricultural development since partition* (Aldershot, Avebury, 1996).

Harbinson, John F., *The Ulster Unionist Party 1882–1973: its development and organisation* (Belfast, Blackstaff Press, 1973).

Harkness, David, *Northern Ireland since 1920* (Dublin, Helican, 1983).

Harris, Richard I. D., *Regional economic policy in Northern Ireland 1945–88* (Aldershot, Avebury, 1991).

Hume, David, *The Ulster Unionist Party 1972–1992: a political movement in an era of conflict of change* (Belfast, Ulster Society, 1996).

Jackson, Alvin, *The Ulster Party: Irish Unionists in the House of Commons 1884–1911* (Oxford, Clarendon, 1989).

Jackson, Alvin, 'Unionist myths 1912–1985', *Past and present, a journal of historical studies*, no. 136, August 1992.

Jackson, Alvin, *Colonel Edward Saunderson: land and loyalty in Victorian Ireland* (Oxford, Clarendon, 1995).

Kennedy, Billy (ed.) *Steadfast for faith and freedom: 200 years of Orangeism*

(Belfast, Grand Orange Lodge of Ireland, 1995).

King, Edward, *Old times revisited in the borough and parish of Lymington* (Winchester 1976, 1900 ed, 1st ed. 1879).

Kingsley, Paul, *Londonderry revisited: a loyalist analysis of the civil rights controversy* (Belfast, Ulster Society, 1989).

Lawrence, R. J., *The government of Northern Ireland: public finance and public services 1921–1964* (Oxford, Clarendon Press, 1965).

Loughlin, James, *Ulster Unionism and British national identity since 1885* (London, Pinter, 1995).

Lynn, Brendan, *Holding the ground: the Nationalist Party in Northern Ireland 1945–72* (Aldershot, Avebury, 1997).

Lyons, F. S. L., *Ireland since the famine* (London, Fontana, 1973, 1st ed. 1971).

Lyons, F. S. L., *Culture and anarchy in Ireland 1890–1939* (Oxford, Clarendon Press, 1979).

Maloney, Ed and Pollack, Andy, *Paisley* (Dublin, Poolbeg, 1986).

Maltby, Arthur, *The government of Northern Ireland 1922–72: a catalogue and breviate of parliamentary papers* (Dublin, Irish University Press, 1974).

McAllister, Ian, *The Northern Ireland Social Democratic and Labour Party: political opposition in a divided society* (London, Macmillan, 1977).

McAllister, Ian and Nelson, Sarah, 'Modern developments in the Northern Ireland party system', *Parliamentary Affairs*, vol. 32, no. 3 (Oxford, 1979).

McAllister, Ian, 'Class, region, denomination, and protestant politics in Ulster', *Working Papers in Sociology* (Canberra, 1982).

McCrone, Gavin, *Regional policy in Britain* (London, Allen and Unwin, 1969).

Miller, D. W., *Queen's rebels: Ulster loyalism in historical perspective* (Dublin, Gill and Macmillan, 1978).

Millward, Robert, 'Industrial and commercial performance since 1950' in Roderick Floud and Donald McCloskey (eds), *The economic history of Britain since 1700: volume 3: 1939–1992*, (Cambridge, Cambridge University Press, 1994, 1st ed. 1981), pp. 59–60.

Moore, Chris, *The Kincora scandal: political cover-up and intrigue in Northern Ireland* (Dublin, Marino, 1996).

Moore, Jonathan, 'The Labour Party and Northern Ireland in the 1960s', Eamonn Hughes (ed.), *Culture and politics in Northern Ireland 1960–1990* (Milton Keynes, Open University Press, 1991).

Munck, Ronnie, *The Irish economy: results and prospects* (London, Pluto Press, 1993).

Mulholland, Marc, '"One of the greatest hurdles ...": The recognition of the Northern Ireland Committee of the Irish Congress of trade unions 1963–4.', *Saothar*, 1997.

Nairn, Tom, *The break-up of Britain* (London, New Left Books, 1981).

Nelson, Sarah, *Ulster's uncertain defenders: protestant political, paramilitary and community groups and the Northern Ireland conflict* (Belfast, Appletree, 1984).

O'Brien, Conor Cruise, *States of Ireland* (London, Hutchinson, 1974, 1st ed. 1972).

O Dochartaigh, Niall, *From civil rights to armalites: Derry and the birth of the Irish Troubles* (Cork, Cork University Press, 1997).

O'Dowd, Liam, 'Regional policy', in Liam O'Dowd, Bill Rolston and Mike Tomilson (eds) *Northern Ireland: between civil rights and civil war* (London, CSE

Books, 1980).

O'Dowd, Liam, 'The crisis of regional strategy: ideology and the state in Northern Ireland', in Gareth Rees, Janet Bujra, Paul Littlewood, Howard Newby and Teresa L. Rees, *Political action and social identity: class, locality and ideology* (Hampshire, Macmillan, 1985).

O'Farrell, Patrick, *Ireland's English question: Anglo-Irish relations 1534–1970* (New York, Stocken Books, 1971).

O'Sullivan, Michael, *Sean Lemass: a biography* (Dublin, Blackwater Press, 1994).

Patterson, Henry, *The politics of illusion: republicanism and socialism in modern Ireland* (London, Hutchinson Radius, 1989).

Patterson, Henry, 'Seán Lemass and the Ulster question, 1959–65', *Journal of Contemporary History*, vol. 34, no. 1.

Pašeta, Senia, *Before the revolution: nationalism, social change and Ireland's catholic elite, 1879–1922* (Cork, Cork University Press, 1999).

Phoenix, Eamon, *Northern nationalism: nationalist politics, partition and the catholic minority in Northern Ireland* (Belfast, Ulster Historical Foundation, 1994).

Porter, Norman, *Rethinking unionism: an alternative vision for Northern Ireland* (Belfast, Blackstaff Press, 1996).

Probert, Belinda, *Beyond orange and green: the Northern Ireland crisis in a new perspective* (London, Academy Press, 1978).

Purdie, Bob, *Politics in the streets: the origins of the civil rights movement in Northern Ireland* (Belfast, Blackstaff Press, 1990).

Purdy, Ann, *Molyneaux: the long view* (Antrim, Greystone, 1989).

Quinn, Anthony P, *Credit Unions in Ireland* (Dublin, Oak Tree Press, 1994).

Rafferty, Oliver P., *Catholicism in Ulster 1603–1983: an interpretative history* (London, Hurst, 1994).

Rose, Richard, *Governing without consensus: an Irish perspective.* (London, Faber and Faber, 1971).

Ryder, Chris, *The RUC: a force under fire* (London, Methuen, 1989).

Shanks, Amanda M., *Rural aristocracy in Northern Ireland* (Aldershot, Avebury, 1988).

Short, Con, *The Ulster GAA story* (Ulster, GAA, 1984).

Smiles, Samuel, *Self-help with illustrations of conduct and perseverance* (London, J. Murray, 1st ed. 1859, 2nd ed., with a centenary introduction by Professor Asa Briggs, 1958).

Stewart, A. T. Q., 'The mind of protestant Ulster', in David Watt (ed.) *The Constitution of Northern Ireland: problems and prospects* (London, Heinemann, 1981).

Sunday Times Insight Team, *Ulster* (Middlesex, Sunday Times, 1972).

Thompson, E. P., *The poverty of theory and other essays* (London, Merlin Press, 1978).

Thompson, George, 'The Ulster Folk Museum' in Michael Longley (ed.), *Causeway: the arts in Ulster* (Belfast, Arts Council of Northern Ireland, 1971).

Tobin, Fergal, *The best of decades: Ireland in the 1960s* (Dublin, Gill and Macmillan, 1996).

Todd, Jennifer, 'Two traditions in unionist political culture', in Tom Garvin and Michael Laver (eds), *Irish political studies*, vol. 2, 1987.

Todd, Jennifer, 'Unionist political thought 1920–72' in D. George Boyce, Robert

Eccleshall and Vincent Geoghagan (eds), *Political thought in Ireland since the seventeenth century* (London & New York, Routledge, 1993).

Walker, Brian, *Ulster politics: the formative years 1868–86* (Belfast, Ulster Historical Foundation, 1989).

Walker, Brian and McCreary, Alf, *Degrees of excellence: the story of Queen's, Belfast 1845–1995* (Belfast, Institute of Irish Studies, 1994).

Wallace, Martin, *Fifty years of self-government* (Newton Abbot, David and Charles, 1971).

Walsh, Walsh, *From civil rights to national war: Northern Ireland catholic politics 1964–1974* (Belfast, Athol Books, 1989).

Ward, Alan (ed.), *The selected John Hewitt* (Belfast, Blackstaff Press, 1981).

White, Barry, *John Hume: statesman of the Troubles* (Belfast, Blackstaff Press, 1984).

Whyte, J. H., 'Intra-Unionist disputes in the Northern Ireland House of Commons, 1921–72', *Economic and Social Review*, vol. 5, no. 1, October 1973.

Whyte, John, 'How much discrimination was there under Stormont 1921–68?', pp. 1–35 in Tom Gallagher and James O'Connell (eds) *Contemporary Irish studies* (Manchester, Manchester University Press, 1983).

Whyte, John, *Interpreting Northern Ireland* (Oxford, Clarendon, 1990).

Wichert, Sabine, *Northern Ireland since 1945* (Essex, Longman, 1991).

Wiener, Ron, *The rape and plunder of the Shankill: community action: the Belfast experience* (privately published, 1976).

Wright, Frank, 'Protestant ideology and politics in Ulster', *European Journal of Sociology*, xiv (1973). p. 221.

Wright, Frank, *Northern Ireland: a comparative perspective* (Dublin, Gill and Macmillan, 1987).

Theses

Gallager, Frank, 'Cleavages and consensus: Craigavon Borough Council 1973–81', unpublished MSc thesis (Queen's University of Belfast) 1983.

Gillespie, Gordon, 'The Ulster Liberal Party 1956–73', unpublished MSc thesis, (Queen's University of Belfast, 1984).

Graham, J. A. V., 'The consensus forming strategy of the Northern Ireland Labour Party', unpublished MSc thesis (Queen's University of Belfast, 1972).

Kennedy, Henry, 'Politics in Northern Ireland: a study of one-party domination', unpublished Ph.D. thesis (The University of Michigan, 1967).

Lewis, W. A., 'Northern Ireland Unionism 1963–1990: an examination of the liberal and conservative patterns within Unionism' (unpublished M. Phil., Trinity College Dublin, 1991).

McMillan, P. H., 'The New Ulster Movement and the formation of the Alliance Party of Northern Ireland', unpublished MSc thesis (Queen's University of Belfast, 1984).

Mengal, Hagal, 'Sam Thompson and modern drama in Ulster', unpublished PhD thesis (Frankfurt au Main, 1986).

Miracle, Amy, 'A liberal in spite of himself: Terence O'Neill and moderate Unionist politics', unpublished MSc thesis (Queen's University of Belfast, 1987)

Interviews

Austin Ardill, 10 August 1998.
Rt Hon. David Bleakley, 27 August 1995.
Sir Kenneth Bloomfield, 20 May 1995.
Rt Hon. Robert Cooper, 24 October 1996.
Reginald Empey, 7 December 1995.
Richard Ferguson, QC, 27 March 1996.
Lord Brian McConnell, 17 February 1995.
Rt Hon. Basil McIvor, 3 November 1995.
Lord Moyola, the Rt. Hon. James Chichester Clark, 9 November 1995.
Rt Hon. Ivan Neill, 15 August 1995.
Rt Hon. Harry West, 15 December 1995.

Index

35992769